Help and Hope
Book and CD Set

Staying Off The Wheel Of Misfortune

(the book half of *Help and Hope*) was created to provide practical resources for people living through difficult times. Culled from a lifetime of experience, study and observation, it offers insights and concrete strategies for managing challenges, avoiding obstacles and creating the life you want, including the latest strategic thinking on how to put your best foot forward – emotionally, mentally and socially – no matter what life throws at you. Everyone can learn to stay off the Wheel of Misfortune!

Piece of the Puzzle – 12 Songs of Hope

(the music half of the set, available separately) is Christopher's fifth CD – a fully produced collection of original songs, including many fan favorites, that celebrate human strength, insight and heart. The title song, *Piece of the Puzzle,* includes wit and wisdom from dozens of well-known individuals, from Einstein to George Burns. The songs remind us that no matter what the challenge, we can prevail!

> The audio version of this book is available at *christopherkent.com*. **Piece of the Puzzle** can be sampled and/or purchased at *christopherkent.com* or through your favorite online music outlet.

Staying Off The Wheel Of Misfortune

How to remain passionate,
effective, adaptable and caring –
no matter what life throws at you

CHRISTOPHER KENT

*To Lynn,
for everything*

© 2013 Christopher Kent
First Edition 2013
Valley Vista Press LLC
christopherkent.com

All rights reserved. No part of this publication may be reproduced, distributed, or transmitted in any form or by any means, including photocopying, recording, or other electronic or mechanical methods, without prior written permission from the publisher, except in the case of brief quotations embodied in critical reviews and certain other noncommercial uses permitted by copyright law. Please obtain only authorized electronic editions, and do not participate in or encourage electronic piracy of copyrighted materials. Your support of the author's rights is appreciated.

Books are available at quantity discounts for promoting products or services, or for corporate events by contacting the publisher. To arrange a speaking engagement for the author, please visit *valleyvistapress.com*.

Although the author and publisher have made every effort to ensure that the information in this book is correct, the author and publisher do not assume, and hereby disclaim, any liability to any party for any loss, damage or disruption caused by errors or omissions, whether such errors or omissions result from negligence, accident or any other cause.

Set in Times New Roman
Jacket and interior design by Lynn Yost
Jacket photo and cover art by Lynn Yost
All illustrations © 2013 Christopher Kent
Wheel of Misfortune concept © 2013 Christopher Kent

Kent, Christopher; 1952-

Staying Off The Wheel Of Misfortune:
How to remain passionate, effective, adaptable and caring – no matter what life throws at you

Includes 15 illustrations, endnotes and bibliography.

ISBN: 9780615865652

Acknowledgements

In many respects, writing a book is a solitary process. Nevertheless, I would be remiss if I didn't acknowledge the support provided by a number of individuals, and the contributions made by others whose insights, research and personal stories helped me to understand and convey the ideas in this book.

First and foremost, I have to thank my wife Lynn for both emotional and editorial support over the many years leading up to the completion of this book. She's always been willing to listen to my ideas, make thoughtful suggestions and help me stay focused; she also edited the book more than once and assisted with the charts, not to mention designing the cover and interior of the book. I'm lucky beyond words to have such a loving and talented companion.

Special thanks go to Steven Charles, M.D., psychotherapist Marilyn Ingber, and writer and editor Nadine Kofman for reading and critiquing the next-to-last draft of the book. Their insightful suggestions (and astute eye for typos!) helped make the book coherent, complete and readable.

I'd also like to thank the individuals whose stories I retold in brief in this book. Some stories were told to me in person; others were recounted in books written by the individuals who lived through them. I've done my best to do their stories justice in the retelling, and I've referred the reader to the original source wherever possible.

Special thanks also to the individuals whose quotes appear throughout this book. Your wisdom does us all proud.

Many people contributed to this book indirectly, including my parents, who raised me to ask questions and search for patterns in life; the teachers who inspired me to write and encouraged my interest in science and psychology; the writers and editors I've known over the years who shared their "tricks of the trade" with me; and the many individuals who unintentionally helped me learn valuable life lessons, many of which appear in these pages.

To all of the above I give my thanks. I couldn't have done it without you!

  – Christopher Kent, May, 2013

Table of Contents

Introduction xi

Chapter 1.
Keep Your Perspective. To choose the best action to take, you need to have an accurate perception of what's going on 1

Chapter 2.
Keep Growing. Learn to avoid the mindset that says you can't go beyond your existing talents or skills 25

Chapter 3.
Hold Onto Your Personal Power. Don't take on the role of victim 59

Chapter 4.
Communicate Clearly. Pay attention to what the other person is hearing, not just what you're saying 83

Chapter 5.
Focus on the Right Thing. Instead of resisting what you don't like, put your energy into creating what you'd like to have 103

Chapter 6.
Take Advantage of All of Your Mind's Resources. Don't rely solely on one type of thinking 123

Chapter 7.
Maintain Healthy Relationships by Avoiding Emotional Crises. Learn to express your emotions constructively, so they don't backlog into destructive "emotional stacks" 171

Chapter 8.
Always Try To Understand the Reasons For Behavior. Understanding the reasons for behavior makes it far easier to get what you need from other people – and from yourself 197

Chapter 9.
Let Go of Certainty. Remain flexible: Assume that everything you have accepted as a "fact" – scientific, religious, or otherwise – is at least partly wrong. And keep asking questions 227

Chapter 10.
Create the Future You Want. Avoid being trapped by your feelings about the past or future. Instead, use the power you have in the present to begin achieving your goals 271

Afterword 325

Bibliography 331

About the Author 337

Illustrations

The SEICR Cycle (diagram)	13
Consequences of Having a Fixed Mindset (wheel)	35
Two Ways to React When Someone Mistreats or Harms You (table)	63
Consequences of Taking On the Role of Victim (wheel)	73
How Does Communication Work? (diagram)	87
Consequences of Focusing On What You Don't Like (wheel)	111
Five Ways to Focus Your Attention (table)	119
Nine Things the Greater Mind Does For Us (chart)	153
11 Ways to Make the Most of Your Greater Mind (chart)	163
What Are Emotional Stacks? (chart)	175
Five Ways to Ensure That Emotional Stacks Don't Cause Relationships to Break Down (chart)	193
Consequences of Not Understanding Behavior (wheel)	205
Consequences of Certainty Syndrome (wheel)	237
How a Special Interest Group Can Manipulate Certainty for Profit – With Dire Consequences (flow chart)	251
12 Strategies for Creating the Future You Want (game board)	315

Introduction

"Opportunity often comes disguised in the form of misfortune."
– Napoleon Hill

"Knowledge is that possession which no misfortune can destroy, no authority can revoke, and no enemy can control. This makes knowledge the greatest of all freedoms."
– Bryant H. McGill

The idea of a "wheel of fortune" has been around since ancient times. It usually symbolizes the belief that events occur randomly – as if determined by the spinning of a wheel. In many cultural references, the wheel has been spun by a mythical blindfolded woman, such as the goddess Fortuna, sometimes portrayed as standing on top of an ever-rolling stone. The blindfold, of course, is meant to emphasize that the lady spinning the wheel can't influence the outcome of each spin.

Historically, the wheel of fortune has been mentioned when something unpleasant has befallen someone, as opposed to when great good fortune occurs. That may be because there's a lot less hand-wringing when something good happens; in that situation, most of us are content to conclude that we deserved our good fortune and leave it at that. On the other hand, when something bad happens, the wheel of fortune provides a more palatable way to explain it. Several characters in Shakespeare plays, including Hamlet and King Lear, make comments about the fickle nature of Fortune and her wheel – almost always when someone has suffered an unjust turn of fate.

Of course, all of us have experienced such "turns of fate," when something happens that seems totally unfair and we find ourselves dealing with circumstances we would have preferred to avoid. But if we're going to blame this on a random spin of a fateful wheel, I think the wheel might more accurately be thought of as a wheel of misfortune.

It's true that when negative circumstances befall us they often seem to arise for reasons beyond our control. Whether or not that's true is a matter for debate, but either way, when something bad happens it can really set us back. We may suddenly lose something we thought we couldn't live without. Our long-term plans may suddenly become irrelevant. We may find ourselves forced to do without everyday comforts and resources that we've become accustomed to. The "rules of the game" that we're expected to live by may suddenly change.

Furthermore, when we find ourselves riding the wheel of misfortune, the stakes can be high and our decisions may have much more significant consequences. When money is tight, for example, one false move can leave you penniless. Accurate communication also matters more; when there's little room for error, being misunderstood can lead to disaster. Likewise, maintaining good relationships matters more when times are hard because you need all the friends and support you can get.

There are three key premises that underlie the ideas you'll find in this book:

1) The events we experience are not really random, as if determined by the spinning of a wheel. On the contrary, it's within our power to avoid many of the problems that can befall us.

2) The way we perceive and react to the difficulties we sometimes face is a key factor in how our lives go. Do we see the difficult circumstances as a disaster, or a challenge? Do we decide to change course, or do we fight to maintain our current direction? Our perception of the situation and choice of response make all the difference in the way things finally turn out.

3) When bad things do happen, it's within our power to create something positive from those circumstances, no matter how challenging they are.

In order to create the life we'd like to have, avoid unnecessary problems and see the problems we can't avoid in a useful way – no matter how tough our current situation may be – we have to use effective strategies. That's where this book can help; in the 10 chapters that follow, you'll find a host of helpful strategies. At the end of the book, I'll sum up the key points from each chapter and add a few final thoughts about how these ideas can help each of us stay off the Wheel of Misfortune.

For what it's worth, I make no claim to be offering the final word on any of the subjects we'll be discussing. What I do claim is that these ideas have made a huge difference in many lives, including mine, and hold the potential to do the same for you.

Here's hoping that the ideas and strategies you find here will help you stay off the Wheel of Misfortune and create the life you really want to be living.

– Christopher Kent, May 2013

PS: This book is half of the book and CD set *Help and Hope*. If you've heard the title song from the CD, *Piece of the Puzzle*, (and/or seen the music video), you know that I'm fond of quoting the wisdom and insights other people have shared through their comments and observations. In that same spirit, I've placed a few of my favorite quotes at the beginning of each chapter in this book, and sprinkled additional ones throughout the chapters where appropriate. The quotes help to capture the spirit of each chapter – more pieces of the puzzle, as it were. I hope you enjoy them as much as I have.

1.
Keep Your Perspective.

To choose the best action to take, you need to have an accurate perception of what's going on.

"Some people feel the rain; others just get wet."
– Roger Miller

"Two boys arrived yesterday with a pebble they said was the head of a dog until I pointed out that it was really a typewriter."
– Pablo Picasso

"It's not what you look at that matters, it's what you see."
– Henry David Thoreau

"There will come a time when you believe everything is finished. That will be the beginning."
– Louis L'Amour

When I first moved to New York City in the 1970s, I worked at a small publishing house with a smart and charming fellow whose hobby was gourmet cooking, and who had an unusual laugh – unusual enough that if you didn't know him and heard him laughing, you might have wondered just who this guy was.

One day, he told me the following story: The night before, he had been in his apartment, preparing a gourmet meal. He had purchased a huge side of beef, and was using a meat cleaver to chop it up for a special culinary dish. Because this was a messy operation, he was wearing a butcher's apron, and after a bit of chopping, the apron was splattered with blood from the meat.

Midway through this process, he heard a scream. He recognized the voice; it was a little old lady who lived on the same floor, down the hall and around a corner. It sounded like someone was trying to force his way into her apartment, and she was resisting.

Without a second thought, he rushed out the door and down the hall to come to her aid. Had he thought about it, he might have hesitated; he wasn't big or muscular, and might not have fared well in a fight. But he reacted without thinking and went running down the hall.

Midway down the hall, not yet having reached the corner to turn down the other corridor, it dawned on him that he was still holding his bloody meat cleaver and wearing a blood-stained apron. This struck him as pretty funny. So, he began to laugh – his lovely, strange laugh.

As he rounded the corner, he saw that a man was indeed trying to force his way into the elderly woman's apartment. The man in question looked up and saw my friend running down the hall toward him, laughing like a lunatic, soaked in blood, carrying a bloody meat cleaver.

The intruder may very well have peed in his pants as he ran for the stairwell!

Events vs. Experience: The Importance of Perception

My friend, of course, wasn't nearly as big a threat as he seemed, but the intruder responded to his perception of what he saw. As far as he was concerned, he was about to be unceremoniously slaughtered by an escapee from a grade-B horror movie. And therein lies an important lesson: If you want to choose the best response to a situation, you have to perceive the situation as accurately as possible. (Of course, it was probably a good thing the potential mugger had a slightly inaccurate perception!)

Consider another example: A couple I know bought an old house in a residential part of a big city. Because the house was old, the plumbing was old, and the water in the house had a high level of lead in it. Consuming lead is bad for any human being, but it's especially bad for young children. So, when they had their first daughter, they knocked themselves out to make sure their drinking water was filtered to eliminate as much lead as possible.

After a couple of years they had their daughter tested, and discovered that she had an elevated level of lead in her blood. They were crushed and depressed; they felt that they had failed their daughter. But when they told me the story, I had a very different perspective. "Look," I said, "that just means the problem is far more serious than you realized. If you hadn't done all that you did to eliminate lead from the water, your daughter might have been gravely harmed by now. You may not have eliminated all the lead from the drinking water, but what you did probably saved her life." We interpreted the exact same less-than-ideal situation in very different ways. (Their daughter is doing just fine, by the way.)

Does perspective really make a difference? Indeed it does. For example, a 1997 study done by psychologist Amy Wrzesniewski surveyed people's feelings about their jobs; she grouped them based on whether they saw their job as

1) a job,
2) a career, or
3) a calling (i.e., something they felt they were meant to do).

Many different types of jobs were included, but the study found that regardless of the type of job the person had, those who saw the job as part of their calling in life were happier and more satisfied with their lives.[1] The exact same job seen from a different perspective was associated with a very different level of happiness.

Some might argue that our perspective is not something that we can control, but that's not the case. Every time you gain an insight into something in your life, your perspective changes. Furthermore, you can consciously choose to see something differently. In the case of a boring or unpleasant job, for example, you can choose to see it as a challenge in order to make it less boring or unpleasant while you wait for a better job opportunity to present itself. The same thing is true for any situation, whether it involves a relationship, money, health or surviving a disaster.

I'm not suggesting that when circumstances are horrible we should all "try to be more optimistic and look for the bright side." That sort of feel-good advice is very easy to give – and very difficult to execute. What I am suggesting is that our lives aren't really made up of the things that happen to us. Instead, our lives are made us of our experiences, and our experiences are not the same as the events unfolding around us. Two people experiencing the exact same events can have completely different experiences, just as the study mentioned earlier showed that a person in a challenging job has a completely different experience depending on whether he thinks of it as a job, a career or a calling.

If our experience of events is so important, what determines our experience? Two things: 1) what we pay attention to, and 2) what we believe about the thing we're paying attention to. For example, if you ignore something that's happening around you, it won't have much impact on your experience. On the other hand, a small thing that other people may not care about can become a major part of your experience if you constantly pay attention to it. We'll talk more about the importance of choosing what you pay attention to in Chapter 5 (Focus on the Right Thing). Here, I'd like to talk about the second thing that determines our experience: What we believe about the things we're paying attention to. We can call this our perspective.

When we live through a major upheaval in our lives, for example, there are many ways to perceive what's happening. Losing your home could be perceived as a devastating loss from which you'll never recover; a random act of a cruel universe; a punishment sent by God for earlier "bad behavior;" an indirect result of the actions of a politician or political party; a chance to reap a windfall from an insurance policy; or an opportunity to start over and build a new life. (The possible ways to interpret an event like this are limited only by your imagination.)

The important thing to understand is that you're likely to choose your next action based on your perception about what the loss of your house means. A person who sees a tragedy as a punishment sent by God will behave very differently than someone who sees the same tragedy as an opportunity to start over and create a better life.

For that reason, one of the most important things we can do when we find ourselves on the Wheel of Misfortune is to keep our perspective. Merriam-Webster's Collegiate Dictionary defines perspective as the capacity to view things in their true relations, or relative importance. In fact, our peace of mind and effectiveness depend on our perspective, because if our perspective is reasonably accurate and we process the information in ways that reinforce our personal power, our choices are far more likely to produce the kind of results we really want.

Since our perspective is so important, it's helpful to have accurate information about whatever it is you're paying attention to. (The more accurate your information, the more likely your beliefs will reflect what's really going on.) This is especially important when we're going through a crisis, because we tend to be upset and perhaps overwhelmed when a crisis has occurred. At the same time, in a difficult situation a lot can be riding on our choosing the right response. But if our interpretation of what happened is based on inaccurate or biased information, our response may end up making things even worse.

My purpose in this chapter is to change the way you perceive one of the toughest types of misfortune: watching something you care about or depend upon fall apart. Of course, every major unexpected life change is different, and there's no way to address them individually here. But catastrophic change, in general, does follow certain kinds of patterns that most people are not aware of. Understanding those patterns can change your perspective when you're living through tough times. That change in perspective, in turn, can make a big difference in the actions you choose to take. And better choices will lead to more of the kind of results you want – and more control over your life, helping you to get yourself off the Wheel of Misfortune.

The Cycle of Change

The events that challenge our ability to respond well are usually the traumatic ones, such as the loss of someone or something that we highly value – basically, any dramatic upheaval in our life that forces us to change the way we live, whether we like it or not. These are the kind of circumstances in which our perception and resulting choice of action matter a great deal. And the bigger the crisis, the more our reaction matters.

One of the most important things you can understand about a crisis is that the kind of wrenching change that we think of as a crisis happens periodically in all of nature – at least within "open systems," meaning those that exchange energy and information with surrounding systems. (Examples of open systems would include relationships, countries, individuals and even belief systems.) Furthermore, that kind of wrenching change occurs in a repeating cycle.

We tend to think of the process of growing as a slow, steady upward climb, but it's not. The natural process of growing can be more accurately described as "three steps forward, one step back." The "one step back" is a periodic system crash caused by problems in the system – and no system is without problems. Both parts of the cycle – the steady growth part and the system crash part – serve important purposes. Growing for a while without a major crisis allows us to spend time in a fairly stable situation, learning to deal with the conditions and limitations of that situation, whether it's a relationship, a new form of government or a set of ideas (that's the three steps forward). Then, when major problems cause the system to destabilize and fall apart to some degree (maybe completely), we're forced to address those major problems. (That's important, because addressing major problems within a system can be difficult or impossible when the system is stable and slowly moving forward.) The falling apart segment of the growth cycle, at least for us human beings, is often unnerving and can be very upsetting. That period of crisis is the "one step back."

Fortunately, once the system has gone through the crisis phase, a new, revised system emerges from the crisis and another extended period of relatively stable forward momentum begins – i.e., three steps forward, this time in a new direction.

This cycle is so much a part of life in our world that it can be found everywhere: in biological systems as they grow and develop, in chemical reactions, in evolution, and even in the workings of stars and galaxies. Perhaps more important for our purposes, it's also found throughout human experience at all levels – from small, relatively unimportant experiences to personal life-changing experiences, to global, historical changes that take decades or even centuries to occur and affect millions of people.

Understanding that a crisis in our lives or in the world at large is part of a natural cycle won't lessen the sometimes drastic changes caused by the crisis. Nor will it necessarily shorten the tough times that can follow the initial events of the crisis. But it can alter our outlook on what these events mean. In other words, instead of perceiving hard times as "the end of the world," we can perceive them – and react to them – as a difficult but natural change that has the potential to lead to something better. That can make a big difference in our choices when we're reacting to hard times, and a big difference in the events that our reaction sets into motion.

How the Cycle of Change Works

This recurring cycle follows a predictable pattern that's easy to miss if you're not looking for it, and each part of the cycle serves a different purpose and has different consequences. To understand how a cycle works, let's consider several examples, starting with a very simple one.

A number of years ago when I worked in an office cubicle, I kept several house plants on my desk. One of them had three tall stalks that put out large leaves. Even though my plant was confined to a plastic pot, it did well; the stalks kept growing taller and taller. But because the three stalks were crowded into one pot, they tended to push each other a bit to the side as they grew and put out more leaves. The result was that the stalks were tilted, and getting taller and heavier every week.

After a while I realized that the stalks were in danger of breaking off, so I created a system of supports using small sticks and tape. As the plant continued to grow, the supports became bigger and more elaborate, causing amused looks from my officemates. The system was becoming shaky, but since it was still working, I kept using the same strategy.

Finally, one day, my "fix" for the problem wasn't sufficient any more. Two of the stalks broke off. A little research on the Internet, however, told me that I could root the stalks by placing them in water. Sure enough, in the water they put out new roots where they had broken off, and I was able to plant each one in its own pot. The problem was solved, and a whole new situation was begun. I now had three healthy plants, with no crowding problem!

This is a very simple example, but it's easy to see how the cycle unfolded. When the "three steps forward, one step back" cycle is working, some set of conditions (or ideas) becomes the basis for a functioning system; in this case the "system" was a large plant with three stalks crowded into one small pot. Over time, the system grows and develops following the set of ideas or conditions that underlies the system, as my plant grew. This is the stable part of the cycle. This stable, steady-growth period might go on forever, except for one thing: Every set of ideas has flaws and imperfections, and as the system develops and expands, so do the flaws. In this case, the flaw was overcrowding.

For a long stretch of time, the problems resulting from those flaws can be fixed by simple patches, without making fundamental changes to the system. For example, I managed the increasing imbalance of the plant stalks by using sticks and tape to keep things going. This is true of any open system that's growing, whether it's a potted plant, a relationship, a social system or the world economy. As a stable system grows, problems grow too, but for a long time the problems can be solved with small, relatively simple fixes that stay within the original premise of the system.

However, as the system evolves and grows, the problems become harder to solve, as it became harder and harder to keep the plant from breaking apart. At some point, the problems become too great for the existing system to manage without making fundamental changes to the system itself. That's the point at which the system goes into the collapse or crisis phase of the cycle. This phase usually begins with a significant event that sets the breakdown in motion. In the case of my plant, two stalks finally broke off.

During the breakdown part of the cycle the system is forced to recreate itself with a different – hopefully better – foundation; a different set of conditions or ideas or assumptions that will truly solve the problems that the old system couldn't solve. Once this part of the cycle starts, the familiar, stable system falls apart. In the case of my plants, this period was brief and not particularly traumatic. But when a cycle is occurring in a society over a period of decades, the breakdown part of the cycle can be very traumatic indeed. This part of the cycle often brings about drastic change – at least, relative to the level of change taking place when the system is stable and growing.

How long will a breakdown phase last? That depends on the size of the cycle in question (among other things). If you're talking about a social cycle that takes 80 years to go full circle, the breakdown phase could last for 10 or 20 years. In that situation, enormous numbers of people may simultaneously experience this period as being "hard times." A cyclical change like this led to the stock market crash and Great Depression in the early 1930s in America; the economic collapse took about three years to occur, but the hard times resulting from it lasted another decade after that.

In most cases – at least when we talk about the cycle in connection to human beings – the new foundation or premise that ends up being the bedrock of the next system first appeared during the stable part of the old cycle – but it didn't gain much traction. The reason a new premise for a system doesn't have much impact until the existing system falls apart is that a stable system doesn't change easily. As long as the larger, existing system is still working, new ideas tend to be prevented from full-scale development. They stay "below the radar," no matter how good they are. But when the stable system is finally faced with flaws too big to repair and falls apart, new and improved ideas quickly rise to the surface where they have a chance to become the basis for the new system that will emerge from the ashes of the old system. (This has some important ramifications that we'll talk about shortly.)

For example, consider the story of Elon Musk, CEO of the Tesla Motors car company. With money he made as cofounder of PayPal (the internet-based payment system), he had started Tesla Motors with the dream of making electric automobiles a reality in the mass marketplace. Within a few years he developed a very expensive electric, high-performance sports car; now he was working on creating a low-cost electric car that the average American could afford. But he had a major obstacle in his way: He needed a really big factory like the ones the existing car companies owned. They were valued at prices as high as $1 billion, and he didn't have anywhere near that kind of money.

Then, the existing automobile manufacturing companies fell on hard times – i.e., the system began to crash, in part because of the economy, and in part because of poor judgment by the major car manufacturers about the kinds of cars they should be making. One of the biggest car plants in the world, owned jointly by Toyota and General Motors, suddenly was up for sale. Recently valued at $1 billion, GM had pulled out after declaring bankruptcy, and Toyota was ready to jump ship.

Previously, as a potential competitor, Musk hadn't been allowed near the place. Now, out of the blue, he was being courted as a potential buyer. (People interested in buying billion-dollar car plants were suddenly few and far between!) He had already budgeted $42 million in hopes of buying a small factory, so he submitted that offer, not expecting them to accept. (It was, after all, less than one-twentieth of the recent value of the plant.) To his astonishment, they accepted. The crumbling of the existing system made a key resource available to the man with the new idea. Until then, the new idea was simply squashed by the inertia and power of the existing system; once the cycle moved on to the breakdown phase, the new idea, already present but unable to make real headway, suddenly was able to get a major foothold.[2] (As I write this, it remains to be seen whether Tesla will become one of the pillars of the next automotive "system" – but I won't be surprised if it happens.)

The drastic changes that occur during the breakdown part of a cycle can – and usually do – lead to a much better new system arising. That may explain why natural systems and creatures seem to follow this cycle. Without a drastic change from time to time, natural systems and living creatures would stay pretty much the same indefinitely. Nature, it seems, doesn't want that; it wants to see growth and development. And that means an occasional setback that forces us to change direction and try new things.

To make it easier to remember the steps in this repeating process, I refer to it as the SEICR (pronounced "seeker") cycle. The letters

S-E-I-C-R stand for:
S*tability,*
E*xpansion,*
I*nstability,*
C*ollapse and*
R*ebirth*
– the basic steps that unfold, in that order, during a cycle.

Examples of the SEICR Cycle in Action

Let's look at a few more examples of the SEICR cycle, at different levels of size, scope and importance.

• ***The SEICR cycle in American history***. The SEICR cycle can be found repeating throughout American history every 80 or 90 years (as has been documented by William Strauss and Neil Howe in their book Generations: The History of America's Future, 1584 to 2069.)[3] Here's how it has worked, in abstract terms:
– One set of ideas about "how things should be" takes hold and becomes the basis for the behavior and attitudes of our culture for a period of time.
– After 50 or 60 years of relative stability, the social system based on that set of ideas begins to fall apart. This happens because of problems inherent in the underlying ideas that have gradually become too big for the culture to resolve without making major, fundamental changes.
– As the existing system starts to break down, a period of uncertainty and chaos ensues. This period usually begins with one pivotal, sometimes catastrophic event that abruptly changes the public mood from frivolous to serious. During the ensuing period of chaos and change, the old system comes to be seen as no longer workable, and a new set of ideas about "how the world should be" emerges and takes hold. This new set of ideas was germinating during the previous cycle, but couldn't take hold as long as the old system was stable.
– After a 10- to 20-year "chaotic" period, the new system becomes formalized and stable, and a new cycle begins. Almost always, the new system is an improvement on the old one, solving many of the problems that overwhelmed the old system. However, the new system has flaws of its own. So…
– After 50 or 60 years of stable growth based on the new set of ideas –

the first phase of the new cycle – the flaws result in problems that cause this system to break down in the same way, and the cycle repeats.

A classic example of the chaotic part of the cycle is the Revolutionary War period in American history. The problems between Britain and the Colonies finally grew so serious that they could no longer be easily fixed; at that point, the colonial system broke down and collapsed. This resulted in a period of chaos that allowed a new system – the United States of America – to emerge. (Interestingly, the breakdown of the old system happened fairly quickly, within a few years, but the creation of the new system – deciding on the details of an independent democracy – took more than a decade.) Of course, even after the new system stabilized it had flaws, several of which led to the next system breakdown at the time of the Civil War. (For more examples of how this pattern runs through American history, check out Strauss and Howe's Generations book, mentioned earlier.)

- ***The SEICR cycle in relationships.*** Anyone with experience in a long-term relationship knows that some crises take a long time to "come to a head" and erupt into a huge fight (or a divorce). In many instances, the same SEICR cycle is at work.

Perhaps the classic example is a new couple in a romantic relationship. When most of us first become part of a new relationship, we're anxious to please the other person. So we go out of our way to be nice, helpful and cheerful. We make small sacrifices to maintain harmony in the relationship. In essence, we patch small disagreements and overlook things we don't really like rather than trying to dig deep and uncover potential major problems – even though such problems may very well be the cause of the smaller issues. So we create a system – "the relationship" – that's stable and growing, but a system with flaws. As the relationship grows, the underlying flaws also grow and become more problematic. We apply more band-aids, and things keep going...for a while!

Sooner or later, the problems caused by the underlying flaws become too big to be resolved with "quick fixes." That's the point at which the relationship is likely to go into crisis. Depending on how badly both parties want the relationship to continue, it will either disintegrate, creating two new separate systems, or the parties will negotiate a new set of "rules" for the relationship that both individuals can live with. Those new rules become the basis for a better relationship between the couple. Things become stable again, and the previous problems are now (hopefully) solved.

Of course, the cycle may repeat again, but every time the next set of underlying flaws is addressed, the foundation of the relationship becomes stronger. As with the other examples, being aware of the cycle can make a big difference in how we react – and a big difference in the final outcome.

• ***The SEICR cycle in the economy.*** Spending and debt can follow the same cyclical pattern – something we've seen a lot of in the United States. If you build your lifestyle around borrowing money using credit cards, for example, problems will start to show up over time. The amount of money you owe every month may increase, for example. You may be able to find ways to avoid a crisis for a while – but living on borrowed money is a flawed premise for sure, especially if you keep borrowing!

Following the SEICR cycle, at some point the monthly payments for the debt will become greater than you can manage, or your creditors will come and demand their money back. That's the point of system breakdown. Painful though it will undoubtedly be, it will do what this part of the cycle always does: It will force you to make fundamental changes that solve the underlying problem (living off of borrowed money) and start over with a better premise.

Sadly, our country (the United States) has engaged in this same type of debt behavior, especially since the year 2000, leaving us incredibly far in debt. As I write this, the resulting breakdown is already underway; and when a problem exists on such a grand scale, the crisis and the period of disruption following it is never pretty. However, a good perspective can help. Every economic collapse, including the Great Depression in the 1930s, has only lasted for a relatively short time. Plus, most of them have resulted in changes that set events on a better course in the years that followed, as often happens in the SEICR cycle.[4]

• ***The SEICR cycle in the environment.*** The cycle also can be seen in environmental degradation. Because our culture has acted as if natural resources are unlimited and nature is too large to be adversely impacted by our actions, we have done considerable damage to our air and water – not to mention causing the decline and extinction of tens of thousands of species that used to share the planet with us. As most people are

Chapter 1: Keep Your Perspective 13

The SEICR* Cycle
(*pronounced "seeker")

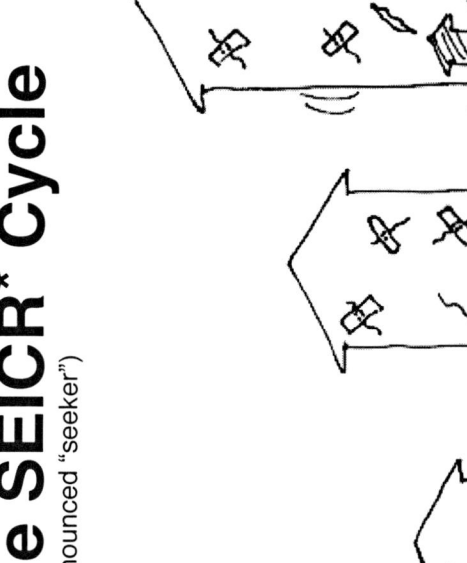

The point of crisis and opportunity →

Stability
A new system arises that has solved the problems that caused the previous system to break down. The new system's flaws are barely noticed. The system is stable.

Expansion
The stable system grows. The system's flaws become noticeable, but the consequences of the flaws can be "fixed" without making fundamental changes to the system.

Instability
As the system grows, the consequences of its flaws grow, too, and become harder to manage. New ideas appear that might eliminate the flaws, but they can't get much traction because the system is still stable—and hard to budge.

Collapse
The consequences of the system's flaws become too great to fix without changing the system. The system collapses. The new ideas suddenly become the focus of attention. Small forces can suddenly have a major impact.

Rebirth
A new system based on one or more of the new ideas begins to form. The old flaws are addressed, but different flaws in the new system will eventually grow along with it and become problematic, causing the cycle to repeat.

realizing, we are a part of nature, and when we cause problems for nature, they eventually come back to impact us.

Our civilization's use of fossil fuels may be following this kind of cycle. For the past 200 years or so we have increasingly relied on coal and oil, and it's not hard to understand why; burning them provides a relatively inexpensive source of heat and energy. That heat and energy can be used to warm homes, power transportation and power huge industrial machines and systems that manufacture the goods much of the world relies on for both sustenance and amusement.

Of course, use of fossil fuels comes with downsides. For example, it's difficult to get them out of the ground; it's difficult to transport them; refining them to make them useable produces toxic waste products; and burning them pumps chemicals into the air. When this "system" first became the primary energy source for civilization, these problems were easily managed because they happened on a small scale. So, the system expanded, and use of fossil fuels proliferated exponentially.

Predictably, as the system has expanded, the problems associated with it have become more difficult to solve. Supplying enough oil and coal to meet ever larger demands has caused us to drill ever deeper for oil (leading to disasters such as the huge, destructive 2010 spill in the Gulf of Mexico) and led to practices such as the complete demolition of mountains to get to the coal inside them. Transporting huge quantities of oil has resulted in giant pipelines that leak and disasters like the Exxon Valdez oil spill. The quantity of toxic waste from coal plants has become a threat to nearby communities, and the air pollution from burning coal and oil has gone from mainly being a problem for people with breathing trouble to altering our climate in ways that could soon be catastrophic. To top it all off, the value of oil is now the cause of wars. In fact, the consequences of relying on coal and oil are now reaching the point at which the system may very well soon collapse. At that point in the cycle it's likely that almost everyone will agree that we have to change the type of energy we use and how we use it – or face dire consequences.

Luckily, as the SEICR cycle predicts, new ideas for sources of energy and heat have appeared in response to the growing problems in the old system. If the fossil fuel system collapses, one or more of those ideas will then become the basis for the next cycle. Living through such a collapse will undoubtedly be traumatic, but it will be important to see it for what it is: nature's way of forcing us to start fresh with a better premise.

The Power of Change (When the Time is Right)

It's especially important to understand that where you are in a cycle has a huge impact on your ability to make changes to the system. When a system is in the stable part of the growing cycle, it's always hard to make major changes to the system. That includes implementing new ideas that might solve fundamental problems caused by the system's flaws. During the stable phase, if you "make waves," the system just absorbs the disturbance without really changing. In the case of a large social system like ours here in America, for example, trying to get fundamental changes made to the structure of government or our national economic policy or our approach to the environment is nearly impossible during the stable part of a cycle.

That changes completely when the system goes into the breakdown phase. At that point everybody realizes that the old system is broken, and something needs to be done. Suddenly, new ideas look really good. For that reason, a small force for change will have very little impact during the stable part of the growth cycle, but can literally change everything during the breakdown phase.

In a way, the breakdown part of the cycle is the most important part, because once it has occurred, major new ideas can be implemented – ideas that would be stymied during the stable phase of the cycle. That means that as painful as this part of a cycle may be, it's absolutely essential. Without it, major changes might never be made. We might be stuck with existing ideas – and their flaws – forever.

Consider the American revolution. The Founding Fathers were alive before the revolution, and some of them probably would have loved to change the existing political system much sooner. But as long as the existing system was stable, their ideas didn't have any significant effect. However, that changed the moment the system went into the breakdown phase. Suddenly a small group of people with a good idea were able to alter the course of history.

The fact that small forces can have a huge impact at these points in the SEICR cycle has important consequences at a more personal level: This means that a crisis in your life is a chance to make major changes that you couldn't have made so easily at other times. You've probably heard that in the Chinese language, the symbol for "crisis" is the same as the symbol for "opportunity." The SEICR cycle is the reason that symbolism makes sense: If you have a good idea that isn't getting traction, or you need to make changes but face too much resistance, a crisis period removes many of the obstacles and gives you the opportunity you've been waiting for. As Albert Einstein once noted, "In the middle of difficulty lies opportunity."

Furthermore, the outcome is likely to be a completely different ballgame than before. So, if you see the crisis you're dealing with as an opportunity of comparatively enormous proportions – rather than seeing it as the end of the world – you can make changes that will benefit you for the rest of your life. It won't be comfortable at first – change never is – but it could turn out to be the best thing that ever happened to you, if you make the most of it.

You could almost think of the breakdown part of the cycle as the reason that nature has adopted this process. It does two absolutely crucial things:

1) it tears down systems that have become riddled with problems, so they don't continue endlessly, causing ever-increasing negative consequences; and

2) it allows better ideas to come to the forefront, and gives them the opportunity to become the foundation of a better system – something that would be nearly impossible without having the existing system fall under its own weight. Put another way, the breakdown/crisis part of the cycle does major housecleaning and opens the door to new worlds.

One other important thing to remember: This is a case of "three steps forward and one step back." Even though the breakdown phase of the cycle can feel like a setback, you won't be starting over from zero. You have the benefit of all the positive developments that were part of the stable section of the previous cycle. In other words, seen from a larger perspective, everything is ultimately moving forward as the cycle repeats. In American history, for example, it's not too hard to see that despite the crises – the revolutionary war, the civil war, the Great Depression, and so forth – our country became stronger as time went by. In fact, we became stronger in part because of the crises we experienced and dealt with creatively.

So, don't despair when you face a crisis in your own life. No matter what you've lost, you're not going to be starting over from scratch.

The Unpredictability Factor

There's another interesting aspect of the breakdown phase of the cycle, noted by Belgian physicist and Nobel Laureate chemist Ilya Prigogine, who has observed and described this kind of cycle in several natural systems.[5] Prigogine notes that while the future is relatively easy to predict during the stable part of a cycle, knowing what direction the system will take after the breakdown has begun (which he calls the bifurcation point) is nearly impossible. This is the point at which abrupt, unexpected changes take place.

To put it another way, the stable part of the cycle is like playing poker; the breakdown part is like throwing the deck of cards in the air. For example, almost no one predicted the outcome of the American revolution before it took place; many thought the war couldn't be won, and if it was, they assumed we'd have a king over here! That was, after all, how Europe had functioned for centuries. (After the war, George Washington made history and set an astounding precedent by declining that very offer from the Founding Fathers.)

That's why past predictions of what the future would be like often look ludicrous in hindsight. Our ideas about the future are usually based on extending whatever is currently happening, and that's where they go wrong. When society goes through a cyclical breakdown, as it does on a regular basis, the new version that comes out the other side seldom resembles the version that existed beforehand. Since the new version of society that arises after the "bifurcation point" is so different from the old system, past predictions suddenly look absurd.

When a Crisis comes Out of the Blue

Although it's not too hard to identify the SEICR cycle of growth and change in many situations once you know what to look for, some situations involve drastic change that seems to come out of nowhere. For example, consider what happened to an acquaintance of mine who was the victim of a violent crime. Walking down the street one evening, he was arbitrarily selected to be the target of someone's rage. He barely survived.

Needless to say, he was severely traumatized; it took him years to deal with all of the resulting wounds and emotions. But when he talks about it now, many years later, he has a surprising perspective on the experience. Although he says he wouldn't wish such a nightmare on anyone, he feels that it was a positive turning point in his life. It forced him to rethink everything about who he was and what he'd been doing.

As a result, he made dramatic changes in his life. Those changes, he says, helped him to find fulfillment he would otherwise never have found.

In circumstances like these, the crisis may seem unconnected to what was happening beforehand; there's no obvious set of flaws in some life system leading up to a collapse. But it's still true that a crisis is one of the ways nature allows beneficial growth. Any drastic change is a window of opportunity for something new and better to emerge.

And that's the point. Seen in hindsight, traumas and tragedies often turn out to have been powerful opportunities for positive change. If you realize this when you're in the middle of an ongoing painful situation, rather than figuring it out years later in hindsight, it can make a huge difference in how you react. If you can only see that you're in a crisis, you may respond by taking drastic actions to retaliate against the perceived cause, or to try to hold on to whatever is falling apart – with terrible consequences. If you see it as an opportunity for change, you can turn it into exactly that.

Yes, seeing a calamity from a different perspective may not make it more fun. But it will change the way you react to it. If you understand that a crisis can have huge positive ramifications, that attitude puts you in charge: There is a solution to the crisis, and you'll find it; and the sooner you do, the sooner you're out of there. It means the end of the problem is comprehensible and within your control, at least to some degree. And that can make a HUGE difference in how well things turn out for you.

So: Treat a difficult situation as a challenge and opportunity for change instead of a meaningless cause of undeserved suffering. If you do, you'll stop suffering, take charge of your life and resolve the situation. And you'll be smarter and better able to handle future problems, as well.

Side-Stepping the SEICR Cycle

Can the breakdown part of the cycle be avoided? This is essentially the same thing as asking whether a problem can be solved before it becomes a crisis. The answer is yes, and that's especially true when human beings are involved. All that's required is to grasp how the cycle works and take action to solve underlying problems before they force a system-wide breakdown. Re-pot your plant before the stalks break under their own weight! Negotiate with other countries and get to the heart of a problem before a crisis occurs. Make a point of tackling some of the serious underlying problems in your relationship before a huge fight makes it unavoidable. Change the way you're managing money before your debt gets out of hand.

Consider the infrastructure that supplies most Americans with drinking water, takes away our waste water and manages storm water overflow. This infrastructure was largely built decades ago – more than a hundred years ago in many cities. Most of it is buried underground, out of sight and mind. The kind of lifestyle most Americans have enjoyed during that period of time has been far more comfortable and economically productive than the lifestyle of most other countries, and that has been at least partly the result of having that water-and-sewage-managing infrastructure. But, like everything else, pipes and pumps clog and deteriorate over time – especially when we don't see the deterioration taking place! So, our water supply is going through the same SEICR cycle, and we're in danger of letting things reach the breakdown part of the cycle. Going through that part of this particular cycle will not be pretty.

Is it inevitable? Hardly. In New York City, for example, water from higher-elevation upstate reservoirs ends up running through two enormous water tunnels underneath the city. The water has never been shut off for tunnel checking and repairs because many millions of people depend on keeping the water flowing. But those in charge of monitoring the situation realized years ago that the system would eventually reach a crisis point and break down. So they thought of a way to (hopefully) avoid reaching the point of system collapse: They began building a third tunnel under the city. It's a huge project that's already been under construction for decades, but clearly they have the right idea. The third tunnel will allow the water to be diverted so that the system won't have to fail in order to get our attention and be upgraded during a full-fledged water and sewage catastrophe.

If a personal crisis seems to come out of the blue – for example being mugged or being in an accident that you didn't cause – it may have been impossible to side-step a system breakdown by somehow preventing the events in question. But then, life throws a few curves at us no matter how diligent we try to be. That doesn't change the fact that we can save ourselves from some system breakdowns. And we can understand the nature of the growth cycle, so that when we are faced with a crisis, we're not overwhelmed; we understand the context and make the best possible choices when we respond to it.

Living in "Interesting Times"

We're living in a era when many very large SEICR cycles that involve the entire planet seem to be approaching the breakdown phase. "May you live in interesting times" is a well-known ancient Chinese curse, and unfortunately, that's exactly where we find ourselves living! That makes it all the more important to remember that this is part of a natural cycle. No matter how big a disaster befalls us, it's nature's way of getting us to start over again with a better premise.

Perhaps even more important, remember that the actions of an individual usually have only a small impact when a system is stable. But during these periods of change, an individual can have a huge impact, just as the Founding Fathers did once the colonial system finally collapsed. That means that, during the next several years, people of good faith and a vision of a more humane world – people like you and me – will be able to have a profound effect on the future that wouldn't have been possible even 10 years ago.

Let's not waste the opportunity.

It's All About Perspective

The bottom line here is that all difficult events – as well as long stretches of hard times – can be seen in different ways. The way you choose to see them will play a major part in determining your response, and that, in turn, will play a big part in how well you come through them.

The following story captures the importance of perspective well. I've run across it several times, with no one credited as its author (although one source claims it's an ancient Taoist proverb):

An old man and his son lived on a small farm near a village. They had little money, but the old man was wise. One day they discovered a white stallion grazing in one of their fields. They captured it, and when the news filtered out to the local community, people came to see the horse. They congratulated the man and his son on their good luck. The man just said, "Good luck? Maybe. Time will tell."

A few days later, the horse escaped and disappeared. The old man's friends told him they were sorry about his misfortune. The old man, however, wasn't upset. He said, "Bad luck? Maybe. Time will tell."

Some time later, the stallion returned, bringing a herd of mares with him. When the local people saw the new horses they congratulated the old man and his son once again on their amazing luck. The man said, "Good luck? Maybe. Time will tell."

The son was given the task of taming the horses so they could be ridden, but one of the horses threw him. The fall broke his leg severely, and it was clear that he would be crippled for the rest of his life. The neighbors came to the farm and helped with the horses, but many had to be sold. The neighbors offered sympathy and said how sad this turn of events was, and how it would now be hard for the old man and his crippled son to manage the farm. But the old man didn't despair. He just said, "Bad luck? Maybe. Time will tell."

Soon thereafter, a war broke out with a neighboring state. Soldiers came to the village and conscripted all the young men who were able to fight, but the old man's son was left behind because he was crippled. A few days later, all the boys who had been taken off to war were killed in a bloody battle.

The point, of course, is that difficult events can have long-term positive consequences that are impossible to foresee when you're in the middle of them. So when you're caught up in a crisis or hard times, keep these points in mind:

• ***Don't despair.*** Remember that everything that grows and develops over time will periodically fall apart under the weight of its problems. It's a natural cycle that affects everything. So, a crisis (or the aftermath of a crisis) is usually not the end of the world, even though it may seem that way when you're in the middle of it. If you play your cards right, the outcome of a crisis can be a far better situation than the one you had before the crisis happened.

• ***Learn as much as you can about the crisis or situation you're dealing with.*** Having an emotional reaction to the situation is perfectly normal and understandable, but don't confuse the perspective you have when you're in the throes of emotion with an accurate understanding of what's happening. It takes a calm mind and some time and effort to get a clear sense of what needs to be done.

• ***Remember that turmoil and instability are an opportunity to make big changes that would otherwise be difficult or impossible to make.*** Of course, a crisis often happens because big changes really needed to be made. So don't sit passively by feeling overwhelmed; see the crisis as an opportunity to find a new, more effective premise that a better system can be based on.

• ***Don't try to recreate what you had before the crisis.*** The idea is to create something better than what you had before the crisis.

• ***You don't have to let a cycle reach the collapse stage if the system in question is under your control.*** All systems tend to follow the SEICR cycle: Stability, Expansion, Instability, Collapse and Rebirth. But it is possible to avoid the collapse by addressing system flaws before they drive the system to the point of breaking down. (For example, in a relationship, look for the problems that are growing and make the effort to solve them before they lead to a system collapse and a heart-wrenching breakup.)

Of course, if the system in question is really big – say, the world economy – you may not be able to prevent the system from experiencing a collapse every so often. It's just too big for most of us to change. In that situation, the best any of us can do is keep our perspective, understand what's happening, and make constructive choices that lead to the best possible outcomes for ourselves and those we care about.

※ ※ ※

Once more, in brief

Here are the key points to remember from Chapter 1:

• ***Our lives are not made up of events; they are made up of experiences.*** What we experience in any given situation depends on: 1) what we're paying attention to and 2) how we interpret the thing we're paying attention to – i.e., our perspective regarding that thing.

• ***When we react to a crisis or difficult situation, we're actually reacting to our perception of it.*** So, perceiving the situation as clearly as possible is crucial to choosing the response that will benefit us the most.

• ***Growth in our world occurs in a repeating cycle that I refer to as the***

SEICR cycle: Stability, Expansion, Instability, Collapse, and Rebirth.
The cycle involves long stretches of relatively steady growth, during which problems are gradually increasing, but are still small enough to be solved without making fundamental changes to the system. Those long stable periods are followed by a shorter "crisis" period, triggered when the problems become too big to fix without making major, fundamental changes to the entire system. During the crisis or breakdown period, the old system falls apart. A new system eventually "emerges from the ashes" – a system based on ideas that were forced to stay "below the radar" until the crisis occurred.

The crisis or breakdown period can be very brief or last for years, depending on the size and scope of the cycle in question; it eventually resolves into another long period of more-or-less steady growth, based on an improved premise that has solved most of the old problems.

• ***Making large-scale changes is difficult during the steady growth part of the SEICR cycle, but during the crisis phase, major, abrupt changes can happen easily.*** This allows sudden changes in direction and leaps forward that were impossible during the stable phase.

• ***Even if a crisis you're experiencing is not part of an identifiable SEICR cycle, acting as if the crisis is an opportunity for change will produce better results in your life than acting as if it isn't.***

• ***It IS possible to sidestep the crisis part of a SEICR cycle by recognizing problems and make fundamental changes to the system before the system crashes.*** However, this can be difficult, because a stable system is highly resistant to change.

• ***Right now, many societal and global systems are unstable and beginning to collapse.*** Remember that the world WILL come out on the other side, quite possibly on a better footing than it was before. And remember that crises represent opportunity to make sweeping, badly needed changes for the better.

NOTES for Chapter 1.

1. Wrezesniewski A, McCauley C, Rozin P, and Schwartz, B. "Jobs, careers, and callings: People's relations to their work." Journal of Research in Personality 1997; 31:21-33.
2. For more details of this story, see the article Supercharged, published in the October 2010 issue of WIRED magazine.
3. Strauss and Howe's book Generations: The History of America's Future, 1584 to 2069 (William Morrow & Co., 1991), discusses the unfolding of this cycle throughout the course of American history in great detail, although in slightly different terms. They divide the cycle into four phases, each encompassing one generational group. Nevertheless, the process of evolution they describe is fundamentally the same as the one described here.
4. For an economic perspective that is based on a similar cyclical observation, check out Conquer the Crash: You Can Survive and Prosper in a Deflationary Depression by Robert Prechter (John Wiley & Sons, Inc. 2002) a past New York Times bestseller. This summarizes some of the work being done by the Elliott Wave school of economics. Their focus is on repeating waves of growth and collapse in economic systems that follow this same pattern – as well as social mood shifts that also follow the cycle, and how those shift connect to the economic changes.
5. Ilya Prigogine, the author of Exploring Complexity: An Introduction (W.H. Freeman & Company;1989) is a Belgian physicist and Nobel Laureate chemist noted for his work on dissipative structures, complex systems, and irreversibility; he won the Nobel Prize in chemistry in 1977. He has identified the growth-and-breakdown cycle in natural systems, although his work has often been described as bridging natural science and social science. Exploring Complexity: An Introduction provides a detailed, scientific description of his work. (This book is a little less mathematically and conceptually difficult than some of his other books.) For a more basic, easier-to-understand summary of Prigogine's ideas in this area, check out the descriptions found in Marilyn Ferguson's books The Aquarian Conspiracy: Personal and Social Transformation in the 1980s (J.P. Tarcher, 1980) or Marilyn Ferguson's Book of Pragmagic (Pocket Books/Simon & Schuster, 1990).

2.
Keep Growing.

Learn to avoid the mindset that says you can't go beyond your existing talents or skills.

"When you're finished changing, you're finished."
  – Ben Franklin

When times are tough, opportunities are usually limited. People can't find jobs, money is scarce and a lot of hopes and dreams end up being postponed indefinitely. So you might think that when an opportunity *does* present itself, any sensible person would grab it.

In fact, people often don't take advantage of opportunities, even when they could provide enormous help in a dire situation. Suppose you believe that you only have a certain amount of talent and ability – the amount you were born with – and you believe that nothing is going to change that. If you accept this premise, then many opportunities are going to appear very threatening to you. If a job offer requires skills you don't have, for example, you may see that job as a situation that will expose your limitations, leading to embarrassment and failure. If it's going to place you among people more skilled than you, you may believe that you'll look inferior in comparison. Many people avoid taking advantage of opportunities for exactly this reason – even when the consequences of turning down the opportunity are very negative indeed.

Consider a study conducted by psychologist Carol Dweck and three colleagues a few years ago at the University of Hong Kong, where all classes are taught in English. The researchers spoke to students coming in who were not fluent in English. First they asked key questions to determine whether the students believed their abilities were preset and unchangeable, or changeable with time and effort. Then, they asked whether the students would be interested in taking a course to improve their English – something that would clearly help them with their education and their grades in English-speaking classes. The students who saw their learning capacity as flexible said they'd be interested in taking the course; the students who believed their skills and abilities were fixed mostly said no. In other words, to avoid facing a "deficiency" in their "innate" abilities, the latter group of students were willing to turn down opportunities to improve, even though turning down that opportunity would mean doing more poorly in school.[1]

Of course, when times are tough, even people who don't believe they can really change might take a job that requires them to change or grow, just because they really need the job. The problem is, those people probably won't do well in that job. As long as they believe they can't learn substantial new skills, they'll focus on maintaining an *image* of competence and success, rather than actually trying to change or grow in ways that would lead to success. They'll be scrambling to avoid being "found out;" they may try to make others look bad so they'll look better by comparison; and they certainly won't be happy. Critical feedback from a boss or fellow employee will seem threatening, and they may react as if their critic is an enemy who's deliberately trying to make them look bad.

Most people who've been in the workforce for a few years have encountered people who handle their jobs this way; it's not a rare phenomenon. In fact, when times are good and jobs are plentiful, focusing on maintaining an image of competence instead of learning and growing to meet challenges may enable someone to get by. But when times are tough, jobs are scarce. That puts a person with this philosophy even more on the spot, leading to more defensive behavior and an even greater likelihood of losing his or her job when the folks in charge realize that the person is focused on defending his position rather than on trying to learn to do the job better.

Two Perspectives, Two Different Mindsets

There are two fundamental ways of thinking about our human capacity for learning and growth. Some people believe that we are born with limited, innate talents and abilities, and that trying to move beyond those limits is a waste of time. As a result of that belief, they adopt a defensive life strategy: "Changing myself to deal with this is a waste of time because people can't really change; therefore, I'm going to defend my current status." However, other people believe that it's impossible to know how far we can go before we reach our limits; to these individuals, growth in any area is possible. When faced with a challenge, these people tend to adopt the progressive strategy: "I will deal with this by doing my best to change and move forward."

These two opposing ideas can be encountered in nearly every area of our lives, sometimes on a small scale, sometimes on a grand scale. For example, a person might think that, in general, people can learn new skills, but only people born with special abilities can become really good craftsmen. Or, our belief may encompass the human condition as a whole: We may believe that human beings as a species have unlimited potential – or that human beings are permanently limited in almost every area.

It turns out that which of these two perspectives we adopt can enable us to succeed, or completely derail us. Luckily, it's a choice that can be turned to our advantage once we see it for what it is.

Why is this so important? How good we are at mastering new skills and adapting to new situations is a key factor in how well we do in life – and how well we navigate through hard times. If a key relationship in your life disappears, for example, being able to adapt to new relationships will be essential to rebuilding your personal social circle (and being socially connected has been shown to be a significant factor in happiness and success).[2] If you're forced to take a new job, being able to pick up new skills can make the difference between keeping food on the table and going hungry. Which of the two mindsets is governing your thinking in that area will help to determine whether you change and adapt, or dig in and remain stuck in the situation you don't like.

For example, suppose you're in a relationship and your partner says to you: "We have a serious problem. You're not contributing nearly as much to this relationship as I am." Suppose that, in this hypothetical scenario, this statement is clearly true. How will you respond? If you believe that you're capable of changing, you may respond by saying, "Okay, what do you think I should do? How can we make this better?" But if you believe that you're fundamentally stuck the way you are, you may react defensively and say, "Well, this is the best I can do," and provide a list of arguments to support that claim.

It's not hard to see that choices like this – "Should I make changes, or defend my current position?" – come up constantly as we go through life. Ironically, most of us make these choices totally unconsciously, because no one has ever told us that we're actually making a choice – or even that there's a different choice we could be making. In fact, understanding the nature of these two alternative beliefs can turn a person's life around completely. It certainly can have a profound effect on how well we survive when times are tough.

These two alternatives – "I can deal with this challenge by growing and changing," or "I'm stuck the way I am" – are what psychologist Carol Dweck calls *mindset*. When we believe we're limited and choose to defend our position, that is what she calls the *fixed* mindset; when we believe we are not constrained by limits and choose to move forward, she says we are in the *growth* mindset. Whether we hold the fixed or growth mindset about a single, specific situation or as a sweeping belief about human capabilities in general, these mindsets produce very different priorities, concerns and choices of action. In particular, the growth mindset puts the focus on moving forward, while the defensive, fixed mindset puts the focus on everything *except* moving forward.

For example:

- ***Your mindset affects whether or not you take on new challenges.*** In the fixed mindset, it makes sense to avoid taking chances and trying new things because doing so might reveal your lack of expertise or ability in a given area (which you believe isn't changeable). It also leads people to discourage others from trying to accomplish things, on the grounds that they have no innate talent. In the growth mindset, there's nothing especially threatening about taking on new challenges, and no reason to discourage others from trying new things.

- ***Your mindset affects what you focus on.*** If facing a challenge is unavoidable, and you believe that you're stuck with your current abilities, you're likely to focus on how this challenge will affect your image or reputation – whether the outcome will show your worth or reveal your shortcomings. If you're in the growth mindset, you're more likely to focus on figuring out what you need to do to handle the challenge and create a good outcome.

- ***Your mindset affects what you base your self-image on.*** If you believe that you're stuck with your talents and knowledge as they are, then how others see you will become crucial. You'll only feel smart and capable if others see you that way. If you're in the growth mindset, how others see you is far less important; you're likely to feel smart and capable regardless of how you appear to others. In the growth mindset, your self-image will tend to be based on what you're doing, not on how others see you.

• *Your mindset affects how you react to being tested.* People with a fixed mindset often believe that a single test measures a person forever. After all, they don't see themselves as being on the road to becoming better, because they don't believe it's *possible* to become better. So tests are very scary: They could reveal your shortcomings – which the fixed mindset says you're stuck with. On the other hand, people with a growth mindset usually see a test as only a measure of where they are right now; they believe that their relative position will change with time and effort. So in the growth mindset, tests aren't especially scary.

• *Your mindset affects how hard you work towards a goal.* People in the fixed mindset tend to think that if you're truly good at something *you shouldn't have to work at it*. In fact, people in the fixed mindset often believe that having to put serious effort into something is equivalent to admitting that you're a failure at it. So, they don't work hard to reach goals because they don't think they should need to. And, they don't ask for help when they need it, because that would be an admission of failure.

In contrast, people in the growth mindset believe that having to work at something is the normal way to proceed. To them, working hard towards a goal simply means you want to succeed at it; it's not seen as an admission of failure or inadequacy. And there's no stigma attached to asking for help.

• *Your mindset affects what makes you happy.* When we're in the fixed mindset, happiness is most likely to be generated by an impressive outcome. When we're in the growth mindset, happiness is more likely to result from a satisfying journey than from the end result.

• *Your mindset affects how easily your confidence can be shaken.* People can be confident about their skills or status in either mindset – but in the fixed mindset that confidence is fragile and easily undermined by anything that makes us appear inadequate.

• ***Your mindset can determine how you treat others.*** The fixed mindset can have profound consequences for those we interact with. In this mindset we become focused on comparing ourselves to others. After all, if you can't *improve* in order to impress others, then you have to impress them by comparing yourself to less-capable individuals. The need to appear better by comparison can lead to all kinds of distortions – and in situations involving social, business or political power, it can lead to actions designed to make others look bad or prevent them from moving forward, all in the name of making the fixed-mindset person look better in comparison.

• ***Your mindset can make you more judgmental.*** In the fixed mindset, where we stand relative to others seems incredibly important; so, we tend to perceive ourselves as always being judged, even when we're not. That – ironically – also encourages us to constantly judge others.

In short, spending time in the fixed mindset – accepting the idea that our prospects are limited by our inborn talent – has a lot of serious consequences. But so far we've been talking in generalities. Let's look at what the results of studies carried out by Dr. Dweck and other psychologists have revealed about the consequences of mindset.

What the Studies Show

Researchers, including Dr. Dweck, have become very interested in finding out how the growth and fixed mindsets affect people's lives and behavior. To do this, they've conducted studies comparing the results of being in the two mindsets in different situations. The studies use one of two models: They either find out what mindset the subjects are already in before looking at the outcomes, or they deliberately influence the subjects to put them into one mindset or the other.

In the first model, the subjects answer written questions about what they believe, which usually makes it clear which mindset they've adopted in that situation. In the other experimental model, subjects are exposed to information that leads them to believe that one philosophy or the other is factually correct – at least regarding the task in question. (For example, before learning a new skill such as juggling, one group might read an article proclaiming that skills in this area are fixed; you're either good at juggling or you aren't. The other group might read an article saying that people get better at juggling the more they work at it.)

The results of these studies are worth reviewing, because the studies show that the impact of the two different mindsets is very real – this isn't just some abstract concept. Your mindset can make all the difference in whether you succeed or fail at any given task or relationship.

For example:

• ***People with a fixed mindset turn down challenges as a way to avoid looking bad – even when they pay a very high price for turning down the challenge.*** We saw this in the study described at the beginning of the chapter, where fixed-mindset students wouldn't learn English even though it would help them in school, and it's been confirmed by other studies as well. For example, in several studies, students with the fixed mindset taking important courses or solving puzzles lost interest in the classes or puzzles once they began to find them to be difficult. Students in the growth mindset did not lose interest when the difficulty increased.[3] In another study involving negotiation skills, half of the people in the fixed-mindset group chose negotiating challenges that would show off their skills rather than challenges that would require them to learn something or improve their skills. In contrast, 88% of those who were in a growth mindset chose challenges that would help them improve.[4]

• ***People with a fixed mindset are generally bad at evaluating their skill level.*** One study found that people in the fixed mindset tended to overestimate their skill level when analyzing their learning status. That makes sense, because people in the fixed mindset are focused on appearing competent in order to maintain their self-image. In contrast, growth-oriented people in the study tended to evaluate their skill level accurately. They weren't defensive about their skill level because they didn't see themselves as stuck there. Furthermore, they recognized the need to see their current level accurately in order to know how to move forward and improve.[5]

• ***People with a fixed mindset choose unrealistic goals based on ideals of achievement rather than goals based on growing and contributing.*** A study of college students found that those with a fixed mindset chose goals that were impossible to work toward, such as to be someone who was "born with great talent." Furthermore, having this unachievable goal made them frustrated, demoralized and stressed; they didn't believe they could ever be a person with great talent. In contrast, students with the growth mindset chose striving goals – the goal was to *work toward* something. They knew they weren't masters yet, but the goal of working toward greatness inspired them (instead of leaving them demoralized and stressed).[6]

• **People with a fixed mindset respond to negative feedback by withdrawing.** Asked how they would react to a bad grade on a test, seventh-grade students with the fixed mindset said they would study less (!); students with the growth mindset said they would study more.[7] Another study found that in junior high, when classes usually become tougher than in earlier years, children with a fixed mindset showed a drop in grades; children with a growth mindset earned better grades.[8] (Dr. Dweck also notes that children with a fixed mindset tend to choose less effective learning strategies, creating yet another obstacle to their own success.)

• **People with a fixed mindset focus their attention on those who make them look good in comparison, not on those they could learn from.** In one study, students with the fixed mindset preferred to compare themselves to others who had done poorly on a test, making them feel better by comparison. Students with the growth mindset compared their work to those who did better than them – which is a great way to learn.[9]

• **People with a fixed mindset boost their self esteem by supporting negative stereotypes.** In another study, boys with the fixed mindset got a boost in self-esteem when they endorsed the stereotype that girls were inferior. Boys with the growth mindset were less likely to agree that girls were inferior, and even when they did believe girls were inferior, the researchers found no increase in the boys' self esteem as a result of that belief.[10]

• **People with a fixed mindset tend to be more depressed – and more overwhelmed when they experience depression.** One study found that fixed-mindset students were more depressed overall, and the more depressed they felt, the more they withdrew from responsibilities. Growth-mindset students did experience some depression, but the more depressed they felt, the harder they worked to pull themselves out of it and fulfill their responsibilities.[11]

• ***People with a fixed mindset try to avoid honest discussion of problems that needed to be addressed.*** One study followed two groups of people working in a corporation. The study found that individuals in the fixed-mindset group were too concerned about how they would appear to risk honest and open discussions. The growth-mindset group were much more likely to express honest opinions and disagree in meetings. Not surprisingly, they did better over time, profiting from feedback and mistakes.[12]

• ***Fixed-mindset boys take offenses more personally and are more likely to want violent revenge.*** A study of eighth-grade students regarding bullying found that fixed-mindset boys saw being bullied as equivalent to being judged, and they were very focused on the idea of getting revenge for the bullying. Growth-mindset boys tended to see the situation as the bully's problem, not as a judgment; they felt the solution was to talk to the bully, not take revenge.[13]

• ***People with a fixed mindset primarily pay attention to judgmental feedback; they ignore useful feedback.*** During a study of brain wave patterns, subjects were asked challenging questions; the brain scans revealed when the subjects were paying attention. Those with the fixed mindset paid attention when they were told whether they were right or not, but did not pay attention when offered information that would help them do better. The growth-mindset people paid attention to both types of information.[14]

• ***People with a fixed mindset hope for unrealistic relationships.*** Young adults were asked what kind of relationship they would like to have. Those with the fixed mindset said they wanted to be with someone who would put them on a pedestal and admire them. Those with the growth mindset said they wanted to be with someone who would challenge them and help them grow.[15]

• ***Students in a fixed mindset do worse in school***. This isn't that surprising, given the other study results we've already described. However, several studies have found that students who take a workshop designed to change their minds about their ability to learn and grow did significantly better in school afterwards. One study showed that switching to a growth mindset raised the math and English scores of seventh graders[16]; another found that college students' grades improved (along with their enjoyment of schoolwork) after a similar workshop.[17]

Another study by Dr. Dweck and two colleagues compared two groups of students, one of which received study skills training, while the other received training in study skills *and* a mindset workshop. As the semester progressed, the grades of those who only received study skills training dropped. The grades of the students who also took the mindset workshop improved. Even the teachers, who did not know which students had taken the mindset workshop, reported noticing changed behavior in those students.[18]

To sum up: The studies above found that people working with a fixed mindset made self-defeating choices, evaluated their situations poorly, did worse in school, were more depressed, took offenses personally and then focused on revenge. They retreated in the face of obstacles, had unrealistic goals and only paid attention to feedback that related to how well they did, instead of information that would help them improve. Talk about keeping you stuck on the Wheel of Misfortune!

A Fixed Mindset Also Affects Those Around You

Studies have found that being in the fixed mindset can also have a dramatic effect on those with whom you interact. For example, the mindset of your teacher affects how well you do in school. A study in Germany found that students who studied with teachers in the fixed mindset ended the year at the same level they began – whether they were considered high ability or low ability at the start of the year. In contrast, students who studied with a growth-mindset teacher all ended up doing well, regardless of how they were categorized at the beginning of the year.[19]

The consequences of what this study found (along with the studies of students' mindsets) could be enormous. Given that the fixed mindset is so widespread, how many teachers out there are operating on the premise that students are either "smart" or "dumb" and nothing the teacher can do will change that? This study suggests that students in those classes won't progress, *because the teacher doesn't believe they can*. How much better could students in schools across the country and around the world

Consequences of Having a Fixed Mindset

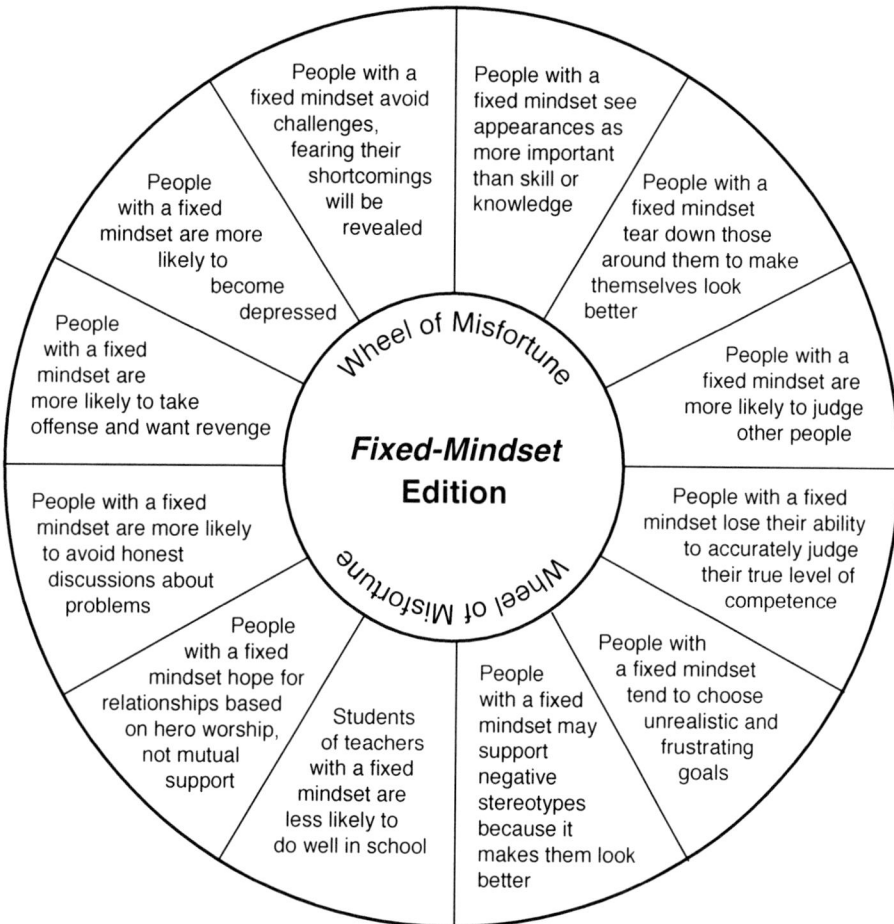

do if every teacher learned that this kind of belief has a powerful effect on how well people do in school (and by extension, how well they do later on in the real world)? Remember, *every student in classes taught by a teacher with the growth mindset progressed.*

Interestingly, a landmark study of how some people become "masters" in their fields, conducted by Benjamin Bloom – described in his classic book *Developing Talent in Young People* – found that highly successful individuals had early teachers who did not judge their students. That's a characteristic associated with teachers who are in the growth mindset, not the fixed mindset. This very likely contributed to putting these future masters on the road to success. Who knows how many more "masters" in every field we might have if all teachers were in the growth mindset?

The mindset of parents also affects children – and the children then affect other children. A study of abused young children – those who were judged and punished by parents for crying or engaging in other normal early childhood behaviors that irritated the parents (a parental behavior associated with the fixed mindset) abused other children the same way the parents abused them.[20] Add to this the fixed-mindset tendency to respond to offenses by wanting revenge, the unwillingness to participate in honest discussions that might make them look bad, and the tendency to endorse stereotypes and hold others back as a way of looking better in comparison, and it should be abundantly clear that being in the fixed mindset is not only dangerous to an individual, it's dangerous to those around him or her.

In fact, the fixed mindset may have a lot to do with bigotry, class war, and hatred of other social, political and religious groups. The reasoning goes as follows: If a group seems inferior in terms of accomplishment, this means they have an inborn, innate inferiority. (After all, those in the fixed mindset believe we're all stuck the way we are.) That "innate inferiority" then justifies treating the people in that group differently than the people in your own group – rather than seeing them as a product of their environment and potentially deserving of your help.

It's important to remember that we're not talking about some serious psychological problem or disorder here; *we're talking about a framework of understanding that almost all of us carry around to a greater or lesser extent.* Believing that we are limited and must defend our current position – because trying to improve would be a waste of time – is not some rare phenomenon. It's a part of the human condition that is everywhere around us, something we're likely to encounter on a daily basis.

A number of factors help to determine which mindset we choose at any given time or in any given situation, and we'll talk more about those factors shortly. But one thing is certain: The mindset we choose will have a direct and profound impact on whether we grow or stagnate in any given situation – and whether we fail or succeed. The defensive choices made in the fixed mindset place limitations on us. The growth mindset says, *there are no limitations, so let's go for it and see what happens.* Furthermore, as noted earlier, mindset can also become an all-encompassing life philosophy. When that happens, the consequences go beyond a single situation and affect our entire lives, dooming us to spend our entire lives on the Wheel of Misfortune.

However, all of this begs an important question: Despite the downsides of being in the fixed mindset, what if it's really true that we're stuck with limited abilities? Can human beings actually change and grow in most situations, or is that just optimistic nonsense? Let's see what the evidence says.

Is It True That We're Limited? Growth, Change, Mastery and Creativity

Despite the demonstrably negative consequences of believing that we can't grow and change – the basic belief behind the fixed mindset – some would argue that this belief is fundamentally true; that talent is the "biological destiny of the few." Is it?

Three very good pieces of evidence suggest that it is not. First, experts studying individuals who excel in different fields have found almost no evidence that this level of achievement is the result of innate talent. Second, contrary to the once widespread belief that the brain was unchanging after the first decade or two of life, the latest brain research shows that learning and practicing at any point in life causes dramatic changes in the brain. And third, there are documented cases of people with no apparent talent in a given area becoming world champions by putting in sufficient time and effort practicing. (A quick note about the word *talent*: For simplicity, when I refer to talent in this chapter, I'm referring to the idea of *innate* talent, a gift you are born with, unless otherwise specified.)

Let's look at each of these pieces of evidence in detail.

One of the things that convinces people that we're stuck with some innate level of ability is the existence of people who seem to be incredibly talented, who are masters in their fields – and who seem to be different from the rest of us. Seeing individuals who apparently have a special gift gives credence to the idea that we either are born with a gift or we aren't. (And the idea that if you weren't born with it, you're wasting your time trying to get it.)

In fact, the evidence from careful studies suggests that this idea is flat-out wrong. When scientists go searching for evidence of innate talent or ability in exceptionally "talented" individuals, as Benjamin Bloom and his colleagues did in the study described in *Developing Talent in*

Young People, they are hard-pressed to find it. Superstars in any field – sports, science, music, chess, you name it – seldom turn out to have been identified as gifted when they were children. In fact, parents and teachers frequently identified *other* children in the same family as being more gifted than the child who grew up to be the "superstar." Furthermore, few "child prodigies" end up being highly successful in their area of expertise when they grow up, so if there is some innate talent there, it seldom leads to adult "master" status.

So what do the "extremely talented" adults have in common? They have all put in *thousands of hours of focused practice* in their area of expertise. Focused practice does not mean simply doing something over and over for years (which would be true for many employed people); it means practicing skills with the specific intention of getting better at them – and doing it for years on end.

In fact, as at least one researcher has noted, the skills that cause most people to classify someone as "talented" are almost always complex skills you *have* to develop through extensive focused practice – they're not skills you can be born with. Researchers have found this over and over again, and the conclusion they've come to is this: Ending up with an outstanding gift is largely about being motivated to work hard at developing a skill and having the opportunity to do so; it's not about being born "gifted."

Yes, personal and physical characteristics are a part of the success equation; a short person is less likely to become a basketball star. But if the parents of a short person are athletic and the opportunity and motivation to practice endlessly are present, a short child will find a way to pursue something athletic where height isn't as much of an issue. Furthermore, looking at it from the other side, being born with a "gift" such as good vocal chords, larger hands, or better physical appearance (according to the social standards of the day), isn't even remotely a guarantee of success or great achievement. Without thousands of hours of focused practice using them, physical gifts don't lead to success.

Mozart is often cited as an example of an innately gifted individual. This idea is supported by his writing a lot of music at an early age, as well as the existence of a letter in which Mozart claimed that large, complex pieces of music came to him whole; his job was simply to write them down. A closer look, however, reveals that his father was a well-known music teacher who forced young Mozart to start writing and practicing constantly at the age of three; his father made him maintain an intensive program of this throughout his early life. Furthermore, much of Mozart's early work is largely derivative of others' music, and his father appears to have "edited" a lot of it. In addition, the letter citing his seemingly magical ability to generate music is now generally acknowledged to be a forgery – which is supported by looking at Mozart's manuscripts. The manuscripts are full of corrections and rewrites; hardly a simple transcription of music that came to him "from the ether." In fact, by the time Mozart was writing his most original and innovative works, he was 20 years old and had spent the required tens of thousands of hours doing focused practice.

The data from both clinical studies and historical research is clear: If you go looking for "innate talent," you're almost certain to find the *appearance* of an innate gift that's actually been generated by years of hard work.

Benjamin Bloom, the architect of the landmark study of how people become "masters" that we mentioned earlier, says in his book *Developing Talent in Young People*: "What any person in the world can learn, almost all persons can learn if provided with appropriate prior and current conditions." He adds that there may be 1% or 2% of individuals who do have some special, innate talent, and 2% or 3% who have mental or physical impediments that make it impossible for them to master some skills. But his research clearly indicates that 95% of people can learn to be good at anything, provided that the right conditions allow the person to master it. (The right conditions meaning, for example, having the time and interest to put in those many hours of focused practice.)

A second key piece of evidence that the fixed mindset is wrong comes from recent research on the brain. For decades it was believed that the brain could not generate new cells or change substantially in response to selective use of it's parts. We now know that's not true. Studies have not only demonstrated that the brain does produce new neurons throughout life, but that people who use one part of the brain more tend to have many more neurons – and far more *developed* neurons – in that area. Taxi drivers in London, for example, whose job requires learning an enormous number of details about the city, were found to have greatly enlarged hippocampi, a part of the brain crucial to memory.[21] The left angular gyrus, a part of the brain essential to language, contains significantly more grey matter in people who speak two languages than in those who speak only one.²² Heschl's gyrus, a cortical area used in sound processing, is twice as large in musicians as in nonmusicians.²³

Someone playing devil's advocate might suggest that people could be born this way and end up in those fields as a result, but the evidence disagrees. The size of the hippocampus in London cab drivers was found to be proportional to the number of years the driver had been on the job. In musicians, the greater the amount of practicing the individual did in the previous 10 years, the larger the size of Heschl's gyrus. And one study demonstrated that when volunteers were trained to juggle, the related areas of the brain increased in density over time as the training continued. Furthermore, the related areas *decreased* in size after a few months of not practicing!²⁴

In fact, practice causes physical changes in both individual neurons and in the way the different parts of the brain are utilized. Research has found that not only does practice cause the relevant area in the brain to get bigger, but after a while the neurons in that part of the brain become more efficient. As a result, fewer neurons have to be involved in order to complete the task.²⁵ (That's part of the reason we don't run out of brain space as we continue to add skills to our repertoire.) A similar change sometimes happens at the physical level as well, as practice leads to completing physical motions more efficiently, using fewer unnecessary muscles and with less anxiety. (Those changes, in turn, lead to using fewer neurons.) Furthermore, even individual neurons change when a skill is practiced. When monkeys were trained to master a task involving very specific touch sensitivity, individual neurons in the area of the brain responsible for that task gradually became more selective about when they would fire, responding only when they received increasingly specific input from other neurons. In other words, their response became more precise over time.²⁵

A third piece of evidence that innate talent is not the reason for exceptional ability is that individuals without any particular reason to excel in a given area have shown that it is possible to rise to the top of a field simply by following the formula discovered in Benjamin Bloom's study: thousands of hours of focused practice. It's not too hard to see how that can be the case in sports – lots of examples of focused practice turning people into top athletes can be found. But the same is also true for skills that are primarily mental.

A classic example is the achievements of the daughters of Laszlo Polgar, a Hungarian who firmly believed that anyone can master anything. In the 1960s he set out to prove this by turning his daughters into world-class chess champions. He and his wife had no particular talent for chess (actually, his wife had none at all), nor was there any chess talent of note among his or his wife's ancestors. In addition, it was widely believed at the time that women could not become chess masters. But starting from an early age, the Polgars taught their three daughters to play chess and got them to practice for several hours every day. They also accumulated a library of ten thousand books on the topic.

Guess what? At age 21, the eldest daughter became the first woman to reach grand master status (the highest possible world ranking). Soon after, the third daughter became a grand master at age 15, beating Bobby Fischer's record for the youngest person ever to achieve that ranking. As a team the three girls competed in the Women's Olympiad and scored Hungary's first victory against the Russians, making them national heroes.[26,27]

And then there's the story of Rudiger Gamm, a young German who started out without any noteworthy mathematical ability. At the age of 20, he began doing four hours a day of calculation practice. Within six years he became a phenomenon, able to very quickly calculate complex numerical functions and solve mathematical problems in his head. He got to be so good at it that he was able to make a living showing off this skill on television! Did his brain change in response to all of that practice? Indeed it did; brain scans showed that he was now recruiting much more of his brain than an average person does each time he performed a mental calculation.[28]

The bottom line? Careful research has only found evidence that skills and talent are *not* innate, at least in terms of becoming really good at something. What makes people excel is an *enormous amount of focused practice*.

Or, to put it another way, the fixed mindset is completely wrong.

Buying the Myth of "Talent"

If the fixed mindset belief – that we're limited in terms of how much we can learn and improve at a given task – is untrue, why do we so often buy into it?

We've already mentioned a number of things that help to perpetuate the idea of "innate talent," but there are at least three more factors worth mentioning:

1: The feedback factor. When we're young we get a lot of "fixed-mindset" feedback from other well-intentioned people whose approval we need – in particular, parents, teachers and peers. This may continue when we're adults; most of us find ourselves interacting with peers, bosses or spouses who believe that our skills are limited, and whose behavior pushes us to treat this world view as valid – or risk giving up our relationship with them (by being fired, for example).

2: The culture factor. Our culture is permeated with beliefs that tend to support this idea – that our abilities are limited to those gifts we're born with, and fundamental skills such as creativity are only available to those who are "gifted."

3: The self-serving factor. Believing in limitations can be self-serving: It lets us off the hook by justifying not "wasting our time" trying to improve in areas in which we don't already show promise.

Let's look at each of these more closely.

Fixed Mindset: The Feedback Factor

It's a basic principle of psychology that a potent way to alter behavior is to reward behavior you like and punish behavior you don't like. Parents and teachers do this to us all the time when we're growing up, in an attempt to push us in what they see as a positive direction. For example, they may praise us or give us rewards for doing well on a test or for behaving in a way they consider appropriate. However, the process of rewarding or punishing is not foolproof, for a parent or anyone else. It turns out that the way we *express* our pleasure or displeasure, for example, has a dramatic effect on whether we actually succeed in encouraging or discouraging the behavior in question.

Suppose you have a child who is attending school. If your child comes home after taking a test and shows you a good grade, that's something you probably want to reinforce, so you praise the child for getting the good grade. The question is, what exactly do you say? Many of us would say, "Wow, you're really good at this subject!" or "You're really smart!" But some might frame their praise a little differently. They might say, "This is great – I can tell you worked really hard on this!" or "I'm really proud of you – you keep getting better!"

All of these bits of praise may sound pretty much the same, but they're actually not. It turns out that these word choices represent two very different ways of offering praise. The first two comments praise the child for being smart or talented; they convey the message that you have evaluated the child based on the good grade, and you like what this grade says about *who the child is*. The last two comments praise the person for what he or she *did* – the behavior they have exhibited – *not* the kind of person you think they are.

This turns out to be very important, because praising the person tends to reinforce the fixed-mindset view of the world. In contrast, praising the behavior instead of the person tends to reinforce the growth mindset perspective; it says, not only can you grow and change, you're already doing it and I'm rewarding you for it. And guess what: You'll almost certainly get a very different response depending on which message the child hears, even though both types of message are meant to encourage more of the same behavior.

Here's why: When we receive positive feedback, such as praise from someone whose opinion matters to us (for example, a parent or teacher when we're young), we like it and we want to get more of it. The specific wording of that praise sends us a message about *what we have to do to get more praise* (or avoid punishment). If the praise says that what matters to the feedback person is our effort and our growth, then we know that we can get more praise by putting out more effort and continuing to grow. But if the feedback tells us that the parent or teacher now has a good opinion of us and thinks that we're talented, the way we can keep the praise coming is to *maintain that image in the eyes of the teacher or parent*. In the latter situation, the goal is not to keep doing good work – the goal is to maintain an image! That might involve doing more good work – or it might not.

Think of it this way: Suppose you want your dog to learn a trick. When he does it correctly, you give him a reward, whether it's a food treat, a pat on the head or just talking in a warm, positive way. That's a pretty effective way to alter your dog's behavior. But what exactly are you rewarding? You're not rewarding him for the kind of dog he is; you're rewarding him for what he did, and he knows it. That's why the reward produces more of the behavior you like. The same thing is true with people: If you want to encourage or change behavior, you have to give feedback about the behavior, not the person.

Telling others *what you think of them* in response to their behavior doesn't reward the behavior directly – and it won't necessarily lead them to produce more of the behavior you like. Instead, it will tend to reinforce the kind of behavior exhibited by people in the fixed mindset.

Furthermore, once someone praises us by saying we're smart or talented, the way we go about trying to maintain that reputation will depend partly on whether we agree with what the person said. If we don't think we really deserve the praise, we'll probably try to avoid any more tests of our ability. Why risk disillusioning the parent or teacher by trying something new that might reveal the truth – that you're not really so smart or talented? In other words, in many situations this kind of feedback can motivate us to *avoid* challenges and avoid trying anything new. It can motivate us to duck out on the things that might help us to continue growing and improving. This is typical fixed-mindset behavior, and it's probably the opposite of what the well-intentioned person providing the feedback is hoping for.

Even if you agree with the praise that says you're smart or talented, the outcome isn't likely to be good. Agreeing with the praise may very well inspire you to take on another challenge, but now you'll have the idea that this should be easy for you because you've been told that you're good at it! So, ironically, you're not likely to work hard at the new challenge. You've inadvertently been set up to not do as well on the next challenge – for example, the next test. And if you don't do as well, you're probably going to conclude that your good reputation may not be deserved. As we've already noted, the safest strategy in that situation is to avoid taking on any further challenges, and instead focus on maintaining your good reputation by other means. And once again, the self-destructive fixed mindset ends up being encouraged.

The irony here should be obvious. A parent or teacher who compliments a child by saying the child is smart or talented is trying to encourage the child. We've all said these kinds of things with the very best of intentions. But if we reward the *child* instead of the behavior, we may actually be throwing up roadblocks to the child's future success.

The same thing applies to punishment. What is the object of our disapproval? Is it the child, or the behavior? If the message is that the child is bad or stupid, that won't alter the child's behavior in a positive way; you're not criticizing the behavior that needs to change. Instead, you're sending the message that it isn't growing and working hard that matters, its *who you are* that matters – and you're telling the child that he or she has a fundamental flaw.

It's hard to imagine a better way to get someone to stop trying.

Again, what we say to people in response to their behavior can make a huge difference in the response we get. Most of us think that when it comes to feedback, the big distinction is between praise and punishment. However, that may not be what matters the most. Instead, what probably matters the most is: Which are you praising or criticizing – the behavior, or the person?

The impact of this difference was well demonstrated by another of Dr. Dweck's studies, in which adolescent students were asked to solve ten problems from a nonverbal IQ test. All of them did fairly well; but those who were praised for their *ability* afterwards turned down the opportunity to try challenging new tasks that they might have learned from. Furthermore, they lied about their scores to make them appear better! *This behavior was not seen* in students who were praised for having worked hard to earn their scores. Praising the work they put in led to constructive choices afterward; saying the person was especially smart or capable led to self-defeating choices and actions.[3]

Of course, "fixed-mindset" feedback not only has the wrong effect on behavior and self-confidence, it also teaches us about what's important to the person giving the feedback, and by extension, what's important in life. So: When we're young, well-intentioned feedback we receive that's phrased the wrong way from parents, teachers and peers may not only change our behavior in a negative way, it can also help to convince us that we really are fundamentally limited, and that the only thing that matters is how others see us – *not* what we're actually doing.

This subtle difference in feedback doesn't just affect us when we're kids. If we *consistently* receive feedback of one kind over a long period of time – such as the message that what's important is who we are, rather than what we do – we may generalize that into a philosophy of life, a belief system we carry around with us that affects everything we do throughout life. We may conclude that preexisting talent really is the deciding factor in life, and that it's a waste of time to try to improve in areas in which we don't seem to have talent. And unfortunately, as adults this may be reinforced by feedback we receive from spouses, bosses and friends who have been swayed to believe the same thing.

Fixed Mindset: The Culture Factor

The second major factor that contributes to shaping our beliefs about life is what we pick up from the society we live in: in other words, the beliefs that most of the people in our culture share. For example, if everyone says that having children is the most fulfilling thing we can do, we're likely to believe it. If everyone around us thinks that money leads to happiness, we're likely to believe it. And if everyone around us says that innate talent is the key to success in life, we're likely to believe that, too.

The idea that innate talent is the key to success is pervasive in our society. It turns out that there are many reasons for this, besides possibly picking up this idea from parents, teachers and other adults.

For example:

– ***It's often a mystery how superstars got to be so good.*** It's rare to hear about the years of work that went into developing the physical or mental skills that make someone seem "talented." In addition, there's a certain cachet to the idea that someone was *born* with great talent – that he or she didn't have to work for it. It makes that person seem extra-special. (And publicists are happy to promote that belief since it works in their client's favor.) This reinforces the belief that you have to be born with talent or you're out of luck. But, as noted above, that's not what people who have studied talent have found.

If we saw all the years of hard work that went into making those people seem so "talented," we might not buy into the idea that you have to be born with talent. But in most cases, we don't see those years of hard work.

– ***"Talented" people usually aren't good at explaining how they do what they do.*** Being very good at something is not the same as being good at explaining how you do it. That's why, for example, many experts in a field who are trying to teach their skill set will simply say, "Watch me do it.... Now you try!" They may not have a clue about how their mind has learned to process the information about the baseball coming toward them, or the status of all of the pieces on the chess board, or how they created that nice melody, or what makes them incredibly good at managing other people. It *is* possible to analyze and understand what's going on in their minds and/or bodies, thanks to the sophisticated tools and better understanding psychologists and sociologists have today. But very few of the talented people out there actually understand in great detail exactly what's going on in their mind or body when they display their skill.

Even in those rare instances in which a "master" really does understand how he or she accomplishes the feats that impress everyone else, he or she may not be good at communicating that knowledge to help other people learn the same skills. That lack of understanding and/or ability to communicate helps perpetuate the idea that there really *isn't* any explanation for their impressive skill, except that the "master" must have been born with it.

– Superstars often buy into the belief that they were born with a gift that sets them apart. This isn't a question of ego; many superstars simply accept what others have always told them about themselves – that they must have been born gifted.

Renowned neuropsychologist Elkhonon Goldberg described a symposium he once attended on the secrets of extraordinary achievement. The symposium panel included a host of superstars in their fields – scientists, athletes, corporate leaders and artists, among others. They took turns sharing their insights into their own successes, and the result was a general agreement that it required two basic things: motivation – i.e., ambition, drive and focus – and innate talent that the individual had to be born with. As Dr. Goldberg says, "The symposium participants agreed that without a special talent there can be no achievement, and that the special talent is something one is born with, the biological destiny of the few."[29]

The evidence from studies of people just like those extraordinary overachievers at that symposium says otherwise. But the fact that superstars themselves often believe that they have an innate gift goes a long way toward perpetuating the idea of innate talent. It helps to support the belief that we either have it or we don't.

Ironically, buying into the fixed-mindset perspective makes it harder to stay on top in your field, should you manage to get there, because it leads to the idea that your success is the result of your "innate ability" rather than the work you've done. That's a recipe for stalling in your career rather than continuing to advance – and continuing to advance is the only way to stay on top in this highly competitive world.

Not everyone has bought into the myth, however. Tiger Woods is a classic example of someone who fully appreciates that talent isn't innate; he was willing to stop and work tirelessly to improve his golf swing *even when he was the number one player in the world.* And shortly before his death, Einstein said, "I know quite certainly that I myself have no special talent. Curiosity, obsession and dogged endurance, combined with self-criticism, have brought me to my ideas." And when Warren

Bennis interviewed great leaders around the world, they all agreed that great leaders are made, not born.[30]

– *Creativity seems to come from nowhere, as if by magic.* As Arthur C. Clarke famously noted, any sufficiently advanced technology is indistinguishable from magic. Creativity, as it turns out, is a very advanced technology – one that happens to be part of the bank of capabilities we're all born with. Creativity still has not been fully explained – at least not enough that most people see it as an understandable process. So, for most of us, creativity still seems like magic. And when someone exhibits creativity that we believe we could not match, the easiest explanation is that the person was born with a gift.

In truth, we're all being creative almost all of the time; we all solve problems and make choices every day. How noteworthy our creativity appears to be is simply a question of degree, and the ends to which we use it. Michelangelo painting the ceiling of the Sistine Chapel and you or me making dinner don't seem like different levels of the same thing – but in fact, they are. They're both expressions of creativity, just on very different scales.

Creativity of the artistic variety can easily be enhanced with practice. And much of what may be seen as a "creative gift" is actually an intimate familiarity with a particular creative process. If you work with a truly excellent teacher, almost anyone can pick up some of that knowledge and suddenly "become more creative" in that area. Betty Edward's work teaching people to draw (described in her book *Drawing on the Right Side of the Brain*) is a classic example; simply conveying a few basic facts about the way an artist sees shifts her students from drawing like five-year-olds to creating drawings that look professional. (For more about Edward's work, see Chapter 6.) Creativity seems mysterious, but it's a skill that can be developed, just like any other. The fact that it seems so mysterious, however, helps to perpetuate the idea that talent is something you have to be born with.

– *Superstars really do seem to be different from the rest of us.* They probably *are* different from the rest of us by the time they're experts in their field. The question is not whether they're different – the question is, *how did they become different?* Many assume that masters in a field were born different, when in fact it's been shown that in almost every case, it's the thousands of hours of focused practice that cause those changes in an individual. This is obvious in the case of building muscles, but, as noted above, it has also turned out to be true in the brain.

So, masters in a given field may, in fact, be different from the rest of us, not only in physical terms, but mentally as well. However, the evidence suggests that this is because of the flexibility and continuing growth of the brain and body, as shaped by their ongoing, focused practice. Most of those differences were not there at birth.

– *Masters do complex tasks with an ease that seems incredible.*
Another thing that makes experts seem different from the rest of us is their mastery of feats that the rest of us would find incredibly difficult to duplicate. For example, masters are often able to remember enormous amounts of information specific to their area of expertise, as when a chess master glances quickly at a complex chess board and can then recall the location of every piece. Feats of memory such as this help to perpetuate the idea that some masters have "mutant" brain abilities that help to account for their success – and leave the rest of us out of the running.

Once again, careful studies have shown that such feats of memory don't signify greater mental capacity than the rest of us have. What they signify is *different ways of organizing information* that make it possible to remember much more than the rest of us – at least in that one area of expertise. Those different ways of organizing information were learned during those years of practice.

Some of this relates to the capacity of human short-term memory (i.e., the ability to capture information and hold it in our minds just long enough to be useful right now). The average capacity of human short-term memory is between five and nine units of information. (That's the reason for the length of phone numbers.)[31] It often seems like masters can remember far more than that – which would support the idea that they have a special innate talent. But they actually have the same memory limits as the rest of us. The reason they can remember so much more is that they've learned to comprehend the information in their field of expertise in much larger "units of information."

For example, when I glance at a chess board with the intention of trying to remember where all the pieces are, I see a huge amount of information about multiple pieces, and it's way too much for me to hold in my mind. I can't easily recreate the way the chess board was set up, after only one glance. But a chess master can, and that's because he (or she) recognizes *patterns* of pieces across the board. In other words, to a chess master the entire board may represent a familiar, single unit of information. The proof? If the chess pieces are arranged randomly on the board – in ways that wouldn't make sense in an actual chess game – a chess master's ability to recreate the chessboard drops to that of a novice.[32]

In addition, practiced individuals may be using different memory strategies that they've learned or developed over time. Remember the story of Rudiger Gamm, the fellow who practiced doing math in his head until he became a phenomenon because his skill was so far beyond what most of us can do? Psychologist Anders Ericsson demonstrated that Gamm, as well as many other "experts," learn to use long-term memory to aid in doing tasks that the rest of us would only use short-term memory to accomplish.[33] In other words, they're using their mental resources in ways the rest of us don't – at least for that particular skill or task – helping them to leapfrog ahead of the rest of us in that area. Learning to enlist an unusually great percentage of our mental resources in the service of a particular skill takes time, and a lot of practice. But once we've learned to do it, our abilities in that area may seem like a miraculous level of "innate talent" to everyone else.

There's also the issue of shortcuts. When you've done something intensively for years, you learn how to do it quickly by grasping details and using processes that someone without your experience wouldn't have a clue about. As a songwriter, I've had people marvel that I sometimes can create a very complex piece of music in a matter of hours – maybe even minutes. They react as if I must have been born with a great gift. I usually go out of my way to point out that I've been doing this intensively for decades – I've even taught classes in it. I know all the creative shortcuts; I know what will almost certainly work or not work. In short, I know that my ability to occasionally create something wonderful in a short period of time is not the result of some innate gift I was born with. It's a skill that I developed as a result of extensive, focused practice.

Superstars may also seem to have greater perception than the rest of us, as when a tennis star reacts incredibly quickly to move to intercept a ball being returned by the opposing player. Does that signify some innate talent – some ability to see more quickly or respond more quickly when the ball is hit? It turns out that thousands of hours of experience enable people to notice cues that the rest of us less-experienced people miss. In the case of tennis, the superstars know where the ball is going to land before the amateurs do, not because of some innate talent, but because they've learned to "read" the position and movement of the other player's body *before the ball is hit*.[34] It's another advantage that comes from practice, not from talent they were born with. The rest of us have to see the ball start to travel towards us before we react.

It's like the old joke about the plumber called in when the plumbing in an entire skyscraper stopped working. The plumber arrives, surveys the situation, goes into the basement, pulls out a hammer and gently taps once on a pipe with the hammer. Everything starts working again. On his way out, he hands the building owner a bill for $10,000. The building owner stops him, and says, "Wait a minute! All you did was tap on a pipe! How come you're charging $10,000?" The plumber says, "Okay, let me give you an itemized bill." A minute later he hands the owner a new bill that reads: *Tapping on pipe: $1. Knowing where to tap: $9,999.*

We're not usually surprised when a craftsman can do "miraculous" things after years of experience. We know that an expert carpenter is expert because of years of focused practice. But most of us have trouble seeing that the same thing is true when we marvel at the abilities of a star athlete, a brilliant scientist, or some other "master."

Again, the bottom line here is that masters, experts and superstars always turn out to have put in thousands of hours of focused practice and hard work. Furthermore, most of them didn't show any sign that they were destined for greatness when they were very young. So the fact that they seem different from the rest of us may be an accurate perception – but it's merely evidence of the time and effort they've put into practicing their area of skill or expertise. It's *not* evidence for an innate gift that the rest of us missed out on and can never hope to match.

All of the factors we just discussed encourage people to buy into the fixed mindset – the idea that trying to learn and change is futile, and the idea that you're either born with talent or you're not. And as we've seen, that's a major reason people end up stuck on the Wheel of Misfortune.

Fixed Mindset: The Self-Serving Factor

There's another reason the fixed mindset is popular: It can be self-serving. After all, if success is out of our hands – if we're either born with great skill or we aren't – then we don't have to do anything! In contrast, the studies of talented individuals indicate that excelling at something requires a lot of work. Yes, if you really love what you're doing, putting in that much work may not seem like a huge imposition. But if you're not thrilled with what you're doing, you'll *never* put that kind of effort into it. And if you don't, believing that the resulting lack of mastery or superstar status isn't your fault lets you off the hook. You can simply say, "I wasn't born with that gift."

Needless to say, very few of us reach the level at which other people think of us as very talented or gifted, much less a "master" in our field. So believing that talent is something you have to be born with works in our favor, psychologically speaking. It saves us from fretting about the fact that we haven't matched that level of achievement.

Meanwhile, it translates into two self-defeating ideas: First, if we don't have obvious skill in some area of life, it's not worth even trying to accomplish anything in that area. This causes people to stagnate, and leads them to encourage others around them to "accept their limitations" and not "waste their time" trying to excel (unless some amount of skill is already evident). Second, it leads people to conclude that *effort doesn't really matter* – that if you don't have innate talent in some part of your life, no amount of effort will lead to success. If you buy into that idea, you may end up not working hard at *anything*.

How Can You Change a Fixed Mindset?

By now it should be obvious that changing your thinking from the fixed mindset to the growth mindset could make all the difference in how well you do in life – especially when misfortune seems to be dogging your footsteps. But how easy is it to change?

The answer depends on what's driving your mindset in any given situation. Our mindset about some things can be changed by something as simple as reading an article telling us that people can learn to do it – as many of the studies described earlier demonstrated. That's true because we probably don't have a preconception about whether or not we can learn to do that particular thing (for example, juggling), and if an "expert" says we can or can't, we'll probably take his or her word for it. Of course, if the word of an expert can put us into one mindset that easily, contradictory information can change it back just as quickly.

Kids also seem able to change their mindset without too much difficulty, given the right information. That may be the case because they haven't fully developed their "life philosophy" yet. As we discussed earlier, Dr. Dweck helped design a workshop for adolescent students that explained how the brain changes when a person learns, and how the different beliefs about limitations affect our choices and eventually our achievement level. The course also taught good study skills and habits. Meanwhile, they created a similar course for another group of students that taught the good study skills and habits but didn't give the students the information about mindset and our ability to learn and change.

Even though the courses only lasted eight sessions, the kids in the mindset workshop reported feeling very differently about learning; those who had previously thought of schoolwork as pointless now said they understood why studying wasn't a waste of time. At the end of the school year, the researchers compared the grades of the kids from the two classes, especially their grades from math class, which was seen as the hardest class. The students who took the mindset workshop all showed a jump in grades. The other students didn't, even though they were taught the same helpful study habits. Changing the kids' ideas about their ability to grow and change made all the difference – and Dr. Dweck's workshop succeeded in bringing about that change in a relatively short time.

But what happens when a person has adopted the fixed mindset philosophy as a basis for understanding life? Then we're not just talking about changing beliefs relating to one area of ability. It's like the difference between changing your shirt and changing your entire physical appearance. When the fixed mindset has colored someone's entire world view, making the change is a far bigger challenge.

You might expect that simply showing someone the evidence that we really can – and do – change and learn and grow when we make the effort, would be sufficient to shift someone from the fixed mindset into the growth mindset. The problem is that when you're talking about a pervasive philosophy of life, a multitude of things have become part of the equation, such as what we consider important, how we evaluate ourselves, how we interact with others, and so forth. And unfortunately, the human mind always has trouble making big changes. (That's one of the reasons for the Japanese philosophy of *Kaizen*, which we'll be talking about in Chapter 10. Kaizen emphasizes making changes in small increments, to avoid creating the internal resistance that arises when we face big changes.)

It's no secret that when faced with facts that disagree with our world view, rather than cheerfully altering everything we believe, most of us will scramble to dismiss those facts. So changing someone's mindset when it has reached the level of a philosophical world view may not be easy.

In fact, the very reality that our brains change as we learn new information and practice new skills may work against us in this situation. When the fixed mindset becomes an overriding philosophy, our behavior reflects that in a host of different ways – and the longer we follow those behavior patterns, the more our brain's patterns and structure change to accommodate them. The rut we're in gets deeper and deeper, and it becomes tougher and tougher to get out of it. Once an adult has spent years behaving according to the dictates of the fixed mindset, it will require more time and effort to change that mindset. The brain has molded itself to accommodate the behaviors that the fixed mindset produces.

It's possible to make the change, but it's likely to take time and effort.

That leads us to two other problems that may arise when making this kind of change, as Dr. Dweck has noted.

– ***Problem #1***: Even if we understand that making a change would benefit us, we may underestimate how much help we need to make the change. Underestimating how much help you may need is actually encouraged by the fixed mindset, which includes this idea: *If you're good at something, you shouldn't need help doing it*. So even if you come to realize that the fixed mindset philosophy is bogus, you may still believe that you shouldn't need help changing your philosophy. Unfortunately, not getting any help could guarantee that you fail at changing it.

So, if you find yourself wanting to change your world view to the growth mindset, don't be shy about enlisting others that you trust to help you. Explain the situation in detail and ask them to point out when you're falling back into old habits of thinking and behaving in limiting ways. (Dr. Dweck herself had a fixed mindset for much of her early life; she reports that she still falls back into those patterns from time to time.)

– ***Problem #2***: Once people do make a change, they often see the new, growth-mindset state as a *fait accompli* and expect it to continue without further attention. In reality, old habits die hard. This is especially true if you've been inspired to change because you've realized that your fixed mindset is having a negative effect on others. For example, if you make the effort to change the feedback you're giving, you <u>will</u> get a changed response from those around you – *but only as long as <u>your</u> new behavior continues*. If you like the changes your new mindset and behavior are eliciting from other individuals (better work, better grades, a different reaction to you, etc.) you may think you've conquered the problem, and as a result stop being vigilant. But old habits of thinking and behavior can easily reappear if you haven't fully established your new habits.

What will almost certainly happen if you stop being vigilant about your new attitude is that your earlier behavior and thoughts patterns will re-emerge. As soon as that happens, the people around you will revert to their previous behavior, too. For example, if you decide that you're being held back by a fixed mindset and decide to change your attitude, you might also realize that your child has adopted the fixed mindset and isn't trying to get better in school subjects in which he believes he has no talent. (Plus, when he has gotten good grades, you've rewarded him for "being smart" rather than for working hard.)

Now, let's say you deliberately change that and do your best to convince him that we *do* grow and become better when we put in the effort; and you decide to reward him on the basis of effort, not because he's "smart." After a little while, you'll almost certainly see a positive change, just as Dr. Dweck's workshops caused students to do better. But if you then relax and stop paying attention, you may fall back into your old habits. Your child will soon respond in kind. In that situation, when you realize your child's behavior has gone back to the behavior you don't like, you may throw up your hands and declare that the whole mindset idea doesn't work. (That's always the easy thing to do.)

So be forewarned: If you manage to change your mindset and you like the results you experience, you'll need to stay on the case for the foreseeable future. If you can manage to do that, perhaps with some help from friends and family, the improved results in your life – which may include moving ahead in your career, more successful relationships, less depression and better work from the people around you – should continue as well.

Once more, in brief:

Here are the key points to remember from Chapter 2:

• Whenever we have to decide what we're going to do in response to a given situation, there are two fundamentally different strategies we can employ: changing to meet the needs of the situation, or remaining as we are and defending our position. The option we pick often depends on our "mindset" about the situation. The fixed mindset says, "People are fundamentally stuck as who they already are, so trying to change is a waste of time." The growth mindset says, "People can indeed grow and change."

• Mindset may be specific to a given situation (*as in the case of believing that only a person with inborn talent could learn to do a particular task*), or, it may be a general philosophy of life (*as when someone believes that people can't really change in any fundamental way*).

• A long list of negative consequences can occur when we make choices based upon the fixed mindset. In the fixed mindset we tend to avoid challenges; we focus on appearances; we judge others; our goals become unrealistic and frustrating; we're more likely to become depressed; our relationships are less likely to succeed; and if we're teaching others, our students are less likely to progress.

• The evidence overwhelmingly supports that the growth mindset – the belief that almost any skill or knowledge can be enhanced with focused practice – is accurate. People are not stuck at one level; we have remarkable capacity for growth in virtually any area. Our culture supports the idea that talent is innate, but the evidence does not. Instead, the evidence says that superior ability results from thousands of hours of focused practice.

• A fixed mindset is easy to change if it's based on limited experience and has not already shaped our behavior to a large degree. In contrast, if we've held a belief for a long time, it will have shaped our behavior, and that repeated behavior will have caused changes inside the brain. Those changes can only be undone with time and effort.

- If you want to change your mindset from "fixed" to "growth" but find it's not easy to do so, enlist appropriate help. Remember that as soon as you stop being vigilant, your behavior may revert to the earlier mode, taking any positive external improvements with it. But if you stick with it, enlisting the help of friends if necessary, your brain will eventually adapt to the new outlook and behavior patterns and you won't have to worry about falling back into old fixed-mindset habits.

✳ ✳ ✳

NOTES for Chapter 2

1. Study described in Carol Dweck's *Mindset,* Chapter 2
2. For example, see: Deiner E, et al. Wealth and Happiness Across the World: Material Prosperity Predicts Life Evaluation, Whereas Psychosocial Prosperity Predicts Positive Feeling. *Journal of Personality and Social Psychology* 2010:99;1;52-61.
3. Mueller CM, Dweck CS. Praise for intelligence can undermine children's motivation and performance. *J Pers Soc Psychol.* 1998 Jul;75(1):33-52.
4. Kray L, Haselhuhn M. Implicit Theories of Negotiating Ability and Performance: Longitudinal and Experimental Evidence. *Journal of Personality and Social Psychology* 2007:93:49-64.
5. As shown in the work of David Dunning. For example: Ehrlinger J, Dunning D. How chronic self-views influence (and potentially mislead) estimates of performance. *J Pers Soc Psychol.* 2003 Jan;84(1):5-17.
6. Study done by Carol Dweck and Bonita London, described in Chapter 7 of Dweck's Mindset.
7. Blackwell LS, Trzesniewski KH, Dweck CS. Implicit theories of intelligence predict achievement across an adolescent transition: a longitudinal study and an intervention. *Child Dev.* 2007 Jan-Feb;78(1):246-63.
8. ibid
9. Study by Carol Dweck and David Nussbaum, described in Dweck's *Mindset*, Chapter 2.
10. Study conducted by Shari Levy, PhD, described in Dweck's *Mindset*, Chapter 6.
11. Study conducted by Carol Dweck, Allison Baer and Heidi Grant, described in Dweck's *Mindset*, Chapter 2.
12. Wood RE, Williams-Phillips K, Tabernero C. "Implicit theories of ability, processing dynamics and performance in decision-making groups." Australian Graduate School of Management, Sydney, Australia.
13. Study conducted by Carol Dweck, described in *Mindset*, Chapter 6.
14. Study conducted by Carol Dweck, Jennifer Mangels and Catherine Good, described in *Mindset*, Chapter 2.
15. Study conducted by Carol Dweck, Stephanie Morris and Meliss Kamins, described

in *Mindset*, Chapter 2.
16. Good C, Aronson J, Inzlicht M. Improving adolescents' standardized test performance: An intervention to reduce the effects of stereotype threat. *Applied Developmental Psychology* 2003:24;645-62
17. Aronson J, Fried CB, Good C. Reducing the Effects of Stereotype Threat on African American College Students by Shaping Theories of Intelligence. *Journal of Experimental Social Psychology*. 2002:38;113-125.
18. Blackwell L, Trzesniewski K, Dweck CS. Implicit Theories of Intelligence Predict Achievement Across an Adolescent Transition: A Longitudinal Study and an Intervention. *Child Development.* 2007:78;246-263.
19. Falko Rheinberg. Achievement Evaluation and Motivation to Learn. Gottingen: Hogrefe, 1980. 87, 116. Also reported at the conference of the American Educational Research Association, Seattle, April 2001.
20. Main M, George C. Responses of Abused and Disadvantaged Toddlers to Distress in the Day Care Setting. *Developmental Psychology* 1985:21;407-412.
21. Maguire EA, et al. Navigation-related structural change in the hippocampi of taxi drivers. *Proc Natl Acad Sci USA* 200:97;8;4398-4403.
22. Mechelli A, Noppeney U, et al. A Voxel-Based Morphometry Study of Monolinguals, Early Bilinguals and Late Bilinguals. Presented at the ninth annual meeting of the Organization for Human Brain Mapping, New York City in 2003.
23. Schneider P, Scherg M, et al. Morphology of Heschl's gyrus reflects enhanced activation in the auditory cortex of musicians. *Nat Neurosci* 2002:5;7;688-694.
24. Draganski R, Gaser C, et al. Neuroplasticity: Changes in grey matter induced by training. *Nature* 2004: 427;6972;311-12.
25. Jenkins WM, Merzenich MM, et al. Functional reorganization of primary somatosensory cortex is adult owl monkeys after behaviorally controlled tactile stimulation. *Journal of Neurophysiology* 1990:63;1;82-104.
26. Flora C. The Grandmaster Experiment. *Psychology Today* July/August 2005.
27. *Queen Takes All*. The Telegraph, January 16, 2002.
28. Pesenti M, Zago L, et al. Mental calculation in a prodigy is sustained by right prefrontal and medial temporal areas. *Nature Neuroscience* 2001:4;1;103-7.
29. In his book *The Wisdom Paradox* in chapter 1.
30. Warren Bennis. *On Becoming a Leader*. Basic Books. Fourth edition, March 2009.
31. As noted in George Miller's essay "The Magical Number Seven, Plus or Minus Two: Some Limits on Our Caapacity for Processing Information." *Psychological Review* 63 (1956): 81-97.
32. Chase WG, Simon HA. Perception in Chess. *Cognitive Psychology* 1973:4;55-81.
33. Ericsson KA, Kintsch W. Long-term working memory. *Psychol Rev.* 1995 Apr;102(2):211-45.
34. Jones CM, Miles TR. Use of Advanced Cues in Predicting the Flight of a Lawn Tennis Ball. *Journal of Human Movement Studies*. 1978:4;231-35.

3.
Hold Onto Your Personal Power.

Don't take on the role of victim.

"All blame is a waste of time…. The only thing blame does is keep the focus off you when you are looking for external reasons to explain your unhappiness or frustration. You may succeed in making another feel guilty of something by blaming him, but you won't succeed in changing whatever it is about you that is making you unhappy."
– Wayne Dyer, Your Erroneous Zones

The one thing all of us need, and want, is personal power – the power to shape our own lives. We want to feel that we can influence the direction our lives are taking, even though we obviously can't control everything that happens to us. Not surprisingly, it turns out that the positive impact of feeling that we do have power over at least some part of our lives can be profound. Not only can it affect our happiness, it can dramatically affect our health, and even help determine how long we live.

Consider a study involving residents of a nursing home, who – as you might imagine – already had the deck stacked against them in terms of controlling their lives. In this study, volunteers visited residents on a regular basis. The residents were divided into two groups. In one group, the timing and length of the visits were controlled by the residents. In the other group, the timing and duration of the visits were controlled by the person who was visiting. The researchers wanted to see whether just being able to control this one aspect of their lives would have a measurable positive effect on the residents, compared to the group that didn't have control over the visits.

Although the two groups were very similar at the outset, two months into the study the researchers found that the residents who controlled the timing of the visits were healthier, more active, happier and taking fewer medications than the other group of residents. And sadly, in a startling after-effect of the study, the researchers found that once the study ended, a significantly greater percentage of the residents who had been controlling the timing of the visits died. Apparently the loss of the visits – and the little bit of control over their lives that came with them – was much more depressing for those residents than the loss of the visits was for the others.[1]

Many other studies have given some indication of the importance of a sense of control. For example, Michael Marmot, a professor of epidemiology and public health at University College London, has done extensive work on the ways in which a person's social status affects health.[2] After years of investigation, he concluded that what makes a job dangerous to your health – and can make you more likely to die younger – is not so much stress as it is the amount of control you have. People with high-stress jobs who have a lot of control are far less likely to suffer ill effects from working than people who have less control. And this is true even when other aspects of their jobs, such as the salaries, are similar.

It's important to realize that we're talking about a *sense of control*, as opposed to actual control. In other words, the control that counts is the control you *believe* you have, regardless of the outside circumstances. That's one reason some people live through a horribly traumatic situation while others succumb to it: If you believe that you have the power to influence events to some degree – whether or not other people would agree that you do – your happiness and health and motivation to keep going will surpass that of people who see themselves as powerless.

It's also important to note that having some control over the events of your life is not the same as *having power over other people*. There are plenty of people with unlimited financial resources who have lots of power over other people's lives, who are nevertheless miserable and feel that their own lives are out of control. The reverse is also true; someone who appears to be without power over other people may actually have plenty of personal power. It's your sense of personal power that counts, not how much power you have over anyone else.

In fact, an absence of a sense of control is one of the main things that leads people to think of themselves as being trapped on the Wheel of Misfortune. Given that reality, you might assume that maintaining personal power would be very high on everyone's "to-do" list. The last thing people should want to do is *deliberately* give up their personal power. But amazingly, that's not the case. Many people give up personal power quite willingly, without even realizing it.

They do it by *taking on the role of victim.*

What Makes Someone a Victim?

The truth is, everybody has been treated unjustly from time to time. The things that happen to us range from distasteful experiences to those that truly can be life-shattering (for example, being sexually assaulted all through childhood; being unjustly imprisoned; or losing everything and everyone close to you in an accident or disaster). Regardless of the level of tragedy you've experienced – hopefully nothing on the scale of those last examples – everybody knows the feeling of being treated unfairly, maybe by another person or group, or maybe by events beyond your control.

The catch is that *not everybody takes on the role of victim.* Seeing yourself as a victim is one way to respond to being treated unfairly, but it's not the only way.

Suppose you've just been mistreated by someone. You could react by thinking: "This person clearly has power over me and is using that power to harm me." If you decide to view the situation in that way, you are framing the experience as reflecting *a specific type of power relationship* with the person who did you wrong. You are choosing to take on the role of victim in your relationship with that person. But you don't have to react that way. You could react by thinking, "I've been treated unfairly, so I'm going to use my personal power to change the situation and make sure this never happens again." That perspective doesn't create a victim/victimizer relationship at all. That reaction frames the experience as an event that you need to respond to. It doesn't put you in the position of victim.

Taking on the role of victim has serious consequences, because when you take on that role you change your beliefs about who you are and where you stand in relation to the other person. Then, your behavior – *and the other person's behavior* – change in response to your interpretation of what happened. In essence, you're creating a self-fulfilling prophecy. You are, in fact, *giving that person power over you*. And you don't have to do that.

Those who take on the role of victim in response to being treated unfairly create all kinds of further problems for themselves. To help clarify this, let's consider three questions:

1. Why do some people take on the role of victim?
2. Exactly how does taking on the role of victim backfire?
3. If you already see yourself as a victim and decide you want to change, what can you do?

Why Do People Take On the Role of Victim?

When victimization has been overwhelming and life-altering, it's easy to understand how people might come to think of themselves as victims. However, many people don't require overwhelming abuse to take on the role of victim. That's true because in the short run, taking on the role of victim has some payoffs. In many situations, those payoffs are more than sufficient to inspire people to opt for seeing themselves as victims.

For example, if people perceive you as a victim, some of them will try to help you out with emotional or financial support. They'll pay attention to you and defend your feelings. If you've been in an accident or feel that a professional has failed to live up to his or her commitments, you may be able to sue the other person and profit financially. And, as we've all seen at one time or another, some people use this role to manipulate others through guilt, or by insisting that they're unable to take action on their own because of the harm that has befallen them – so someone else has to do things for them.

There's also often an avoidance payoff: Being a victim may get us out of having to do something scary. We don't have to confront the bully. We don't have to go out on our own, which may be scarier than staying with an abusive partner. We don't have to risk making a parent angry by making life choices he or she might disapprove of. You get the idea.

Furthermore, suppose your own behavior helped to cause the negative thing that happened to you. Contemporary culture teaches us that we're not responsible for whatever happened to us, unless it's *inescapably obvious* that we, and we alone, caused it to happen. So if you're a victim, you can avoid taking any responsibility for what happened. You can see the person who wronged you as the only person who "has a problem." You don't have to look closely at yourself or make any changes in your own behavior or attitudes. Plus, you have an excuse to be righteously

Two Ways To React When Someone Mistreats or Harms You

	1. You take on the role of victim	2. You don't take on the role of victim
Overall attitude toward the situation:	This person has power over me; I'm a victim	This situation is unfair; I will change the situation or leave it
Focus:	Being angry and blaming	Getting out of the situation
Perception of the other person:	He (or she) is a bad person	He (or she) has a problem
Main emotion:	Anger and frustration	Determination
Plan of action:	Getting revenge	Changing the situation
Relationship perspective:	This person has power over me	This situation needs to change
Personal power:	Given to the other person	Not given away

angry, which always feels good – at least at first.

These kinds of perks make the role of victim seem like a reasonable choice. Furthermore, our culture supports the idea that seeing yourself as a victim is perfectly legitimate, so taking on this role is acceptable – as long as you have an unhappy experience to justify it.

The reality is that being a victim is *easier* than working to change things in your life. After all, if you decide that you're a victim, you're defining yourself as a person who needs someone else to come to your rescue. The alternative – taking control and making changes in your life – can seem very hard. Staying in an emotional or physical rut as a victim may be embarrassing, but it's safe. (That's not true, of course, if you use being a victim as an excuse to take revenge. That can be a lot of work, and it is definitely *not* safe.)

So there are a number of reasons people take on the role of victim. Some people are overwhelmed by what has happened to them; others take on the role of victim because it seems reasonable; and still others do so because it provides them with subtle but real benefits which seem desirable – if you don't look at those "benefits" too closely.

So: What's the Problem?

Here are a few of the reasons that being a "victim" backfires big-time:

1. Taking on the role of victim keeps you focused on the wrong things, so you don't learn how to get out of your situation and create the life you want. By definition, playing the victim means blaming someone or something else for your misfortune. If you focus on blame, you expend your energy being angry, thinking about the past, and thinking about how unjust the world is. It puts your conscious energy on the apparent source of the injustice – instead of on what you should be doing to get closer to the things you want out of life.

Furthermore, playing the role of victim can become a form of "tunnel vision" that blocks out important information that could help you get out of your situation. Because you're focused on the idea that someone else is to blame, you may totally miss seeing ways in which *you* could change things for the better and prevent the bad thing from happening again. (That's especially likely to happen when our own actions helped to make the bad situation possible. At some level we know our behavior contributed to the problem, which provides an additional motivation to focus intently on the other person so we don't have to admit our part in it.)

For example, if you walk down an unlit street in a bad part of town and you get mugged, yes, the mugger is to blame. But if you don't take responsibility for choosing to put yourself in a dangerous position in the first place, you're going to end up doing the same thing again later – maybe with an even worse outcome. Or, suppose you're in a relationship in which you get beaten by your spouse. Yes, your spouse is to blame. But you're helping to perpetuate the situation by making the choice not to leave, whatever your reasons may be. Being focused on blaming can blind us to changes that are well within our power to make – changes that might prevent a repeat of the unhappy event.

Another way focusing on blame can backfire is by causing us to incorrectly identify the source of a problem. For example, suppose you experienced a victimization in the past for which you clearly had no responsibility, such as being abused during childhood. If you let that experience define you as a victim for the rest of your life, you may begin to feel that your past victimizer is to blame for your *current* troubles. If you do, you'll direct your energy toward resenting the past, and away from your responsibilities to yourself and your loved ones in the present. Both you and your loved ones may suffer as a result.

Noah Levine, American Buddhist teacher, counselor and author of *Against the Stream* and *Dharma Punx*, says he had a moment of clarity about this that changed his life when he was 17. He'd been drinking and getting high since age 12, and had been arrested for his third felony. After a failed suicide attempt, he suddenly had a life-altering insight: He'd been blaming everyone else for his problems. He realized that this idea had kept him from focusing on the present and addressing his personal issues. At that moment, he realized he was responsible for his life. "I was not a victim," he says. "I had created the situation and I had the power to get out of it. I had hope."[3]

2. Taking on the role of victim generates "learned helplessness." Several decades ago, psychologists Martin Seligman, Steven Maier and Richard Solomon at the University of Pennsylvania observed an interesting phenomenon in the laboratory.[4] If you put an animal in an unpleasant situation – for example, in a cage that delivers an electric shock periodically – the animal will try to get out. But if you prevent the animal from escaping, after a while the animal stops trying to escape.

The interesting part is this: Once the animal has given up trying to escape, even if you *do* provide the animal with a way out, *he won't take it*. In most cases, the animal just sits there and takes the shocks, even if he now has a way to get out of the cage.

This is called "learned helplessness," for obvious reasons. And guess what? People do the same thing. Put someone in a situation in which he's helpless, and he'll try to get out of the situation. If he fails to get out of the situation after repeated tries, he stops trying. Then, when an easy way out of the situation shows up, *he doesn't take it*.

This has a lot to do with what we mentioned earlier about perspective: What really matters is *the amount of control you perceive yourself to have*. I believe that learned helplessness happens because repeated, failed attempts to get out of a bad situation lead us to believe that we don't have the power to escape. And once we perceive ourselves as powerless, we effectively *become* powerless. Then, when the situation changes and does provide a way out, our perception that we're powerless overrules the new reality. We stay in the situation and continue to suffer.

It shouldn't be hard to see the connection to taking on the role of victim. If you perceive yourself as helpless in some area of your life, you won't take advantage of opportunities to make positive changes when they finally do come along. To put it another way, once you step into the role of victim, it's not easy to step back out. If anything, your victimhood may spread to other areas of your life, and voila, you're giving up more and more control over your life. And you'll be more likely to stay in situations that cause you to suffer – even when a way to escape them is right in front of you.

3. Taking on the role of victim gives the "victimizer" power over you. The idea that the person who abused you has power over you is an illusion. It's a popular idea for sure, but just because someone hurts you – or is in a position to hurt you – *doesn't mean that he or she has power over you.*

In truth, power over you is something *you allow others to have.* Regardless of the circumstances, you always get to choose how much power someone has over you. People who realize this are able to retain their power, regardless of their circumstances.

Suppose, for instance, you were held prisoner in a concentration camp. You could choose to see your tormentors as having power over you, and yourself as a victim. On the other hand, you could see yourself as a person caught in a bad situation and making the best of it, but *not see yourself as a victim.* If you didn't see yourself as a victim, you'd be looking for opportunities to improve your situation by using the power that you did have.

Glenn Frazier, an American soldier, became a prisoner of war in Osaka, Japan, during the early days of World War II. In his autobiographical book about the years he spent in captivity, *Hell's Guest*, he tells how he was pulled from a line of prisoners on a forced march and taken before one of the officers in charge, for the crime of putting his hands in his pockets. He was asked (through a translator) why he had put his hands in his pockets. He said his hands were cold. He was told angrily that he had broken the rules, and was taken outside to be executed.

The officer pulled out his sword and held it at Frasier's throat. He asked Frasier if he had any last words. Frasier said to the translator, without taking his eyes off of the officer holding the sword, *"He can kill me but he will not kill my spirit and my spirit will lodge inside him and haunt him for the rest of his life! Any Japanese who kills an American without just cause will have his spirit haunt him forever!"* Upon hearing the translation, the officer was taken aback, and after a moment's thought he angrily sheathed his sword. Thanks to Frasier's not thinking like a victim, he survived that encounter – and many others during four years of captivity – and was able to make a good life for himself after the war.

Again, it's an issue of how you choose to interpret your situation: If you see yourself as a victim you are giving away power that you could use to improve your situation. Or, to put it another way: *The fastest and surest way to lose your personal power is to believe that someone else is responsible for your problems.*

4. Taking on the role of victim makes it possible for the victimizer to maintain his (or her) role. When one person abuses another, that's a single event. But when a person takes on the *role* of victim, he or she is adopting a semi-permanent position relative to another person or group of people. It sets up a psychological framework for future behavior and choices, a game that automatically involves the other person. Once the "game" is underway, the person who sees himself as a victim provides an ongoing target for the abuser. The apparent victim becomes what is sometimes called an "enabler" – a person who makes it possible for the other person to continue acting in abusive ways.

In other words, in this situation the other person gets to treat us as a victim *because we let him or her do so*. This may sound contrary to common sense: If someone is mistreating us, it must be their fault, because we'd never let someone continue to do that if it was in our power to stop it! Sadly, human behavior is not that straightforward. We *almost always* have the power to change an abusive situation, but multiple factors – such as learned helplessness and the payoffs that come with being a victim – may cause us not to. So we stay in the role, keep playing the unhappy game, and allow the person who is abusing us to continue abusing us.

However, if either person stops playing, the game can't continue. For example, consider the possible responses to being bullied in school. Psychologists have observed that the target of bullying often ends up playing a predictable role that allows the situation to continue. If, instead, the person who is being bullied refuses to fall into the role of victim, he or she can seek outside help and find creative ways to interrupt the "game," so the bully changes his or her behavior.

Early in my life I was often bullied. I was a tall boy, good in school but lousy at sports. That made me a perfect target for bullies, because they got credit for pushing around a tall, seemingly more imposing kid; it made them seem more powerful than pushing around a smaller kid. But on several occasions I figured out ways to break the game pattern, sometimes with outside help. (My dad had a degree in psychology and offered me good advice more than once.)

The last time I was bullied in school was when I was a freshman in high school. By then, I was fed up with playing the victim and decided not to let myself be put in that position. During a workout with the soccer team – sports were a requirement – a muscular senior starting pushing me around. Rather than taking the punishment, I pushed back and let it escalate into a minor scuffle – with the coach in sight. The coach rushed over and said angrily, *"All right, who started this fight?"* In truth, the coach knew perfectly well who had started the fight. I was several years younger than the other kid and clearly not in good enough physical condition to be starting a fight with him.

The way this little game would normally have played out was that the bully would have taken the blame and then, after the teacher was gone, he'd have let me know he'd be kicking my ass for the rest of the year. But the moment the coach asked the question, I said, *"I started the fight, sir!"* I remember the coach's jaw dropping, since he knew I was lying. The bully's jaw also dropped as he turned and stared at me in complete surprise. After a minute the coach told us both to run a few laps around the field. And you know what? Because I made it clear I wasn't willing to play that game, that senior never bothered me again.

Please note that this particular strategy won't work in every situation. Part of the reason it worked for me at that time is that the coach could plainly see that I hadn't started the fight. If you were to try this strategy and the authority figure nearby (coach, teacher, policeman, etc.) thought you were telling the truth, it could backfire badly! So, I'm not suggesting you try exactly what I did if you're being bullied. I *am* suggesting that if you're being repeatedly abused, you're caught in a psychological game that's allowing the abuser to continue to play his or her role. If you choose to step out of the role of victim and refuse to play the game, the victimizer can't continue to follow that pattern of interaction with you.

However, in some situations, the bully may have a lot to gain by keeping the game going. If that's true, and you stop playing your part, he or she may try to change the nature of the game – perhaps by escalating the abuse. For that reason, if you're in an abusive situation that's really dangerous, you may need outside help to break the pattern and get out of danger. (One very helpful resource you can easily refer to for advice on preventing or managing any bullying situation is www.stopbullying.gov on the Internet.)

Either way, deciding that you don't want to play the role of victim anymore is the first step toward ending the cycle of abuse.

5. Taking on the role of victim encourages other people (besides the abuser) to victimize you as well. People have an amazing capacity to pick up on your self-image when they encounter you, and they'll treat you according to the way you see yourself. That's not a good thing if you see yourself as a victim. For example, experienced muggers look for people who have the body language of a victim, because they know those people will be easy to rob! So seeing yourself as a victim makes you a target for manipulation and abuse, even by people you've never met before.

6. When you take on the role of victim you increase your own sense of powerlessness. In addition to needlessly giving power to others, seeing yourself as a victim positions you as relatively powerless in your own mind. It's the ultimate self-fulfilling prophecy: If you believe you're powerless, then you are – and feeling that way will have immense effects on your happiness, your health and even how long you're likely to live. It will certainly undercut your ability to take effective action in your own behalf, and make it infinitely harder to get off the Wheel of Misfortune.

7. Taking on the role of victim undermines your physical and mental health and drains your energy. If you take on the role of victim, you get to be angry at your "victimizer." Righteous anger feels good – at first. The problem is, people often maintain righteous anger for long periods of time, and that is very bad for their physical and mental health. Plenty of clinical studies have confirmed this.

For instance, when you're angry, you go into a high-stress state – which is useful if you need to run like crazy or fight for your life. It's not useful at all if you *don't* need to run like crazy or fight for your life. When you're in that high-stress state, your body chemistry changes dramatically; your adrenal glands pump large doses of adrenaline and cortisol into your bloodstream. The pounding heart and raised blood pressure triggered by those hormones can produce tiny erosions in the walls of your arteries. Then, adrenaline causes the platelets in your blood to clump together at those damaged areas.

Adrenaline also causes your fat cells to empty extra fat into your bloodstream to provide extra energy for running or fighting. But if you're just angry and you don't actually need to run or fight, those fats aren't used up right away. To manage that, your liver converts some of the extra fat in your bloodstream into cholesterol. Some of that cholesterol will then be attracted to the clumping platelets inside your arteries.[5] In short, you're creating conditions that make it more likely you'll have a heart attack. Meanwhile, as you remain in your angry state, your brain restrains the calming forces of your parasympathetic nervous system which would normally counteract those stress changes after a little while. At the same time, the hormones reduce the effectiveness of your immune system, leaving you more vulnerable to other health problems such as infections.

This "fight or flight" body chemistry was designed for short-term use. Staying in that state all the time not only damages your body and mind, it also drains a lot of your energy, leaving you tired and irritable. Other health issues also increase with ongoing anger. For example, a 2005 study found that wound healing was dramatically affected by the level of hostility in a couple's relationship; injuries healed *twice as fast* when couples had low levels of hostility compared to couples with high levels of hostility.[6] Other studies have confirmed that people under stress get more respiratory infections, decreased immunity, higher blood pressure...you get the idea. This effect has been demonstrated many, many times.[7]

So, being angry at another person or group (or fate, or God) because you feel you've been victimized can easily be justified, and it may feel good at first, but if it continues long enough it begins to eat away at you from inside. The real irony, of course, is that being angry at someone doesn't do a thing to the person you're mad at – it only hurts *you*. Besides, as Phil McGraw (aka "Dr. Phil") has observed, *you don't have to be angry just because you have the right to be.*

8. Taking on the role of victim causes good people to avoid you.

Have you ever known someone who perceived himself or herself as powerless? If you have, then you know how unpleasant it can be to spend time with a person in that state.

When we see a person who has been victimized, most of us want to help, just as we would want to *be* helped if the situation were reversed. In the case of a straightforward one-time victimization, offering help or friendship has mostly beneficial consequences. But when people see someone who has a reputation for thinking of himself as a victim being mistreated, they're much less likely to help. That's because they know there's a game being played – that the person who sees himself as a victim prefers not to take responsibility for bad situations he finds himself in. They know that offering help can entangle them in a complicated psychological game that may become an energy drain and a source of trouble. And it's often the smartest and most capable people – the ones who would make the best friends and be the most helpful resources – who are most likely to see this potential trouble and back away.

Here's another way to think of it: Saying you were victimized tells people something about what happened to you. Saying *you are a victim* tells people how you see yourself, a vastly different thing with far greater consequences and ramifications.

Of course, not everyone will back away from you because you've taken on the role of victim. Some people you encounter will also see themselves as powerless in some area of life. In that case, you may provide confirmation and approval for each other, making you both feel comfortable. (And keeping both of you stuck in powerlessness.)

As unpleasant as it is to spend time with someone who sees himself as a victim, it's even more unpleasant to be around someone who is using this role as a means to manipulate others. Many people avoid panhandlers on a city street or in a public place for exactly this reason: They suspect they're being manipulated by someone who isn't really a victim at all. Even an ordinary person in our family or social circle may occasionally try the same strategy on a more subtle scale. Sometimes it works for a while, but sooner or later it backfires, leading to avoidance. Others eventually realize what's happening and distance themselves from the "victim" who's doing the manipulating.

The importance of a good social network – *especially* when you feel trapped on the Wheel of Misfortune – can hardly be overstated. Good advice, companionship, emotional and physical aid and comfort, and just being able to share resources, are invaluable when times are tough. If you take on the role of victim, you are effectively cutting yourself off from all of those resources, which you would otherwise have at your disposal.

9. When you take on the role of victim, bitterness and anger tend to spread into other parts of your life. An emotional state doesn't stay restricted to one area of your life. If you're unhappy or frustrated about one thing and the feeling is part of a long-standing role you've taken on, your whole life will eventually be affected by it. The same is true of an attitude; if you focus on the idea that one part of your experience was unjust, you'll start to find evidence of injustice in other parts of your life as well. Your life experience will be fundamentally altered. It may take a while for the anger or bitterness to spread into other parts of your life, but when it happens, it will not make you a better person or increase your chances of happiness and success. Just the opposite.

10. When you take on the role of victim you're more likely to take actions that, at best, will not improve things, and at worst will backfire and make your situation more dire. If you see the world as unjust and you see yourself as being at the mercy of at least some part of it, it will be easy to justify attitudes and take actions that you would never take if you weren't seeing yourself as a victim.

For example, taking on the role of victim often leads to:

– *Attacking the source of your victimization instead of solving the problem.* This is part of righteous anger: "You [the victimizer] are guilty, I had nothing to do with it, so you are a monster and it's my job to punish you." Pushing your energies in this direction does absolutely nothing to solve the problem and prevent the victimization from continuing. In all likelihood it will simply lead to the next item on the list:

– *Taking revenge.* Seeing yourself as a victim can be used to justify doing something terrible to the other person – the "eye for an eye" school of thought. The problem is, this makes the other person feel justified in doing something even worse to you in response. Pretty soon you have a war going on with lots of people being victimized, violence escalating and no end in sight.

A common rationalization in this situation is that if your attack on the other person is harsh enough it will be "the final blow." But a quick look at world history will show you that half of the hatred in the world today is being justified by events that took place years, decades, even centuries

Consequences of Taking On the Role of Victim

ago. So even if the "final blow" you try to deliver actually does end the back-and-forth vengeance in the short run – and there's no guarantee that it will – it will almost certainly escalate things in the long run.

To put it another way, the actions you take should be aimed at *preventing more abuse in the future*. If your choice of action is to "get even" by hurting the other person, then you're causing *more* abuse to take place – the opposite of what you should be trying to do. Taking on the role of victim also leads to:

– *Making extreme choices.* Being a victim puts you in the position of being helpless, and helpless people, by definition, can't do anything about their situation. Anything *reasonable*, that is. So, this perspective can be used to justify taking extreme actions – burning someone's house down, murdering people, etc. And any time a person chooses an extreme action because of feeling helpless, things go downhill quickly. Innocent bystanders can get hurt, and the damage can be astronomical.

People who choose to see themselves as bearing at least some small part of the responsibility for being victimized seldom choose to take extreme actions. They don't see themselves as helpless and in need of lashing out. Instead, they focus on actions that really do prevent future abuse – *without* generating more abuse in the process.

Ironically, even if your anger is not directed at a person or group, seeing yourself as a victim will still cause you to take unhelpful actions. In that situation, rage often ends up being directed randomly against others in your life – terminating friendships and marriages and leading to destructive life choices. All that righteous anger doesn't magically evaporate. So, the "choice of extreme action" becomes nonspecific, but it ends up being extreme action, nonetheless. And it's just as awful in its consequences, because innocent bystanders end up getting hurt.

The bottom line is that taking on the role of victim:
- makes you focus on the wrong things
- undermines your personal power and credibility
- allows victimizers to continue in their role
- invites others to join in abusing you
- leads to anger that can undermine your mental and physical health
- tends to spread negative emotion into other areas of your life
- pushes away people who could be good friends and associates, and
- provides justification for actions that can be highly destructive to yourself and others.

Getting Out of the Victim Role

Suppose you realize that you've taken on the role of victim and you decide you want to change. Making fundamental changes to the way we see ourselves and interact with those around us isn't always easy. Here are five strategies that may help:

Strategy #1. Find out what payoffs you're getting for staying in the victim role. As noted in Chapter 8 (Understanding Behavior), nobody stays in a situation unless there are one or more payoffs. These may be direct payoffs, such as being treated in a certain way by others. Or, they may be avoidance payoffs – aspects of the situation that "help" you by keeping you from having to deal with some other even more scary situation.

As long as you don't consciously identify the payoffs, you'll never be able to move yourself out of the role of victim. But once you identify the payoffs that are rewarding you for staying in the role of victim, you can make a conscious choice to change, and you'll know exactly what you're giving up in exchange for your new-found freedom.

Strategy #2. Recognize that feeling trapped is an illusion. Remember that the psychological condition known as "learned helplessness" is often part of being in the victim role. In other words, the feeling that you're trapped is a natural part of being in that position, but it is *not* an accurate analysis of your situation. As long as you're alive and able to make choices, you have options.

One way to help get past the feeling that you're trapped is to make a conscious effort to replace that perspective with the idea that your situation is a *challenge* – a puzzle to solve rather than an inescapable trap. This change in perspective can go a long way toward freeing up your ability to find a way out. Besides, it's a much more realistic way to view your situation.

Strategy #3. Take some responsibility for the situation so you can learn from it. When you feel that you've been victimized, it's useful to look for ways in which your actions helped make the event possible. Some people call this "blaming the victim," but it's really just about taking responsibility for your life. In fact, you may not be to blame for your misfortune, but looking for ways in which your own actions may have inadvertently contributed to what happened does two things: It gives you tools to prevent further victimization in the future, and it gives you back some of the personal power that you otherwise lose.

For example, many Americans in the first decade of the 21st Century lost their homes because they signed up for mortgages that turned out to be predatory. Clearly, many people could justifiably blame this misfortune on business people who lied and said the buyer would be able to refinance the house before the rate went up, or misstated the realities of the situation in other ways. You could also blame the politicians who, at the end of the year 2000, revoked the banking laws that had been in place since the Great Depression, thus making it possible for banks to engage in unethical practices that had been outlawed for decades.

All of this may be true, but it doesn't help the buyer much. If the buyer looks beyond blaming the business people or politicians to see how his own actions helped set him up to be in this situation, some helpful lessons might emerge that could prevent a similar event from happening again later. For example, such a situation might have been avoided if the buyer had read the mortgage papers more carefully to see whether the mortgage really did guarantee the buyer's right to refinance. Realizing that tells you what to do the next time around, so you don't get victimized again.

Every specific situation will be different, but the principle is pretty fundamental: If you think only in terms of blaming the person who profited at your expense, then you won't gain any insight into how you can avoid being scammed in the future. If you take some amount of responsibility for your behavior, you can find ways in which you contributed to the situation, learn from those insights and save yourself from future suffering.

The second point about taking some responsibility for the situation is that it gives you back a sense that you do have some power over what happens to you. It's a way of reaffirming and acknowledging that *we don't have to be victimized.*

The change in your attitude that results from adopting this strategy will relieve some of the emotional burden that comes with feeling powerless. Furthermore, it will impact your relationships in a positive way. The people around you will pick up on the fact that you've stopped seeing yourself as a victim, and instead of seeing you as a potential liability, they'll begin to see you as a self-reliant, capable person who got into a bad situation and learned from it. Good people will be more likely to respect you and see you as their peer, someone they can rely on. And that will make them more likely to help you, if and when you really need help.

Strategy #4. Take action to change your position. If you're in an ongoing abusive situation, having a non-victim perspective is important, but it's equally important to take action to change your situation. Any situation can become comfortable, no matter how unpleasant it may be; that's one reason so many people remain in the role of victim. (You may be getting abused, but at least you know what to expect.) It's a part of the "learned helplessness" phenomenon: It's easy to stay where you are, even if you're miserable.

Of course, when you do take action, it matters which action you choose to take – and this will be dramatically affected by whether or not you see yourself as a victim. For example, a woman who perceives herself as a victim may escape an abusive relationship only to end up in another abusive relationship; or, she may try to take revenge against the abusive partner. Neither choice of action ultimately solves her ongoing problem. On the other hand, if a woman caught in an abusive relationship sees herself as at least partly responsible, she's likely to see *changing her own behavior* as part of the solution, and that could make all the difference in actually preventing more victimization in the future.

One final important note: If you believe that the person who has abused you is a serious threat to other people's lives or safety, not just your own, you might want to take action beyond simply protecting yourself. But your judgment about whether this kind of action needs to be taken – and what exactly you should do – will be far more reasonable and realistic if you avoid taking on the role of victim, and avoid focusing on blaming the other person for the abuse. And, if you don't see yourself as a victim, the actions you choose will be much more likely to help the other people you're worried about.

Strategy #5. Get outside help. The more overwhelming and destructive the abuse you've suffered, the more you'll probably need help to end the habit of seeing yourself as a victim, especially if you've been in that position for a long time. Some people can make major changes without outside help, but there's no shame in getting help when your safety could be at stake, or when the result could be a huge turnaround in your life.

If the victimization is still going on – if you're unable to leave a relationship that routinely causes you physical harm, for example – help isn't far away; our society offers many resources to help someone in this situation. But you first have to decide that the payoffs you're getting for staying in the situation are not worth the suffering you're enduring. If you keep returning to the same situation, you're making a choice with predictable, harsh consequences. *You do not have to make that choice.* Again, help is out there in many forms, but you won't get that help unless you ask for it.

What About Forgiveness?

Great religious and philosophical leaders throughout history have urged us to forgive others. Of course, it's not a particularly popular idea, or we wouldn't have to be reminded over and over again! Many people just dismiss forgiveness as being "for sissies," and a cowardly way to get out of what they see as the risky but righteous business of issuing retribution.

Here's a big secret about forgiveness: It's not about letting the abuser off the hook – *it's about letting yourself off the hook.* When you haven't forgiven someone for a perceived abuse, you're carrying around anger and resentment. And that's one of the ironies about seeing yourself as a victim: Your anger does nothing to the person or thing you're mad at. It just eats away at *you.* It allows the victimizer to continue to make you suffer, to control part of your life – in many cases even after he or she is no longer a part of your life. As Oprah Winfrey has noted, if you're holding a grudge, that grudge is really holding you.

Think of it this way: Forgiving someone is making a decision that *you're not going to continue suffering because of what happened.* That's why forgiving is a valuable thing to do. As D. Patrick Miller says in his wonderful *Little Book of Forgiveness*, "To carry an anger against anyone is to poison your own heart, administering more venom each time you replay the injury in your mind." Ironically, some people see forgiving a villain as being a miscarriage of justice. In actuality, *refusing* to forgive someone simply compounds the injustice done to you. In contrast, forgiveness lifts a huge burden from your shoulders.

Furthermore, forgiving the person who abused you allows you to base your future actions on a less-angry analysis of the situation. Without forgiveness, people often choose actions that start a cycle of retaliation and escalation. With forgiveness, people tend to choose their actions in ways that address the root problems – actions that *don't* make matters worse.

Again, the idea is not that you're going to pretend that you were never wronged; you certainly want to protect yourself from a repeat offense. (And in some situations, you may need to protect others as well.) The saying "forgive and forget" may have gotten it wrong; it makes more sense to forgive and remember. (As John F. Kennedy once said, "Forgive your enemies, but never forget their names.") What's important is the *way* you remember it. If you remember it in terms of you being a victim, you're perpetuating your own suffering. If you remember in terms of knowing you have a pitfall to avoid in the future, you're doing yourself a service.

Interestingly enough, relieving your internal anger and suffering by forgiving the victimizer may also cause changes in the other person, if you're still interacting with him or her. If the other person senses that you're no longer responding with anger, the entire dynamic between you may shift. As Dr. Philip McGraw often says, *we teach people how to treat us.* People don't interact with us in a vacuum; they see our reactions to what they're doing and saying, and that guides their choices about what to do and say when they interact with us in the future. So, once you relieve yourself of the internal suffering that comes with being angry about a victimization, your words and actions will let the person who abused you know that you're not playing the same game any more. Abusers continue to abuse because they're getting some payoff from the situation; if you change, it's likely that the payoff they've been getting will disappear, and their behavior will change as well.

A good example of the power of forgiveness to lift a burden off of our own shoulders is found in the story of concentration camp survivor Eva Mozes Kor. Before World War II, Eva and her twin sister spent their childhoods living with their Jewish family in Hungary. At the age of 10, the entire family was sent to Auschwitz. She and her sister were subjected to humiliating and deadly medical experiments by Dr. Josef Mengele, who used 1,500 sets of twins as guinea pigs at Auschwitz; less than 200 survived to see Auschwitz liberated. She survived by force of will: She decided early on that she would survive this, no matter what. And she did.

Many years later, she did something remarkable: She decided to forgive Josef Mengele. In fact, she forgave *all* of the Nazis, despite the slaughter of her family and the torture endured by her and her sister. (That decision became the subject of the documentary *Forgiving Dr. Mengele* which was released in 2006.)

Her decision came about because of her interaction with a former Nazi doctor 50 years after the end of the war. She was surprised to find that he was human – it was clear that he had spent most of the years since the war horrified by what he had done. Eventually, he helped her document a history of Auschwitz.

That experience caused her to rethink her position as a victim. She decided to forgive this doctor, making it official with a public declaration of forgiveness. Later, she decided to forgive Dr. Mengele and everyone else as well. Some people were incredibly angry that she would do this; they saw it as the equivalent of denying that the atrocities took place. In fact, it was a decision to alleviate her own suffering and thereby release herself from the final lingering abuse tied to the experience.

"I ... realized that I had the power to forgive," she said at a presentation explaining her decision. "No one could give me the power and no one could take it away. And for a little victim, who was a victim for almost 50 years, to realize that I have the power [to forgive] made me feel very good." Indeed, signing her declaration of forgiveness was a turning point in her life. "I felt immediately a burden of pain was lifted from my shoulders," she said. "[I felt] that I was no longer a prisoner of my tragic past. That I was no longer a victim. That I was finally free."

Today she shares the message she learned from this experience: "Forgive your worst enemy," she says. "It will heal your soul. It will set you free."

Moving Out of the Dark

If you've taken on the role of victim in some area of life, whatever benefits have made that position seem attractive will eventually be overshadowed by the long list of downsides we've discussed. Seeing yourself as a victim – or letting others see you that way – can keep you trapped on the Wheel of Misfortune and unable to move toward the better life you'd like to have. In contrast, taking some responsibility for your life – even the parts in which you felt abused – will help you prevent further abuse and change your situation for the better.

Last but not least, if you can eventually forgive the person who abused you, you'll lift a huge emotional burden from yourself and be able to address what happened – or is happening – with a clear mind.

Once more, in brief:

Here are the key pionts to remember from Chapter 3:

- Being wronged does not automatically make you a victim; you *always* get to choose whether or not or not you're going to respond to a negative event by seeing yourself as a victim.

• When you choose to take on the role of victim, you change your beliefs about yourself and you change your behavior. Other people – including the person who wronged you – also respond to the way you see yourself.

• Taking on the role of victim is encouraged by our culture, and a natural response when you're overwhelmed by events that seem unjust. Plus, it has some short-term benefits: You get out of having to look at your own behavior; you avoid all responsibility for what happened; you get to be righteously angry; and you may get sympathy and/or pity from others. However, it backfires in multiple ways: It alters your focus and your emotions; it undermines your physical health; it undermines your personal power and credibility; it invites further abuse from others; it pushes away potential friends and associates; and it provides the justification for highly destructive actions.

• If you've taken on the role of victim and you want to change that:

1. Find out what positive or negative payoffs you're getting for staying in that position.
2. Remember that feeling trapped is an illusion.
3. Look for ways in which you're inadvertently allowing the abuse to continue. This will help you find ways to prevent it from recurring, and will remind you that you're not powerless in the situation.
4. Take action to change the situation. However, choose your actions from the perspective that you are *not* a victim. Choosing your actions from a "victim" perspective can lead to doing things that make the situation worse.
5. If you're in a dangerous or difficult situation, get outside help.

• Remember that forgiving someone who has abused you is not about letting him or her off the hook – it's about ending your own anger and suffering, which is the final, lingering part of being victimized. Forgiveness lets *you* off the hook, and if further action needs to be taken, forgiveness makes it far easier to choose the most constructive, realistic action to take to make things better.

NOTES for Chapter 3

1. This and other related studies are described in Ellen J. Langer's book *Mindfulness*.
2. For example, see his book *The Status Syndrome: How Social Standing Affects Our Health and Longevity* (Holt Paperbacks).
3. From an interview in the article *The Spiritual Connection* in *Oprah* magazine, May 2008. (See p. 286.)
4. Dr. Seligman has published dozens of articles on this topic. To see summaries of many of them visit http://www.ncbi.nlm.nih.gov/sites/entrez and enter *Seligman learned helplessness* in the search window.
5. For a more complete detailing of this process and an excellent summary of how anger can erode your health, see Chapter 2 of *Anger Kills* by Redford Williams, MD, and Virginia Williams, PhD.
6. Kiecolt-Glaser JK, Loving TJ, Stowell JR, Malarkey WB, Lemeshow S, Dickinson SL, Glaser R. Hostile marital interactions, proinflammatory cytokine production, and wound healing. Arch Gen Psychiatry. 2005;62:12:1377-84.
7. Many books have been written on this topic. For example, see *Who Gets Sick: How Thoughts, Moods and Beliefs Can Affect Your Health*, by Blair Justice, or Bernie Siegel's classic *Love, Medicine and Miracles*.

4.
Communicate Clearly.

Pay attention to what the other person is hearing, not just what you're saying.

"The single biggest problem in communication is the illusion that it has taken place."
– George Bernard Shaw

"The two words 'information' and 'communication' are often used interchangeably, but they signify quite different things. Information is giving out; communication is getting through."
– Sydney J. Harris

"I know that you believe you understand what you think I said, but I'm not sure you realize that what you heard is not what I meant."
– Robert McCloskey

Musicians John Lennon and Yoko Ono were always a controversial couple in the eyes of the public. John, of course, became world famous as a founding member of the Beatles. An outspoken, strong-willed woman, Yoko Ono was perceived as having caused the breakup of the Beatles when she became involved with, and eventually married, John. She was not well-loved by John's fans – but she was very well loved by John.

At the end of the 1970s, long after the breakup of the Beatles, John Lennon had gone several years without recording any new music; he was staying home with their child, enjoying a completely different life than the one he had lived as a member of the Beatles and then as a solo star. (His wife, Yoko Ono, handled their business affairs during this time, which often ruffled feathers because everyone expected that they'd be dealing with John, not Yoko.) Eventually, John felt ready to record again. In an unusual move, John and Yoko not only decided to share the creative duties on the record, but decided to record the album on their own, financing it themselves. (Professional-quality home recording was almost unheard of at that time, and few could afford the $50,000 it cost to make an album in a professional studio.) John and Yoko created the album *Double Fantasy*, to which they each contributed half of the material.

Once the new album was completed, John and Yoko let it be known that labels could bid on the right to release the recording. Every major label was interested, of course, and they contacted John with their offers. Only one record label president addressed his offer to Yoko Ono instead of John – David Geffen, former owner of Asylum Records, who had just started a new label, *Geffen Records*.[1]

Guess which record label John and Yoko chose?

David Geffen won that battle by using the most important communication secret in the world: Don't just think about what you're saying – *think about what the other person is hearing.*

Communication: A Two-Way Street

Most of us think of communication as sending out a bit of information to someone else. For example, if we need something, we generally ask for it; if we see something that deserves everyone's attention, we point it out; if we have an opinion, we share it. The problem is, the people hearing us don't always get the message we expect them to get. They may misunderstand what we asked for and give us the wrong thing; they may believe we're trying to deceive them or simply ignore what we're pointing out; they may totally misinterpret the opinion we state and react very differently than we expected.

Most of us have had this kind of experience many times. Sometimes we realize that a misunderstanding has occurred; sometimes we don't. (Sometimes we find out the hard way, when a misunderstanding leads to a disastrous event later on.)

The reason this kind of misunderstanding happens as often as it does is that most of us have accepted a not-very-useful idea of how communication works: the "one-way street" model. This model says: *I say something, you hear what I said.* End of story. In fact, that's not a good model of how communication works. I can talk to someone who doesn't speak English and he may hear me perfectly well, but he probably won't have a clue as to what I said. Communication involves *being understood* – and being heard is not the same as being understood.

Here's a better model of how communication works: 1) You send out a message; 2) the other person receives the message; 3) something happens inside the other person's mind; 4) the other person gives you back a response. This is what I call the *two-way street* model of communication. The reason this model works better than the one-way street model is that it takes into account that something happens inside the other person's mind; the other person is not just a passive receptacle for your message.

Words and ideas mean different things to different people, so what happens to your message in the other person's mind will determine whether or not your intended message gets through. To put it another way, what the other person is hearing may be very different from what you thought you said. In that case, the response you get back will probably not be the one you wanted.

The originators of a branch of psychology called Neuro-Linguistic Programming have a saying they use when making the same point: *The meaning of your communication is the response you get.*[2] In other words, the meaning that counts is not what you think you said, but what the *other person* thinks you said. The reaction you get back tells you how the listener interpreted your communication – and that's what matters.

Unfortunately, how your communication will be heard isn't always easy to predict, because human beings experience and interpret the world – including things that are said to them – through very personal internal filters. Those filters can include:

• **The filter of past experience.** If a man dating a woman says, "I love the way you smile," he probably expects her to hear it as a compliment; but that comment could be heard as a veiled insult if she has been told in the past that she has a terrible smile.

• **The filter of sensory limitations**. If you tell someone that he received an important phone call, but he's paying attention to something else when you say it, he may hear your voice but still not realize what you said.

• **The filter of mood.** If you say something witty to a person who is in a really bad mood, he may take your comment as showing a callous disregard for his feelings and get angry.

• **The filter of culture.** Communication styles and specific ways of interpreting words (including nonverbal) can be dramatically different in different cultures – and even different genders!

For example, if you try to be gracious by saying you're sorry in certain parts of the world, it may be taken as a sign of weakness. Similarly, Japanese anthropologist and translator Tomoko Hamada's book *American Enterprise in Japan* details a host of ways that communication between Japanese and American businessmen is befuddled by cultural "filters" that can cause people to take a very different meaning from your words and actions than the one you intend. According to the author, for example, food and drinks are often prepared in advance for a business meeting in a restaurant, and everyone is expected to eat what they are served. At one such luncheon, an American businessman asked for decaffeinated coffee – a simple and common request in the United States. But in this instance, the Japanese restaurant didn't have decaffeinated coffee. The remark was taken as pointing out poor preparation and thoughtlessness on the part of the host, resulting in a commotion and acute embarrassment among the Japanese. Had the businessman done more research ahead of time, he might have known that a special request in this situation could be heard as an insult (perhaps unintended, but an insult nevertheless).

Differences in "gender culture" are more common; most men and women have encountered more than one misunderstanding caused by a difference in the way men and women "hear" the same words. For example, psychologists have found that if a wife asks her husband to do a chore, she may interpret a positive response as a sign of love – and a negative response as a *lack* of love. It probably doesn't mean anything of the sort to the husband, so he may not realize that he's communicating a "lack of love" if he postpones the chore until another day because he has other priorities.

It's important to understand that miscommunication because of internal filters can't be eliminated by being incredibly intelligent or the world's greatest speaker or writer. You can *minimize* the problem, but you can't totally avoid it. Why? Because the other person's filters are different from yours, and they may even change over time (the mood

How Does Communication Work?

The conventional assumption:

 *I say something and assume the other person hears me and understands me.*

A better way to look at it:
Communication as a two-way street

 *I say something, the other person hopefully hears me.....*

 *What the other person does hear is filtered through distractions, mood, past experience, cultural beliefs, etc., and interpreted accordingly...*

 *I get back a reaction/response that gives me some idea whether or not the other person understood me correctly....*

 *If I suspect the other person didn't get the message I intended, I try again, expressing my meaning in a different way. I repeat this until I get back the response I want.*

filter, for example). So even if you're talking to your best friend or the loving spouse you've been married to for 30 years, misunderstandings are going to happen.

Making the Two-Way Street Work

Communicating clearly is essential if you want to stay off of the Wheel of Misfortune. Since misunderstandings are inevitable and communication really is a two-way street, you have to be both proactive and reactive to make sure communication is happening the way you intended. This means taking three steps: First, plan ahead – make an effort ahead of time to anticipate how the other person may interpret what you say. Second, pay attention to the response you get. Third, if you get back the wrong response, change the way you're expressing your message.

Let's look at each of these steps a little more closely.

Step 1: **Plan ahead.** In many situations it's possible to at least partly determine ahead of time what effect the other person's internal filters are going to have. Sometimes you can make a good educated guess about what the other person's filters are by knowing as much as possible about the other person's situation and experience. For example, you can notice that someone is in a bad mood and adjust your comments accordingly. Or, if you know he comes from a different culture, you can learn about his culture before you interact with him. David Geffen used this type of planning ahead when he decided to send his offer to Yoko Ono instead of John. He realized that Yoko Ono had been treated with disdain by many people, and that this would play a part in how John and Yoko reacted to the record company offers. Sending his offer to Yoko would tell them that he "got it" about their partnership. Because he thought about this ahead of time, his communication produced the response he wanted – a deal with John and Yoko.

Step 2: **Pay attention to the response you get.** To make sure communication is happening as you intended, *watch the other person's response*, to make sure it's the response you wanted. People who know that communication is a two-way street are always paying attention to the other person to make sure their message gets through. Because they're thinking this way, if the message doesn't get through, they find out about it right away. On the other hand, people who think of communication as a one-way street often simply *assume* that they've been understood. If they're wrong, they'll find out eventually, but that time delay – during which they've been misunderstood – may put them at a huge disadvantage. And it may cost them dearly.

The renowned film director Alfred Hitchcock (known for films such as *Psycho* and *The Birds*) learned this lesson early in his career, and it changed the way he made his films. He actually made one of his early films twice – *The Man Who Knew Too Much*. Asked in an interview what inspired him to make a second version of the same story, he explained that after he'd finished the first version, he came to understand that he had not been thinking about the audience's internal experience as they watched the movie; he was just making the movie the way he thought was best. The realization that he had to *try to get the right response from the audience* was so profound that he made the movie over again! Of course, he went on to be considered one of the greatest filmmakers ever – which is, among other things, a pretty high recommendation for that little insight he had.

A few years ago, someone in the field of medicine noticed that even when a person is anesthetized during surgery, the nervous system can respond to stimuli such as pleasant music.[3] Thus, some surgeons began playing music during surgery. Unfortunately, it turned out that this didn't always have the right effect. That's because there's a caveat to this idea: *Music means different things to different people!* So during surgery you might play a sweet, upbeat song that cheers most people up, hoping to sooth the patient's autonomic nervous system. But the patient may actually hate that type of music, in which case it could have the opposite effect. Or, that song may have been the favorite song of his sweetheart who died in a car crash. Playing relaxing music during surgery is probably a good idea – but only if you take the other person's internal filters into account when you choose the music. If you don't, you may get a very different response than the one you intended.

There's another good reason to pay attention to the response your communication gets: It may warn you when something is not right, even if the other person correctly understood your communication. For example, if you ask a stranger for help, or tell a salesperson you want to buy something, they might be happy to help you – or they could see it as an opportunity to rip you off. Their reaction to your request – carefully observed – may tell you which thing they're thinking. In other words, observing a person's reaction to your communication can do more than just tell you whether you've been understood; it can tell you when your communication has an extra meaning for the other person that you were not anticipating. It's in your interest to pick up on that possibility.

Step 3: **If you get the wrong response, change the way you're expressing your message.** This does *not* mean *changing your message* so you just say what the other person wants to hear. It means putting your message into a form that will be correctly understood by the other person. It's like speaking to a Frenchman in French instead of English – you don't change the content, you change the presentation. (David Geffen didn't change what he was offering John and Yoko in order to get the right response; he just changed a key part of the way he presented his offer.)

Indeed, the reason Alfred Hitchcock's revelation made him a better filmmaker was not that he tried to give the audience exactly what they expected or wanted from him; it was that *he changed what he did in the film* until he got the reaction he wanted. This is not "pandering to the public;" this is *good communication*. And it's not "selling out;" it's making sure you're understood.

To reiterate: A good communicator knows that getting a message across is a two-way street. So,

1) he'll plan ahead by doing his best to anticipate ways his message might be misunderstood; then, he'll present his message in a way that avoids those misunderstandings;

2) while he's communicating, he'll constantly monitor the other person's response so he can tell whether the other person is correctly understanding him; and

3) if the response he gets back is not the right response, he'll change the presentation of his message immediately and do his best to get the response he wanted.

Six Universal Communication Strategies

The perception filters that your message goes through when you're communicating with another person may be unique to that individual. However, some things in the environment, and some basic strategies, can alter the other person's perception of what you're saying in ways that are pretty much universal. In other words, there are some factors that affect how others hear what you say that are consistent in almost any situation and have a highly predictable effect. Because these are pretty much universal, you can use them to help ensure other people understand you correctly, whether you know the other person's background and mood or not.

Here are six universal communication strategies that apply in almost any circumstance:

Strategy #1. Be wary of communicating with someone in front of others. When you speak to someone in private, the other person's reaction will depend entirely on his background, beliefs, relationship to you, and so forth. But the exact same communication done in front of other people can drastically change the way your comments are heard by the person you're addressing. That's because the person you're talking to will now be conscious of what the third parties who are listening in are likely to think. This can be particularly damaging if it sounds like you're criticizing the person you're speaking to. If other people overhear your critical comments, the person you're addressing may lose face in front of those other people. That can alter the person's response dramatically and have far-reaching consequences.

This is true in the workplace, for sure. When I was having difficulty working with a boss at one particular job, I wrote him a letter detailing why I was frustrated and asked him to consider changing some of his behavior toward me. But before reading the letter, he passed it along to the head of the human resources division, assuming it was a company issue. Consequently, several people I never intended to see those critical comments read the letter before he did. As a result, he felt that I had embarrassed him, although that was never my intention. And instead of being able to resolve my complaints with him in private, the equation changed. He lashed out at me in self defense, criticizing my work, and things deteriorated. Eventually I had to change jobs.

Luckily, in most situations we have control over the circumstances in which we express something to another person. You can use that fact to your advantage by making sure that the presence of others is taken into account when you decide what to say, how to say it – and *when* to say it.

It's worth noting that even *praise* given in public may have different consequences than praise given in private – possibly beneficial, but not necessarily, depending on the circumstances. Praising someone in front of peers could generate jealousy, for example.

The key point is that the presence of others may alter the meaning of your message dramatically. If there's any chance that this might happen, it's worth making sure that your communication takes place privately so this factor is eliminated from the equation.

One important corollary involves the same principle: It's almost always a bad idea to criticize someone in any form that can't be retracted later, whether it's in a letter, an electronic message sent over the Web, a voicemail, or something even more permanent such as an article, recording or book. When you express a criticism in any format that will go beyond your ability to control who reads it or hears it, it's very likely that others you didn't intend will eventually hear it or read it, and the person you criticized will lose face in ways you didn't intend. Even worse, if the person you're criticizing is not a friend, he or she may use your words against you. (More than one celebrity and politician has been humiliated by a leaked voicemail, email or letter.) So, when you need to provide feedback – especially negative feedback – it's best to do it in person and in private, where other people's reactions will not be part of the equation.

Strategy #2. If you want someone to change his behavior, don't confront the person with an accusation. Instead, state how the behavior is affecting *you*. If you try to change someone's behavior by saying something judgmental about the person or accusing him of something, your comments will be perceived as an attack and defenses will fly up. The content of your comment will be overshadowed, maybe even lost, in the emotional, defensive reaction you'll trigger.

For example, when someone's behavior is upsetting, many people will say, "You shouldn't do that!" or the popular variation: "You always do that!" Instead, you can say, "It really upsets me when you do that." The first two statements are judgmental and accusatory. They're guaranteed to cause a defensive response that will keep your meaning from getting through. (Besides, a blanket statement about the other person's behavior, like "You always do that" can easily be dismissed as simply being untrue.) On the other hand, a statement about how the person's behavior is affecting you can't be brushed off in the same way; it won't cause the same kind of defensive reaction. At the very least, it lets the other person know that he or she is affecting you negatively.

Of course, the other person may not change his or her behavior in response, no matter how well you communicate. But if you state the issue in terms of how the other person's behavior is affecting you, your communication will have a much better chance of being understood. Your message is far less likely to be interpreted as an attack, allowing the person to at least hear what you're saying.

Chapter 4: Communicate Clearly 93

Strategy #3. If you need to ask for something, mention how your request will meet the <u>other</u> person's needs. This puts a whole different cast on asking for something, because you're communicating that the other person stands to benefit from helping you. It's a classic negotiating tactic.

For example, when I first moved to New York City, I stayed with a school chum while I looked for a more permanent roommate situation. I used a service that connects people to potential roommates, and after a few meetings with people I didn't care for and visits to apartments that I didn't think I could live in, I found a roommate situation in a great apartment with a sunken living room and access to a nice roof in a nice part of town. However, I wasn't the only person who thought it was a great situation. I found myself competing to get the person making the decision to choose me as his roommate.

I could have told him how much I really wanted to get the apartment, but instead, I called several times and mentioned things that I knew would make him happy to have me there, such as that I enjoyed his favorite music (which was playing when I saw the place). I also went out of my way to be pleasant and easy-going, because that's the kind of roommate *I* would have wanted.

My strategy worked. He knew I really wanted to be chosen – I did call several times – but I focused on letting him know that he would benefit if he gave me what I wanted. If the other person picks up that you care about his needs, it changes the way he hears what you're saying.

Strategy #4. If you're asking someone to do something, make sure you communicate not only what you want the person to do, but also the goal you're hoping to achieve with that person's help. Instructions given without a reason are an invitation to not getting the result you want. If you don't explain what your goal is, and circumstances turn out not to be exactly the way you thought they would be, the other person may simply *guess* what your overall intention was and execute your instructions as if *that* were your goal. If the other person guesses wrong, the consequences can be dire.

Consider the story told of a doctor doing surgery on a patient with an anesthesiologist monitoring the patient's vital signs while the patient was anesthetized.[4] The surgeon decided he needed to lower the patient's blood pressure and asked the anesthesiologist to give the patient a specific drug that would have that effect – *but he didn't explain the reason he wanted this done.* So, the anesthesiologist gave the patient the drug; then he saw that the patient's blood pressure had dropped. Since he didn't know that this was the reason the surgeon asked for the drug, the anesthesiologist gave the patient a different drug to bring the blood pressure back up again. (After all, part of the anesthesiologist's job is to keep the patient's vital signs stable.) When the surgeon realized the pressure still wasn't as low as he wanted, he asked the anesthesiologist to give the patient a little more of the first drug. The anesthesiologist did, and then compensated with more of the second drug.

After a few more rounds of this, the conflicting drugs overwhelmed the patient's system and the patient died.

When your purpose in asking someone to do something is not completely clear, the other person has to engage in what author Gary Klein refers to as *mind-reading*.[5] If you send someone to the store to buy something and it turns out the store doesn't have what you asked for, the person you sent has to guess what you wanted the item for in order to know what to do next. If you explained the reason you wanted that item, the person can find an appropriate substitute that may accomplish the same purpose. But if you didn't explain the reason for your request, the person has to guess. You may end up with something that you can't use at all.

There are other advantages to stating your goal up front, as well. If the person knows why you're asking him to do something, he can foresee potential problems and ask you about them before setting off on the mission. While he's executing your request, he can recognize opportunities to accomplish your goal that you couldn't have foreseen, and take advantage of them. But the most important advantage is that he won't make a bad decision because of a lack of information.

Here are five things you can do to make sure your instructions are complete:

1) Don't just specify the result you want; explain the bigger picture – the reason you want that result.

2) Don't provide too many step-by-step details about how the person should do what you're asking. Those details might be valuable *if everything goes exactly as you think it will*, but it probably won't. So the most valuable piece of information to share is the big picture. In addition, too many details about how the person should fulfill your request may obscure the whole point of the mission. Understanding the

big picture enables the person to improvise successfully when things *don't* go exactly the way you thought they would.

3) If you suspect that problems may crop up while the person attempts to do what you're asking, talk about those potential problems up front and suggest what the person could do if they occur. For example, if you send someone to the store, suggest an alternative item he can buy if the item you want turns out to be unavailable. Or, suggest how the person might proceed if public transportation breaks down and he can't get to the store in question.

4) Make it clear what you *don't* want. This helps to clarify your goal and minimizes the chance of an outcome you don't want.

5) Invite the other person to ask you questions. That can avoid a host of problems by revealing misunderstandings and allowing you to address potential problems you might not have thought of.

Strategy #5. Remember that actions speak louder than words. Words are usually a good place to start, but there are other ways to communicate. Well-known comedian and television host Jay Leno says that when he was young and looking for work in Boston, he saw a Mercedes/Rolls-Royce dealer and decided he'd like to work there. (Leno is well-known for his life-long love of elegant cars.) When he inquired about a job, the owner told him they weren't hiring. Leno's clever response was to *show* the boss that he was worth hiring. The next Monday morning, he showed up at the car wash section of the dealership and told the person in charge that he was the new guy. Then he proceeded to work hard for several days, until the owner noticed that he was there. The car wash supervisor told the owner what a hard worker Leno was. Leno said to the owner, "I figured I'd work here until you hired me." The owner hired him.[6]

Strategy #6. Beware of trying to share contradictory information with someone who has absolute certainty about his opinion. We'll talk more about this in Chapter 9, but it's highly relevant when you need to communicate with someone, so it's worth mentioning here. Being certain that we're absolutely right about something – that we have the final word on it – leads to a host of negative consequences. Ironically, this is true even if we are, in fact, right. One of the consequences of being certain about something is an automatic tendency to ignore or dismiss information that contradicts what we are sure is true. Another consequence is a tendency to divide the world into "those who agree with me" and "those who don't" – and then lower your opinion of those who disagree, sometimes to the point of contempt. My term for this is *Certainty Syndrome*.

If you're trying to share information with someone who has Certainty Syndrome, beware: If what you're sharing contradicts what that person is certain about, you're not likely to get the response you're hoping for. Instead of processing your information at face value, such a person will immediately categorize what you're saying as being flat-out wrong, no matter how obvious or persuasive you may think the information is. Furthermore, the person may dismiss you as ignorant, or begin to treat you with contempt – definitely not an ideal response.

Of course, you can't always know when someone you're communicating with has certainty about the topic you're discussing. But in many cases you will know, or you can guess. Political and religious discussions, in particular, often fall into this category. Certainty about political opinions, for example, accounts for most of the bitter divisiveness and politically-related contempt seen in the United States in recent years. You may feel strongly that the person you're trying to communicate with is overlooking facts, but if the person in question has Certainty Syndrome, you're probably wasting your time trying to sway him by pointing out those facts. And, you may put yourself in a bad position merely by doing so. For that reason, if you're about to share information with someone you know or suspect has Certainty Syndrome, and disagrees with what you're about to say, you should probably reconsider.

This raises an important question: How do you get through to someone who is certain that he has the final word on a given subject? There are some communication strategies that may work, and we'll talk about that in Chapter 9 when we discuss Certainty Syndrome in more detail. For now, suffice it to say that the direct approach will probably backfire and should be avoided.

Keeping Delayed Communications Clear

When you're communicating with someone face-to-face, you have a fallback mechanism that can help you out if the listener doesn't hear what you wanted him to hear: You can see his reaction and immediately change your presentation in response. But what if you're not present when the person reads or hears your words?

When I was in college, I took one class at a nearby school. As it turned out, the professor was not only brilliant, he was a great showman. The subject was dry and potentially deadly – something about the neurobiology of psychology that I'm sure I needed to take to graduate – but he made it *exciting!* He rushed back and forth in front of the class, gesticulating wildly and raising and lowering his voice with emotion like a great Shakespearian actor. He wrote his notes on the board in different bright colors of chalk. He really was fascinated by this stuff, and he made us think it was pretty amazing, too!

At the end of the semester we had to write a review of the teacher; I was happy to write that he was the best teacher I'd ever had, which was absolutely true. Shortly thereafter I had to take my final exam in his office, by myself, because I wasn't enrolled at his school. He asked me whether he should read my comments before he graded my test or after. I told him either way was fine with me, so he pulled out my review and read it while I took the exam.

I did very well on the exam, but I got a mediocre grade for the course. The professor interpreted my high praise as a blatant attempt to butter him up and get a better grade, which pissed him off....so he lowered my grade!

In hindsight, I can see why he might not have believed my review; why would he? If I'd had more insight into human behavior I might have foreseen the potential for misunderstanding and told him to grade my test *before* reading my review of his teaching. But I naively thought that he knew how good a teacher he was (and knew how honest I was!) And so, a heartfelt compliment was interpreted completely the wrong way.

This is a classic example of delayed communication and the special problems that come with it. Had I been talking to him and said that he was my favorite teacher, he would either have picked up on my sincerity, or I would have seen his response and realized right away that he had taken my comment in a totally different way than I intended. But that feedback loop wasn't there because the communication was delayed. He read my comments several days after I had written them, and he read them when I wasn't able to see his reaction and correct for his misinterpretation.

When a message you're trying to communicate will be delayed, you need to make a special effort to minimize the odds of a misinterpretation. If you write a letter, or an article or a book or a song, or you post a video online, you may not experience the response until later – and that's a serious problem if the response turns out to be negative. Once something is out in the world, you can't take it back, and it can require a huge effort (or be impossible) to undo any unexpected damage from people not "getting it" the way you intended. (I certainly couldn't get my grade changed.)

This is where a "feedback person" comes into the picture. If a communication is important, and you can't be present when it's received, bounce the intended message off of someone else before sending it. This isn't foolproof, but in most instances, if a misinterpretation is possible, your "feedback person" will catch it – especially if you choose your feedback person wisely. This will let you revise your choice of words before you send the message.

For example, when I worked as a magazine editor, my boss told me one day that he had received a resume from someone looking for an editorial job. The resume was full of typos and misspellings, even in the headlines at the top! Needless to say, the message my boss "heard" was not the one the applicant thought he was conveying. If that person had shown his resume to a feedback person, his typos would most likely have been pointed out; he would have corrected the errors in the resume and stood a far better chance of being considered for the job. (If you're trying to stay off the Wheel of Misfortune, you *definitely* don't want to make that kind of mistake.)

Not conveying what you mean to say can go far beyond missing a typo. Occasionally I've said or written something that seemed totally innocuous to me, only to have someone who heard or read my words be offended because of some meaning my words had that I didn't even think of – but which others assumed was my intended meaning. Comedians often get big laughs pointing out headlines that have meanings the writer clearly didn't intend. The lesson is a good one: Get feedback *before* you publish anything!

This is one of the reasons writers have editors: so that someone else experiences your communication before it goes public. Again, it doesn't matter how experienced or brilliant you are; *you can never be sure how others will hear what you have to say*. The only way to get some idea of the reaction you'll inspire is to try your communication out on someone *before* it goes public. Some of the most successful creative people in the world have come out with major works that bombed, even at the peak of their careers, because there was some basic aspect of the work that the public didn't react to the way the creator thought they would. (Actually, this can be even more of a problem when someone is very successful. Very successful people sometimes end up surrounded by "yes-men," who tell them that everything they're doing is great, instead of giving them realistic feedback that would alert them to a potential misunderstanding.)

Choosing a Feedback Person

In order for this "early warning" system to work, you need to pick the right person (or people) to give you feedback. Some helpful tips:

• *Pick someone who is representative of the audience you hope to reach.* If your resume or video or letter is aimed at a person or people of a certain age or background, make sure you get your feedback from someone in that category. Otherwise, the feedback (positive or negative) may be partially or completely irrelevant.

• *Pick someone who is perceptive and experienced enough to catch a potential problem in your communication.* For example, suppose you're writing something offering advice on how to repair the reader's home plumbing, and your advice will be published somewhere online or in a magazine. You should have at least two feedback people look over your work before you publish it: first, an experienced plumber, who can tell you if you skipped a step or got some small but important detail wrong; and second, a person who has *never* repaired his own plumbing, because he can tell you whether your advice makes sense to an inexperienced person. Similarly, if you're publishing something that you believe is a new idea, run it by someone trustworthy who has enough experience in that field to know if someone else, unbeknownst to you, actually thought of it first.

A feedback person with experience in the area you're writing about can make a big difference. When I'm finishing up a new song, I've always found that I get the most useful feedback from friends who have taken a songwriting course. As a songwriting teacher, I know the principles of good songwriting very well; but that doesn't change the fact that I need to have someone besides me hear my work before it's published. People who have studied songwriting make good feedback people in this case because they have better tools to identify potential problems in a song than the average person would. If they have a different reaction to the song than the one I was hoping to get, they're better equipped to explain to me *why* they're having that reaction. That helps me to know how to revise the song so I'll get the reaction I wanted.

• ***Pick someone who is not out to attack you.*** You won't get reliable feedback from someone who has a motive to undercut you.

• ***Pick someone who does not have an unrealistic picture of you as being perfect.*** It's easy to ask for feedback from people close to you, such as a family member or spouse. But be careful: getting unrealistically positive feedback defeats the purpose of getting the feedback in the first place. You want to uncover potential communication *problems* before you put your creation out into the world, and anyone who is too big a fan may miss or overlook important details that will come back to haunt you later.

• ***Pick someone who can tell you the truth without risking your relationship.*** If the feedback people you choose are astute, you're going to hear some negative feedback sooner or later. (And that's the whole point – to hear it *before* your work goes out into the world and can't be altered.) Unfortunately, when you have a lot invested in something you've worked on, negative feedback can be hard to take, even if you asked for the feedback and you know that it will help you out. Some of my favorite feedback people cringe when they have to point out something I've overlooked or need to rewrite, because they know I'm not going to be happy about it!

The point is that this can be an uncomfortable process, and if your relationship is shaky, it can put a strain on it. So, it's helpful to pick a feedback person who (in addition to the other characteristics) has a solid relationship with you that won't be damaged if he or she has to tell you what you don't want to hear. Either that, or the person is a neutral party who *doesn't* have a personal relationship with you that could be affected as a result of them giving you unpleasant feedback.

Getting Your Message Through

As the world becomes more complicated and our ability to communicate with each other increases geometrically, the importance of communicating clearly can hardly be overstated. So, whether you're trying to get work, asking for help, trying to borrow money, expressing your needs, apologizing, trying to get someone to change his behavior, or simply trying to get someone to stand up for you, make sure the other person really understands what you're trying to say. And when your communication will be delayed – so you won't have the opportunity to revise your word choice based on the other person's reaction – use a feedback person as a way to make sure you're understood *before* you send your message on its way.

After all, when you're trying to stay off the Wheel of Misfortune, being understood can make all the difference.

Once more, in brief:

Here are the key points to remember from Chapter 4:

• A key part of successful communication is realizing that your meaning will be altered by the other person's internal filters. Those filters may include mood; past experiences; cultural differences; or simply hearing you incorrectly.

• It's not enough to think about what you're trying to say; you have to also think about *what the other person is hearing*. A good rule of thumb is: *The meaning of your communication is the response you get.*

• To avoid misunderstandings, do the following three things:
1) Make an effort ahead of time to anticipate how the other person might interpret what you say.
2) Pay attention to the response you get. This tells you if your meaning didn't come across.
3) If you get the wrong response, change the way you're expressing your message. This doesn't mean changing your message; it means *changing the way you present it*, so you're understood correctly.

• Ensure that your communications produce the response you want with these six strategies:
1) Be wary of communicating in front of others.
2) If you want to change someone's behavior, state your concern in

terms of how the behavior is affecting <u>you</u>.

3) Show an interest in meeting the other person's needs.

4) When asking someone to do something, communicate the reason you're making the request – the goal this action is intended to achieve. If something goes wrong, the person will have a better chance of improvising appropriately.

5) Remember that when you're communicating, actions speak louder than words.

6). Beware of trying to share contradictory information with someone who has absolute certainty about his or her opinion.

• If a communication won't be read or heard until later, get feedback about your communication from a trusted *feedback person* before sending your communication out into the world. Make sure your feedback person is:

– representative of the audience you hope to reach;

– perceptive and experienced enough to catch a potential problem in your communication;

– not out to undercut you;

– someone who has a realistic understanding of who you are;

– someone who can tell you the truth without risking your relationship.

NOTES for Chapter 4

1. The full story is recounted in the book *Starting Over: The Making of John Lennon and Yoko Ono's Double Fantasy* by Ken Sharp. (Gallery Books 2010).
2. For more on Neuro-Linguistic Programming and the idea that the meaning of your communication is the response you get, see *Frogs Into Princes* by Richard Bandler and John Grinder. (Real People Press, 1979)
3. Many studies have been done supporting this finding. For a review of many of these studies, see: Nilsson U. The anxiety- and pain-reducing effects of music interventions: A systematic review. AORN J. 2008;87:4:780-807.
4. Related by Gary Klein in *Sources of Power.*
5. ibid. See Chapter 13, "The Power to Read Minds."
6. As related by Jay Leno in an interview printed in Parade magazine, September 6, 2009.

5.
Focus on the Right Thing.

Instead of resisting what you don't like, put your energy into creating what you'd like to have.

"Most of us serve our ideals by fits and starts. The person who makes a success of living is the one who sees his goal steadily and aims for it unswervingly."
– Cecil B. deMille, American film director and producer

"Don't let what you can't do interfere with what you can do."
– John Wooden, American basketball coach

"If you're going through hell, keep going."
– Winston Churchill

Chris Gardner, whose autobiography *The Pursuit of Happyness*[1] was excerpted (and slightly rearranged) for the feature film of the same title, came from a disadvantaged background. His father left when he was an infant; his mother was sent to jail for allegedly earning money while on welfare when he was two years old. He lived in a foster home until his mother returned when he was five, but she brought with her an abusive, alcoholic step-father who threatened, humiliated and beat him and his mother.

Nevertheless, as he grew it became clear that he was smart and talented, and although he didn't go to college, he showed so much talent for medical surgery in the Navy that he was offered a job in San Francisco assisting a surgeon who had been impressed by his abilities.

Eventually he had a son with a woman he lived with, and then the limited wage ceiling associated with his medical job became a problem. Unfortunately, he realized he couldn't afford the years of education he'd need to become a surgeon himself.

Around that time, he discovered that he had an affinity for being a stockbroker; it was stimulating, used abilities he already had, and had huge earnings potential. The only problem was, to become a stockbroker it was usually necessary to have a college and/or business degree – and it was helpful to have connections and money. He had none of these.

Despite these obstacles, his gut told him that this was his ticket out of poverty. From that moment on, it became his goal to achieve financial success as a stockbroker. He began doing one interview after another at different firms, but everyone turned him down as being unqualified. (The fact that he was African-American certainly didn't help.) One person offered to get him into a training program, but when he showed up for the program, his benefactor had been fired. Another dead end.

To make money during this time, he worked at odd jobs – painting, roofing, cleaning homes. Finally he got an interview, but before the day of the interview his current live-in partner who was angry with him had him arrested for unpaid parking tickets. Since he had no money to pay the tickets, he had to spend a week in jail – which meant he would miss his interview. However, he convinced a guard to let him make one phone call, which he used to move the interview later by a few days. (He didn't mention the reason!)

When he got out of jail and returned to his house, his partner had taken his son and all of his possessions (clothes and car included) and changed the locks. So he had to find friends who would loan him clothes, provide a little food and let him sleep on their floor. Wearing clean but entirely inappropriate clothing, he made it to his last-chance interview, and miraculously impressed the fellow enough to get accepted to that company's training program.

For the next several weeks, he carried all of his worldly possessions with him, sometimes discreetly sleeping under his desk at night, as he worked hard to master the training program. Even though the final exam was notoriously difficult, he passed.

At this point he began to receive a small salary and was able to rent an apartment. But then, after weeks of working hard in the training program, his former live-in lover showed up just long enough to return his young son to him. Having been fatherless as a child, Gardner had vowed to always be there for his own kids, so he was overjoyed and relieved to finally have his son back. Unfortunately, however, no children were allowed in the apartment building where he was living. So, having his son back instantly made him homeless again.

His salary at this point was so small that he could just pay for low-cost daycare for his son and food; they spent their nights in cheap hotels, shelters, on park benches if weather permitted. A few times they even had to sleep in a small, lockable bathroom in the local subway station. He had no place to leave their belongings when the boy wasn't in daycare, so he now had to carry *both* of their worldly goods with him when they walked around town. Through it all, he ferociously protected his son and still managed to be at his desk every day, gradually getting better at his job.

Sure enough, over time his salary increased until he was able to rent an apartment for himself and his son, put his son into a better daycare center and live a life more like the one most Americans are accustomed to. As time went by, he kept working and developing his skills and business connections until he was at the top of his field.

Today, Gardner owns his own multimillion dollar brokerage firm and has become a renowned philanthropist, helping to pull other disadvantaged people out of poverty in this country and around the world.

I believe it's fair to say that most of us would have thrown in the towel at some point if we had to go through everything that Gardner did as he tried to reach his goal. It's true that Gardner had courage, determination, talent and intelligence. But when circumstances are stacked against us, talent, intelligence and desire are not always enough to achieve success. There's another equally important factor: *The way we think about our situation.*

What does Gardner say about how he prevailed against those seemingly insurmountable odds? He says that whenever his worries began to get the upper hand, *it was his focus that saved him*. He devoted his attention to simply moving forward, one step at a time – he didn't dwell on the obstacles he faced. He kept his focus on the things he could control, and that focus kept his fears and worries from overwhelming him.

The moral of the story? If you want to stay off – or get off – the Wheel of Misfortune, the things you choose to focus on can make all the difference.

Choosing Your Focus

Basically, when you're working to achieve a goal and you face serious obstacles, there are five different things you can focus on:

1) You can focus on the things you don't like in your current experience – the things that provoke anger or frustration because they're making your life difficult.

2) You can focus on how far away the situation you'd rather be in appears to be.

3) You can focus on the things that make you happy in your current experience.

4) You can focus on the positive situation or goal that you hope to reach. And/or

5) You can focus on the steps you're taking to move toward your goal.

Focusing on either #1 or #2 – the things you don't like, or how far away your goal is – will almost certainly be self-defeating. Focusing on any of the last three – the things you like, your goal, or the movement you're making toward your goal – is much more likely to help you make it successfully through the obstacles you face.

Let's look closely at the consequences of focusing on each option.

1. Focusing On the Things You Don't Like

When people are unhappy, they often focus on whatever is provoking their anger or frustration. This is understandable; we all feel justified being angry and resentful when we believe we've ended up in a situation we don't deserve to be in. Furthermore, if you're into playing the role of victim (see Chapter 3), focusing on what you don't like can be a very reinforcing part of the game; it helps to confirm and justify your belief that you're a victim.

Strangely enough, we human beings actually have a biologically based tendency to notice and remember things we don't like more than things we *do* like. In psychology, this concept is referred to as *negativity bias*.[2] The classic example is a compliment versus a critique. If three people tell you how much they like your work, and one person tells you your work is terrible, which comment is going to run through your mind later? Events (or aspects of events) that we perceive to be negative upset us, triggering chemical reactions in our bodies and minds that imprint them in our memory more deeply than positive events. Positive events tend to evoke a less-dramatic physical reaction and therefore don't embed themselves in our memories to the same extent.

Paying more attention to troubling details has some practical advantages in many situations. It may be that the things that trouble us are the things we *need* to pay attention to and fix. And maybe the person who hates your work is more likely to cause trouble down the line, so it's worth paying more attention to him or her. However, this natural tendency to notice and remember the bad things has a major downside: It causes us to focus more on the negative aspects of our experience, biasing our perspective in that direction.

There's nothing wrong with being realistic, but there is something wrong with only noticing the negative side of a situation: Doing so can alter our perspective in a way that doesn't balance the good and bad, making us more pessimistic, more angry and more impatient. And, the actions we choose to take in response will be very different – and probably less effective.

Here are a few negative consequences of focusing on what you don't like:

- ***When you're focused on the negative, you can easily miss other things – such as information and opportunities.*** A few years ago, Dr. Daniel Simons, a psychology professor at the University of Illinois, conducted a very interesting experiment with Christopher Chabris at Harvard University. They showed subjects a video of two small groups of people playing basketball and asked the viewers to pay attention to specific things taking place in the video, such as counting the number of passes made by one of the teams. In the middle of the video, a woman wearing a gorilla suit walks slowly through the scene, among the players, stopping to face the camera and thump her chest before exiting the scene.

After the viewing, the subjects were asked if they had seen the gorilla. *Half of them had no recollection of the gorilla,* and when shown the video a second time, many insisted it was an altered video with the gorilla added in.

On the other hand, the same video was shown to a different group without instructions to pay attention to specific things, and everyone saw the gorilla.

The point? When we are paying attention to something, we can become *totally oblivious* to other things that are right in front of us – even if they would ordinarily draw our attention. When the Titanic set sail for America in April of 1912, the owners were focused on doing everything possible to generate extra headlines. (Being the maiden voyage of the largest and most luxurious ship ever built apparently wasn't sufficient.) So, the captain cranked the engines and sent the ship across the ocean at top speed, attempting to set a new ocean-crossing record. They should have been focusing more on practical issues like icebergs. Because they weren't, 1,500 people died.

When times are tough it's easy to fall into the habit of focusing on what you don't like. But that will cause you to miss other things that are happening – and the gorilla you fail to see could be the key to changing your situation for the better.

• *Focusing on what you don't like brings more of it into your experience.* Contrary to what many people believe, your experience is not determined by what's happening to you – it's determined by *what you're paying attention to.* If someone says to you, "The world is a cruel and cold place," they're not describing the world – they're describing their *experience* of the world. They are paying attention to negatives, so their experience becomes negative.

No matter how dire your situation, you always have a choice about what you focus on. Focusing on the worst part of your experience has the effect of making it the centerpiece of your world. For example, imagine living with someone who has one small, irritating habit. If you ignore it, it's not a big deal. But the more you focus on it, the more it will drive you crazy. Many otherwise compatible relationships have been brought to ruin because of a minor problem that one party chose to focus on.

Again, paying attention to what you don't like makes it a bigger part of your experience. That, in turn, generates anger and frustration. This easily can escalate into a spiral of increasing fury, followed by increasingly bad choices of action that make things worse, not better.

• *Focusing on perceived limitations helps to make them real, and keeps you from putting your energy into creating what you want.* Often, especially when we're struggling to stay off the Wheel of Misfortune, the list of things we don't like includes perceived limits on our resources and options. Focusing on those limitations is a great way to give them far more power than they really have. Focusing on them not only makes them the center of our experience, it also gives them legitimacy they don't deserve.

Suppose you're walking down a path and find a huge tree has fallen in your way. You won't benefit from focusing on your misfortune, or how big the tree is, or how this is going to make you late for an appointment. The more you think about the limitations produced by the obstacle, the bigger the obstacle will seem. You'll do far better if you focus on how to get around the obstacle.

Suppose you need to travel a long distance, but have no money to buy gas or a bus, train or plane ticket. If you focus on the lack of money, you may remain angry and stuck in your current location. (You may even stoop to violating your standards by trying to steal money from someone else, in desperation.) If you stop focusing on the lack of money, you'll do a much better job of finding an alternative, such as looking for another person traveling to that location, finding someone who needs something delivered to that location, or offering a service to someone in exchange for the use of their vehicle.

In order to succeed, Chris Gardner had to put his focus on improving his job skills during the day and finding food and shelter at night. If he had focused on all of the other, more abstract obstacles he had to surmount every day, such as the sheer difficulty of what he was trying to do, he would have wasted all of his energy being angry and frustrated. He would never have been able to accomplish what he did.

The bottom line: One of the greatest obstacles to solving a problem is focusing on the limitations you think you have, instead of focusing on looking for solutions. As author Richard Bach says in his novel *Illusions*, "Focus on your limitations, and sure enough, they're yours."[3]

• ***Focusing on what you don't like leads to attacking it, which is seldom the best strategy***. Two problems result from attacking what you don't like. First, attacking something directly often makes it stronger, just as when an infection attacks the body and the body responds by juicing up its defenses. Second, the attacking process can become a major energy sink.

I once was hired for about a month to organize old legal files in a warehouse. I shared the job with a guy a few years younger than me who enjoyed irritating me. (It seemed to be the only way he knew to create a sense of personal power – make the people around him angry.)

Soon after we began the job, he brought a boom box to work and proceeded to play loud music that I really didn't like. The more I asked him to turn it down or play something else, the louder he cranked it, with obvious satisfaction. For a while, I was angry and I focused on how to get him to stop playing his music so loudly. Of course, nothing I tried worked; the more I tried to get him to stop, the more he enjoyed himself. I was quite frustrated.

I finally decided to stop focusing on what I didn't like and start focusing on what I'd prefer to experience and how I could create it. It didn't take me long to think of a solution: I went out and bought myself a portable CD player with headphones. From then on, I listened to music that I enjoyed as I worked, easily drowning out the boom box with my headphones. And my co-worker finally gave up trying to irritate me. By withdrawing my energy from the problem, I caused it to disappear – where before my *attack-what-you-don't-like* energy had been making things worse. Focusing on what I wanted led to a satisfying solution, without any negative consequences.

The second downside to attacking what you don't like is that it can really eat up your time and energy; it can become an obsession. And, whatever you attack is likely to rally its defenses and may try to fight back, causing the drain on your time and energy to increase dramatically. History is full of examples of individuals (and whole societies) that became obsessed with putting all of their time and energy and resources into attacking something they didn't like, a bit like Captain Ahab in Herman Melville's novel *Moby Dick*, who becomes so focused on the white whale that caused him to lose his leg that he ends up sinking his ship and killing all but one member of his crew trying to get his revenge. If you fall into that trap, you may end up with not only a negative view of the world, but little time and energy to think about creating a better alternative.

In reality, the best way to lessen or eliminate something you don't like is often to simply withdraw your support and attention from it, just as I did in the warehouse. This is not an appropriate strategy in every situation – for example, if you need to fight against something or someone in order to save a life. But whenever you're faced with an ongoing situation that's making you miserable, it's worth looking carefully to see whether there's a way to defuse some or all of the negatives by simply withdrawing your support and attention.

One argument that might be made in support of focusing on the things you don't like is that you need to understand those things better

Consequences of Focusing On What You Don't Like

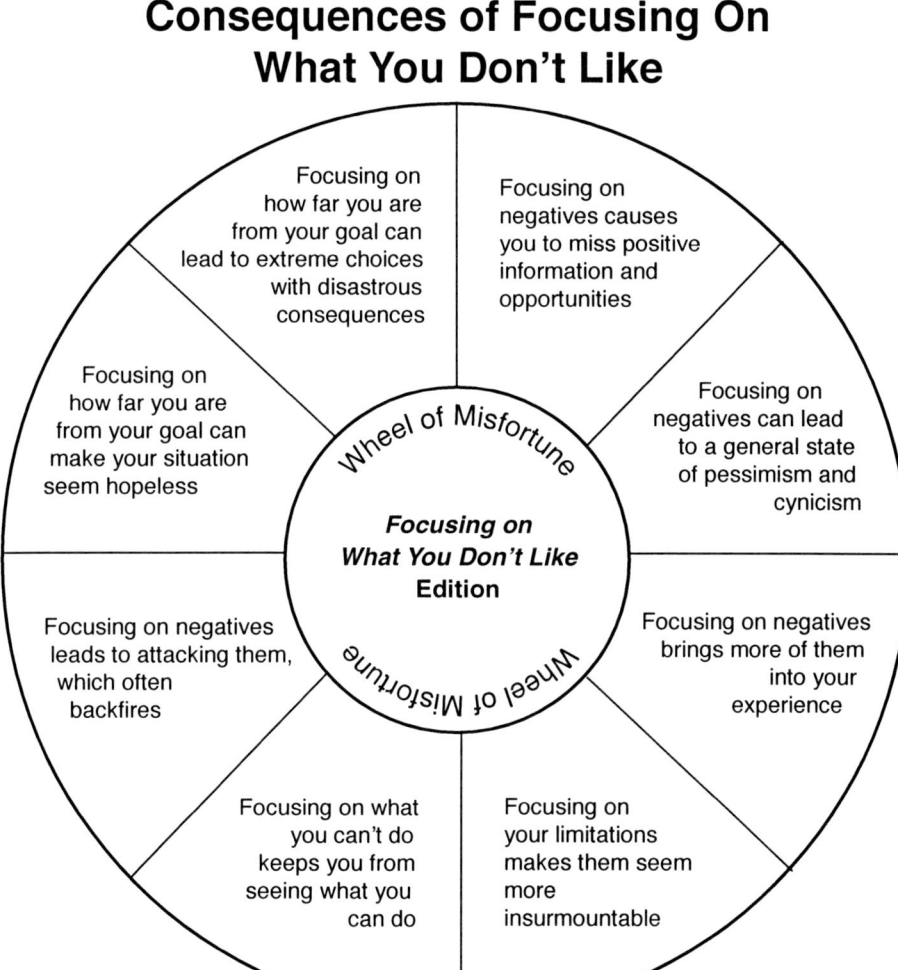

in order to change them. However, it's important to remember that there's a difference between *knowing about* something and *focusing* on it. Knowledge is a tool, but devoting unnecessary energy to dwelling on something you don't like doesn't increase your knowledge. Instead, it tends to distort your perspective and provoke emotions that are probably not helpful, such as anxiety and anger.

Here's another way to put this: *Make peace with what you've got.* Letting yourself be angry about your current situation pumps energy into it and helps keep it going. (Resistance, as they used to say on *Star Trek the Next Generation*, is futile.) Instead of resisting what you have, put your energy into creating what you want.

That brings up another important point: Some things that affect us negatively are within our ability to change – *but others are not*. It's important to make that distinction, because if you can't change something you are definitely not helping yourself by dwelling on it. Doing so will simply cause you to feel frustration and anger without producing any positive result. Alcoholics Anonymous has its well-known serenity prayer that reflects this distinction: *God grant me the serenity to accept the things I cannot change; the courage to change the things I can; and the wisdom to know the difference.* If you definitely cannot change the thing that's making you miserable, you're doing yourself a major disservice by focusing on it any more than you have to.

So, if you find yourself focusing relentlessly on things in your experience that you don't like, ask yourself whether it's within your power to do anything about them. If it isn't, then you won't gain anything at all by dwelling on them.

One last point: As mentioned earlier, human beings automatically tend to notice and remember negatives more than positives. How can we keep this innate tendency from leaving us depressed and angry? By remembering that this is the way the human mind is designed to work, and by going out of our way to compensate for it. In other words, be conscious of the fact that positive aspects of your situation will tend to slip by with less fanfare and remain relatively unnoticed – unless you go out of your way to notice them. *Make a point of paying attention to the positives in your experience as well as the negatives.* This isn't just "goody-two-shoes" advice: It's a way to compensate for one small downside of the way your brain works. Plus, making a conscious effort to do so will leave you with a more accurate picture of what's happening. It will make it easier to maintain a positive frame of mind, and it will help you make better choices about what you need to do.

2. Focusing on the Gap Between What You Have and What You Want

Have you ever set out on a long trip in a car with young kids? If you have, you know what you're likely to hear soon after you get underway: *"Are we there yet?"* It's a cliché, but it's true....I even remember saying it on long car rides when I was a kid!

This, of course, is a classic example of focusing on the gap between where you are and where you want to be. For a child it's easy to focus on the seemingly endless time that's left before you get to your destination. (Unfortunately, the result of that focus can be a very unhappy child for the duration of the trip, and corresponding pain for the parents.)

It's also easy to fall into the same habit as an adult – focusing on how far you have to go and how many obstacles you have to overcome before you can get to the place you want to be. But there's one big difference between an adult doing this and the kids in the car: The kids will eventually reach their destination, barring a major catastrophe. So, their obsessing about how long it's taking to get there is just an annoyance. But if you're an adult trying to reach a goal and it's *not* guaranteed that you'll succeed, focusing on the distance between where you are and where you want to be is a good way to *totally derail your chances of reaching your goal at all.*

This is actually one of the worst things you can do when you're in a situation you don't like. The more you focus on the gap between what you have and what you want, the more hopeless the situation will seem. That will not inspire the confidence you need to move forward – or inspire good choices about what action to take.

Among other things, this focus can warp your perspective about how far away your goal actually is. When you obsessively focus on an obstacle or a series of obstacles, they can begin to seem bigger and more significant than they really are. Then, the odds of your reaching your goal start to seem smaller and smaller; the mountain you have to climb just looks so big! That, in turn, can lead to feelings of despair, being overwhelmed and becoming immobilized.

It's a little bit like having to walk across a log bridging a deep canyon between two precipices in the mountains. What will you focus on? What a long distance it is to the other side? How far you'll fall if you slip? You don't have to be a genius to know that you won't make it across the gap if you focus on those things. You have to focus on the destination, or on the small steps you're taking and how you place your feet, so that you maintain your balance and don't become overwhelmed.

For many people, focusing on the gap between where they are and where they'd like to be makes the journey toward the goal a lot more unpleasant and nerve-wracking than it needs to be, but it doesn't actually cause them to fail or lead to any horrifying side effects. However, for some individuals, focusing on that gap can go from being a minor hindrance to becoming a major problem for them and everyone around them. That makes these individuals deserving of a closer look.

The goals that may lead to this kind of bad outcome are not usually specific, concrete, short-term goals. Instead, they are very general, idealized future versions of the world in which a specific perceived problem – or *all* problems – have been solved. When these individuals look at the current situation, which they don't like, they focus on evidence of ignorance or malice, exaggerating that aspect of the present until the existing situation is seen as intolerable. They come to think of the existing world, and the people they believe are responsible for what they don't like, as hopelessly evil, ignorant and corrupt.

The combination of a very negative perception of the current situation and an idealized image of "what should be" creates an impossibly wide gap between the two. In this situation, focusing on the gap amounts to thinking: "This glorious goal is impossibly far away – *but we desperately need to reach it or all is lost.*" The more a person in this position focuses on that imagined gap, the worse everything seems, and the more the person feels powerless to reach the goal. And the more powerless the person feels, the more it seems justifiable to take *extreme actions*. Taking normal, small steps toward the goal ends up looking like a waste of time. (The popular phrase for this type of reasoning is "the end justifies the means.")

Unfortunately, the extreme actions taken by a person who is caught up in this focus almost always contradict the person's idealistic goal. Furthermore, the extreme actions taken will probably cause a huge setback in terms of actually *reaching* the goal. For example, on a small scale, this kind of thinking can justify actions that are mean-spirited, as when someone who feels he's been given a "raw deal" cheats someone else in the name of "making things fairer." On a larger scale, the frustration caused by this focus can lead to justifying actions that the person in question would never *dream* of taking under other circumstances. Those actions may include murder, as when someone kills an abortion doctor in the name of "stopping the killing," or self-destructive acts such as suicide (even mass suicide, as happened at Jonestown in 1979). It can also lead to acts of terrorism, shooting innocent bystanders in a public place, starting wars and justifying almost anything, *no matter how far from the person's ideal vision those actions may be.*

All of this is a consequence of focusing on the gap between an overly negative interpretation of the current situation and an overly idealized version of what could or should be happening instead.

Author Jane Roberts expressed this idea very well in her book *The*

Individual and the Nature of Mass Events.[4] She uses the term *practicing idealist* to describe someone who avoids falling into this trap by focusing on the goal – instead of focusing on the gap between the present situation and the goal – and then chooses appropriate actions to take on that basis. In other words, by not dwelling on how far away your goal seems to be, and instead *consciously choosing your actions specifically so that they are in sync with your goals and highest ideals*, you create a situation in which every action you take will be worthy of your real goal – and every action you take will move you toward creating that ideal, instead of undermining it.

So, the next time you feel a wave of despair about your situation, check to see if you're dwelling on the gap between what you have and what you want. If you are, remember that this focus isn't going to improve things – quite the opposite. Make a conscious effort to change what you're spending your time and energy thinking about. For example, focus on small steps you can take to help bring your preferred situation into existence. At the same time, make a commitment to avoid taking any actions *unless they are worthy of your goals*.

3. Focusing on What You *Like* in Your Current Situation

No matter how bad the situation you find yourself in, there are almost always some aspects of your situation that are positive. Yes, when we're suffering it's hard to notice the aspects of our lives that are still pretty good. For starters, our brains all have the "negativity bias" described earlier, which makes us notice and remember unpleasant things more readily than positive things. Furthermore, in some situations we may actually *need* to pay close attention to the negative things we're experiencing in order to survive.

Nevertheless, it's important to go out of your way to notice whatever good things still exist in your life. Spiritual leaders talk about this in terms of gratitude – being grateful for what we have. Mainstream culture sometimes refers to this as "counting your blessings," which can sound like sappy and unrealistic advice. However, there are very good, practical reasons for making a special effort to focus on the positive aspects of your current experience.

First and foremost, your experience as a human being consists of what you focus on. Do you want your experience to consist entirely of things you don't like? That's what you get if you let your brain's negativity bias take charge. To avoid that you have to *consciously choose* to take the time to notice and think about the positive parts of your experience.

Second, we tend to create more of what we focus on, so it's important not to let the things you like slip away from your attention. By focusing on them – at least part of time – you'll help to draw more of those positives into your life.

So, spend some time each day paying attention to whatever positives are still in your life. It's not just sentimental claptrap; it will really work to your advantage.

4. Focusing On What You Want (i.e., Your Goal)

The fourth option, focusing on what you want, has the ultimate advantage: It sets the process of creating that better situation into motion, and keeps the process going. If you stay on track, the result will be the eventual creation of the situation you'd like to be in. (Of course, before you can focus on your goal, you have to know what it is! For more about figuring out what you want, and more about the process of reaching your goal, see Chapter 10.)

The one drawback to focusing constantly on what you want is that it's easy to fall back into focusing on the gap between your goal and where you are right now. For that reason, the fifth possible choice of focus may be the best choice of all….

5. Focusing on Taking Small Steps Toward Your Goal

In 1985, mountain climbers Joe Simpson and Simon Yates decided to attempt to climb the west face of Siula Grande in the Peruvian Andes – a feat no one before them had successfully accomplished. They made the attempt alone; they had one friend at the base camp, but otherwise had no one to count on if they needed help. Within two days – after some terrifying close calls – they made it to the summit. Then came the most dangerous part: getting back down.

Not long into their descent, Joe slipped. During his brief fall, he sustained a devastating injury to his right leg; the impact pushed the lower part of his leg up through his kneecap, shattering it. In overwhelming pain, he was nearly unable to move. His partner Simon chose to attempt a rescue by lowering him down the length of the rope that tied them together; once Joe had secured his position and taken his weight off the rope using his good leg, Simon would climb down to Joe's level and lower him again. The lowering down parts went faster and faster, nearly a free-fall slide, as both men were losing strength and time was of the essence.

Although excruciatingly painful for Joe, this strategy worked for a while. They got a good part of the way down the mountain face before flying snow made it impossible to see what lay ahead. Then Joe was lowered at top speed down an incline and over a precipice, jerking to a stop hanging over a crevasse (a deep fissure in the ice) far below. The impact didn't pull Simon off the mountain, but it made it impossible for him to move; Joe's weight never came off of the rope.

Unable to see anything, Simon maintained his position for about an hour. By then he realized that whatever had happened, Joe was clearly helpless. If nothing changed, Simon would slip and they would both die. So he decided to cut the rope, knowing at least one of them would survive.

When Simon cut the rope, Joe dropped into the crevasse below him. Amazingly, he wasn't killed by the fall. Meanwhile, Simon eventually climbed down past the spot where Joe had gone over the precipice and realized what had happened. However, it seemed impossible that Joe could have survived, so Simon returned to base camp believing he was responsible for his friend's death.

After some hours of unconsciousness, Joe, waking up in the crevasse, realized that Simon wasn't coming for him. But instead of giving up, he decided to try to make it back to base camp. Since he couldn't climb up to get out of the crevasse, he did the only thing he could do: He lowered himself down further into it. Miraculously, he found an opening through which he was able to crawl out into daylight. Nevertheless, he still had to traverse miles of ice and then rocky terrain to make it back to base camp – hungry, extremely dehydrated and in incredible pain. He couldn't walk; he couldn't even crawl. But by pushing himself up and hopping one step and then falling (with excruciating pain), he was able to inch forward.

How did he manage to traverse miles of icy, rocky terrain in this condition? He picked out some feature in the landscape that lay in front of him and decided he would force himself to reach it within a certain number of minutes. (Luckily, his wristwatch was still working.) He repeated this strategy over and over, and slowly but surely he moved toward the base camp. Had he focused on the larger distance that he had to cross, he probably would have given up hope. But by breaking his seemingly impossible journey into smaller, extremely difficult but not impossible pieces, he moved forward, and within a couple of days got close enough to the camp that they could hear him yelling. They heard his cries just hours before they were to leave the area for good.

Joe's story, captured in his book *Touching the Void*,[5] and the movie of the same name, makes an invaluable point. When your goal seems distant and difficult or impossible to reach, break it up into smaller steps that will challenge you but not overwhelm you. As you reach those goals one by one, you'll find yourself well on the way to the greater goal that once seemed impossible.

Many wise individuals have recommended this strategy. Mark Twain said, "The secret of getting ahead is getting started. The secret of getting started is breaking your complex, overwhelming tasks into small manageable tasks, and then starting on the first one." And Henry Ford observed the same thing: "Nothing is particularly hard," he said, "if you divide it into small jobs."

Chris Gardner, whose story we talked about at the beginning of this chapter, certainly used this strategy to beat the odds; he focused on the details of his current surroundings and the fact that he was making headway toward his goals. That saved him from becoming overwhelmed by the odds stacked against him.

It's also important to note that the two main alternatives to taking small steps forward are to do nothing, or try to take huge leaps toward your goal. If you're following the first alternative – not doing anything to create what you want – you're liable to start believing that you *can't* do anything. That leads to more frustration and focusing on your feelings, and that can lead to actions that make things worse. If you try the second alternative – taking huge leaps toward your ideal that probably aren't practical given your current circumstances – there's a good chance you'll fail. This will leave you increasingly likely to focus on negatives and push you toward actions that will undermine the end result you'd like to see.

For all of these reasons, the best thing to focus on is small, manageable steps that you can take every day that will move you slowly but surely toward your goal. This will not only have a powerful cumulative effect over time, but will also help prevent frustration. After all, it's pretty hard to see yourself as helpless or powerless when you know you really are moving forward.

5 Ways to Focus Your Attention

Focus	Consequences
Focus on what you don't like (negativity bias tends to make us do this)	Causes you to miss other things
	Fills your experience with what you don't like
	Makes perceived limitations seem more real
	May inspire attacking what you don't like, which can become an energy sink and tends to make the thing you don't like stronger
	Diverts your energy away from creating what you want
Focus on how far away your goal seems to be	Warps your perspective about how far away your goal actually is
	Leads to feelings of despair, being overwhelmed and becoming immobilized
	Leads to justifying extreme actions that ultimately undercut your chances of reaching your goal
Focus on what you do like in your current situation	Offsets negativity bias, making your daily experience more positive
	Helps you to create more of what you do like
Focus on your goal	Helps keep you moving in the right direction
	Helps you make choices of action that are in line with your goal
Focus on the small steps you're taking toward your goal every day	Minimizes frustration and hopelessness because you can see that you're moving toward your goal
	Encourages you to continue taking small steps toward your goal
	Avoids the pitfalls that arise when you try to take giant leaps toward your goal

So, come up with some simple things you can do to move in the direction you want to go; things that make sense for you right now, working with your current situation and abilities. Those small steps will have positive consequences that you may not even be aware of, and if you persist, they'll eventually lead you to your goal.

The Bottom Line

When you're faced with serious obstacles and challenges, make sure to *pay attention to what you're focusing on* – especially when you're feeling frustrated or angry about your situation. This is a really important part of staying off the Wheel of Misfortune. Keep your ultimate goal in mind – the situation you'd like to end up in – and then focus your attention and energy on small, manageable steps you can take on a daily basis that will move you slowly but surely toward that goal. Don't focus on the obstacles you face and how terrible they seem, any more than you need to in order to survive. You'll only cause them to loom larger in your experience and appear more difficult to surmount. Make peace with your current situation instead of resisting it. And don't allow yourself to dwell on the gap between where you are right now and where you'd like to be. That's a recipe for frustration and hopelessness, and those emotions can lead to very counterproductive choices that will make your situation worse, not better.

Just say: "My situation is what it is; I'm going to focus on creating something better, and move towards it one step at a time." If that's your focus, something better is exactly what you'll get.

Once more, in brief:

Here are the key points to remember from Chapter 5:

When you're in a tough situation, you have five options to choose from when deciding what to focus your conscious energy on. The first two backfire; the last three work to your advantage:

1) You can focus on the things that are provoking your anger or frustration because they're making times hard. This backfires in multiple ways. Paying a little bit of attention to the things you don't like is OK; doing so might help you change those things for the better. But don't dwell on them. And be especially carefully not to get sucked into focusing on things you don't like that are beyond your ability to change.

2) You can focus on the gap between the current situation and what you'd rather be experiencing. Focusing on that gap leads to feelings of despair, misjudging the difficult of reaching your goal, becoming immobilized, and in some cases justifying extreme actions because the gap seems so large and insurmountable – the classic strategy of *using the end to justify the means*. So if you catch yourself dwelling on the gap between where you are and where you'd like to be, stop and shift your focus to one of the next three choices.

3) You can focus on whatever you do like in your current situation. This helps to offset our innate negativity bias – the human tendency to notice and remember the things we don't like more than the things we do like. Deliberately focusing on the things we like shifts at least part of our experience toward the positive; and it helps us bring more of those positive things into our lives.

4) You can focus on the positive future alternative you'd rather be experiencing (i.e., your goal). Among other things, this has a powerful, positive effect on your odds of reaching your goal.

5) You can focus on the small steps you're taking to bring your goal into reality. This encourages you to keep moving forward; it minimizes frustration and hopelessness because you'll see progress; and it keeps your focus on concrete things you can manage. And remember: Trying to take a huge leap toward your goal can seriously backfire – if you fail, you'll just get discouraged.

So: Be aware of what you're focusing on, *especially* if you're feeling angry and frustrated. Focusing on your ultimate goal and the small steps you can take toward it every day is the least frustrating choice, and it produces the best results.

✻ ✻ ✻

NOTES for Chapter 5

1. Gardner C & Troupe Q. (2006) *The Pursuit of Happyness.* New York: HarperCollins.

2. For more on this, see: Baumeister R, Bratslavsky E, Finkenauer C, Vohs K. Bad is Stronger than Good. Review of General Psychology 2001;5:4: 323–370.
   or
   Rozin P, Royzman EB. Negativity bias, negativity dominance, and contagion. Personality and Social Psychology Review 2001;5:296–320.
3. Bach R. (1977) Illusions: The Adventures of a Reluctant Messiah. New York: Dell Publishing.
4. Roberts J. (1981)The Individual and the Nature of Mass Events. Amber-Allen Publishing. San Rafael, Calif.
5. Simpson J. (2004) Touching the Void: The True Story of One Man's Miraculous Survival. New York: Perennial.

6.
Take Advantage of All of Your Mind's Resources.

Don't rely solely on one type of thinking.

"The intuitive mind is a sacred gift and the rational mind is a faithful servant. We have created a society that honors the servant and has forgotten the gift."
– Albert Einstein

"Civilization advances by extending the number of important operations which we can perform without thinking about them."
– Alfred North Whitehead

As noted in my song *Piece of the Puzzle*, psychologist Abraham Maslow once observed that if a person only has a hammer, he tends to see everything as a nail. In other words, if we only have one tool for dealing with the world, we may try to use it to solve every problem – whether it's the right tool for that purpose or not.

Now suppose you *believe* you only have a single tool to work with – but in reality, you have a bunch of tools you're not aware of. You might continue to use the one tool you know you have, blissfully unaware that you could be doing a far better job of managing your life with the other tools you possess….if you only knew you had them!

When we talk about the human mind, this is the situation in which many modern people find themselves. Our culture encourages us to believe that our intellect is what makes us different from the animals – that our ability to consciously analyze a problematic situation and think carefully about everything before we act is what makes us the dominant life form on Earth. If you accept that idea, you may see your intellect as your one great tool for dealing with life's challenges, including staying off (or getting off) the Wheel of Misfortune.

Since most of us identify with the part of our consciousness that thinks verbally and can ponder whatever topic we choose – the part we call our "intellect" – it's easy to believe that this really is our most powerful survival tool. However, it turns out that there's a lot more going on here; the mind uses a lot of other tools, skills and strategies to help us manage our lives. In fact, the verbal, analytical part of the mind has some serious limitations, and the rest of the mind does a pretty good job of compensating for those limitations, often without us even realizing it.

Sherlock Holmes and characters like Star Trek's Mr. Spock epitomize the idea that logic and intellect are greatly to be desired and the best way to approach a problem. But are they?

In her bestselling book *Drawing on the Right Side of the Brain*[1], one of the definitive books on learning to draw, Betty Edwards shares an interesting experiment that anyone can try. (If you've never experienced this, I encourage you to take a few moments and try it.) Find a picture of a common object, such as a chair (a magazine ad might be a good place to look). Take a pencil and a blank piece of paper and try to draw an accurate copy of the chair. Most people who are not experienced in the art of drawing will create a fairly sloppy picture of the chair.

Now *turn the picture you're copying upside down*, and try doing it again, using another piece of blank paper. When you're done, turn your drawing right-side-up, and compare it to the picture you were copying. If you're like most people, you'll discover that the second drawing, done with the object upside down, is a much more accurate drawing of the chair!

The explanation is simple: Our minds use many different types of thinking, even though we're usually not conscious of it. In this instance, when we see the picture right-side-up, we recognize the object as a familiar item. The image we're seeing connects to similar reference images in our minds, and we identify the object as a member of a category: *This is a chair.* At least for those of us not skilled at drawing, that knowledge actually *interferes* with the kind of thinking that would help us make a good drawing. Instead of looking carefully at the shapes and spaces that make up the image and trying to duplicate those, as an experienced artist would, we try to draw a chair – which ends up producing a sloppy drawing. In short, the way we're thinking about what we're looking at undercuts our ability to draw an accurate picture of it.

In contrast, when we turn the image upside down, the usual brain connections that identify the object as a chair don't work as well; we're not accustomed to seeing the world upside-down. *So we shift into a different mode of thinking* in order to recreate the image. Instead of "drawing a chair," we're forced to actually look at the shapes and spaces and relative sizes of the parts of the image. As a result, we produce a copy of the image that's far more accurate – and looks more like a chair when it's turned right side up!

This experiment makes three important points:

1) We're capable of using many different types of thinking. In fact, we constantly process information in a number of ways that do not involve our conscious, verbal selves.

2) The way most of us think on a daily basis is often *not* the best way to solve a particular problem or deal with a given situation. For example, as we've just seen, logical, analytical thinking doesn't produce good drawings. (As Betty Edwards points out, many people believe they don't have the skills required to draw well, when in fact they do have the skills – they're just using the wrong thought process.)

3) Our standard way of thinking can actually *interfere* with more effective ways of functioning that would better meet our needs in a given situation. For that reason, sometimes we're more effective when we *turn off* our standard thinking apparatus so that a more effective mode of thinking can come to our rescue, as we did in this exercise.

When trying to stay off the Wheel of Misfortune, we need all the skills and talents that are available to us to help us make smart choices and interact with other people effectively. That includes using alternate ways of thinking, perceiving and analyzing, such as intuition and gut instinct. Unfortunately, we have not been taught to take them seriously or use them effectively, and that has put us at a disadvantage.

The Mind as a Team Effort

Psychologists often talk about the unconscious and subconscious mind – labels used to refer to parts of the mind responsible for mental operations that occur outside of our usual consciousness. I believe these parts of consciousness are every bit as conscious, alert, present and competent as the part we think of as our "identity." They just don't communicate or show their presence in the same verbal way.

In the course of daily living, we constantly perform mental calculations and operations that are crucial to our ability to function well, but have nothing to do with "conscious thought." We move our limbs in coordinated ways; we maintain our balance as we walk or stand; we know how fast to run to intercept a moving target without consciously calculating anything; we answer questions and carry on conversations without having to think about every word we say.

In fact, some have argued that these operations are managed outside of our "normal" consciousness because our normal consciousness would be overwhelmed! For example, it's widely accepted that the "rational" mind can only keep a limited number of things in mind at one time – approximately seven things[2] – which means our day-to-day mind can't possibly manage all the details of the monitoring, analysis and responding to our surroundings that we do every day. Instead, the parts of our mind that aren't verbal take care of these tasks outside of what we think of as consciousness, so our verbal, analytical self can focus on managing the most pressing decisions without unnecessary distractions. It's almost as if the conscious self that we normally identify with has a supercomputer at its disposal that constantly performs important functions for us – but without drawing any attention to itself.

The "silence" of these other parts of the mind may lead us to think that they don't exist...or if they exist, they aren't all that valuable. But our "conscious" mind is like the tip of an iceberg; it may be all that's visible, but it's only a tiny fraction of the whole story.

I find it useful to think of the mind as being like a team, rather than a single player. Suppose you're the coach of a small group of individuals who work together. One person in the team does all the talking and is generally the center of attention. That person happens to be very good at logical, step-by-step analysis and connecting details of current experience with past experience. He (or she) is always talking to you, and occasionally jumps up and down and yells and waves his hands to make sure you're hearing him! But the other team members have equally valuable skills – different skills – and they're working for the team just as hard. If one of them periodically taps you on the shoulder and presents you with information – nonverbally – are you going to ignore that information because it didn't come from the talkative, attention-grabbing member of the team?

The Mind's Team Members: VAM and GM

For practical purposes, let's call our standard day-to-day consciousness the *verbal, analytical mind*, or VAM. And let's refer to the rest of the consciousness "team" that includes all of our "unconscious" abilities as the *greater mind*, or GM.

So what exactly does this "greater mind" do for us? The list is pretty impressive: Research has shown that it perceives things in our experience and environment that our conscious self (the VAM) misses; it does a better job of many kinds of problem-solving than the VAM; it manages thousands of operations inside our bodies and reacts to external events in ways that our VAM couldn't begin to keep track of (much less constantly make decisions about); it can be highly creative, supplying us with bursts of inspiration; it's a repository for our learned skills and abilities; and much more. (We'll discuss these and other abilities in more detail in the next section.)

Even some activities that most of us believe only our conscious mind can do, such as reading or writing, can be done without using our usual conscious mind. Famed author Gertrude Stein conducted several experiments when she was studying psychology at Harvard in the 1890s. Among other things, she demonstrated that both she and a colleague could, with practice, write down what someone else was reading to them while she and her friend were reading and paying attention to something completely different. Afterwards, they had no conscious idea what they'd written down, although they were quite aware that they'd written something. Stein and her colleagues also found that they could read a book out loud while devoting their full conscious attention to a different story someone else was reading to them. In both cases, they were able to get the seemingly nonverbal greater mind to read and write without their conscious mind being involved.[3]

Some researchers go so far as to argue that the conscious mind doesn't do *any* of the real analysis or decision-making in our lives. They suggest that the parts of our mind outside of normal consciousness do all the real thinking and simply drop the result into our conscious mind; then the conscious mind just has to come up with a rationale to explain why it made that decision![4] I'm not sure I'm willing to go that far – but there's no question that a large part of the "thinking" we rely on is not done by what we consider to be our conscious mind.

Author Jonah Lehrer compares the contemporary human mind to

the cockpit of a modern commercial airliner.[5] The pilot is surrounded by extremely sophisticated computer systems. Those systems manage enormous numbers of details without the captain's involvement; they note internal and external changes and respond to them; they can even fly the plane without the captain's assistance at times. But the captain makes all the crucial decisions and monitors everything. The captain and the computers work together to keep the flight safe and smooth.

That's important partly because, despite expertise and careful programming, both the captain and the computer systems are fallible. So, they constantly monitor each other. The captain, of course, is like our verbal, analytical self; the banks of computers can be seen as similar to our greater mind. Imagine how much difference it would make to fly in a plane if the pilot had no idea that this sophisticated battery of computers was doing all of this for him. He'd be wasting his time worrying about details that the computers were already handling. Furthermore, he wouldn't take advantage of the information and warnings provided by the computers.

Many of us walk through our lives that way, ignoring much of the information provided by the greater mind.

Let's look in more detail at the ways our VAM and GM interact. To do that, we'll divide our discussion into four sections. First, we'll talk about how the greater mind shares information with the verbal, analytical mind. Second, we'll focus on some of the specific abilities the greater mind has, and how those abilities help us in day-to-day living. In that section we'll discuss some of the research that's been done in this area and what it's found. Third, we'll talk about why we often don't heed the "intuitive" advice and gut feelings we receive from the greater mind. And finally, we'll talk about specific strategies that can help us make our mental "team" work together more effectively.

How Does the Greater Mind Share Information?

There are two reasons many of us go through life without even realizing how much is going on in our greater mind outside of our conscious awareness.

First, the GM is usually nonverbal. When it needs to pass information along to the VAM, it almost never uses words to communicate. Instead, it gives us a surge of emotion or a physical feeling – for example, a knot in the stomach if it's trying to tell us that something is wrong or that something bad is about to happen. That's why such communications are often referred to as "gut feelings." (When the gut is not involved, people sometimes label such nonverbal information *intuition*. For our purposes, I'll use *gut feelings* and *intuition* interchangeably.) These feelings can be pretty subtle, but if you're paying attention you'll notice them. Sometimes, they're not subtle at all!

Second, the greater mind is *designed* to work without attracting attention to itself. The VAM, as already noted, has a limited attention span, so its assistant *has* to be able to work without attracting attention. The fact that the greater mind does its job unobtrusively helps to make the partnership between VAM and GM work very smoothly – but it also may lead us to miss the fact that we have a silent partner who is providing us with enormous help.

Interestingly, in a serious crisis, the GM may resort to far less subtle forms of communication. It may even break its normal non-verbal limitation and literally appear as a voice in our minds. For example, when climber Joe Simpson was struggling to survive after his disastrous climbing accident (as described in Chapter 5), he was severely injured, exhausted and dehydrated. But each time he felt he couldn't go any farther, a voice called out to him in his mind, egging him on and giving him instructions. His normal consciousness was overwhelmed, nearly non-functional – but that voice from outside his normal consciousness saved his life.[6]

In the early 1980s, researcher Weston H. Agor conducted two large studies of how executives, including 88 CEOs, made decisions. (The studies are described in detail in his book *The Logic of Intuitive Decision Making*.[7]) He was especially interested to see how they used nontraditional, nonanalytical thinking – i.e., trusting their gut or intuition – when they had to make important choices. The first study involved more than 3,000 executives; his second study took the 10% from the first study who scored highest in intuitive decision making and asked them for detailed reports on how and when they used this kind of thinking. Most of the executives readily admitted that they used nonanalytical thinking to make major decisions involving millions of dollars, and trusted their intuition in situations in which their decisions would have huge consequences.

Another study called *How Senior Managers Think* conducted by Professor Daniel Isenberg in the 1980s confirmed this.[8] Isenberg's study found that many managers and executives were using intuitive thinking instead of the analytical process to make decisions. The study noted five different ways intuition was being used: 1) to sense when a problem existed; 2) to execute familiar behavior rapidly; 3) to integrate isolated pieces of information into a coherent picture, often abruptly, in what we might call an "aha" experience; 4) to see whether the person felt positive or negative about a decision he'd already made in a more analytical way; and 5) to simply bypass the analytical approach to problem solving and jump to a solution.

One of the questions Weston Agor asked the executives who participated in his study was how they received the intuitive information. Not surprisingly, they reported knowing whether a decision was good or not-so-good based on the *feelings* that accompanied it. If they felt a sense of excitement, commitment, internal harmony, warmth and confidence, or sometimes a burst of energy, that told them they were making the right decision. When they were inclining towards a decision and felt anxiety, discomfort or an upset stomach, they knew that it wasn't a good choice; at the very least it needed to be considered further before taking action. In other words, the information almost always came in nonverbal form, but it was very real and had a profound impact on the decisions the executives made. In fact, Agor's studies found that the CEOs' rise to the top of the corporate ladder had a lot to do with their ability to recognize valuable information that didn't come from the conscious mind.

What the Greater Mind Does for Us

Recently, a number of popular books have promoted the idea that alternate ways of thinking are valuable and should be treated as such. They've noted the value of fear (when it's prompting us to take action in response to a real threat), the value of seemingly instant judgments, and the value of "gut" feelings. Yet this is a nebulous subject: There's no definitive chart explaining exactly what's going on outside of our verbal, analytical mind.

Given that, I'd like to offer one possible list of the services that seem to be provided to us by the GM. These helpful functions can be seen as falling into a couple of broad categories:

1) managing sophisticated skills we've learned that would overwhelm the VAM;

2) refining our skills by figuring out shortcuts and implementing them;

3) picking up on information the VAM misses;

4) drawing useful conclusions from our experience much faster than the VAM;

5) helping us make decisions of many types, and under many different conditions;

6) working on problems while our conscious mind is busy with other things, or asleep;

7) providing us with creative bursts and flashes of insight;

8) providing us with impulses to take beneficial actions that our VAM would have overlooked; and

9) warning us with feelings of discomfort when we're about to do something that we don't consciously realize is a mistake.

This list, of course, is somewhat arbitrary; the processes on the list overlap, and I may be omitting some that deserve to be included. Also, keep in mind that the items on this list may involve different skills and mental operations – which means they may come with different caveats about their accuracy and limitations. (The greater mind is far brighter than many of us think – but it certainly isn't infallible.)

With that noted, let's consider each category in more detail.

Service #1: *The greater mind manages sophisticated skills we've learned that would overwhelm our VAM.* One of the steps in any learning process is the gradual sublimation of newly learned skills and abilities out of consciousness and into the GM. For example, someone learning piano starts out consciously selecting each note and using many muscles to play the notes. Soon, the need to consciously select each note disappears, and the muscle movements used to play the notes become streamlined and automatic. This is reflected in brain structure changes as well: Not only do the areas of the brain involved with a task we're learning get larger with practice, but the neurons respond to increasingly specific stimuli, and they fire faster and more efficiently.[9]

This process also applies to learning a language. Learning a language starts out as a very conscious process, memorizing words and phrases; but after a while understanding and speaking happen automatically. Management of the details is gradually taken over by the GM, so the VAM doesn't have to expend its time and energy deciding what word to use.

In fact, once skills are taken over by the GM, letting our VAM try to help use those skills or guide them can backfire. Studies have shown that when experienced golfers, for example, are made to think about their swing, they make significantly worse shots.[10,11] The act of consciously thinking about what they're doing interferes with the learned process that's already quite well managed by the GM. The reverse is true for novice golfers; in general, the more they think about their swing, the *better* they do. They have to take things step by step because they have no experiential resources. Their VAMs are not interfering with an established process, because they're new to playing golf.

This runs counter to what many people assume. It sounds sensible to say that amateurs make decisions by just following their impulses, while experts work things out carefully, step by step using their experience. But the reverse is true.

In another study, novice and experienced golfers were given more time or less time to make their swings. Novices did better when they were able to take more time; experienced golfers did better with less time.[12,13] One reasonable explanation for this is that the more time you have before doing something, the more your VAM begins to consider your options. That works for novices, because they don't already know which option is best. But experienced players tend to choose the best option right off the bat without thinking about it because of their experience (stored in the GM). Having time to think before taking the shot allows other options to creep into their minds. Then the VAM kicks in, trying to decide which option is best, muddying the waters and increasing the chance that the pro golfers won't go with their first impulse.[14]

In short, once we've learned a skill, the GM manages it without the VAM needing to be involved. And, as these experiments demonstrate, when the greater mind already knows what it's doing, letting the VAM get involved tends to interfere and cause us to screw up!

Service #2: *The greater mind refines our skills by figuring out shortcuts that work and learning which things we need to pay attention to. However, it <u>doesn't</u> usually share what it's figured out with the VAM.* That last fact is one reason that "experts" are seldom ideal teachers; much of the skill that makes them an expert has been refined outside of consciousness, so they're actually not fully aware of how they do what they do. This not only makes it very difficult to transfer their skills to someone else, it invites the expert to try to come up with rational explanations for the skills that sound reasonable. Then, they teach those rationalizations to others, instead of teaching the actual processes they're using (which they're not fully aware of). This type of teaching or coaching can produce lousy results, unless the explanation the expert's VAM comes up with is actually correct – which it often is not.

For example, few baseball players can explain how to catch a fly ball. So, when trying to teach someone to do it, they may encourage the learner to run faster or slower, along with keeping his or her eye on the ball. In fact, researchers have found that when someone is good at catching fly balls, the GM is using two simple rules of thumb that get the person to the right place at the right time to catch the ball:[15]

Rule of thumb 1: If the ball is rising as you look at, run so that the relative speed at which it appears to be rising stays the same. (This works because if its rising rate appears to be slowing, it's going to fall somewhere in front of where you're standing; if its rising rate is *increasing* as you watch, it's going to end up coming down behind you. Either way you need to move or you won't be in the right spot to catch it.)

Rule of thumb 2: If the ball is coming down, keep your eye on it and run at whatever speed makes the angle of your gaze stay the same. (If you have to bend your head back farther to see the ball as you run, it will land behind you; if you're looking lower to follow the ball as you run, it will land in front of you.) Again, few ball players are aware that their GM has figured out these shortcuts and is using them. But that's how the GM gets them to the right place to catch the ball.

Another example is the way in which expert tennis players judge where a ball hit by the opponent will land. Few of them could explain how they know this; most would probably attribute their skill in returning the ball to "quick reflexes." In fact, as we discussed back in Chapter 2, studies have found that these experts have learned to pick up on details of the other person's body movements as they *prepare* to hit the ball, so their GM already knows where to go to successfully return the ball *even before it's hit*.[16,17] (What they're actually doing is a little like what jugglers do: Jugglers don't look at the balls coming down into their hands; they look at the top of the arc the balls make as they fly back and forth.)

The GM develops these approaches over time as we practice a skill. But it seldom, if ever, spells out in words what it's doing, for the benefit of the "team captain" – the VAM. As noted earlier, this is the main reason that a skilled person may not a good teacher. To be really successful at sharing a skill, you have to be conscious of what your GM is doing when you use that skill. Most people, including experts, are not.

So: If you want to learn a skill from someone who has already mastered it, try to find someone who's not only good at the thing in question, but also *consciously knows* what his or her GM is doing. Such individuals are not always easy to find, but it's worth looking for them. (And if you have to choose between learning a skill from someone who is a really good teacher or someone who is a "superstar" at doing that thing – but not such a great teacher – you should probably choose to learn from the really good teacher.)

Service#3: *The greater mind picks up on information our VAM misses.* Can the greater mind really do this? Indeed it can. Here are just a few of the things that the GM may pick up on that our VAMs usually miss:

– *Information we weren't consciously able to take in.* In one experiment, subjects watched a ticker tape of stock market information scroll across the bottom of a television screen, just like the one you might see on a cable news channel. It indicated what hundreds of stocks were doing – i.e., going up or down in price. There was so much information going by that after a few minutes subjects couldn't answer questions about which stocks were doing better or worse. The VAM couldn't manage the sheer volume of information. However, the information *was* registering in the subjects' greater minds; when asked which stocks triggered the best *feelings* – a favorite way for our greater minds to share information – subjects did remarkably well at identifying the stocks that the ticker tape had said were doing better.[18] So other members of our mental "team" have far less trouble capturing large quantities of information than the VAM does, and they can share what they've learned by giving us positive or negative feelings.

– *Microexpressions.* If you've ever spoken to someone and had an uncomfortable feeling that the individual might not be telling the truth, it's possible that your greater mind is picking up on signals we all tend to give off when we lie – signals that the VAM doesn't normally perceive unless it's been trained to do so. Apparently, the mental gymnastics involved in telling a lie cause us to have difficulty maintaining our facial expressions (an important part of successfully telling a lie).

Because it's difficult to maintain the appropriate bogus emotion on our faces when we lie, the real emotion we're feeling often flashes onto our faces for a microsecond as we tell the lie. It happens so quickly that most of us can't see it. But if you film someone telling a lie and slow down the film, you'll see it. Interestingly, psychologist Paul Elkman, who has done much of the groundbreaking work in this area[19], has shown that with as little as 35 minutes of training, most of us can learn to consciously notice these "microexpressions." But if you haven't done the training, and your gut becomes uneasy when talking to someone, your GM may be doing what your VAM can't – it may be picking up on this kind of fleeting microexpression indicating that the person is lying, and telling you to proceed with caution.

– **Upsetting information**. This is another type of information our VAM may miss – or deliberately choose to ignore. Dr. Phil McGraw (aka Dr. Phil) has described an experiment he conducted while in graduate school.[20] Using a high-tech slide projector, he showed a series of words and short phrases to a group of conservative elderly women from a local church. The projector allowed him to show the words for different lengths of time, even as brief as one-hundredth of a second. The ladies were asked to report what they saw – and they were also wired with equipment capable of detecting the most minute changes in their physiology, such as an increase in heart rate.

Most of the words and phrases were totally neutral in terms of emotional content, but a few were very risqué. It turned out that the women were able to recognize and report words very accurately, even when they were only flashed onscreen for extremely short times. However, when the *risqué* words were flashed onscreen, the accuracy of their reports plunged; the women reported not seeing them. This was true even when the terms were on screen ten times as long as benign words that they had no trouble seeing. In short, their conscious minds simply edited out the words that were upsetting.

Did the greater mind do the same? No. The sensors recorded definite skin temperature changes, heart rate increases and other changes when the risqué words and phrases were flashed on the screen, *even when the women said they hadn't seen them and showed no visible signs of embarrassment*. So the conscious mind edited out the uncomfortable experience, but the greater mind did not.

Our verbal, analytical mind does many things to help us get through life with minimal discomfort – apparently including editing out experiences that make us uncomfortable. As a result, it's not hard to imagine a situation in which we might miss important information about the world around us. Luckily, unlike the VAM, the greater mind doesn't edit out that disturbing information or experience – one more reason to pay attention to the signals your GM is sending you.

Service #4: *The greater mind draws useful conclusions from our experience much faster than the VAM*. Both the VAM and the GM have talents that make them particularly useful in specific situations. One of the greater mind's talents is very rapid pattern recognition; it's able to notice a pattern more quickly than the VAM (although there may be exceptions to this), and it also quickly notices when a familiar pattern has been broken.

A classic experiment proving this point was conducted by a group of researchers at the University of Iowa College of Medicine in the mid-1990s.[21] They had subjects play a simple card game involving four decks of cards. Turning over some cards – those in decks A and B – produced a payoff of $100 (in play money, sadly). Turning over cards from decks C and D produced a smaller payoff of $50. However, all four decks also contained some cards that triggered a penalty, a financial loss, and the penalty was much bigger in decks A and B than in decks C and D. That was the catch; although you'd make more money each time you turned over a "good" card from decks A and B, you'd take a much bigger loss when you turned over a "bad" card from A and B. So the solution to "winning" the game was to figure out that it was a better strategy to pick from decks C and D, even though the payoffs came in smaller amounts.

The people playing the game didn't initially know any of this, so the object was to see how long it would take them to figure out the winning strategy. Although some people took longer than others to figure it out, on average, by the time they were turning over the 50th to 80th cards, the subjects had a strong feeling that decks C and D were the better bet – but they couldn't explain why. It took until the 80th card, on average, for the VAMs of the subjects to be able to explain why C and D were the better choice.

Here's where it gets interesting. In addition to periodically asking the players about their understanding of the game and what strategy would allow them to win it, the researchers also measured how many cards the subjects were actually picking from each deck at any given time, and how much the palms of their hands sweated each time they chose a card to turn over. What they found was that, on average, subjects hands began to sweat more when reaching for the unfavorable decks after only a few losses. That physical, nervous reaction to choosing from the more unfavorable decks took place all through the period between the 10th and 50th cards picked, when the subjects didn't even have a conscious hunch about what was happening. Furthermore, the subjects began picking more cards from the "good" decks during this same period – again, when the subjects still insisted they didn't have a clue about what was happening.

Clearly, at some level the subjects' brains had detected which of the four decks were a bad bet as early as 10 cards into the game. Their sweating patterns and favoring of the good decks demonstrated that. Yet it took until the 50th card, on average, for the subjects to consciously recognize that they had a good or bad feeling about each deck, and until the 80th card to be able to explain the reason decks A and B were the poorer choice. The VAM took *eight times as long* to figure out what was happening and how to win the game. As you can see, sometimes our verbal analytical mind is the last to figure something out.

In other situations, where there isn't a puzzle for the VAM to solve, the greater mind still can help us pick up on information very quickly. In a series of studies done by Nalini Ambady and Robert Rosenthal at Harvard,[22] the data showed that people could judge the effectiveness of teachers after being shown extremely brief, silent clips of the teachers in action – clips as short as two seconds. Even more impressive, their evaluations were about the same as evaluations made by people who worked with or studied under those teachers extensively.

Apparently, this was related to movements the teachers made – agreement in evaluations plummeted if the subjects only saw a still photo of the teacher. But the evaluations *didn't* correlate with easily identifiable behaviors, such as whether the teacher was smiling – things the *VAM* might be able to identify consciously and quickly. Instead, the subjects simply made their judgments based on overall impressions; just the kind of thing the GM excels at. And their judgment based on three two-second silent video clips was about the same as the judgments of others who had spent months studying with the teachers!

Service #5: *The greater mind helps us make decisions in a number of different situations.* It helps us make quick decisions in a crisis, such as when our conscious mind may be overwhelmed; it also does a huge amount of the work when we're not in a crisis and we have plenty of time to make a decision. It's much better than the VAM at making decisions about what will make us happy. And, it provides crucial support to the VAM when a decision involves a large number of options, or the options are complex.

Let's look at some of these decision-making situations in more detail.

– ***The greater mind helps us decide what action to take in a crisis.*** Because of our culture's current bias toward VAM-style thinking, many people have the impression that making an important decision about what action to take comes down to using our intellect to avoid being swayed by untrustworthy emotions and feelings. As you might suspect, given what we've already discussed, our feelings are not as "untrustworthy" as they are often portrayed. Feelings can represent very sophisticated information coming from the GM.

The greater mind has a talent for identifying patterns very quickly. It also has a talent for drawing conclusions quickly – something the VAM can take a long time to do. For that reason, the greater mind may advise us on how to respond to a situation by sending us gut feelings long before the VAM has even begun to figure out exactly what's happening. In fact, there are times when the GM gives us good advice and our VAM *never* figures out why the "hunch" was right – or how it is we knew what to do.

Consider the following two classic examples, which have been discussed in several previous books on this topic. A lieutenant firefighter who participated in a study of decision-making conducted by Gary Klein[23] reported a situation in which his team was trying to fight a fire inside a house. The fire wasn't responding as it should have been, based on his extensive experience. He became gripped by the feeling that something wasn't right, so he pulled his team out of the building to regroup; shortly thereafter, the floor they'd been standing on collapsed.

It turned out that the fire had been raging on the floor below, out of sight. At first, after this event, the firefighter assumed that he had an intuitive gift, because he had no idea what had produced the uneasy feeling that saved his team. But eventually it became clear that his GM was perceiving and analyzing details that his VAM couldn't process that quickly, such as the warmth of the floor they were standing on. The parts of his mind outside of normal consciousness made the connections and sent a danger signal in the form of a strong uneasy feeling, while his VAM was still puzzling about the odd behavior of the fire they could see in front of them.

Another classic example from the same study involves an officer aboard a British destroyer involved in a battle near the end of the Persian Gulf War.[24] As planes flew to and from the ship carrying out bombing raids, someone onshore fired a silkworm missile at the ship. The missile was capable of sinking the ship, and it was picked up on the ship's radar.

The problem for the officer in charge of air defense was that the radar screen showed many other blips that represented friendly aircraft making runs through the same airspace, and there was no apparent way to tell them apart. This type of missile was the same size and traveled at the same speed as the friendly aircraft. Yet somehow his gut told him that this particular blip was a missile, not an aircraft, and he ordered it shot down, saving the ship. However, he couldn't explain how he knew this, and for many hours before the truth was confirmed, he had to deal with the possibility that he had ordered one of their own aircraft shot down.

In fact, it took a group of people working on the puzzle long after the event to finally figure out how the officer "knew" that this wasn't a friendly aircraft. His GM (but not his VAM) had noticed that the blip first appeared on the screen a little farther from the coastline than the blip produced by an aircraft would have – indicating lower altitude. (The radar signal took longer to appear because of ground clutter.) Again, this was so subtle that the officer couldn't figure out how he knew something was wrong, even months later. But his GM noticed the difference immediately, and the fact that the officer trusted his gut saved the lives of everyone onboard that destroyer.

The bottom line here is that your GM may be noticing, and responding to, information that your VAM misses (or chooses not to notice, or simply doesn't have time to analyze). This ability is very real, and we ignore it at our peril. In both of the latter two examples, the greater mind's ability to connect the dots outside of consciousness saved the lives of many individuals.

– **The greater mind helps us make decisions even when we have plenty of time to think.** The examples above demonstrate that the greater mind has a talent for quickly detecting key information and drawing conclusions that the VAM might take a long time to manage. But what about when we're not in a crisis? Isn't logical analysis our most powerful weapon in that situation?

Not always. I don't want to downplay the power of the VAM, but there's good evidence that even when we have plenty of time to think about a decision, the GM is often the primary decision-maker rather than the VAM. Consider this example: Peter Soelberg taught a course in decision-making at MIT's Sloan School of Management, in which students learned how to execute what is called the *rational choice strategy* – a precise use of rationality to choose between options. For his PhD dissertation, he decided to try an experiment: He asked students to choose the job they would like to pursue as they finished earning their degrees. Then, he monitored how they went about making the decision.[25]

Did the students use the rational strategy they were now experts at using? The results suggested that they didn't. Soelberg interviewed the students a few weeks before they had consciously made a decision and discovered that he could predict with 87% accuracy what their decision would be. The students were adamant that they had not made a decision – yet at some level they had. What Soelberg found was that their intellectual process was primarily about *justifying* their choice, not about *making* the choice.

Author Gary Klein relates a story from his own experience showing the value of trusting input from the GM, received in the form of feelings.[26] At one point in his career, weary from the stress of running his own small business, he considered selling his business to a larger company. In short order he was in discussions with a company recommended by a friend, which led to a better offer from the company than he had expected.

The problem was that every time he met with the manager who would be taking over, he came away feeling tense and agitated. When he spoke about how pleased he was to have this opportunity, friends said he didn't *sound* pleased. (That's a dead giveaway that your intellect is ignoring warning signals from your GM. If you ever have mixed feelings about a decision even though your intellect believes it's the right decision, and friends tell you that you don't sound happy when you talk about it, your friends are picking up on warning signals your analytical mind is choosing to overlook.)

Even though he couldn't think of any logical reason to do so, he eventually turned the offer down. Later, he discovered that the manager who would have taken over created a very tense atmosphere in his own office; Klein's employees would have been thrown into a difficult and unpleasant situation. He didn't detect this consciously, but his GM picked up on signals indicating trouble. (Interestingly, the company's branch that Klein's group would have become part of closed down a few years later.)

In fact, some evidence suggests that intellect working alone, without "gut feeling" input, may have an extremely hard time making decisions. When brain damage causes some individuals to be unable to access their feelings, they often become *unable* to make simple decisions – even when their intellect is completely functional and their IQ is high.[27] Apparently, a fundamental part of most decisions we make is input from our GM – input that comes to us in the form of *feelings*. Rational analysis is fine, but decision-making seems to be highly dependent on those messages that the rest of our mental team is providing.

One reason many people find this difficult to believe is that our culture's glorification of the analytical, comparative approach to making a decision has led us to believe that *having more information will lead to a better decision.* If that's true, then it makes sense to let the VAM take its time and gather as much information as possible and think it all through very carefully. However, it turns out that having more information does not always lead to a better solution to a given problem. In fact, most good decisions are based on knowing only the *crucial, most relevant* information; knowing more than that confuses our thinking process by distracting us from the key information we should be paying attention to. The extra information also slows the decision process down, and it tends to short-circuit whatever helpful input our GM has to offer.

For example, doctors tend to think that life-or-death decisions should be made after assembling the maximum amount of information. But simple formulas that ask only the key information have been shown to save more lives in many situations. Cardiologist Lee Goldman spent years developing a formula for determining whether or not a patient who came into an emergency room complaining of chest pain was really having a heart attack. It was based on knowing four things:

1) the results of an electrocardiogram;
2) whether the patient had unstable angina;
3) whether there was fluid in the patient's lungs; and
4) whether the patient's systolic blood pressure was below 100.

Most doctors thought it was crazy to make such a decision on the basis of so little information when so many other factors could be involved, such as age, history of smoking and gender. But when the formula was finally tested in an emergency room, it turned out to be significantly more accurate at determining whether a patient was really having a heart attack. The experts were being handicapped by extra information that seemed important but actually undercut their accuracy.[28]

The same effect has been shown in other situations. In one study, college counselors were given lots of information about high school students – transcripts, test scores, essays written by the students, and personality and vocational test results. Plus, they were allowed to interview the students. The object was to predict the students' grades in their first year of college. For comparison, the researchers also predicted the same students' grades using a formula based on only two pieces of information: the students' grade averages and their scores on one standardized test.

As you might suspect, the counselors with lots of information made far less accurate predictions than the simple formula did. They were processing so much information that their conclusions were swayed by less important or completely irrelevant details, such as personality, or whether the essay the student had written was good. Nevertheless, the counselors were very confident about their conclusions because their conclusions were based on so much information. They had no idea that the extra information was a handicap, not an advantage.[29] Numerous other studies have demonstrated the same thing.[30]

In fact, many processes in the brain work well *precisely because* they are adept at identifying and ignoring information that's not relevant. In the case of vision, during early childhood our visual cortex learns to distinguish between information that matters and information that doesn't matter. Without that ability, our vision would be far less useful.

For example, our visual system is designed to perceive boundaries between shapes, which helps us to identify the thing we're looking at. However, some boundaries in a given image matter more than others. Suppose we see an animal standing in the sun. We need to know what kind of animal it is, what he's doing, whether he represents a danger to us, and so forth. If the animal casts a shadow because he's standing in the sun, our eyes pick up on all of the boundaries that mark visual edges, including the edges of the animal and the edges of the shadow. However, an experienced visual system knows that not all visual edges are equally important; it can tell that only certain boundaries are connected to the animal, while some boundaries mark the edge of the animal's shadow. That distinction enables us to identify the animal, his position and other relevant information. In other words, our visual system has learned to identify and disregard information that's less relevant to our needs.

In contrast, when a child has been blind since birth and his vision is surgically restored (as sometimes happens when a child in a poor country is born with congenital cataracts that are later corrected), his visual brain hasn't learned from experience to identify and ignore irrelevant information. To him, the animal and the animal's shadow may appear equally relevant, making it very hard for him to identify the animal's shape, which now includes the shadow. Because he can't tell which information is irrelevant, he can't make a good decision about what he's seeing and what he should do in response. This is very much like inundating yourself with information, believing that you need every possible piece of information to make a good decision. In fact, you need the *right* information, not every possible piece of information.

Ironically, the one thing having more information does do – as happened with the college counselors – is increase our confidence that we've made the right decision. That's not a good thing, given that the information overload may actually be having the opposite effect. As author Malcolm Gladwell has noted, *understanding* is the key to making a good decision, not knowledge – and having a huge amount of knowledge may only serve to interfere with our understanding. So, a key theoretical advantage our VAM should have when it comes to choosing a course of action – being able to carefully consider a large amount of information – *isn't* an advantage at all, at least in many situations.

This may be part of the reason our GM often makes better decisions than our VAM: It's so good at pattern recognition that it often zeroes in on the information that really matters, while our VAM drowns in a pile of excess information that obscures the important data.

As noted earlier, Weston Agor's studies of business executives support the idea that successful people really do trust their gut feelings more than their intellectual conclusions. One of the things revealed by Agor's research was that the top executives in his study were significantly better at using this type of non-VAM thinking than other individuals who were lower on the corporate ladder. Furthermore, this was true *in every organization he studied*, even though some types of organizations did work that was less conducive to so-called intuitive thinking (for example, engineering, financial management and law enforcement). Even in those organizations, the people at the top scored higher on intuitive thinking those than those working under them. In addition, all of those who used this type of intuitive thinking reported that the decisions they made in this way had been successful in the long run. Not surprisingly, when asked about decisions they made that had turned out poorly, they almost all reported that those decisions had been made when they *didn't* follow their "gut instinct."

– *The greater mind is usually better at choosing what will make us happy.* I suspect the reason for this is that happiness and satisfaction are usually more emotion-based than intellect-based. "Feeling good" about something is, by definition, a feeling – not an intellectual conclusion. So, when the intellect gets involved, we tend to make choices that don't have a lot to do with emotional satisfaction. The result, of course, is that when we have to live with those choices, we end up not-so-happy.

Several clever studies done by Timothy Wilson at the University of Virginia have illustrated this point.[31,32] In one, he asked students to rank their preference for four different brands of strawberry jam, comparing their preferences to those of a panel of experts who had ranked 45 brands in an earlier study conducted by *Consumer Reports* magazine. He found that when choosing impulsively, the students' rankings were in pretty good agreement with the experts. Then, he took a second group of students and repeated the experiment – but this time the students had to fill out a questionnaire explaining the reasons for their choices. In other words, he forced them to bring the VAM into the choice-making process. What happened? Their rankings were totally different. They sometimes gave the "best" ranking to the jam that the experts (and the previous group of students) had considered to be the worst.

Wilson conducted another similar experiment in which women college students had to choose one poster from a selection of five to take home. Some were prints of fine art paintings; others were just humorous posters. One group simply ranked them by how they felt about them and took home the poster that appealed to them the most; they mostly chose the fine art prints. The other group had to fill out a questionnaire explaining why they liked or disliked each poster before making their choice. Forced to consciously explain their feelings about the posters, the second group found many reasons for not liking the fine art prints and frequently choose the humorous posters.

When Wilson interviewed the participants later, he found that a much greater number of students in the first group were happy with the poster they took home. In fact, no one who took home a fine-art print was sorry about the choice, but three-quarters of the people who took home the humorous posters regretted their choice.

The problem, it seems, is that our VAM is not an expert on what makes us happy. And why should it be, if our gut already knows? Part of what the GM does for us is take care of a lot of mental functions so the VAM is free to handle day-to-day matters. So, the VAM doesn't need to be an expert on why we like what we like; if we simply trust our gut feelings about what we like, they usually lead us in the right direction. On the other hand, as soon as we drag the VAM into the decision process, we start trying to *figure out* what's likeable and unlikable about our options, and we may override our gut feeling. We end up making choices based on reasons that sound logical but don't actually have much to do with what makes us feel good.

The GM may not *always* make the best choice – every part of the human mind is capable of making mistakes – but these experiments suggest that choices made by the GM are far more reliable than choices made by the VAM, at least when it comes to deciding what will make us happy.

– The greater mind helps us make a decision when the options are numerous or complex. One of the limitations of the VAM is that it has difficulty dealing with large quantities of information. So, when we're confronted with having to choose one item out of a large group, our conscious mind has to start deciding which characteristic matters the most, just to narrow down the choices. This idea actually makes sense, because in most situations the best decision can be made – and should be made – on the basis of a few key considerations.

The problem is that if we're inundated with information, a lot of which isn't very important, the VAM can get bogged down trying to sort out what's important from what's not. We may not end up focusing on the information that really matters. When buying something, for example, we often decide to focus on a detail that's far from being the most important. We may choose a cereal at the supermarket because of the packaging or the fact that it has added vitamins, instead of more overriding nutritional considerations such as an excessive amount of sugar and corn syrup; we may choose a wine because it's more expensive instead of because it tastes best; or we may choose a house because it has extra rooms, instead of thinking about how far it will force us to commute to work. Unfortunately, our VAM is not well-equipped to make choices when the number of factors that need to be considered is very large. The large number of details exceeds our limited capacity for processing.

Similarly, the VAM even has trouble choosing between a small number of options if each option involves a host of details. If you're deciding which one of three cars to buy, for example, the numbers of factors you should *ideally* take into account is enormous, and your VAM will have a hard time making a good selection because of that.

Ap Dijksterhuis, a psychologist at the University of Amsterdam, did a series of studies that illustrate this nicely.[33] In one, subjects had to choose which of four used cars they would buy based on information about the cars provided by Dijksterhuis. (One of the hypothetical cars was deliberately chosen to be a better all-around choice.) One group of subjects was given four key pieces of information about each car – enough to be able to tell which car was the best choice. So they had to make their choice using 16 pieces of information. The question was: Would the VAM or the GM be better at picking the best car? To find out, he gave one group four minutes to consciously think about it and then decide. A second group saw the information, was then distracted for the same amount of time, and was then asked abruptly to choose. This forced the GM to make the choice, since the VAM had no time to think about it.

In this situation, the VAM did far better than the GM. The subjects who had time to think picked the better choice more than half of the time. The other group hardly ever picked the best car.

Then, he repeated the experiment – but this time he gave the subjects *12* bits of information about each car (which is probably much closer to a real used-car shopping experience). This meant they had *48* pieces of information to weigh before deciding. This time, the group that had a few minutes to consciously think about it was *much less likely* to pick the best car; in fact, they would have picked the best car more often by throwing darts at a board. How did the group forced to use the GM do? They picked the best car almost 60% of the time. So when the amount of detail was overwhelming, the VAM fell down on the job, but the GM did a respectable job.

How can this be? If the greater mind can pull the best choice out of a big pile of details, why didn't it pull the best choice out of a much smaller pile? Right now, I doubt that researchers can answer that question conclusively, but here's my guess: It may be that the VAM sends out a "request for help" signal to the greater mind when it senses that it's in trouble. We all know when a choice is going to be tough because a lot of information is being thrown at us. That may be sufficient to get the GM working on the problem. On the other hand, when a choice seems manageable – as it apparently did when the subjects only had to consider four things about each car – the GM may not bother to work on the problem.

Whatever the explanation, this experiment suggests that the GM is better than the VAM at handling choices when the amount of information is overwhelming. To pursue this idea, Dijksterhuis did a follow-up experiment, interviewing people who went shopping to buy items for their homes. Based on interviews done right after shopping and several weeks later, he found the same thing. When a purchased item was simple, with only a few things to consider before making the purchase, the people who thought carefully about their choice were happier with their choice later than the people who made these purchases on impulse. But when people were shopping for more complicated items, such as furniture, the reverse was true. Those who based their choice on a rational analysis were *less* happy than those who made their final decision by gut feeling.

This does raise one other question: Does the GM need time to process a large amount of information, or can it select the best choice right away?

Dijksterhuis did one other experiment that suggests that the GM benefits from having time to process the information.[34] This experiment was similar to the poster experiment done by Timothy Wilson, but he added a third group of choosers. The third group didn't have to explain their choices consciously the way the second group did. But instead of choosing by impulse right away like the first group, they were given several minutes before making their choice between options. During that time they were given puzzles to solve so they wouldn't be analyzing the data with their verbal, analytical minds.

Dijksterhuis found that the subjects who had to explain their choices before making them were still the least happy with their choice a few weeks later. But of the two groups who chose by gut feeling, the happiest group was the group that made their choice after a few extra minutes had gone by. So the GM refined its choice when it had a few minutes to process the information. (And all of this happened while the VAM was kept busy solving puzzles!)

In short, it appears that when the conscious mind is overwhelmed by facts relating to a decision, it calls upon the greater mind to help out – and the GM does a better job of making the choice, especially if we give it a little time to process the information.

So: If you're faced with a simple decision, thinking it through may be the most effective approach. But if you're faced with a complex decision, your best strategy may be to 1) look at all of the information, 2) let your conscious mind do something else for a while, and then 3) go with your gut feeling about which choice is best. Do remember, however, there is no guarantee that the GM will make the best choice every time. These studies only found that the GM did significantly better than the VAM, assuming that the number of details people had to process was large. They did *not* find that the GM made the best choice *100%* of the time.

Service #6: *The greater mind works on problems while our VAM is busy with other things – or asleep.* Everyone is familiar with the phenomenon of solving a problem by "sleeping on it." Essentially, this is an acknowledgement that our minds can work on a problem even when our waking consciousness is out of the picture.

In fact, this process is so effective that we can put it to conscious use. If you can't seem to solve a problem in your daily life, when you're falling asleep at night ask your GM to offer you some help. You will likely wake up in the morning with insights you didn't have the night before – and possibly even a solution. (I'm not aware of any clinical studies proving this, but it's easy for anyone to try, and it often works miraculously well.)

This is a great illustration of the greater mind's ability to function on its own, without our conscious guidance.

Service #7: *The greater mind can produce creative bursts and flashes of insight.* Any person who makes his or her living being creative knows that ideas often appear in the conscious mind as if out of thin air. It seems that the GM is often being creative for us; it helps us out by solving what might be thought of as "creative problems." Sometimes, it gives us solutions to creative problems we didn't even know we had!

A classic example happened to me one night in 2007. My wife had taken a bus to New York City, which was about four hours away from where we were living in central Pennsylvania. But her return bus ride from New York to our town was abruptly cancelled. So she found a different bus option; one that went from New York to Philadelphia,

Philadelphia to Harrisburg, and then Harrisburg to our town. Unfortunately, the bus broke down when it was leaving Philadelphia. By the time another bus was sent to replace it, the travelers were two or three hours behind schedule. As it turned out, the travelers had to make a connection to a different bus at Harrisburg to make the final leg of the journey – but that bus didn't wait for them to arrive. So, my wife found herself stranded at a bus station in Harrisburg at 11:00 pm. She couldn't find a hotel nearby with a room costing less than a small fortune, so she called me and asked me to drive down and pick her up – a two hour drive each way, if driving conditions were good.

As you might expect, I wasn't thrilled about making a four-hour round trip in the middle of the night, and I had never driven *into* Harrisburg – only past it. To make matters worse, by the time I got near Harrisburg, a thick fog had moved in. As a result, it took me an extra hour to find the bus station, and the drive home was harrowing because of the fog. By the time we finally reached home and went to bed, I was totally disoriented – literally in an altered state from being thrust out of my normal routine into such a strange situation (not to mention being wide awake when I would have preferred to be asleep).

But then, something strange happened; as I lay in bed feeling dazed and hoping I could fall asleep, huge chunks of a new song popped into my head, whole. The song incorporated three different dramatic experiences from my life, and even came with some ideas for an appropriate melody and chords. What surprised me the most was that this was not the solution to a creative problem – except perhaps the most general one: "I can always use a new song!" I hadn't been trying to create a song like this. And yet there it was. I knew it was "mine," because these were experiences from my life, and the song followed all of the "rules" and conventions that I rely on as a songwriter. (Such experiences are not uncommon; Paul McCartney has related on many occasions that the music to his record-breaking hit song *Yesterday* came to him in a dream. He was so taken aback that it took him some time to be convinced he hadn't unconsciously copied an existing tune.)

This became, for me, a classic example of how the GM can work for us – even when we haven't asked it to solve a specific problem. Like any good team, the VAM and GM working together can produce results we aren't expecting, as long as we're clear about our goals and we've put in the time and effort to ensure that the GM has learned the necessary skills and has the tools to do the job.

Service #8: *The greater mind provides us with impulses to take beneficial actions that our VAM would have overlooked.* Sometimes we're not making a decision, per se, when we get information in the form of an impulse from the GM. For example, when you're in a bookstore you might have an impulse to pull down a certain book from the shelf. Or, you might have an impulse to say hello to a stranger that you can't otherwise explain, or an impulse to call an old friend. You might suddenly feel that you should walk in one direction instead of another, or buy a specific item in a store, or avoid eating a certain piece of food.

Impulses to take action are one of the main ways the GM passes along information and pushes us in directions the VAM might never think of going. In these situations, the GM may be picking up on information that our VAM has missed or isn't able to process for some reason. Sometimes we can figure out the reason for the impulse in hindsight; in other cases we may never find an explanation for it. But such impulses can be very valuable advice from the "silent" member of your team. If you ignore a strong "gut" impulse to do something simply because you know there's no logical reason for it, you may be doing yourself a serious disservice.

For example, a friend of mine in New York City was apartment hunting with her boyfriend when they found an apartment that was a great space in a good location. However, the apartment needed a tremendous amount of work to be comfortable. She liked the place and knew it wouldn't be available for very long given its advantages, but her boyfriend didn't like it. So they didn't take the apartment.

It wasn't long after that that she broke up with her boyfriend. Then, a few days after the breakup, she had a strong impulse to call about the apartment again – even though she knew it had almost certainly been taken by someone else almost as soon as she said no.

Wisely, she followed her impulse and made the call. The landlord confirmed that the apartment had been snatched up shortly after she and her boyfriend had turned it down. "However," the landlord said, "the couple that took the apartment just discovered that they can't get their piano in through the door and as a result, they've changed their mind. Do you want the place?" She lived there happily for 20 years.

Author Philip Goldberg relates another story like this in his book *The Intuitive Edge*.[35] While writing the book he began interviewing potential agents, which usually involved going to their office. In most cases he felt mixed after the interviews, but he recalls that in one instance his gut told him immediately that this person should *not* be his choice. His conscious mind couldn't see anything that would explain the feeling, but he trusted his gut.

However, when he was leaving this person's office, having already decided that he wasn't going to choose her to be his agent, he had an overwhelming feeling that he should leave a copy of his book's outline on the woman's desk. Not only did this seem nonsensical – after all, he had already decided that he didn't want this person as his agent – but it seemed doubly crazy because he had to go across the street and make an extra copy of the outline to leave on her desk, and he was already late for another appointment that he considered very important. Nevertheless, he chose to follow his impulse. He made the copy of the outline, returned to her office and left it on her desk. He says that he felt like an idiot for the rest of the day because he'd followed an impulse that logically made no sense.

The next day, however, he got a call from an editor friend. She suggested he call publisher Jeremy Tarcher, whom she had run into the previous evening. Tarcher had mentioned seeing Goldberg's book outline lying on an agent's desk. Tarcher eventually published the book.

As Goldberg notes, it's easy to resist an impulse when it doesn't seem to make sense, but the evidence suggests that we should give impulses like these the benefit of the doubt. "With intuition," Goldberg writes, "you, the magician, are surprised by the rabbit, which seems to be in the service of another, superior sorcerer."

Service #9: *The greater mind provides us with a warning when a conscious choice may get us into trouble.* This is the flip side of an impulse to action: a warning to *avoid* taking action, whether it be walking down a street, saying something or making a purchase. As with the more positive impulses, we ignore such warnings at our peril, even when we know there's no logical explanation for the bad feeling. The executives in Weston Agor's study commonly reported stopping and reconsidering their actions when they got a bad feeling about a choice – and if they ignored the warning, they regretted it later.

Sometimes these impulses seem to be based on intuitive knowledge that can't be explained by previous experience or current information. For example, a few years ago a friend of mine who lived in New York City decided to give his wife a helicopter ride over the city as a birthday present. His wife was excited and pleased. But when the time came, she suddenly announced that she wanted to visit his parents that weekend instead. He was dumbfounded; she did get along well with his parents, but asking to visit them was highly unusual, to say the least. He knew she wasn't afraid to go up in the helicopter, and asked why she wanted to postpone. She didn't offer a reason, except to say that it just felt like something they should do. Since it was her birthday, he agreed to her request.

They had a pleasant, uneventful weekend visit with his parents, but on Monday morning they were shocked to see the newspaper headlines: The helicopter ride they'd been planning to take had crashed into the East River. She denied having any conscious knowledge that this might happen; she said she just felt like they were supposed to visit his folks that weekend.

Most of us think of ourselves as being just our conscious self – the verbal, analytical mind. But as you can see, our minds do all kinds of things for us that the VAM simply can't manage, including using complex skills we've learned, finding shortcuts, noting things around us that the VAM misses, drawing conclusions very quickly, helping us make decisions, solving problems while we're asleep, providing us with creative bursts, giving us impulses to take actions our VAM wouldn't think of taking, and warning us against taking actions that will backfire. The truth is, our conscious minds are just the tip of an iceberg. The rest of that iceberg, hidden from view, is a very powerful team that's supporting us.

Understanding that this is true can make a big difference in how we proceed in life – and whether we end up stuck on the Wheel of Misfortune, or end up achieving our goals.

So: Why Don't We Listen to the Greater Mind?

Given the value of this resource, why do we so often let our conscious self overrule the advice our GM is trying to give us?

In my experience, there are three main reasons. The first is that for centuries, intuitive gut feelings have been discredited as being, at best, inferior to analytical conscious thought – and at worst, as being totally bogus, "paranormal nonsense." As a result, many people discount their gut feelings altogether, and others are hesitant to trust them. It's only in recent years that clinical evidence has begun to support the validity of

9 Things the Greater Mind (GM) Does For Us

1. It manages sophisticated skills we've learned that would overwhelm the limited processing abilities of the conscious, verbal, analytical mind (VAM).

2. It refines our skills by figuring out shortcuts that work, and by learning which things are important to pay attention to.

3. It picks up on information in the world around us that our conscious mind misses.

4. It draws useful conclusions from our experience much faster than the VAM.

5. It help us make decisions, both during a crisis and when we have plenty of time to think about the options.

6. It works on problems while our conscious mind is busy with other things or asleep.

7. It provides us with creative bursts and flashes of insight.

8. It provides us with impulses to take beneficial actions that our VAM would have overlooked.

9. It warns us with feelings of discomfort when we're about to do something that we don't consciously realize is a mistake.

non-conscious thought.

Today, there are a number of popular books discussing the evidence that "intuition" is a legitimate form of thinking and a valuable tool. Nevertheless, deeply ingrained ideas can take a long time to change. (Ironically, even people who insist that intuition is nonsense usually know enough to stop and reconsider a decision when their gut goes into a knot!) And many who use intuition to their advantage don't admit it for fear of having their credibility questioned. For instance, when Weston Agor did his study of executives who relied on this type of thinking, most said that they never discussed their decision-making process with their colleagues, out of fear that they wouldn't be taken seriously.

A contributing factor in intuition's poor reputation in some cultures has been the supposed association between women and intuition – i.e., referring to it disparagingly as "women's intuition." Because many cultures have labeled women as inferior to men for thousands of years, it makes a perverse kind of sense that a style of decision-making seen as inferior to logical analysis would be associated with the "inferior gender" – i.e., "women are intuitive, men are not." One consequence of the resulting gender association is that it gives men another reason to avoid admitting that they rely on intuitive gut feelings, because it's still considered humiliating for a man to be seen as doing anything considered too "feminine." Of course, as most people in modern cultures have figured out, the differences between men and women do not make one inferior to the other. And finally it appears that people have also begun to realize that "intuition" is not inferior to analytical analysis. And for the record, there is no evidence that women are more intuitive than men.

The second reason we may let the VAM overrule advice from the GM is that it isn't always easy to tell whether a strong feeling is a legitimate message from the GM, or simply fear or desire on the part of our conscious self. For example, if you have a bad feeling about accepting a new job, is it just nerves and concern about how you'll do in the new position – or is it your inner self telling you that it has picked up on a reason you shouldn't take the job? If someone wants you to do something that might be risky, is the bad feeling in your stomach a warning, or is it just fear? If you meet someone and immediately have a good feeling about him or her, is your GM picking up on something, or are you just attracted to the person because he or she fits some stereotype of desirability? Sometimes it's hard to tell – especially if you haven't ever paid attention to how "feelings" from different sources feel. Those doubts about whether a feeling is truly a "gut feeling" or not can cause us to decide to ignore it.

The third reason we often let our VAM overrule our GM is that the VAM is easily sidetracked, confused, overwhelmed and susceptible to being swayed. As a result, we can be led to feel that we simply *must* make a certain choice or take a certain action, despite our negative gut feelings about it. Fears, desires, questionable logic, ego issues, guilt and strong emotions, among other things, can cause us to overrule our gut. And most of us will let the VAM win any debate in which the VAM and GM disagree.

Ironically, in Weston Agor's study of intuitive executives, the subjects noted that most of their decisions that did *not* turn out well were those in which they disregarded or overruled their gut feeling. Among the factors the executives listed as causing them to overrule their gut feelings were: being unwilling to face the truth about something; having their ego be too involved; being angry when they made the decision; believing they had to make the decision quickly regardless of how they felt; being fearful or anxious; trying to accommodate the desires or feelings of others; being fatigued or not well; or feeling "out of balance" at the time. These are all emotions and circumstances each one of us sometimes encounters. Nevertheless, letting those emotions and/or circumstances persuade us to overrule our gut feelings can lead to some very miserable situations indeed.

For example, consider what happened to Deborah Kiley, an experienced sailor who agreed to help sail a boat from Maine to Florida (a trip described in her book *Albatross*[36]). The skipper was a young man who enjoyed drinking and was very casual about preparing the ship for the voyage; his resume revealed that none of his previous boating jobs had lasted long, apparently partly because of the girlfriend who often traveled with him; they frequently had major arguments. To Deborah's dismay, the girlfriend abruptly joined them.

As their trip began in late September, 1982, Deborah noted that the skipper didn't set the sails the way most captains would, and he forgot to lower the centerboard (which is key to making it easy to maneuver the boat). Despite some uncomfortable experiences, they made it down the coast to Annapolis, Maryland, where the skipper needed to add additional crew. Deborah asked a friend of hers to join them, but he brought along another young man who turned out to be sexually abusive and insulting – and a heavy drinker. Deborah soon discovered the new fifth crew member was lying about his credentials. When confronted with this fact in front of their shipmates, he made it clear he'd get even.

As you might expect, Deborah decided she shouldn't be part of this crew any longer. But if she left, the young skipper would be shorthanded, and he began to pressure her with threats about undermining her future in boating. Everyone told her she was overreacting. And when she talked to the boat owner by phone, he chastised her for not honoring her commitment. Her verbal, analytical self was under assault: She was made to feel embarrassed about breaking her word; she was fearful of the effect her choice would have on her future in sailing; and her trust in her gut feelings was undermined by people telling her she was overreacting. So – you guessed it – she overruled her feelings of dread and stayed on the boat to complete the trip.

Things might have worked out okay despite all of these problems – except that they sailed into a hurricane. With three crewmembers drunk, Deborah kept the boat afloat until she had to stop from exhaustion. She awoke to find the boat sinking.

With nothing left floating but an inflatable runabout with no supplies in it, and the cold air temperature and wind making it impossible to climb aboard, the five of them clung to the runabout in the water. The girlfriend, injured as the boat sank, was bleeding, so they were soon surrounded by sharks, forcing them to climb into the runabout. They floated without food or water for days, until the skipper and the fifth crewmember became disoriented from dehydration and jumped into the water, where they were promptly eaten by the sharks. The girlfriend died from her wounds. After several days, close to death, Deborah and her friend were spotted by a passing ship and rescued.

Years later, author Laurence Gonzales interviewed Deborah and asked what advice she would offer to others. She said, "Trust your gut." She let her gut feeling be overruled by fears about career consequences and embarrassment about not honoring her commitment, and the result was disastrous.

Getting the Most from Your Greater Mind

To learn to take better advantage of this alternate thinking process – i.e., to get better at hearing what your GM is telling you – you can use several strategies:

Strategy #1: *Treat impulses and intuitive feelings as valuable information.* Gut feelings are not always going to lead us to the best possible outcome – they're based on our past experience (among other things) and our past experience may include misinformation and misinterpreted experiences. But intuitive information is not meaningless or random – it's the greater mind at work processing what's happening to us and doing its best to help us out. The GM is imperfect, but it's a powerful resource that we ignore at our peril. For example, if you find yourself feeling uneasy about something, even though you can't think of a logical reason to be uneasy, don't simply dismiss the feeling.

Of course, we don't always have to act on impulses and intuitive feelings; the GM and the VAM are a team, and the VAM has the right to decide that it's OK to ignore a gut feeling. But if you choose to ignore advice from your GM, do so consciously, with full awareness that you're making that choice. Don't just pretend that your greater mind doesn't exist, or that information coming in from the GM is meaningless. You're most likely to stay off the Wheel of Misfortune when you let your VAM and GM work together.

Strategy #2: *Always notice your initial impulse when faced with a new situation.* I've often had the experience of being asked or advised to do something, and my instant reaction was to say no. But in those situations, if I'm asked why I'm reacting that way, I often can't say; my VAM doesn't have a clue. Later, after I've had a chance to think about it for a while, I usually realize what caused my gut reaction. In other words, my GM seems to be able to access all of the considerations almost immediately and sends the result through to my VAM via "gut feelings." It simply takes me a lot longer to run through all the details in my VAM and bring the relevant reasons into consciousness.

This can make life awkward at times – other people may be miffed or offended if you say no to a request without (apparently) having a logical reason. But this is the way the mind often works. If it's at all possible, trust your gut feeling, with the knowledge that it's simply going to take a little while to consciously zero in on what your GM has already figured out. Don't reject your gut feeling simply because you can't explain it immediately – even if it makes someone unhappy when you go with your gut.

Strategy #3: *Learn to tell the difference between feelings that represent information from your GM and less-meaningful feelings or impulses.* Knowing when intuitive information is legitimate takes practice. Suppose you were visiting Earth from another planet and you'd never seen a television before. If you wanted to get useful information from watching television, you'd have to learn to distinguish between news programs, soap operas, movies and sitcoms. In the same way, we have to become sensitive to which of our feelings are information from the GM and which are not.

Probably the easiest way to identify information coming from the GM is that it tends to be visceral – i.e., a knot in the stomach, a rush of warm feeling, a sudden sense of dread, sweaty palms, a strong feeling of joy. And, these feelings tend to come up suddenly, unlike ongoing feelings we may have about a person or situation. One indication that an impulse, for example, is *not* helpful information from the GM would be recognizing that it reflects an ongoing desire you have that you're already aware of. If you love chocolate and you get an impulse to eat a whole bunch, that's probably not your GM trying to help you out. Ditto for having an impulse to grab a cigarette or a second or third beer.

It's very important to remember that not all impulses come from the GM. In particular, there's one impulse you should *never* follow: the impulse to do violence to someone else. As we'll discuss in the next chapter, the impulse to do violence is a sign that you've been ignoring impulses to communicate your dissatisfaction about something. In other words, you've been stifling your anger instead of expressing it. (If anger or dissatisfaction is expressed *when you feel it*, it doesn't backlog and build up into an impulse to do violence.) In other words, an impulse to do violence is not advice from your greater mind – it's repressed emotion that's bursting to get out. Following that impulse is *always* a bad idea. On the other hand, an impulse to speak up and express your dissatisfaction – without violence – is an impulse worth following (although you need to let your VAM decide how to do so in a way that's appropriate). We'll talk more about this in the next chapter.

It can take a while to notice an authentic communication from the GM when the stakes in a situation aren't very high. For example, the people who participated in the study who had to figure out the best strategy for playing a card game didn't consciously realize that they were having a gut feeling until many moves into the game, even though their bodies reacted very early on. Of course, in some situations the feelings sent by the GM are much less subtle. You may meet someone and feel an instant strong kinship with them; or you may turn down a street at night and suddenly feel your stomach tense up.

It's definitely possible to identify which feelings and impulses are information from your GM, as long as you make a little effort. After all, this is your own mind trying to communicate with you! As with learning anything, the key is *paying attention*. The more you pay attention to your feelings and impulses and make the effort to improve communication between your VAM and GM, the clearer that communication will become – to your benefit.

Strategy #4: *Learn to recognize situations in which the alternate thinking modes might give you better guidance than day-to-day VAM thinking, so you use the best source of information.* For example, if you have extensive experience using a skill, let your greater mind do the work when you use that skill; don't try to control everything consciously. *Over*thinking will undercut your expertise.

It's especially important to recognize which part of your mental team is best equipped to help you when you have to make a decision. As we've already seen, many good decisions are made outside of consciousness, with the VAM only stepping in at the end to justify or explain the decision.

In general, your GM will make better decisions than your VAM in these situations:

A) If you have a lot of experience dealing with something and find yourself in a crisis. Your greater mind may be able to access your previous experience to make a decision much faster than your conscious mind can, as the stories about the firefighter and the officer studying the radar screen demonstrated.

B) When a lot of uncertainty is involved. Too much uncertainty can derail our ability to use logical analysis, leading to faulty conscious decisions.

C) When you have to decide which of several things will make you the happiest. Trying to decide what will make you happy using logical analysis can leave you totally focused on details that have little or nothing to do with what will actually make you happy.

D) When a choice is very complex. When you're faced with more details to consider than your VAM can manage, the best way to make a choice is probably to: 1) study the details; 2) think about something else for a while so your GM can process those details; and 3) then let your gut make the decision.

However, the VAM is usually good at making a wise decision when the choice *doesn't* involve a large amount of detailed information.

When deciding which part of your mental "team" is best qualified to make a particular decision, you might want to consider what the executives in the Agor study said. They said that in their experience intuition was a better choice for making decisions when:

- there's a high degree of uncertainty;
- facts and information are limited;
- you don't recall similar situations in your past experience that might have helped to guide you;
- multiple options all seem equally reasonable; and
- time is short and pressure is high.

However, remember that even if the GM is most likely to make a good decision in a given situation, there's no guarantee it will always make the *right* decision. No matter which part of your mental team you rely on when making a decision, always allow for the possibility that the decision could be the wrong decision. There are no guarantees!

Strategy #5: *Know when to put your conscious thinking process on hold so the greater mind can contribute.* Sometimes we try to solve a problem through step-by-step analysis when it really calls for a flash of insight that will change our perspective (something that, by definition, comes from outside of normal day-to-day consciousness). When our VAM is hard at work thinking about something, it can easily drown out helpful input from the greater mind. It's a bit like when we struggle mightily to remember something, but can't; then when we stop trying so hard to remember, the answer pops into our head. It's delivered by the GM, as if by magic.

I've often noticed that when my VAM is working furiously during the day, insights seldom appear. But when I'm lying in bed at night waiting to fall asleep, solutions to problems, new ideas, insights and so forth often pop into my consciousness. It's almost as if they were waiting for me, but as long as my VAM was busy analyzing, talking to myself internally and thinking things through consciously, I wasn't available to receive information from my GM. My "circuits were busy," so to speak.

It's often been noted that taking time to relax and daydream is not a waste, and this may be the reason. If you have a team of people working for you but you never stop working long enough to listen to them, you're wasting your resources. Similarly, the VAM sometimes needs to be quieted with a little relaxing and daydreaming so your GM can get through with helpful information.

Strategy #6: *Consciously invite input from the GM.* One way to do this is to go out of your way to create conditions that quiet the VAM so gut feelings or inspiration can come through. For example, you can:
- try listening to relaxing music;
- exercise;
- look at a peaceful nature scene;
- meditate;
- listen to "white noise" (the sound made by wind, rain or taking a

shower). This has been shown to shift brain activity away from the left brain (which seems to be the primary source of the VAM).

Another approach, already noted, is to simply ask yourself for input when you're falling asleep. A straightforward invitation to your GM to help you out often produces remarkable results.

Another trick that can help if you're faced with a decision is to imagine what will happen if you were to choose each of the alternatives you're trying to decide between. See what gut feelings follow as you imagine each outcome. If your GM has picked up on details you've missed, or has a better idea about what matters than your VAM does, it will let you know by reacting accordingly.

For example, a friend of mine was faced with a choice between two job situations. She was very concerned about which one would provide less stress than her current situation, and it seemed to her that there were too many factors involved to be sure which choice was best – an ideal situation to let the GM have a say. So, she imagined herself in each of the two possible situations. When she imagined herself in the first situation, her stomach tightened into a knot. When she imagined herself in the second situation, her body relaxed. She chose the second alternative, and it seems to have been a wise decision.

When Weston Agor conducted his study of how executives used intuition, he asked them what strategies or techniques they used to help enhance their intuitive abilities. The answers they gave included: meditating; using guided imagery; writing a journal; staying in shape; fasting once a month; praying; using the I Ching; deliberately exposing themselves to novel ideas and situations outside of their normal day-to-day experience; reading science fiction; reading philosophy; looking for patterns in things where none appear to exist; keeping a notepad handy to record creative ideas or insights before they're forgotten; and attending events that focused on intuition-related or "psychic" topics. Any of these techniques might be useful as a way to help you gain access to information from your own hard-working GM, which is, after all, constantly trying to help you out.

Strategy #7: *Use your VAM to support your intuition, not just the other way around.* As author Philip Goldberg observes in his book *The Intuitive Edge*, scientific breakthroughs are often described as if they were made logically, at the end of a careful step-by-step logical analysis of the facts. In reality, scientific breakthroughs usually occur because someone had an intuitive insight. That insight is then eventually supported by logical analysis and accumulation of facts and evidence, *after* the insight has been spelled out. (This misrepresentation of how scientific breakthroughs occur can backfire, because it encourages people who are trying to be creative to overvalue logic and undervalue flashes of insight.)

Instead of thinking of our VAMs as our main resource, with the GM acting as the support team, it may behoove us to see it the other way around. In this view, your greater mind is the primary tool in your arsenal and your conscious self is the support team that keeps things on track. At the least, this attitude will ensure that you don't undervalue the help your GM is providing. It will also ensure that you don't make the mistake of believing problems should only be solved intellectually, using step-by-step analysis, with any other input cast aside.

Strategy #8: *When you can't seem to make a decision, remember that increasing your understanding of the situation is often more useful than trying to weigh all of the options intellectually.* If you're caught in a situation in which you need to decide what action to take, it may not be helpful to get caught up in arguing with yourself about details. That's your VAM struggling to find a "logical" answer to the problem. Instead, when you catch yourself doing this, focus on giving your GM plenty of input to maximize its ability to help you out. If you spend your energy learning more about the situation instead of rethinking it, your entire mind will have more to work with, especially your GM, which may zero in on the best solution much faster than your VAM can.

Strategy #9: *If your experience is too limited for your intuition to be based on pattern recognition, consider asking someone with more experience to share his or her gut feeling.* Your GM relies on your experience when it evaluates a situation or helps you make a decision, and in some situations, your experience may be minimal. If that's true, your gut feelings may not be reliable, and it may make sense to get an opinion – or gut feeling – from someone who has more experience than you do before you proceed. That person's intuition may offer you valuable advice that your own GM can't yet provide – simply because that person's gut feeling is based on more experience.

Of course, be sure you have confidence in the expert in question before relying on his or her gut feeling, and remember that even an expert can

11 Ways to Make the Most of Your Greater Mind (GM)

1. Treat impulses and intuitive feelings as valuable information, and at least consider acting on them—except when you have an impulse to do violence, which is a sign that you've been repressing your feelings and need to do a better job of communicating.
2. Always notice your initial impulse when faced with a decision.
3. Learn to distinguish feelings that represent information coming from your GM from other less-meaningful feelings or impulses.
4. Learn to recognize situations in which the alternate thinking modes might give you better guidance than day-to-day verbal-analytical-mind thinking (or vice versa), so you use your best source of information.
5. Know when to put your VAM on hold so the GM can contribute.
6. Consciously invite input from the GM.
7. Use your VAM to provide support for your intuition, not just the other way around.
8. When you can't decide, remember that increasing your understanding of the situation is often more useful than trying to use the VAM to compare all of the options intellectually.
9. If your experience in a situation is too limited for your intuition to be based on pattern recognition, consider asking someone with more experience to share his or her gut feeling.
10. Remember that useful guidance from the GM may not lead you directly to what you want. An impulse may help you toward your goal by taking you in an unexpected direction.
11. Become more conscious of how your thinking process works. People who pay attention to the way they think make better decisions.

occasionally make a bad call. (If the expert seems to be trying to help you by logical analysis, that may not be as useful; your expert may not be drawing on the experience stored in his or her GM.)

Strategy #10: *Remember that even useful guidance may not lead you directly to what you want. Don't undervalue an impulse just because it takes you in an unexpected direction.* Don't be disappointed when a choice you make based on your intuition results in "learning" instead of leading directly to your desired end result. Looking back later, there's a good chance you'll find that you would not have ultimately achieved your goal without the knowledge you gained from that unexpected side trip.

For example, when I was a young adult, a woman I met triggered a very strong gut feeling that I'd found the "love of my life." That relationship was quite an educational experience, but it ended badly. The gut feeling that she was "the one" could be seen as faulty, since the relationship didn't work out. But the reality is that I learned some of the most important lessons of my life from that relationship, and those lessons have helped me ever since – including making my happy marriage possible many years later. Is that a coincidence? I don't think so.

Sometimes the indirect route is the only way to get where we want to go. So, if your instincts tell you to do something that doesn't seem to lead toward your goal, don't dismiss that impulse out of hand – your GM may be trying to help you assemble the tools you need to reach your goal. Many results can't be achieved without experience, and experience usually involves side trips, failures and mistakes. (As renowned physicist Neils Bohr once noted, an expert is someone who has made every possible mistake in a given field.)

The bottom line is, don't be discouraged if you follow an impulse or let your gut make a decision and it doesn't immediately lead you to the ideal payoff you were hoping for. The GM can make mistakes, but it can also be incredibly clever, helping you out in ways that seem like bad luck at the time. As the Dalai Lama has noted (mentioned in my song *Piece of the Puzzle*) sometimes not getting what you want works out best of all.

A Few Final Thoughts…

There are two ideas that, in general, will help you make the best use of your mental resources.

First, recognize that you have multiple resources working in your behalf – not just the conscious mind you're familiar with (the verbal, analytical mind). As others have said, *you know more than you know*. Don't let those other powerful resources go to waste. Pay closer attention to your internal feelings and impulses; those are the messages that represent your greater mind's contributions to your life.

Second, *think about how you think*. Psychologist Philip Tetlock studied the thinking styles of political pundits in the media, and how good they were at predicting the future. Most of them turned out to be abysmal at correctly predicting what was going to happen; instead, they fell into "certainty syndrome" (see Chapter 9), and as a result made predictions that were *worse* than they would have made by random guessing.[37]

However, a few pundits did much better. What set these individuals apart? Tetlock found that the latter group *paid attention to their own thinking process*, while the former group did not. I'd be willing to bet that one reason they did better was that paying attention to their own thinking process made them more aware of the feedback they were getting from the GM – i.e., their gut feelings. After all, the GM often tries to keep the VAM from making mistakes; if you're not paying attention, those mistakes won't be prevented.

Many of the suggestions in this chapter are based on studies and ideas that are relatively new, so nothing I've said here should be taken as the final word on this topic. Far from it! But you've been put on notice: If you're relying exclusively on your logical, analytical mind – your VAM – you're selling yourself short.

So, look at your own thinking processes carefully, and learn as you go. While we're still figuring out exactly how the mind works and how to make the most of it, one thing is crystal clear: Those who use the resources of their greater minds most effectively do better in life – and are far more likely to stay off the Wheel of Misfortune.

Once more, in brief:

Here are the key points to remember from Chapter 6:

• The verbal, analytical mind (or VAM) that most of us identify with – is only one part of the mind. It's constantly being aided and supported by the greater mind, or GM. Relying too much on the step-by-step analytical process that the VAM is so good at can hold us back, because the GM has many skills and abilities that the conscious mind does not. In fact, step-by-step analysis often is *not* the best way to solve a problem or make a decision, and it can interfere with other legitimate mental processes, preventing them from coming to our aid.

• The greater mind usually communicates through feelings, or by dropping an idea or the solution to a problem into our consciousness.

• The greater mind does many things for us, including:

1) It manages sophisticated skills we've learned that would overwhelm the limited processing abilities of the conscious VAM.

2) It refines our skills by figuring out shortcuts that work, and by learning which things are important to pay attention to.

3) It picks up on information in the world around us that our conscious mind misses.

4) It draws useful conclusions from our experience much faster than the VAM.

5) It helps us make decisions, both in a crisis and when we have plenty of time to think about them.

6) It works on problems while our conscious mind is busy with other things, or asleep.

7) It provides us with creative bursts and flashes of insight.

8) It provides us with impulses to take beneficial actions that our VAM would have overlooked.

9) It warns us with feelings of discomfort when we're about to do something that we don't consciously realize is a mistake.

• To learn to take better advantage of this alternate thinking process:

1) Treat impulses and intuitive feelings as valuable information, and at least consider acting on them. The exception is when you have an impulse to do violence to someone, which is a sign that you've been repressing your feelings and need to do a better job of communicating.

2) Always notice your initial impulse when faced with a decision.

3) Learn to distinguish feelings that represent information coming from your GM from other less-meaningful feelings or impulses.

4) Learn to recognize situations in which the alternate thinking modes might give you better guidance than day-to-day VAM thinking (or vice versa), so you use your best source of information.

5) Know when to put your VAM on hold so the GM can contribute.

6) Consciously invite input from the GM.

7) Use your VAM to provide support for your intuition, not just the other way around.

8) When you can't decide, remember that increasing your understanding of the situation is often more useful than trying to use the VAM to weigh all of the options intellectually.

9) If your experience in a situation is too limited for your intuition to be based on pattern recognition, consider asking someone with more experience to share his or her gut feeling.

10) Remember that useful guidance from the GM may not lead you directly to what you want. An impulse may help you toward your goal by taking you in an unexpected direction.

Also, it pays to become more conscious of how your thinking process works. Studies have found that people who pay attention to the way they think make far better decisions.

NOTES for Chapter 6

1. Edwards B. (1999) *The New Drawing on the Right Side of the Brain.* New York: Tarcher/Penguin.
2. As noted in George Miller's essay "The Magical Number Seven, Plus or Minus Two: Some Limits on Our Capacity for Processing Information." *Psychological Review* 63 (1956): 81-97.
3. Described in "Normal Motor Automatism" by Leon Solomons and Gertrude Stein, first published in *Psychological Review,* September 1896.
4. For example, see B. Libet, *Mind Time.* (Cambridge, Mass.: Harvard University Press, 2004).
5. For more on this concept, see Lehrer J. (2009) *How We Decide.* New York: Houghton Mifflin Harcourt.
6. Related in Joe Simpson's book *Touching the Void: The True Story of One Man's Miraculous Survival.*
7. Agor W. (1986) *The Logic of Intuitive Decision Making: A Research-Based approach for Top Management.* Westport, Conn: Greenwood Press.
8. Daniel J. Isenberg. How Senior Managers Think. *Harvard Business Review.* Nov-Dec 1984;80-90.
9. Merzenich MM, Tallal P, et al. Some neurological principles relevant to the origins of – and the cortical plasticity-based remediation of – developmental language impairments. In J. Grafman and Y Christen, eds., Neuronal plasticity: Building a bridge from the laboratory to the clinic. Berlin: Springer-Verlag, 169-87.
10. Beilock SL, Carr TH, MacMahon C, Starkes JL. When paying attention becomes counterproductive: impact of divided versus skill-focused attention on novice and experienced performance of sensorimotor skills. *J Exp Psychol Appl.* 2002 Mar;8(1):6-16.
11. Beilock SL, Carr TH. On the fragility of skilled performance: what governs choking under pressure? *J Exp Psychol Gen.* 2001 Dec;130(4):701-25.
12. Beilock SL, Bertenthal BI, McCoy AM, Carr TH. Haste does not always make waste: expertise, direction of attention, and speed versus accuracy in performing

sensorimotor skills. *Psychon Bull Rev.* 2004 Apr;11(2):373-9.
13. Beilock SL, Bertenthal BI, Hoerger M, Carr TH. When does haste make waste? Speed-accuracy tradeoff, skill level, and the tools of the trade. *J Exp Psychol Appl.* 2008 Dec;14(4):340-52.
14. Johnson JG, Raab M. Take the first: Option generation and resulting choices. Organizational Behavior and Human Decision Processes 91:215-29.
15. McBeath MK, Shaffer DM, Kaiser MK. How baseball outfielders determine where to run to catch fly balls. *Science* 268:569-73.
16. Jones CM, Miles, TR. Use of Advance Cues in Predicting the Flight of a Lawn Tennis Ball. *Journal of Human Movement Studies* 4.1978;231-35.
17. Muller SB, et al. "Hoe Do World-Class Cricket Batsmen Anticipate a Bowler's Intention?"*Quarterly Journal of Experimental Psychology* 29: 2162-86.
18. Betsch, Tilman et al. Different Principles of Information Integration in Implicit and Expicit Attitude Formation. *European Journal of Social Psychology* 36;2006:887-905.
19. For example, see Paul Elkman's book *Telling Lies: Clues to Deceit in the Marketplace, Politics and Marriage* (New York, Norton, 1995) and *Facial Action Coding System, Parts 1 and 2* (San Francisco, Human Interaction Laboratory, Dept. of Psychiatry, University of California, 1978), coauthored with Wallace V. Friesen.
20. Philip McGraw, Life Strategies, Chapter Five.
21. Bechara A, Damasio H, Tranel D, Damasio AR. Deciding advantageously before knowing the advantageous strategy. *Science.* 1997:28;275(5304):1293-5.
22. Ambady N, Rosenthal R. Half a Minute: Predicting Teacher Evaluations from Thin Slices of Nonverbal Behavior and Physical Atttractiveness. *Journal of Personality and Social Psychology* 1993;64:3:431-41.
23. The study and the incident mentioned are described in Klein's book *Sources of Power*, Chapter Four.
24. As described in Klein's book *Sources of Power*, Chapter Four.
25. As described in Klein's book *Sources of Power*, Chapter Two.
26. See Gary Klein. *The Power of Intuition*. Chapter 7.
27. For examples, see *Descarte's Error* by Antonio Damasio (New York, Penguin, 1995)
28. Goldman L, et al. Prediction of the Need for Intensive Care in Patients Who Come to Emergency Departments with Acute Chest Pain. New England Journal of Medicine 1996:334;23;1498-1504.
29. Grove W, et al. Clinical versus Mechanical Prediction: A Meta-Analysis. *Psychological Assessment* 12 (2000): 19-30.
30. For example, see: Stewart TR, Heideman WR et al. Effects of Improved Information on the Components of Skill in Weather Forecasting. *Special Issue: Experts and Expert Systems of Organizational Behavior and Human Decision Processes.* 1992:53;2;107-34; Lusk CM, Hammond KR. Judgment in a Dynamic Task: Microburst Forecasting. *Journal of Behavioral Decision Making 1991:41;55-73;* Patterson ES, Woods DD, Sarter NB, Watts-Perotti. Patterns in Cooperative Cognition. *Coop '98, Third International Conference on the Design of Cooperative Systems.* Cannes, France, 1998.
31. Wilson T, Schooler J. Thinking Too Much: Introspection can reduce the quality

of preferences and decisions. *Journal of Personality and Social Psychology* 1991;60;181-192.
32. Wilson T, et al. Introspecting about reasons can reduce post-choice satisfaction. *Personality and Social Psychology Bulletin* 1993;19:331-339.
33. Dijksterhuis A Bos M, et al. On making the right choice: The deliberation-without-attention effect. *Science* 2006;311:1005-07.
34. Dijksterhuis A, van Olden Z. On the benefits of thinking unconsciously: Unconscious thought can increase post-choice stisfaction. *Journal of Experimental Social Psychology* 2006;42:627-631.
35. Goldberg P. (1983) *The Intuitive Edge: Understanding Intuition and Applying It in Everyday Life.* New York: G.P. Putnam's Sons.
36. Kiley DS, with Noonan M. (1995) *Albatross.* New York: Bantam Books.
37. Tetlock, Philip. *Expert Political Judgment.* Princeton: Princeton University Press, 2006.

7.
Maintain Healthy Relationships by Avoiding Emotional Crises.

Learn to express your emotions constructively so they don't backlog into emotional "stacks."

"Emotion turning back on itself, and not leading on to thought or action, is the element of madness."
 – John Sterling, 19th Century novelist and poet

"The shut-down-and-suppress strategy should be used with care…. It doesn't do what we usually hope it will do, namely calm us down, lower the tenor of a conversation or bypass a fight."
 – Sue Johnson, Director of the Ottawa [Canada] Couple and Family Institute

It should be pretty obvious that good working relationships are a key to success – not to mention happiness – under any circumstances. When you find yourself on the Wheel of Misfortune, that goes double: Mutually beneficial relationships and support networks can make the difference between survival and disaster.

There are a number of things you can do to help preserve supportive relationships, such as improving communication (see Chapter 4). But one of the most important ways to ensure that those relationships remain strong is to take steps to avoid common problems that often disrupt or terminate relationships. One problem that's particularly destructive is called *emotional stacks*.

If you've ever been in a relationship for an extended period – or, for that matter, if you've ever gotten to observe other people in long-term relationships (your parents, for example) – you may have noticed a phenomenon that relates to how arguments get started. Often, the most ferocious arguments are triggered by a seemingly trivial occurrence. One person leaves the lid off a tube of toothpaste, and the other person explodes in anger, far out of proportion to the size of the offense. Clothing left lying on a chair leads to a screaming match. Something minor said – or not said – in front of other people is followed by anger and tears as soon as the two people are alone, far beyond what you'd expect given the minor nature of the incident. To make matters worse, once an explosion of anger takes place, the person on the receiving end is likely to become upset and may return the anger – and a key justification for this response will probably be the fact that the event that triggered the first outburst was so minor.

What's really going on here?

Emotional Stacks: A Backlog of Unexpressed Feelings

What's happening is that the person who exploded with rage wasn't really reacting to just that one small event. The person who exploded had been holding in anger about a whole series of events. The minor incident in question was simply the trigger that unleashed the backlog of pent-up emotion, like the proverbial straw that broke the camel's back.

In a situation like this, the backlog of feelings that eventually explodes is referred to as an *emotional stack*.

What causes an emotional stack? As human beings, we always get to choose whether we express the feelings we're having at any given moment or hold them inside. Often, we choose to suppress them, for any number of reasons. However, feelings don't go away; emotions are meant to be expressed in some form. If they're not expressed, they begin to pile up like river water behind a dam, and each incident that triggers the same feeling causes the pile-up to get larger. Meanwhile, the emotion can become mixed with frustration and a growing sense of powerlessness because the irritating situation isn't changing; the thing that we find upsetting keeps happening. (Ironically, that's one of the consequences of choosing to suppress the emotions we're feeling; keeping the other person in the dark about our true feelings allows the situation to continue. So the fact that the situation keeps recurring isn't entirely the other person's fault!)

If this continues for a long time, the buildup of emotion, frustration and feelings of powerlessness can eventually become too overwhelming to hold in. Once that breaking point has been reached, the next little thing that triggers a similar feeling – perhaps a chore the other person forgot to do, or a negative comment – causes an explosion of emotion far out of proportion to the incident that actually triggered the explosion. Then instead of a constructive bit of communication explaining that one person hasn't been getting his or her needs met, the other person experiences a major attack – a "stack attack," if you will.

Unfortunately, emotional stacks and the explosions that mark their release are a very common problem. Living or working with someone, it's easy to build up a backlog of anger connected to a series of irritations. Then a minor event triggers a screaming match that ends with your marriage breaking up. Or something that your boss routinely does that's been upsetting you for months leads to an explosion of anger – and you lose your job.

When an emotional stack explodes, the resulting dispute can be difficult to resolve. On the one hand, the person who explodes feels justified; the built-up frustration was very real. At the same time, the person on the receiving end of the explosion may be offended and angry because the event that triggered the outburst was so minor. Furthermore, when a tremendous buildup of emotional energy like that is finally released, the actions the angry person takes can be extreme and totally counterproductive, including irrationality and violence. The consequences can be relationship-altering – in some cases, *life*-altering.

This pattern (the development of an emotional stack and the consequences that follow) is actually an example of the SEICR growth cycle described in Chapter 1. A problem inherent in the "system" – in this case the system being your relationship – slowly builds up over time. Eventually the problem becomes so aggravating that it threatens the stability of the system, forcing the system to break down. At that point, either

A) the relationship re-forms in a better arrangement – i.e., you work things out and come to a new understanding – or,

B) the relationship ceases to exist.

It's worth noting that emotional stacks don't always involve unexpressed anger. *Any* suppressed emotion can lead to a stack. For instance, if you feel really sad about your life but believe that showing sadness is inappropriate, you can spend your entire life pretending you're not sad. But if you don't allow those feelings of sadness to be expressed, the backlog of unexpressed sadness is likely to make you ill or depressed. Or, you may start treating the people around you in ways they find disturbing and inexplicable, ultimately leading to the loss of friends and/or support from your family.

Although unexpressed emotion of any kind can lead to an emotional stack, in this chapter we're going to talk mostly about emotional stacks involving anger. That's because the consequences of a backlog of anger can be especially devastating – not only to the person who explodes, but to those around him or her.

What Happens When We Suppress Our Anger?

Whenever we become angry, it means that something is taking place that we don't like. We may feel that something unjust is happening, or a goal we hope to achieve may appear to be blocked by someone or something. Feelings of anger are a call to action: When you're angry, your body and mind are telling you that you need to do something to change what's going on. That call to action is also meant to push us to communicate what we're feeling, letting others know that were unhappy.

Here's the most important point: Emotions – including anger – are a natural part of our existence. They're supposed to flow through us. When anger is freely expressed each time we feel it, *it doesn't explode*; on the contrary, as long as it's expressed in a way that shows some respect for the other person, it can result in communication taking place and both parties taking action to resolve the situation, often with extremely positive results. It's only when we *don't* express our feelings that they backlog and build up. Furthermore, if allowed to flow freely, any emotion (including anger) will evolve into another emotion as time passes. If we suppress our anger, it doesn't get to evolve into some other emotion; instead, it gradually becomes stronger and begins to generate feelings of frustration and powerlessness, as well as internal stress, both mental and physical.

Because emotions involve a complex web of psychological and physical processes, not letting those processes run their course can have a dramatic negative effect on both our mental and physical health. For example, when something makes us angry, bodily changes occur: Muscles tighten, adrenaline is released into the bloodstream and our heart rate increases. This is what is often called the "fight or flight" response. In this state, neurotransmitters such as epinephrine, norepinephrine and

What Are Emotional "Stacks?"

Emotional "stacks" arise when an emotion is repeatedly experienced but never expressed or acted upon. Stacks can lead to three possible outcomes:	1. Something happens to release the buildup of emotion before it becomes too extreme. An explosion is avoided.
	2. The emotion and frustration build up until they are released explosively in response to a trigger that's relatively minor.
	3. The emotion and frustration are never released, resulting in ill health for the person holding in the emotions, along with behavior that may seem inexplicable to others.

serotonin are released in the brain and the hypothalamic, pituitary and adrenal glands are activated. This, in turn, causes a flood of hormones inside the body, affecting all of our physical systems. (This process is described in more detail in Chapter 3.)

In essence, the tightened muscles and released hormones represent energy the body has made available for our use so that we can take some sort of immediate action to address the situation. If our emotions are allowed to flow freely, we can use that available energy to do something to change the situation and/or express our feelings, which generally benefits our mental and physical health. The adrenaline is used (at least to some degree) rather than left in our bloodstream for the body to deal with. Furthermore, when we use that energy instead of suppressing it, our parasympathetic system is then activated, undoing much of the potential damage the adrenaline and other hormones can cause. Our muscles relax, and our anger shifts into other emotions. If we simply hold that anger inside, all of that adrenaline remains in our system where it can cause our internal chemistry to go out of kilter. Remaining in this state for long periods of time can lead to suppression of the immune system, tissue damage, muscle wasting and cardiovascular changes.

As already noted, an emotional stack can end with an explosion of rage – usually over something trivial. However, it's also possible that a person may contain the buildup of feelings indefinitely without ever taking any action or exploding. If you never let your anger out – if you find some way to contain it no matter how big the backlog becomes – then your repeatedly out-of-kilter internal chemistry can make you physically sick. In today's world, many people attribute their health problems to outside causes such as germs and viruses, but an enormous number of health problems can be triggered simply by routinely stifling our emotions. A highly stressed body is not going to maintain its health as well as an unstressed body does.

Furthermore, bottling up an emotion such as anger also undermines relationships, even if an emotional stack never explodes. That's because feelings, including anger, are a powerful means of communication, and not expressing them shuts down communication. Without communication, whatever is triggering your feelings can't be resolved.

Of course, in some situations it may be appropriate to avoid expressing your feelings or taking action to change things. That's a judgment call you have to make in any given set of circumstances. However, if you choose not to express your feelings, and the situation that's triggering your feelings keeps recurring, it will produce all kinds of undesirable results.

Is Anger the Same as Violence?

A big part of the reason anger has such a bad reputation is because of its association with violence. Ironically, if anger is expressed in a straightforward and non-hurtful way when we first feel it, it actually *prevents* violence by leading us to change a situation that's bothering us. In fact, it usually leads to communication and better understanding. It can be extremely constructive, causing us to make changes for the better, including eliminating injustices and making the world a better place.

Contrary to what many believe, *violence is not usually an expression of anger*. Violence is the release of a buildup of frustration and feelings of powerlessness – feelings that arise, for example, when individuals choose *not* to express their anger over a long period of time. It's important to make this distinction about the nature of violence, because violence in the world we live in is very real and very widespread. If you think that violence and anger are basically the same thing, then you may conclude that the solution to the problem of violence is to avoid anger. *That's backwards*. If you try to avoid anger in the name of preventing violence, you're going to end up suppressing your feelings and trying to get other people to suppress theirs, too. And that is the exact recipe for causing an emotional stack of frustration and powerlessness – an emotional stack that will probably lead to the violence you're hoping to prevent.

So, one key to *preventing* violence is to express your anger when you first feel it – or at least take some action to change the situation so you don't end up repeatedly feeling frustrated. Anger that has not been allowed to build up over time almost never leads to violence.

So: Why Don't People Express Their Anger?

As already noted, we can consciously choose to bottle up our feelings, including anger. Those kinds of choices are made based on what we think will happen if we reveal our feelings. Sometimes we're afraid of negative consequences; sometimes we may simply believe that expressing anger is a bad thing.

Here are some beliefs about anger that prevent people from expressing anger when they first experience it – and tend to backfire.

Belief #1: Anger is dangerous because it's very powerful – much more powerful than positive emotions. We may see the results of a violent explosion of rage on the news, or experience an explosion of rage from someone we know, or remember being on the receiving end of an explosion of rage when we were children. Witnessing these things may lead us to conclude that anger is very dangerous. But a violent explosion of rage isn't ordinary anger; it's the release of a tremendous backlog of frustration and powerlessness that's been building up for a long time.

Unfortunately, believing that anger is dangerous backfires in several ways. First, it leads people to try to suppress their anger. That bottles it up, turning the person into a pressure cooker – which, ironically, reinforces the mistaken idea that anger is dangerous by making it feel more powerful and dangerous as the pressure builds! As we've already discussed, this eventually leads either to an explosion of rage or to the person becoming physically ill.

A second way this belief backfires is that a person who suppresses his or her anger never gets the chance to learn how ordinary anger works. If you politely show irritation or alarm when you feel it, you'll quickly learn that a reasonable expression of anger can be a tool for communication and a way to change a situation for the better. Your own experience with anger as a constructive force will keep you from buying into the erroneous idea that anger is dangerous.

A third way that seeing anger as dangerous backfires is that fear of emotions, especially fear of anger, will lead you to avoid life situations that you think might stir up those emotions. By avoiding any potentially upsetting situations or relationships, you may succeed in reducing the amount of anger you have to stifle, but you'll also reduce the range of experiences that make up your life. You'll cut yourself off from all kinds of people and experiences that might have brought you joy, growth and satisfaction.

Belief #2: Anger is a negative emotion, to be lumped in with fear and sadness – and expressing it makes a bad statement about me. If the only anger you've encountered is the explosive variety – the result of an emotional stack – then it's easy to understand how you'd come to see anger as very negative. But that's like seeing a car wreck and deciding that a car is a negative thing.

Your brain certainly doesn't lump anger in with generally unwanted emotions such as fear or sadness. Brain scans have found that anger lights up the left side of the brain – the same side that's activated when we're amused or showing intense interest. In contrast, sadness and fear activate the right side of the brain.[1] So to your brain, anger is entirely different from fear or sadness. There's nothing inherently negative or undesirable about it.

Ironically, if you believe that anger is a bad thing, then in addition to suppressing it, you'll feel *guilty* about being angry. This may then cause you to feel additional anger towards yourself whenever something makes you angry! Anger isn't negative, it isn't evil, and it isn't wrong to feel it. It's a part of being human, and it's meant to be a useful part of our experience. It only become "negative" when we manage it in less-than-healthy ways.

Does expressing anger really reflect badly on you in the eyes of the people around you? That depends on a multitude of factors, but it's more likely to influence your reputation in other people's eyes if you're a woman. Women, to some extent, are still expected to avoid showing anger; they may be labeled a bitch or rude if they express anger. (In contrast, men are *expected* to be angry – which is a very unfortunate stereotype).

Nevertheless, if you're a woman, even if you're anxious to avoid being labeled a bitch, suppressing your anger is not the right way to address the problem. An explosion of rage from an emotional stack will have a much worse effect on your reputation than finding constructive ways to take action whenever something causes you to feel angry.

Belief #3: Showing anger will disturb the status quo and risk terminating a relationship. If you conceive of a relationship as fragile, the idea of displaying anger may seem like a threat to the stability of the relationship. Depending on the nature of the relationship, you might be afraid that the other person will withdraw, get angry at you or become defensive. In an intimate relationship, you may fear that revealing your true feelings will alter the bargain you implicitly made with the other person – i.e., "I'm not really the person I seemed to be when we got together."

That's ironic, because expressing anger when you initially feel it keeps the lines of communication open; it actually makes your relationship more stable by eliminating misunderstandings and preventing emotional stacks from building up. Yes – an *explosion* of rage can threaten the success of a relationship, but an explosion only happens when anger has gone unexpressed for a long time. (You don't see many people in new relationships dealing with explosions of anger. That's because it takes time for suppressed emotions to build up and explode.)

The reality is that a relationship is far more likely to come to a bad end if you *don't* express your feelings. When we're feeling anger, our brain and gut are telling us that something is wrong. In that situation, pretending that everything is fine is a sure-fire way to make yourself a lot angrier. Furthermore, expressing your feelings allows issues to be resolved. You can't resolve problems if one or both parties are pretending that they don't exist.

Of course, it's possible to have a relationship that really is fragile, where the link between you and the other person is so flimsy that honesty will trash the whole thing. If that's the case with a boss or someone else that you are truly stuck with, then you have to find a way to make the best of it. But if a romantic relationship is that fragile, you need to think twice about continuing it. A relationship that has a solid foundation will *benefit* from a reasonable level of honesty; it will only suffer if one or both parties stifle their feelings.

The other reason not to worry too much about disturbing the status quo in a relationship is that difficult times happen in every relationship, and ideally, they trigger changes for the better. Any long-term close relationship has to go through a period of seeing the less-than-ideal side of the relationship, withdrawing from it a bit, and asking "Is this what I really want?" If you never go through that, you'll never be sure that it *is* what you want, and the relationship will eventually suffer. So acknowledging negatives isn't necessarily a bad thing.

One last thought: If the reason for trying to bottle up your anger is to avoid letting someone else know how you really feel about something, you may be wasting your time anyway. In many relationships, even if you don't express your anger, the other person can tell how you're really feeling.

Belief #4: Expressing your anger will lead others more powerful than you to retaliate. Some people may feel this way because they were punished in the past – for instance, as a child – when they expressed anger. If that's the case, the fear of retaliation in the present situation may be overblown and unrealistic.

Of course, it is possible to be in a situation in which retaliation by the other person is a legitimate concern. This could be true, for example, if you're dealing with someone who already has a huge emotional stack built up; in that situation, you could be on the receiving end when the other person's stack explodes. If the other person is someone who has power over you, such as a boss, that could definitely have negative consequences. So how should you handle that kind of situation?

First, make sure you're right about communication being too dangerous. Fears are sometimes justified and sometimes not justified – and communication, done properly, can prevent a host of emotional stack problems in the future.

Second, if honest communication is truly an undesirable option because of the potential consequences, as might be the case if you're having a problem with your boss, try to find some other way to take action by altering the situation to eliminate or minimize whatever is making you angry. Maybe you can change what *you* are doing in such a way as to minimize or eliminate the frustrating concern. (We'll talk more about this shortly.)

Third, if there's nothing you can do to alter the situation, at least express your anger to someone you can trust so it has some outlet. Just make sure you do it in a way that's respectful to your friend and won't indirectly backfire by getting back to the other person – the very thing you're trying to avoid!

Belief #5: Good mental health means always being cheerful, never sad or angry. In fact, just the opposite is true; good mental health comes from finding constructive ways to express your emotions, not from stifling them.

Belief #6: Spiritual people never get angry. The idea that true spirituality means never being angry may have arisen from the observation that spiritual masters seldom seem to show anger. I would suggest that this is a reflection of their perspective – not an absence of anger, or the result of an attempt to stifle it. In my experience, greater understanding generally alters your perspective in ways that reduce anger.

Spirituality is about fully understanding and using your experience, not about stifling parts of it. As already noted, anger is a part of your being that's meant to help prevent injustice and keep relationships healthy. If you think that anger is something you have to "rise above," then your ideas about the nature and purpose of anger are incorrect. (Remember, anger is NOT the same thing as violence!) Your feelings, including anger, are valid and they need to be treated as such; learning to deal with them constructively is a part of any spiritual journey. The idea that eliminating your emotions makes you spiritually superior is highly questionable, and it can have very serious consequences if it results in building up emotional stacks.

Belief #7: "I'm already too emotional." If you see yourself as "too emotional," that's a giveaway that you have some negative ideas about expressing your emotions. Maybe you're expressing your emotions in awkward ways, or in ways that are not constructive. But that's not a reason to suppress your emotions; it's just a reason to learn different ways to express them.

Managing Emotional Stacks

It shouldn't be hard to see that managing emotional stacks by learning to recognize them, prevent them and resolve them when they occur can give you a huge advantage when you're trying to stay off the Wheel of Misfortune. Having those skills will allow you to sidestep potential breakdowns in important relationships. Instead of losing a friend, partner or job situation when something is wrong, both parties will get their needs met, and emotional explosions – if they occur at all – won't be mysterious, hurtful or violent.

In that spirit, it makes sense to adopt these five strategies:

Strategy 1. Learn to prevent stacks from building up inside yourself.

Strategy 2. Learn to recognize when someone you interact with is building up a stack.

Strategy 3. Learn to defuse an existing stack before it causes trouble.

Strategy 4. Learn to manage the fallout and repair the damage from stack explosions when they do occur.

Strategy 5. Set up ground rules about stacks with people you care about or need support from.

Let's explore each of these strategies in greater detail.

Strategy #1: Learn to prevent stacks from building up inside yourself. The first rule about preventing stacks in yourself is: *Don't stifle your emotions*. That means experiencing your emotions as legitimate and responding to them by either communicating your feelings to whoever is triggering them and/or taking action to alter the situation in some way that doesn't escalate the problem.

Let's assume another person's actions have triggered your anger, and you know it's not the first time and won't be the last time. You could easily fume and do nothing. But since you know that that will result in a stack, hopefully you'll decide to take action instead.

There are three ways you can take action in this situation:

Option 1: Change the situation by negotiating with the other person.

Option 2: If communication won't work, change the situation on your own.

Option 3: If neither of those options will work, change your interpretation of the situation so it no longer evokes that emotional response.

The one thing you *do not* want to do is suppress the emotion and expect it to go away. If the thing that's triggering your reaction isn't going to go away, neither will your emotional reaction.

Let's look more closely at the three options for taking action:

<u>Option 1</u>: The first option is to communicate what you're feeling to the other person and negotiate with that person. If this is a viable way to proceed, it's important to keep in mind that this will only produce a positive result if you communicate your feelings in a way that doesn't come across as an attack or an insult. When you're feeling emotional this can be tough, but it's essential. This means you can't just "vent" by spewing your emotion at the other person; you have to treat the situation as a communications challenge.

Remember: The bottom line here is *getting the outcome you want*. In most situations in which someone is making you angry, that will require a little thought and strategy because you'll need to show respect for the other person, even though you're angry. You'll need to separate your emotions from the communication process as much as possible, so your emotions don't cause you to get carried away. If you accuse the other person of being bad, stupid or inconsiderate, the other person is likely to respond with anger and may even *do more* of the thing that's upsetting you. (And remember: If you have a strong impulse to do something violent or mean to the other person, *you've already built up a stack*. To deal with that, see the section on defusing an existing stack, below.)

So, before you speak you need to think about what you're going to say – and how you're going to say it. In particular, follow the golden rule of communication discussed in Chapter 4: *Don't just think about what you're going to say – think about what the other person is going to hear.*

A practical way to communicate your feelings without making the situation worse is to

1) come up with an *emotionally neutral* statement that communicates how the other person's actions make you feel; and

2) make it clear that you are not trying to deprive the other person of something. You're simply asking for a change.

For example, don't say, "You have a lot of nerve doing that!" Instead, say, "When you do that, it really upsets me. Is there some way you can get what you need without doing that?" There's no blame in this statement, so the other person will hear that his or her behavior is having a negative effect on you, without feeling like you're attacking. Furthermore, it shows that you know the other person is getting something out of the behavior in question, and that you're not trying to deprive the other person of anything he or she wants; instead, you're asking for a change that will let *both of you* get your needs met.

Assuming both of you have an interest in making the relationship work, this should give you a fighting chance to change the situation so you won't be experiencing those negative emotions repeatedly. Then, you won't build up an emotional stack, with all of its unpleasant consequences.

Of course, this won't always work. In some situations, both parties don't have an equal interest in maintaining the relationship, so the other person may not really care about your reaction to his behavior. If communicating and negotiating with the other person isn't practical or fails to work, try the second option.

Option 2: The second option for preventing stacks from building up in yourself is to *change the situation on your own* so you no longer experience the irritating behavior. There are three ways you can do this.

1) The first way is to *remove yourself from the irritating situation.* Even if you can't totally avoid the other person, there may be a way to avoid the behavior or specific situation that's causing you to repeatedly feel upset. Remember the story in Chapter 5 about the time I was trapped working in a warehouse with a kid who insisted on playing loud music on his boom box that I really disliked? Negotiation failed, so I found a way to remove myself from the situation by listening to my own music over headphones. The stack I had begun to build up soon vanished.

2) The second way to change the situation on your own is to *change the other person's behavior by removing your support for the behavior.* In many situations we're unintentionally encouraging the person who is causing us grief. For example, children often repeat behavior that irritates us if they feel that they're being ignored; our upset reaction gives them what they want – our attention. So, think carefully about the situation you don't like. If you realize that you're unintentionally rewarding the behavior that's driving you crazy, the best approach may be to change *your* behavior to withdraw your support for the behavior. That's the difference between a parent yelling at a misbehaving child, and simply grinding everything to a halt for a "time out." If the child really just wants your attention, yelling at him will encourage the unwanted behavior. The "time out" won't give him what he wants, so the behavior will probably stop.

Likewise, it's possible that unwanted behavior from another adult you interact with may be partly an attempt to evoke a reaction from you. If you realize that your reaction is encouraging the behavior, try changing your reaction. Sometimes simply refusing to react to the unwanted behavior *in any way* will cause the other person to lose interest and stop the behavior. (It's certainly worth a try.)

3) The third way to change the situation on your own is to *help the other person find better ways to meet his needs.* If you're smart enough to deduce what the other person is getting from the behavior you dislike, you may be able to help the person get those needs met some other way. For example, if someone is always asking for your help and it's driving you crazy, and negotiating with them doesn't stop them from asking for your help, don't stifle your emotions and build up an emotional stack. Instead, find another way for the person to get the help he needs that doesn't involve you.

<u>Option 3:</u> The third option for preventing stacks from building up in yourself is to *change your interpretation of the situation.* As I noted back in Chapter 1, our lives are not made up of things that happen to us, they're made up of our experiences – i.e., how we interpret the things that happen to us. That's why the same experience can evoke a completely different reaction from different people. Similarly, how we interpret behavior we don't like can totally change the reaction we have to it. Remember: What's evoking your emotion isn't really the other person's behavior – it's *how you interpret* what the other person is doing.

For example, when I first lived in New York City, I shared my apartment with several other guys. One fellow who lived there briefly was younger than me and seemed a little overwhelmed by the uncertainties of life in the big city. One evening he answered the phone and then came into my room looking shaken: He said it was an anonymous caller who was threatening him. To my apartment-mate, this represented a very real threat to his well-being, and he had no idea what to do. My perspective was somewhat different. I interpreted this as a person who wanted some attention and felt powerless and was trying to remedy that by making random calls and hoping to get a response of fear from the person on the other end of the line. I told my apartment-mate to let me take the phone. Before the person on the other end could speak, I said, "It's late; let me tell you a bedtime story." I proceeded to tell a short, amusing story about something that happened to me in school. I finished with, "Sleep well," and hung up.

We never heard from the caller again.

The point, of course, is that our interpretation of the event made an enormous difference in our emotional response. Furthermore, the way I dealt with the situation changed my roommate's perspective about the event. So, even if the stranger had called again, my roommate probably wouldn't have continued to build up an emotional stack of fear, because his interpretation of the event was now different.

Along those same lines, one way to change your perspective when you can't alter or escape unpleasant behavior is to try doing a little homework about the reason for the behavior. Maybe the person who drives you crazy by always talking so loudly is simply hard of hearing. Maybe the person who always treats you badly mistakenly thinks you did something to him. What you find out may shed a different light on the behavior you don't like and eliminate or minimize the painful emotional reaction you have to the behavior. Then, building up a stack will be a lot less of an issue.

Strategy #2 for managing emotional stacks: Learn to recognize when someone you interact with is building up a stack. Defusing a stack before it builds to the breaking point can save you a lot of grief. To do that, first and foremost, you have to become sensitive to signs that someone you interact with is not expressing his or her feelings. Sometimes the signs are subtle. Does the person seem angry or hurt by something you're doing but isn't saying anything about it to you? Does someone start to say something and then pause and walk away? If so, emotions are probably being suppressed, and if you don't encourage the person to share those feelings, an explosion may be waiting down the line.

Sometimes the evidence isn't subtle at all. If someone is fuming at you (or at someone else, for that matter) but not coming right out and putting those feelings into words, that's stack-building in action! And the eventual unhappy result is predictable. So, be on the lookout for cues that someone isn't expressing his or her feelings.

Strategy #3 for managing emotional stacks: Learn to defuse an existing stack before it causes trouble. Sometimes this will mean defusing your own emotional stack; sometimes if will mean defusing someone else's emotional stack. Let's start with the first situation.

If you realize you've been suppressing your emotions – especially anger – and you've already built up a stack, the best thing to do is find a way to begin to express those feelings so they stop backlogging. This may require some careful thought on your part so you *don't* make things worse when you start letting your feelings out. For example, suppose you haven't told your neighbor that his loud music is driving you crazy – even though you've had the impulse to say something many times – and now you have the impulse to do something to retaliate. You know this may start a fight with your neighbor, but you have a backlog of anger and frustration built up.

To avoid an undesirable outcome, begin by acknowledging that you have an emotional stack. Your impulse to do something mean or violent is the result of frustration and a sense of powerlessness that *you yourself* have created by not doing anything to change the situation each time you felt angry about the loud music. So, to resolve the matter without making things worse, defuse your own emotional time bomb *before* trying to deal with the behavior or situation that's been aggravating you.

One good way to defuse a stack that you've already built up is to find a third party that you can share your feelings with. Punching a pillow isn't likely to help much; it may just make you more frustrated. Ideally, you should talk to someone who will have an unbiased perspective on the situation; someone who will appreciate your feelings without goading you into even more anger. This strategy should help to defuse enough of your stack that you can then take action to change the situation – using one of the three options described in Strategy 1 (change the situation by negotiating with the other person, change the situation on your own, or change your interpretation of the situation so it no longer evokes that emotional response).

What if it's not your stack? Suppose you realize that someone you interact with has built up a stack about something you do that bothers him. The most important thing is to address the problem before the stack gets any bigger and the frustration builds up even more. This means getting the other person to express the feelings that are currently being repressed.

Of course, if the other person's stack has been building up for a long time, you're inviting anger and perhaps an emotional tirade by getting him to open up. However, if you *don't* do something, you may end up dealing with an even worse emotional explosion later that might come at an awkward time and permanently damage your relationship. If you take the initiative to resolve this, you have a fair amount of control: You can choose the time the discussion happens, you can choose the way the emotional floodgate is opened, and you can be prepared for the emotional tirade so it doesn't catch you off guard and evoke raw emotion from you in response. In other words, if you play your cards right, you can defuse a ticking time bomb and save the relationship – even though the encounter may be emotional and force both of you to deal with issues you'd rather avoid.

It's a small price to pay to save a relationship, if the relationship really matters to you.

Strategy #4 for managing emotional stacks: Learn to manage the fallout and repair the damage from stack explosions when they do occur. Even in the best of circumstances, when both parties have the best of intentions (for example, in an otherwise happy marriage), sometimes a stack will build up and explode. Luckily, there are a number of things you can do to make it easier to minimize the damage when this happens.

First of all, once an explosion happens, recognize it for what it is. Regardless of whether it's you or the other person who has exploded, the first thing to do is step back for a minute and think: Is this emotional explosion really about the one thing that appears to have triggered it – or is it the result of an emotional stack? It's crucial to stop and figure this out, because if the argument really is just about one thing, you can resolve it by addressing that one thing. But if the argument actually is the result of a stack exploding, you have a larger mess to clean up.

Then, if you realize that a stack is the real problem, stop and address it. Say something like, "Wait a minute. It doesn't make sense that you're so angry about this one thing. Have you been angry about my actions for a while and not telling me?" Above all, don't waste your energy by responding with equal fury and escalating the situation into a relationship-ending screaming match.

If you reframe the argument quickly and accurately, most people will realize that you're perception is correct. Then the argument will shift away from two people shouting at each other, and turn into an opportunity to find out whose needs are not being met. It will give you a chance to come up with a way to negotiate a happy ending.

What if you're the source of the explosion? If you explode at someone else and you realize that you have a stack, stop and call a time out. Say something like, "Wait a minute – I just realized that I'm not really upset about this one thing. I guess I've been holding in my feelings for a while.

We need to talk about the bigger picture, not just this one incident." Do your best to explain to the other person (who may be upset and/or angry because of your explosion) how stacks work, and that you've been holding in your feelings. This will defuse any potential screaming match and lay the groundwork for dealing with the real problem. (It may help to explain the reason you've been holding in your feelings – if that's appropriate, given the situation.)

Important note: *Don't focus on your feelings.* Instead, focus on resolving the situation that's been triggering your feelings. And remember: This is a negotiation, not a blame session.

Another important point: **Don't try to resolve things by offering solutions or advice.** Instead, start the repair process by listening to the other person and acknowledging the other person's feelings. A big part of an emotional stack of anger is a belief that your needs, wishes and feelings have been ignored. So if you want to undo someone else's emotional stack, once the initial torrent of feeling has poured out, show that you understand and acknowledge the other person's feelings. (That doesn't mean saying that you *agree* with them.) It's a way of saying, "Yes, your feelings are a legitimate part of this relationship and I'm willing to negotiate so we find a way to get both of our needs met without repeating the situation that makes you so unhappy." If, instead, you jump right in offering solutions and advice *before you really listen*, the other person will end up feeling that he or she *still* isn't being heard, and the problem will probably just get worse.

Once the initial burst of emotion has been unleashed, ask the other person open-ended questions about his or her feelings. Say something like, "Whoa! What's really going on here? Have you been having these feelings for a while and not saying anything to me? Tell me about how you've been feeling." Open-ended questions – in other words, questions that invite a long reply – will help to draw the other person's feelings out into the open. In fact, sometimes the other person won't even know the reason for his or her anger. If that's the situation, it's *especially* important to ask leading, open-ended questions; the answers the other person gives will probably help make him or her more conscious about what's really been going on and why it led to an explosion of emotion.

It's also imortant to resist the temptation to try to change the other person's feelings. Trying to change the other person's feelings tells the other person that you think his or her feelings aren't legitimate. In other words, don't say, "Wow! Your reaction to what I've been doing is totally unreasonable! How can you possibly feel that way?" Criticizing the other person's feelings will only put the other person on the defensive. If you want to put a stop to the build-up of unexpressed emotions and preserve the relationship, you have to make it clear that those suppressed feelings matter – even if you don't agree with them.

Finally, once the backlog of feelings has been released, you want to change things so that both parties get their needs met, thus preventing any more emotional stack building. That calls for a bit of negotiating.

To be a successful negotiator, it helps to remember these three negotiating tips:

Negotiating tip #1: *Remember that negotiating is not about "winning."* Focus on solving the problem and allowing both of you to get your needs met. Negotiating is not about outfoxing or overpowering the other person, it's about finding a solution that both parties can live with that will prevent future trouble.

Negotiating tip #2: *Treat the other person with respect during the process.* As Herb Cohen points out in his classic book *You Can Negotiate Anything*, the way you go about trying to resolve the problem can, by itself, meet some of the other person's needs and help to defuse the situation. A stack often builds up because someone feels he's not being treated with respect, so if you treat the other person with respect while resolving the problem, you've already dealt with one of his complaints. This is why people are usually far more willing to compromise if they feel you've listened to them and acknowledged their point of view.

Negotiating tip #3: The thing a person *says* he wants is often just his current idea of how to get his needs met. In fact, what's important may be an *underlying* need, not the specific thing the person is demanding. To put this another way, there may be quite a few things that would give the person what he really wants, even though he's focused on demanding that one particular thing. Because this is often true, if you can't give the person you're negotiating with the specific thing he says he wants, you may still be able to determine what his underlying need is and then solve the problem by addressing that underlying need.

Here's an often-repeated story that provides a good example of solving a problem by addressing the issue that was hidden underneath the "surface" problem. (This story has been attributed to many different individuals, so if the story is true, it's not clear who the "hero" of the story really was.)

The owner of a large building in a busy city once had a problem: So many people needed to get in and out of the building at certain times of day that the elevators were overwhelmed. As a result, it took forever to get in or out of the building. When complaints, anger and frustration reached a fever pitch, the building's owner knew he had to do something. However, there was no way to add more elevators or speed up the existing elevators. He asked the building's designer for help.

How did the designer solve the problem? He realized that the speed of the elevators wasn't the real problem – the real problem was that people were frustrated about having to wait so long. So he addressed *that* problem instead of trying to change the elevators. To reduce people's frustration, he installed full-length mirrors around the elevators. Suddenly, people could see how they looked, comb their hair, and focus on their appearance. Their frustration – and the complaints – dropped dramatically. The designer solved the underlying problem by defusing the frustration people felt, even though he couldn't give them the specific thing they said they wanted – a way to get out of the building faster.

So, if you can't find a way to meet the other person's *stated* needs when you're trying to negotiate a solution, look for the hidden needs that underlie what the person is asking for. If you can meet the *unstated* needs, you may be able to get past a negotiating impasse and get both of your needs met.

It's important to note that managing the fallout when a stack explodes will be a whole lot easier if both people already know what emotional stacks are and how they work. In this situation, when an emotional explosion occurs, it becomes possible to stop the emotional outpouring much more quickly and have a good outcome. So, making sure both of you understand the nature of emotional stacks and how they work – before an explosion happens – is a good investment of your time and energy. (For more on this, see Strategy #5, below.)

Strategy #5 for managing emotional stacks: Set up <u>ground rules</u> with people you care about – or need support from – so that stacks don't build up in the first place. Setting up ground rules to avoid future trouble is a powerful strategy, but there's a caveat: You can only set ground rules with someone who has a reason to want to work with you. For example, it may not be possible to do this with an annoying neighbor or a boss (although there could be exceptions).

From here on, I'll assume that we're talking about a situation in which both parties are interested in preventing misunderstandings, and both parties are willing to take some simple steps to do exactly that. Here are some ground rules that will help prevent future stacks from building up:

Ground rule #1: *Make sure both parties understand how stacks work.* If you've read this far, you probably have a pretty good idea of how emotional stacks happen. But if the other person isn't familiar with this idea, you'll have to explain it to him or her – or have the person in question read this chapter.

Ground rule #2: *Agree that both of you will try to express your feelings when you have them.* Once both of you understand the nature of emotional stacks and the negative outcome you'd like to avoid, try to come to an agreement that when either of you finds yourself stifling feelings, you'll stop and ask the other person to help you out. That help will consist of allowing you to share your feelings and working with you to find a mutually acceptable way to change the situation so a stack of suppressed emotion does not build up.

In order for this to work, both of you need to agree that anger is a legitimate feeling, and both of you must be willing to respect the other person's anger if it arises, and be willing to respond to it constructively. (If that's completely impossible, the relationship may not have a promising future.)

Ground Rule #3: *Agree to express your feelings in a way that shows respect.* The idea is to communicate your needs, not to start a fight. We've all seen people vent, and we've all seen emotional stacks explode, but expressing your feelings doesn't mean attacking someone else. The focus has to be on getting suppressed feelings out in the open and finding a way for both parties to get their needs met, not on punishing the other person. So, you need to agree that both of you will do your best to express your feelings and needs in a way that *doesn't make things worse*.

This also means that you shouldn't be indiscriminately honest without regard to the circumstances. Expressing your feelings can be done hurtfully, even used as a weapon. Timing matters, too; expressing feelings at the wrong moment can undercut positive changes. So, you have to use good judgment about how and when to express your feelings. However, if it's clear that the moment *isn't* right to express your feelings,

5 Strategies to Ensure That Emotional Stacks Don't Cause a Relationship to Break Down

1. Prevent stacks from building up inside yourself. The main rule here is: Don't hold in your emotions. Instead, try to communicate and negotiate to change the situation that's provoking your emotions. If that's not possible, change the situation on your own, or change your interpretation of the situation.
2. Learn to recognize when you or someone around you is already building up a stack.
3. Learn to defuse a stack you've discovered before it explodes.
4. When a stack does unexpectedly explode, learn to manage the fallout and, if possible, repair the damage. First, recognize that a stack was the cause of the explosion; don't react to the situation at face value. Second, use your awareness to defuse the situation. Third, try to resolve the underlying problem.
5. Set up ground rules with people you care about—or need support from—so that stacks never build up in the first place.

don't squash them and try to forget about them – just save them for a more appropriate moment.

Ground Rule #4: *Agree that you'll both respond to an expression of feelings by treating those feelings with respect, even if you don't understand or agree with them.* This is the other half of Rule #3: Not only does the person expressing his feelings have to do so in a respectful way, the person who is listening has to respond with respect. If either of you responds to an honest statement of feelings with sarcasm or anger or by acting like you couldn't care less, the other person will feel stung and stop sharing his or her feelings. Then you'll return to stack-building and the relationship will be in danger again.

Ground Rule #5: *Agree that you'll work to negotiate a resolution that gets both of your needs met.* Remember that doing this means looking past the immediate complaint to see if something else is really triggering the emotions. The immediate complaint may not be the real issue at all. If you agree to avoid doing one particular thing that triggered the outburst – for example, agreeing that you won't throw your dirty clothes on the floor any more – but the *real* problem is that the other person feels like his or her feelings are being ignored, then you haven't solved the problem. The stack will continue to build. In other words, *you need to get to the bottom of what's really happening.* Then you can resolve the real problem instead of just wasting time dealing with symptoms *caused* by the real problem.

What If a Stack Has Nothing To Do With You?

So far, we've talked mostly about stacks that have built up because of a repeated interaction between you and someone else. But it's also possible to trigger an emotional explosion of a stack that you were not previously involved in. I think we've all had the experience of saying something perfectly innocent to an acquaintance and having him or her explode at us.

For example, if someone has spent years feeling abused – not by you – and you happen to say or do the one thing that epitomizes the frustration that person feels, you may trigger an explosion of that person's stack and receive the brunt of his or her anger. (In fact, if your acquaintance has been worried about expressing his emotions to the person who is driving him crazy, he may be *more* likely to vent his emotions at somebody else – like *you*. From his perspective, it's probably safer!)

What should you do if an innocent remark or action produces an emotional explosion from someone else? First and foremost, recognize that an emotional stack is behind the explosion. As long as the stack really doesn't have anything to do with you, don't take it personally. Recognize it as being the other person's problem, and strive to avoid triggering the stack a second time.

Should you try to help the other person resolve his emotional stack? That's a judgment call. If you have a compelling reason to try to help, use your knowledge of how stacks work. However, remember that dealing with another person's emotional backlog can be a tall order, so think carefully before you decide to take on the challenge. Trying to undo another person's emotional stack can be a huge energy sink, and might end up putting your own relationship with that person at risk – as well as potentially resulting in problems between you and the third party who was causing your acquaintance's stack to build up in the first place.

Once more, in brief:

Here are the key points to remember from Chapter 7:

• Emotional stacks arise when an emotion is repeatedly experienced but never expressed or acted upon. The emotion then backlogs like water piling up behind a dam and gets stronger. At the same time, it becomes mixed with frustration and a sense of powerlessness.

This can end three possible ways:

1) Something happens to release the buildup of emotion before it becomes too extreme. An explosion is avoided.

2) The emotion and frustration build up until they are released explosively in response to a trigger that's relatively minor.

3) The emotion and frustration are *never* released, resulting in ill health for the person holding in the emotions, along with behavior that may seem inexplicable to others.

• Any emotion can build up into a stack, but anger is the most dangerous. A big enough stack of unexpressed anger can produce violence when it explodes.

• Anger can be constructive when it's expressed each time we feel it; if it's not held in, it doesn't explode. So the best way to prevent violence is to make sure anger is expressed in some form instead of allowing it to be suppressed over and over again.

• If both parties want a relationship to work, there are five strategies you can use to ensure that emotional stacks don't cause a breakdown of the relationship:

Strategy #1: Learn to prevent stacks from building up inside yourself. The main rule here is *don't hold in your emotions*. Instead, try to communicate and negotiate to change the situation that's provoking your emotions. If that's not possible, change the situation on your own or change your interpretation of the situation.

Strategy #2: Learn to recognize when someone you interact with is building up a stack.

Strategy #3: Learn to defuse an existing stack before it causes trouble.

Strategy #4: Learn to manage the fallout and repair the damage from stack explosions when they do occur. When an emotional explosion occurs, recognize that a stack was the cause of the explosion. Don't react to the situation at face value. Then, stop the superficial argument and address the stack. Respectfully encourage the person to express his or her feelings; then use good negotiating techniques to find a solution that prevents future stacks from building up.

Strategy #5: Set up ground rules with people you care about – or need support from – so that stacks never build up in the first place.

❈ ❈ ❈

NOTES for Chapter 7

1. As noted in *10 Lessons to Transform Your Marriage*, by John M. Gottman and Julie S. Gottman.

8.
Always Try To Understand the Reasons For Behavior.

Understanding the reasons for behavior makes it far easier to get what you need from other people – and from yourself.

"Nothing in life is to be feared, it is only to be understood. Now is the time to understand more, so that we may fear less."
 – Marie Curie

"Everything that irritates us about others can lead us to an understanding of ourselves."
 – Carl Jung

A friend of mine reported seeing a situation unfold in the supermarket one day. A mother was shopping for groceries with a two-year-old boy in tow who was whimpering and crying. The mother was clearly frustrated by this and asked the boy to stop crying. But he continued. Finally, the mother began yelling at the little boy: "Stop crying! You're a bad boy!"

To my friend's surprise, the little boy came to his own defense. Through his tears, he said loudly, "I am *not* bad! I'm hungry!"

The moral of the story? If you want to change someone's behavior, you'll have much greater success if you understand the reason for it.

Being able to change problematic behavior can be a crucial skill when you're trying to stay off the Wheel of Misfortune – whether the behavior is someone else's or your own. When circumstances are tough, going it alone is seldom an option; your survival and success tend to be linked to cooperating with others. If a person you need to work with, for example, behaves in ways that don't make sense to you and need to be changed, you can't simply ignore it. Or, in the case of an existing relationship – say, a marriage – the inability to change problematic behavior can lead to a breakdown that costs you dearly in terms of emotional, physical and even financial support.

As I hope to demonstrate in this chapter, the key to changing problematic behavior is understanding the reasons for it. Unfortunately, understanding the reasons for behavior – including our own – is not an easy task. (If it was, psychologists and psychiatrists wouldn't be able to make a living!) Getting even a partial understanding of the reasons behind behavior takes time and effort, and most of us are short on time and energy. So it's quite understandable that most of us, most of the time, don't bother. On the other hand, when a situation involving someone else's behavior is ongoing and problematic, the value of spending the time and effort to understand the behavior increases dramatically.

The time-honored way to try to change someone's behavior, when you don't understand the reason for the behavior, is to resort to punishment. However, punishment often doesn't work. Later in this chapter we'll talk about the reasons for that, but for now let's just say that when you want to change someone's behavior, you're more likely to succeed if you have some idea of what's causing the behavior.

Then, of course, there's the issue of *our own* behavior. What do you do when you need to behave a certain way but can't seem to make yourself do it? Being puzzled by our own behavior is a common human experience, and when times are tough, it can be more than puzzling – it can be life-threatening! The need to understand our behavior in a relationship, for example, may become much greater when day-to-day difficulties increase, raising stress and anger levels.

As with other people's behavior, the better you understand your own behavior and the underlying reasons for the choices you make, the more likely you are to be able to change the behaviors you don't like. Furthermore, if you *don't* understand your own behavior, you may end up judging yourself negatively, which can become a major hindrance to your ability to survive. In the meantime, your behavior may also be pushing away others whose support you need.

Here, I'd like to talk about five different aspects of trying to understand the reasons for behavior (yours or someone else's):

- First, we'll look at the concrete benefits you can get if you make the effort to understand the reasons for behavior.
- Second, we'll examine the reasons people often don't bother trying.
- Third, we'll talk about the problems that come with using punishment as a way of changing behavior.
- Fourth, I'll share some general observations about human behavior that may be helpful when times are tough.
- Finally, I'll offer a few specific suggestions for dealing with behavior that you don't immediately understand – whether it's your own behavior or someone else's.

The Benefits of Understanding Behavior

There are many reasons you should make it a habit to try to understand the behavior of the people around you. Here are just a few:

Benefit #1. *Understanding behavior gives you a fighting chance to change it.* Without realizing the reason for her child's crying, the mother in the grocery store didn't see any option for changing his behavior except to yell at him. Since hunger was the cause of the crying, yelling (or punishment) was not likely to work – and even if it did stop him from crying, the cause of his crying was not being addressed, so he'd probably lash out in some other way.

Of course, it's important to note that understanding the reasons for behavior *doesn't change the behavior* by itself. But it's the first step on the road to changing the behavior, and it may give you the key that will allow you to change it – as the mother in the store hopefully changed her son's behavior by getting him something to eat.

Understanding behavior can also help by removing roadblocks to change. That's especially true when the behavior we'd like to change is our own. For example, if we're continually doing something we know we shouldn't do and we don't know why we keep doing it, we may come up with rationalizations to justify the behavior. We may say, "There's nothing really wrong with this," "Only other people suffer the side effects of doing this," "I'm only doing this because I enjoy it," "I can stop any time," etc.

These kinds of rationalization do reduce our internal stress, so in that sense they serve a useful purpose in the short run. The problem is that they can become very effective roadblocks to change. The more we repeat them to ourselves, the more legitimate they sound. So, they not only make us feel better, they become arguments for perpetuating the behavior.

However, once you understand the real reasons for your behavior, those rationalizations become irrelevant. Yes, you still have to deal with changing the behavior, but at least you won't be sidetracked by bogus rationalizations in your quest to make things better.

Benefit #2. *Understanding behavior can provide motivation to start the process of change.* This is true, in part, because when we don't understand the reasons for behavior it's easy to become judgmental – and negative judgments can be a real motivation dampener. Why try to change someone's behavior if you've already decided that the person is inherently mean or stupid? Why try to change your own behavior if you've already categorized yourself as weak, or a failure, or born with bad genes? In contrast, simply realizing that your own behavior (or someone else's) has a specific, understandable reason for happening can give you hope, and that can free up an enormous amount of energy.

So, even if understanding the behavior doesn't change it, it can jumpstart your quest to make the change – in yourself or in someone else.

Benefit #3. *The better you understand someone's behavior, the easier it is to work with them, resolve disagreements and negotiate with them to get things you need.* It's very difficult to negotiate successfully with someone you don't understand. Negotiating is all about trying to get both parties' needs met. If you don't understand the other person's behavior, you probably don't understand his needs, either.

Benefit #4. *As long as the reasons for behavior remain a mystery, it's easy to judge others and then use that judgment to justify anger and abuse in response to their actions.* A friend of mine, who hadn't been feeling well recently, suddenly began to take things personally and get angry over things said to him that were not meant to be offensive. He and I had several loud arguments as a result – and I almost *never* argued with this person about anything. I began wondering if I really knew him as well as I thought, and my view of our friendship began to change. But after a few days of thinking about it, I realized he had started taking a pain medication a few days before his first outburst. When I pointed this out to him, he looked quite surprised, and then realized that there was undoubtedly a connection. Even though he kept taking the medication for some time after that, we didn't have any more arguments.

One reason we sometimes judge other people is that it's an easy way to eliminate the discomfort we feel when we're troubled by behavior that we don't understand. When we judge someone, we place the person into a category in our mind – enabling us to dismiss the behavior without actually figuring out the reason for it. Doing this reduces our anxiety, but it's pretty much the *opposite* of understanding. As such, it makes us less able to change the behavior.

Furthermore, categorizing someone to explain away or rationalize his behavior often involves dismissing him or lowering our opinion of him – and that can be extended to an entire group of people. Many times throughout history, one population has used behavior they couldn't understand in another population as a justification for declaring that population inferior, or guilty of some crime (for example, heresy). The strategy of categorizing other groups of people negatively because we don't understand their behavior, used as a substitute for actually trying to understand the behavior, can lead to persecution or even genocide. Making the attempt to understand the behavior can prevent that from happening.

Benefit #5. *If you understand the reasons for a particular behavior, you'll have some idea of whether trying to change it is a waste of your time.* In some cases, changing behavior requires a lot of time and work. Understanding the reasons for the behavior will tell us whether it's worth making the effort – or if it's too big a job for us to undertake on our own.

One reason some behaviors are difficult to change is that the human brain physically changes when behavior is repeated over a long period of time. Science has demonstrated that repeated behavior gradually reshapes the brain, altering neural connections and even changing the size of different portions of the brain.[1] Undoing those physical alterations in the brain may require extensive repetition of alternative behaviors. (It really is true that old habits are hard to break.) So if a behavior you don't like is a new behavior, it might be fairly easy to change, but if it's been going on for years, changing it will be a lot tougher.

Another reason changing behavior may require a lot of work is that the payoff for the behavior may be very powerful, such as when the behavior helps someone avoid a deep-seated fear. Or, a physical addiction may be involved, as in the case of constant use of nicotine or consumption of alcohol. Some behaviors may be tied into deeply held beliefs, such as religious beliefs. It's pretty easy to see that these beliefs, and the behaviors they trigger, are not going to change overnight.

Knowing that the reason for the behavior is deep-seated or that the behavior has been going on for a long time can save you years of wasted effort and keep you from making choices you'll live to regret.

Benefit #6. *When people behave in alarming ways, and changing their behavior is beyond your ability, understanding the reasons for their behavior can reduce your anxiety and frustration.* If we guess about the reasons for behavior and we guess wrong, we may subject ourselves to a lot of suffering based on our mistake. And if we don't understand someone's troubling behavior at all – if it seems completely inexplicable – that lack of understanding can be very frustrating and cause a lot of anxiety. Getting a clue about the real reasons for the behavior is the antidote.

I had a woman friend who became seriously ill. When I went to see her, she complained to me that her brother was now avoiding her. She was very hurt and upset, which was understandable because she was sick and really needed his support. Unfortunately, she had no idea how to change his behavior because she didn't have any idea why he was avoiding her. But I knew a little of her family's history, and with an outsider's perspective, it wasn't too hard for me to guess the reason for his behavior. I knew that their mother had died when they were both very young, an experience that can have a life-long impact. Suppose you were a young boy and watched, horrified and helpless, as your mother got sick and died. How might you react when, years later, another woman family member that you're close to falls ill and could die, and once again you can't do anything about it? Many people would react by staying away from the sick person to avoid the frightening possibility of going through that horrible experience a second time. (And they might not consciously know the reason for their own behavior.)

I suggested this possibility to my friend, and I believe it changed her perspective. Hopefully, it helped to reduce the alarm and despair she was feeling.

This can apply to more global behavior as well. For instance, nothing is more unpleasant than feeling that "the world doesn't make sense." I've sometimes been deeply upset watching horrible world events caused by individuals in power; I know that human beings are capable of doing a lot of good, so it can really ruin my day when someone shows contempt or malice towards others. The one thing that helps me "keep my cool" is having some idea of the reasons that people – even honest, well-intentioned people – end up rationalizing and justifying cruelty. I may not be able to change the behavior in question, but having some understanding of the causes of the behavior keeps me from seeing that person's actions as a reason to condemn the entire human race. That perspective keeps my frustration and anger from overwhelming me.

One of the most unfortunate side effects of ignorance about the reasons for people's behavior is that it contributes to the belief that bad behavior is a fundamental, unalterable part of human nature. That belief has numerous negative consequences. Perhaps the worst consequence is that when you're faced with seriously bad behavior, you're likely to have feelings of hopelessness – which is one of the things that pushes people to justify fanatical behavior, where any action is seen as justifiable. (For more on this idea, see the section on *focusing on the gap between what you have and what you'd like to have*, in Chapter 5.)

In contrast, the more you understand the reasons for other people's actions, the more you'll see people as fundamentally the same, and our global problems as solvable (maybe not today, but eventually). After all, if there are *reasons* for someone's behavior, then all is not lost. Plus, you know that the person behaving badly didn't start out that way; something *caused* the behavior. So, understanding behavior can go a long way toward reducing feelings of hopelessness and preventing fanatical choices of action.

Benefit #7. *The more you understand other people's behavior, the better you'll understand your own.* You'd be amazed how often getting to the bottom of someone else's behavior will give you an insight into your own actions. For example, you might wonder why a talented friend keeps turning down opportunities. You might eventually realize that he's carrying around a fixed mindset (as we talked about in Chapter 2), and doesn't believe he can master new challenges. Even if your insight doesn't lead to you helping him change, it might very well cause you to notice some of that kind of thinking in your own life. That could be a wake-up call that ends up changing your life for the better.

Benefit #8. *The better you understand yourself and others, the more other people will be attracted to you.* As noted earlier, knowledge about the reasons for behavior puts you in a far better position to negotiate for things you need and change behavior you don't like. That knowledge, in other words, is a useful tool – *and it has just as much value to others as it does to you.* In a confusing world, who would you rather hang around with – someone who is clueless about human behavior, or someone who has some insight into it? People around you who pick up on your level of understanding will realize you're a valuable resource, someone worth knowing, and worth having as a friend and colleague.

The flip side is that ignorance of the reasons for behavior can push people away. Generally, people who don't understand themselves or those around them deal with the world in one of two ways: They simply judge everyone and every behavior they don't understand; or, they don't pass judgment but feel helpless because the behaviors they're faced with seem inexplicable.

If you fall into the first category – if you simply judge those people whose behavior you don't understand – then people who agree with your judgments will enjoy your company, but people who disagree with your judgments will not. Furthermore, since this type of judging is a protective mechanism (it keeps us from having to spend time and effort getting to the bottom of something), anyone who challenges your judgments will be undercutting your psychological defenses, and you won't see him as a friend. So if you manage your lack of understanding by judging others, you'll push away a lot of people – people who otherwise might have developed into good friends and resources.

If you fall into the second category – being troubled by unexplained behavior even though you don't judge it – your awareness of your ignorance may undermine your confidence and focus. Other people will sense that, and many of them will avoid getting too close to you for that reason.

In short, if you take the time to understand the reasons for behavior, people will pick up on that and see you as a potential resource. As a result, you'll draw more interesting, knowledgeable people into your personal circle, and that can improve the quality of your life considerably – not to mention providing you with much-needed resources and support during hard times.

Why People Don't Bother Trying to Understand Behavior

Since we benefit from a better understanding of the reasons for people's behavior, why don't we spend more time trying to increase

Consequences of Not Understanding the Reasons for Behavior

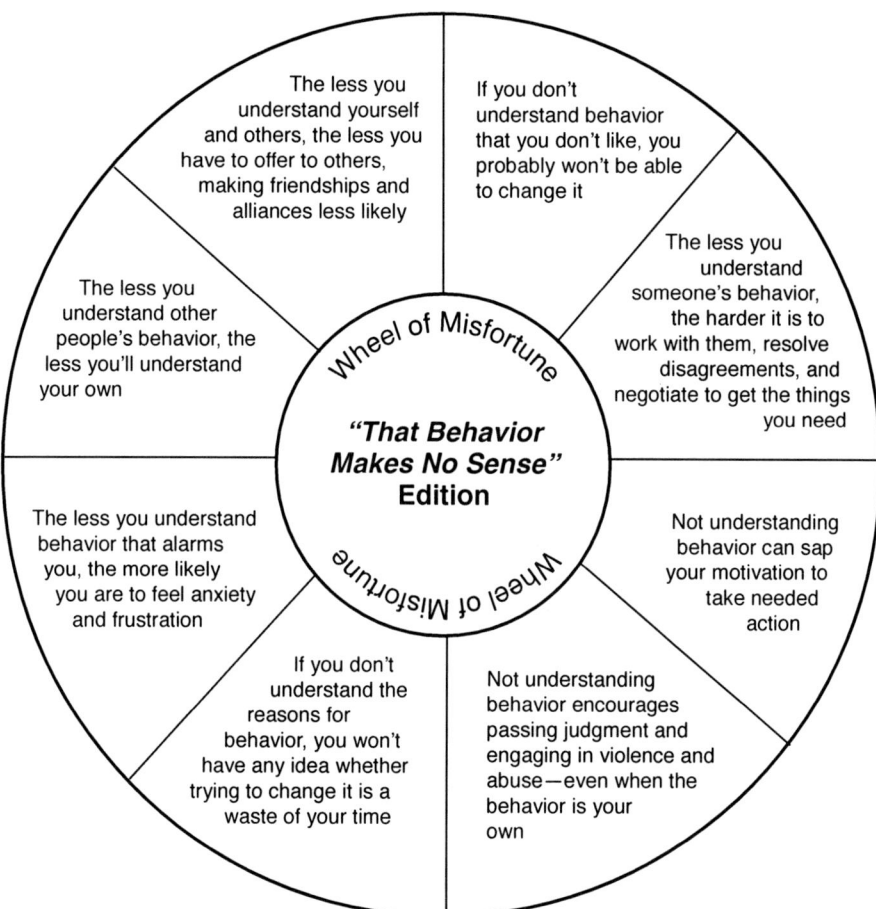

our understanding?

For one thing, it takes too much time and effort. This may be a legitimate reason to skip the understanding process, especially if behavior needs to be changed quickly to avoid a calamity; in that situation you may not have the luxury of taking the time to find out what's behind the behavior. But generally, how we spend our time and effort is up to us, and if understanding people's behavior is not fairly high on your priority list, you're putting yourself at a serious disadvantage. In other words, the payoff for understanding can be enormous. It's worth making the effort, even when circumstances don't give you much time to get to the bottom of the matter.

A second reason we might not want to know the reasons for someone's behavior is that we might find out we have something to do with it! If someone's troubling behavior is a part of his or her relationship with you, you can bet your bottom dollar you have something to do with it. Admittedly, that can be a tough pill to swallow – especially if you're in the fixed mindset.

The fixed mindset springs from the belief that we're stuck with our existing talents and characteristics with no real chance of changing. People who carry this mindset around have a pressing need to blame others for relationship problems – because if you don't believe you can change, the last thing you want to do is see yourself as part of the problem. However, the premise on which the fixed mindset is based is false; we can, and do, change and grow constantly. Furthermore, the idea that one person is solely responsible for how two people interact is *never* true. This doesn't mean that if you're suffering in a relationship you're doing something bad; this is not about "blaming the victim." It's about the reality that when two people relate, both people are part of the equation.

In an abusive relationship, for example, one person may be doing physical damage to the other; but if the person who is being abused stays in the relationship and takes no action, that person is definitely helping to keep the abusive relationship going. And that makes understanding the abuser's behavior a scary proposition for the person being abused; it's likely to make the person being abused realize that she (or he) has to make some changes in her (or his) own behavior in order to stop the abuse. Having to take responsibility for changing our own behavior is sometimes even scarier than facing the harsh realities of our current situation.

So, the possibility that we might be contributing to someone else's negative behavior is enough to scare some people away from trying to understand the reasons for it. It's always easier to see the problem as being entirely the other person's fault – even if doing so deprives you of the power to change the behavior.

Another reason some people don't try to understand the reasons for unwanted behavior is that they believe that doing so is merely a way to excuse it. In reality, understanding behavior has nothing to do with excusing it or letting someone off the hook. For example, if you understand why someone committed a horrible crime, you're not going to say, "Gee, now that I understand why the person did this awful thing I'll have to overlook it!" On the contrary – understanding why someone committed such a crime will put you in a much better position to prevent it from happening again. It's true that this knowledge probably won't provide you with a magic key to instantly stop someone from repeating the behavior, but it will give you a better perspective on what needs to be done, and it may help you eliminate the conditions that lead people into that kind of behavior.

One last point: People may not bother looking for the reasons for behavior if they feel they already *know* the reason. That's one of the potential problems with religion and science: They offer explanations for behavior that people may accept wholesale, leading to the belief that there's no need to look any farther.

For example, some religions teach that "bad" behavior is the result of being controlled by an outside force of evil, such as the devil. A scientific equivalent might be the idea that violence is engrained in our genes, and therefore needs no further explanation. These kinds of explanations for behavior are extremely unhelpful, because they provide an excuse to stop looking for other more immediate causes of behavior that you can actually do something about. Furthermore, they allow people to evade taking responsibility for their own behavior. They get to blame their behavior on the devil, or on "bad genes."

Partly for that reason, blanket explanations also lead to totally inappropriate ways of trying to change the behavior in question. Yes, "coming back to God" may have altered some people's negative behavior. (Quite a few politicians who committed horrible crimes and got caught have experienced religious conversions in jail!) But if your idea for ending corruption in the world is to convert everyone to a particular religion, you're not going to have much luck solving the world's problems. Similarly, if you throw up your hands and declare that human violence is an unsolvable problem because it's coded into our genes, you're not going to solve violence-related problems that most assuredly *do* have solutions. Blanket explanations for behavior from any source are counterproductive.

If you want to change other people's behavior – or your own – you need to start by trying to understand the kind of concrete, experiential causes that lie behind even the most negative or seemingly inexplicable behavior. Without that understanding, you're putting yourself at a huge disadvantage.

The Punishment Paradigm

This raises an important question: Why bother understanding someone's behavior if you can just change their behavior with punishment?

Punishment is a common response to behavior that people don't like. Of course, there are many kinds of punishment – physical, emotional, deprivational – but the idea is the same: Make the person associate something unpleasant with the behavior you don't like so the behavior stops. Resorting to punishment is usually far easier than looking for the reason for the behavior, and punishment can often be justified by falling back on cultural traditions which claim that punishment is honorable and appropriate and should therefore be used without further thought. Some cultures believe, for example, that children should be "taught" by being subjected to physical punishment when they make a mistake. In fact, people in some cultures believe that if you *don't* do this, you're doing the child a disservice. (The evidence does not support that, as we'll see later.)

Even if you have doubts about using punishment, sometimes it seems like the only option. When you need to change behavior in a hurry, or a behavior is deeply ingrained and therefore *can't* be changed quickly (even if you do understand its causes), you may have to fall back on using punishment to try and change the behavior. That's just the way things are – at least at this point in human history.

Unfortunately, punishment has some serious drawbacks when it comes to producing a good outcome, even when it's well-intentioned and seems like the only option you have. Here are a few of the practical factors that can cause punishment to fail to have the desired effect:

Punishment Problem 1: Timing matters. Consider the hot stove analogy: If a child touches a hot stove, he gets the equivalent of punishment – his hand is burned. This is quite effective in terms of changing the child's behavior; he isn't likely to touch the stove again. However, the main reason this works is that the "punishment" occurs exactly when the behavior occurs. If his hand didn't feel burned until some time later, he might never learn to avoid touching the stove.

In contrast, when a person engages in behavior that someone else doesn't like and is punished for it, the punishment often comes hours or days later; it doesn't happen at the time the behavior occurs. So, the person probably gets some immediate *positive* reinforcement for the behavior (which is why it's happening in the first place), but because the punishment is delayed there's no immediate link between the behavior and the punishment. Instead, the person has to *intellectually* connect the behavior and the punishment. That's often not very effective. Consider the religious concept of being punished after death for sinning; that idea has an *incredibly* bad track record for changing behavior. So, the fact that most punishment happens some time after the behavior happens guarantees that it will have limited success as a deterrent.

Punishment Problem 2: There's more than one way to avoid punishment. When punishment does succeed in changing behavior, it does so because the person who was punished wants to avoid experiencing the punishment a second time. With the hot stove, it's perfectly clear that the way to avoid getting burned a second time is to not touch the stove again. However, when someone punishes us for doing something they didn't like, stopping the behavior is not our only option. In fact, the easiest way to avoid getting punished a second time is to *avoid the person who punished us* – or *avoid getting caught the next time.*

This is why laws and jail time do such a poor job of preventing bad behavior; you can avoid punishment by not getting caught! Furthermore, being locked in jail may prevent behavior from happening for a while, but it doesn't address the reason for the behavior at all, so the behavior is just postponed or redirected. The result is that we all pay lots of money in taxes to keep more and more people in jail, who eventually are released and go back to engaging in the behavior that got them in trouble in the first place.

Yes, having laws is necessary at this point in history, because left to our own devices, human beings often behave badly. But the reality is that laws, like threats, don't alter behavior; they simply spell out possible consequences of a behavior. Whether that actually changes the behavior in question depends on a host of other factors that may have nothing to do with the threatened punishment. (Look at how ineffective laws prohibiting drug or alcohol use have been, for example.)

So punishment isn't terribly effective in part because the game it sets in motion is *avoiding a repeat of the punishment* – and there are a lot of ways to do that besides changing your behavior.

Punishment Problem 3: The meaning of the punishment is in the

eye of the beholder. As we discussed in Chapter 1, a person's experience does not consist of what happens to him – it consists of what he *perceives* to be happening to him. In this case, when we're punished – regardless of the reason – we tend to see it as unjust. Furthermore, we may see it as a reason to retaliate against whoever punished us! That's why punishing someone, following the "eye for an eye" school of thought, tends to start a vicious circle, leading to an escalation of violence. This is how wars start, and why they keep going.

In other words, when we try to alter behavior by using punishment, the person being punished may perceive the punishment very differently then *we* perceive it. As a result, there's a good chance that instead of changing the person's behavior, the punishment will only serve to generate anger and resentment, leading to worse trouble later on.

Punishment Problem 4: Delivering punishment is unpleasant for most people, so it tends to be put off until things get out of hand. Many people find punishing others distasteful, so they avoid doing it. Unfortunately, they may not have any other ideas about how to alter the problematic behavior, so not punishing becomes the equivalent of *not doing anything about it.* Thus, the behavior continues, and the bad feelings about it continue.

This can have very negative consequences. Once the delivery of punishment has been postponed for a while because punishment is distasteful, the person who doesn't like the behavior becomes frustrated and unhappy over a *backlog* of "wrongs" and builds up an emotional stack, as we discussed in the previous chapter. Sooner or later, that frustration builds to the point at which punishment *does* happen when the stack explodes – but since it's based on a backlog of anger, the resulting punishment may end up being way out of proportion to whatever offense triggers it. That "over the top" punishment leads to misunderstandings and anger from the recipient, who may not comprehend why the punishment is so great. And, the recipient may then respond with extreme actions of his own.

In addition, others witnessing the harsh punishment, unaware that a backlog of repressed anger was the cause, may also conclude that the person doing the punishing is way out of line. They may even see the excessive punishment as *abuse* of the person being punished, which can have serious consequences for the person doing the punishing.

Punishment Problem 5: Punishing someone sends the message that

punishment is an appropriate way to try to change behavior. By now it shouldn't be hard to see that resorting to punishment as a way to change behavior often doesn't work – which means that teaching others to use it as a strategy will, in turn, put *them* at a disadvantage. Children, in particular, often mimic what is done to them. So if you punish them routinely, they accept the idea that punishing others is the right way to change other people's behavior.

One study that was done compared the behavior of two groups of children in a day-care setting. The children in the first group were routinely judged and punished by their parents for crying or making a fuss; those in the second group were not. In the day-care setting the children who were routinely punished for crying or making a fuss reacted to other children who were crying with anger – in some cases, they even attempted to assault them. The children who had not been punished for crying did not exhibit this behavior. Clearly, both groups were passing along the behavior they had experienced themselves.[2]

Punishment Problem 6: Punishment can have negative long-term effects on the person being punished. This is especially true with children, as numerous studies are finding. One study found that children who were punished by being spanked around one year of age, when observed a year or two later, not only behaved more aggressively than children who were not spanked, but also performed more poorly on cognitive tests. (Some critics suggested that the children being spanked might already have been more aggressive – the "which came first, the chicken or the egg?" argument – but the study was constructed to make sure that was not the case.) Other studies have also found that children who are spanked score lower on IQ tests – and the more they are spanked, the lower they score.[3]

Perhaps more alarming, a major, large-scale study of 20,607 individuals, which focused on the impact of routinely receiving physical punishment as a form of discipline when they were children, found that this was associated with a host of problems as adults.[4] (Note: The study excluded anyone who received more serious abuse, such as sexual abuse, neglect, physical abuse, exposure to violence between parents, and so forth. This was just a study of the consequences of being spanked for unwanted behavior.)

By the time people reached adulthood, simply experiencing harsh physical punishment as a form of discipline was associated with:

- a 41% greater risk of major depression;
- a 59% greater risk of alcohol abuse;
- a 53% greater risk of drug abuse;
- a 49% greater risk of mood disorders; and
- a 93% greater risk of mania.

Please note that this should not be taken as a condemnation of parents who spank their children. Although physical punishment of children is banned in at least two dozen countries, it's consider acceptable in many cultures, including the United States. Nevertheless, this kind of study data is one more piece of evidence that punishment, used as a way to alter behavior, tends to have unwanted side effects – side effects that can negatively affect the entire course of a person's life.

Of course, the reality is that we often need to change behavior quickly and simply don't have the time or ability to get to the bottom of what caused the behavior. So using punishment to change behavior that we don't like may be inevitable, at least in some situations. Nevertheless, there's plenty of evidence that punishment seldom produces the desired result, and alternative means of taking action produce far better results.

Of course, there's another obvious alternative to punishment (besides figuring out what's causing the behavior and addressing that): using *rewards* to alter the behavior instead of punishment. The problem with this approach is that rewards are primarily useful as a way to encourage *new* behaviors, not to stop existing behaviors. The only way to use a reward to try and change someone's existing behavior is to reward the person for doing something *instead* of the behavior you don't like. For example, the mother in the store might have tried to get her child to stop crying by offering him a toy if he stopped.

That approach is problematic for three reasons. First, it doesn't remove the motivation for the unwanted behavior. For example, as long as the child is unhappy because he's hungry, no toy is going to help for long. The underlying reason for the behavior still hasn't been addressed.

Second, in order to have any chance of working, what you're offering has to provide a bigger payoff than the payoff the person gets for engaging in the unwanted behavior. That's tough, because you may not even be sure what the payoff for the unwanted behavior is!

Third, trying to use a reward to change behavior sets up an equation in that person's mind – an equation that may backfire later. This is a complicated point, so we'll discuss it in detail later in this chapter.

The main thing to note is that in many situations, trying to use a reward to change behavior can have just as many unwanted side effects as using punishment. Ultimately, figuring out the real reason for the behavior is far and away the best way to change it.

Note: Changing the behavior of a child is a particularly sensitive issue, and one that's far too large to address in detail here. If you are a parent and would like to avoid the long-term problems that may follow from routine physical punishment, dozens of books and magazines are available to provide guidance on effective alternatives.

A Few Observations About Human Behavior

When you're trying to understand the reasons for behavior, you're probably dealing with a very specific situation. But there are some general principles regarding human behavior that are worth keeping in mind.

Principle 1: *There's always a payoff.* Some behaviors that people engage in seem nonsensical. In fact, some behaviors are so obviously self-destructive that most people are amazed that they continue at all – such as when we watch someone refuse to leave a partner who abuses her (or him). Even more remarkable, this is often a reaction people have to their *own* behavior: Why do I keep eating when I know it's bad for my health and I really do want to lose weight? Why can't I ask that person I like so much for a date? Why do I keep getting into fights with my spouse when I don't mean to?

The answer is that the person engaging in the questionable behavior is getting some kind of payoff for maintaining it, despite the negative consequences. Ironically, the payoff in these cases may also be invisible to the person engaging in the behavior – which is why we can be frustrated and puzzled by our own actions and choices. However, that doesn't change the fact that a payoff is taking place.

This can be very hard for people to accept, especially when it applies to their own behavior. It may seem like a major failing on our part that we'd be doing something we feel bad about just because of a hidden payoff. But that's how human beings work. In fact, realizing that this is true is crucial if you want to take control of your life. If you can find the hidden payoff for your own puzzling behavior, you'll open the door to changing it. Likewise, if you can find the hidden payoff those around you are getting for their behavior, you have a much better chance of changing that behavior.

As already noted, figuring out what the payoff is can be quite tricky. Here are three reasons for this:

Reason #1: The reward that the behavior produces may be purely internal. External rewards such as being paid or getting a pat on the head are fairly easy to see, but a seemingly odd or self-destructive behavior may be accompanied by a rush of good feeling or a reduction of anxiety that an outsider can't see.

Reason #2: The payoff may only be rewarding to that one person, as a result of his or her personal history. Because it's connected to something specific the individual experienced in the past, the payoff may only be evident if you happen to know the person's history. For example, strange or unpleasant experiences we had when we were young may affect what we find rewarding. Brain studies have demonstrated that when two experiences occur together repeatedly, the brain responds by connecting the related circuits in the brain. So if a child is punished painfully, followed immediately by being hugged and treated well because the punisher feels guilty, the child's brain will eventually form a long-lasting connection between pain and feeling good afterwards. This explains many cases of masochism, where individuals seek out pain. To most of us, this kind of behavior is inexplicable. That's because the payoff is based on brain connections formed during repeated early experiences the person had – experiences that we are most likely not aware of. (It's also an internal payoff, making it even harder to deduce.) But the payoff *is* real. If it wasn't, those individuals wouldn't continue to seek out that kind of experience.

Reason #3: Some payoffs are <u>avoidance</u> payoffs. This means the reward is that the behavior keeps the person from experiencing something he doesn't want to experience. In this situation, the behavior may continue indefinitely – even though the behavior causes the person pain or prevents him from reaching a goal. Meanwhile, the big clue that would make the behavior easy for other people to understand never happens! The payoff is *what the person gets to avoid.*

For example, consider overeating. Clearly, there are positive-reward payoffs to eating: Food can be delicious, and a "sugar high" may temporarily lift us out of feeling depressed; in fact, many chemicals in foods have a direct effect on our mood or energy. But there are sometimes avoidance payoffs as well. For example, putting on weight may help us avoid social situations that we don't want to face by making us less stereotypically attractive to the opposite sex. This makes sense if your experiences (for example, past sexual abuse or very low self-esteem) have led you to fear attention from potential sexual partners. Similarly, married people sometimes unconsciously protect their marriage by gaining weight to make themselves less appealing to others, who might become interested and thus threaten the long-term survival of the marriage.

The irony is, people in this situation may feel terrible about their weight because of the social stigma that accompanies being perceived as unattractive. Plus, they can't understand their own behavior, so they feel out of control and anxious....*What's wrong with me? I hate being overweight, but I can't stop eating!*

Or, consider the consequences of staying in an abusive relationship. Yes, there may be a few positive payoffs, such as comfort that's received when the abusive partner isn't drunk or enraged. Or there could be a previously learned belief that abuse will be followed by love, as described earlier. But there may also be avoidance payoffs. If the person has a great fear of being alone, or a fear of having to interact with other people who might be even worse than the current abusive partner, then staying in the abusive relationship may be seen as a way to avoid even scarier situations. (As in the saying, "The devil you know is better than the devil you don't know.")

It's important to remember that these payoffs are often invisible to the person engaging in the behavior. He may have no idea what's motivating him. But even the most seemingly inexplicable behaviors are perpetuated because of a payoff.

That means that if you want to change someone's behavior, it's worth looking for the payoff, whether the behavior is your own or that of someone you're interacting with. If it's your own behavior, discovering the payoff will open the door to changing the behavior. If it's someone else's behavior, understanding it will at least make it far easier to decide what response is in everyone's best interest.

Principle 2: A second general principle of human behavior is this: **When our own behavior conflicts with something positive we believe,**

we'll often eliminate the conflict by redefining what we're doing so that it no longer conflicts with what we believe. Then, we don't have to change the behavior. As a result, some behaviors that are difficult to understand spring from intellectual compromises that people have made in order to relieve the uncomfortable feelings that arise when they do things their beliefs say they shouldn't do.

For example, someone may believe that he is a good, honest person – and then rob a bank. Obviously, that situation has the potential to create a major internal conflict. The most logical way to resolve an internal conflict like this would be to acknowledge that the belief is wrong ("Okay, I'm not really a good, honest person"), or take action to change the situation (give the money back to the bank). But the *easy* thing to do is to simply alter our perspective to eliminate the conflict. In this example, that might mean rationalizing that the bank deserved to be robbed, so you can maintain the belief that you're a good, honest person.

Another example: Suppose a man is caught up in an addiction such as cigarettes, alcohol or pornography. Realizing that he's addicted may be in direct conflict with his perception of himself as a strong, rational person who is in control of his life. One way to resolve that conflict would be to end the addiction, but that's difficult. (That's why it's called an addiction.) Many people in this situation take the easier way out and change their perspective about the addiction. They might say, "I'm not really addicted – I'm just doing this because I want to," or, "The bad things they say this will cause are vastly exaggerated." The new rationale eliminates the conflict and reduces our discomfort.

This way of dealing with things does make us feel a little better, at least in the short run. But it allows the unfortunate behavior to continue, and – perhaps worse – our future behavior then adjusts in response to the new belief. If we're rationalizing self-destructive behavior, for example, that rationalization will then remove some of our motivation to stop the behavior. After all, if you're "not really addicted," why worry about trying to stop?

This mental strategy can also be employed to reduce discomfort caused by situations that involve other people – and the resulting rationalizations can lead to harsh consequences for those other people. For example, suppose you have a comfortable life with plenty of money, and something in your life forces you to come face-to-face with the reality that many people have fewer resources and a harder life than you. That's likely to produce feelings of discomfort. You *could* look into ways that you might help to improve the lives of others, but the easiest way to deal with this is to revise your beliefs about the situation. You could decide – as many people do – that those who have less money and resources are inferior people, or have done something (or failed to do something) which therefore justifies their less fortunate situation. This new way of looking at things eliminates the discomfort of knowing you're better off. Unfortunately, it also eliminates any motivation to help those other people. In fact, it can be used to justify treating those other people with contempt or cruelty.

It's a far-too-common human tendency to make this kind of mental adjustment. It's common because it has a short-term payoff – the elimination of the internal conflict that's making us uncomfortable. But the long-term consequences can be very negative, indeed. Meanwhile, other people who are trying to understand this behavior may be at a loss to explain it, and simply conclude that the person in question is a bad person – or worse, that people in general are cruel and shortsighted.

Sometimes, however, life steps in and forces us to see beyond this kind of rationalization. During my early years in New York City, I worked at some fairly menial jobs to pay the rent so I could write and perform music the rest of the time. Probably the lowest rung of the ladder I ever occupied was Assistant Mail Boy at a huge investment brokerage firm that occupied the top floor of one of Manhattan's tallest buildings. The Mail Boy was my boss (since I was the *assistant* mail boy), and he treated me condescendingly to make sure I knew my place. My jobs involved using a machine to open letters, making Xerox copies of papers, and delivering items to different offices.

Being an aspiring writer, I occasionally read the reports that I was given to copy. One such report was quite interesting and well-written, and when I made the copies and delivered them to the office of one of the VPs of the firm, I told him I thought it was a great piece of writing.

Now, most people in a position like that barely acknowledged my existence; it was part of the accepted behavior that the "important people" didn't interact with the peons. (In fact, I took a risk by even admitting I had read the paper – some individuals might have fired me for such cheekiness.) But to my surprise, this gentleman looked up at me and said, "Really? Are you a writer? What did you like about it?" I told him that I had some experience as a writer and editor, and listed what I thought made his report exceptional.

Then, I added that it was generous of him to be interested in my opinion. In response he invited me to sit down, and told me a story about his life. At one time, he said, he had held a position of considerable influence in Washington, DC. At that time, he said, he never associated with people below a certain station in life. He saw himself as part of a different class, and liked to keep it that way. But then, everything changed. The administration he had been part of was voted out, and he suddenly found himself without a job.

Though he spent considerable time looking for a similar position elsewhere, he found nothing. After several months, his savings began to dwindle, and he became desperate to find work. One dead end after another came and went. Finally, he decided to try working as a laborer, so he got a job on the docks loading and unloading ships. For the first time, he became part of the "lower classes" that he had avoided. To his surprise, he found that the people he worked with were no different from the people he'd worked with in government – some were smart, some not so smart; some were honest and happy to share, others less so.

It was a life-changing experience, he said. He realized that seeing himself as superior to others was nonsense, and he decided never to assume someone was inferior or less competent just because they held a lower-status job. That, he said, was why he could conceive of the possibility that I might be smart and talented, despite my title of Assistant Mail Boy.

Being forced into the trenches, so to speak, changed his perspective in a way that changed his behavior towards others. The rationalization that he shouldn't mingle with the "lower classes" because they were inferior kept him from feeling guilty about his station in life. But that rationalization also held him back. When circumstances forced him to discover that his rationalization was bogus, it opened him to all kinds of possibilities and friendships in the years that followed.

Rationalizing things to minimize the discomfort we feel when our behavior or situation fly in the face of our beliefs is understandable. In fact, a recent study found that individuals who scored higher on measures of rationalizing (which gauged a person's tendency to justify or explain away inequalities) reported greater life satisfaction and well-being.[5] Similarly, looking at it from the opposite perspective, research has found that highly egalitarian women (i.e., those who might be considered "liberated women") were *less* happy in their marriages than traditionalists, because they were less willing to rationalize away the inequalities in the relationship.

This may make the idea of rationalizing your problems away sound like a great alternative. After all, who doesn't want to be happy? Unfortunately, being happier is not necessarily a good thing when it's the result of a bogus rationalization. Many dictators have been quite happy while their contempt for others allowed them to rationalize torture and slaughter. Furthermore, although contempt may lead to a less-troubled view of the world by eliminating some of our internal discord, it can have dire personal side-effects. Studies by psychologist John Gottman have shown that contempt for the partner is the factor most likely to be associated with the failure of a marriage.[6] And contempt is associated with health problems such as heart disease.[7]

In any case, it's useful for us to understand that some of the bad behavior and contempt we see around us is the result of people rationalizing things to avoid internal conflict. Knowing this eliminates some of the mystery behind contempt and bad behavior. It can also help us begin to find ways to change that behavior. Perhaps most important, it can help to keep us from falling into that trap ourselves.

Principle Three: A third general principle of human behavior is that ***people's behavior is often not based on a rational assessment of the facts.*** Although many of us like to think that human beings are generally logical and reasonable, we humans show a remarkable propensity for cherry-picking facts to justify our existing beliefs, even when those beliefs are flatly contradicted by the evidence. Humans have been willing to accept ideas that are not supported by the facts throughout history – and today is no exception. (No wonder "Don't confuse me with the facts!" is a popular ironic saying.)

The reason people are often quick to dismiss evidence that conflicts with their beliefs is that most of us are not willing to deal with the internal discord and discomfort that comes with admitting we might be wrong about something. That's why a lot of the behavior we see around us seems crazy: There's an avoidance payoff. By maintaining the behavior, we get to avoid the internal conflict and discomfort that would come with questioning it – not to mention the effort that would be required to change the behavior if we admitted it wasn't reasonable. (For more on how this particular thinking process works, see the discussion of Certainty Syndrome in the next chapter.)

So if you find yourself frustrated by people behaving in ways that make no sense, rest assured, the behavior probably does make sense.

It's most likely a reflection of an internal process that helps the person avoid feeling conflicted. Of course, that doesn't excuse bad behavior. But it does mean there's an explanation for it – and where there's an explanation, there's hope.

A Few Strategies for Managing Behavior

There's no question that understanding other people's behavior – or even your own behavior – can be challenging. Here are some strategies that may help:

Behavior Management Strategy #1: Make it a habit to think about why you're doing the things you do. It takes a little effort to stop, step back, and ask yourself what payoff you're getting for your own behavior – especially if your behavior is troubling you (or troubling someone else). Nevertheless, thinking about why you do what you do is a worthwhile use of your time, because every so often you'll be rewarded with a real insight that will alter your self-perception and dramatically increase your control over your life. In addition to making it easier to change a behavior you don't like, it may allow you to forgive yourself for things you've done that you're not proud of. Equally important, it may help you to understand other people's behavior. That will put you in a far better position to get the things you need from them.

Behavior Management Strategy #2: Treat behavior as separate from the person. One reason people judge each other so readily is that they fail to separate behaviors they don't like from the person exhibiting the behavior. That backfires, because it's much easier to get to the root of a problem if you focus on the behavior, *not* on the person. Behavior can always be changed (although it may require some time and effort), while the person is pretty much stuck as he is, take it or leave it.

Furthermore, your odds of changing someone else's behavior shrink dramatically once you've judged him. Passing judgment places the other person into a category in your mind, and that effectively eliminates your need to actually understand what caused the behavior. The kind of mental categories we put people into ("that person is just a bad person;" "that person is stupid;" "that person is a communist pinko faggot;" etc.) come with their own pre-decided characteristics. They allow us to react automatically to the person we've categorized without having to make any further effort. It's a mental process that saves us time and effort, which is why we use it. Unfortunately, it leads directly to misunderstandings, dismissing others, trying to change behavior exclusively by using punishment, and a host of other negative side effects. Judging *behavior*, however, has far fewer damaging side effects than judging a person.

In any case, the reality is that these kinds of mental categories don't tell us anything about the person we're judging – or the behavior we don't like. People don't do bad things because they're malicious, perverted or stupid. They do them because they get a payoff of some kind, whether it's internal or external, positive or avoidance-based. Dismissing a person by judging him and labeling him blinds you to the real cause of his behavior and thus makes you powerless to change it. If you judge a person's *behavior* instead of judging him – assuming you feel compelled to pass judgment at all – you'll at least keep the focus on the thing that matters.

Behavior Management Strategy #3: Avoid basing your actions on your initial emotional response to behavior you don't like. There's nothing wrong with having an initial judgmental reaction to a person or to their behavior. The important thing is to avoid *acting* on the basis of that judgment. Cool off, then as much as possible choose your actions on the basis of non-judgmental observation and analysis of what may be causing the behavior. Try to do what's fair, and most importantly, try to do what might realistically change the situation for the better.

Behavior Management Strategy #4: Be wary of "making a deal" with the other person to get their behavior to change – i.e., "you should change your behavior to make me happy" or "you should change your behavior because you know it's the right thing to do." Trying to get someone to change as a favor to you – or to prove they love you, or because they owe you, or because they should do so out of respect for you – is a recipe for disaster. What you're doing is setting up an equation in the other person's mind. The equation says: "I'm making an effort to change, but *only because I'm getting something worthwhile in return* (love, payment of a debt, the knowledge that I'm a respectful person, etc.)."

Setting up this kind of "equation" may get the person to change for a while. The problem is, the equation you've set up can be rewritten in a heartbeat. As soon as the new situation becomes uncomfortable for the other person, all he has to do is downgrade the value of what he's getting in exchange for his new behavior, and *voila,* he has the justification to go back to what he was doing before he made the "deal."

For example, when I was single and living in New York City, I met a young woman who decided I was somebody she wanted to date, and I was interested in dating her, too. However, she was a cigarette smoker, and she felt that because I was a non-smoker I wouldn't want to kiss her or hang out with her. So, she decided to give up smoking "for me." (I didn't ask her to do that, but the equation was set up, just the same.) The equation was: "I'll give up my addition to nicotine in order to get affection from this person."

That bargain held up for a while. However, nicotine addiction is not a small thing, and I'm sure resisting it caused her a lot of grief. Lo and behold, as soon as the relationship began to seem less than perfect, she began to downgrade it, which allowed her to eventually justify returning to smoking. Yes, the relationship probably wouldn't have worked out in the long run anyway, but its demise was hastened as a result of her setting up an equation that connected her giving up smoking to the perceived value of dating me.

Undoubtedly, many relationships have failed for exactly this kind of reason; someone decides to change – or one person asks the other to change – "for the relationship." Later, when the new situation becomes too painful, the value of the relationship is downgraded to justify the person's return to the original behavior.

The moral of the story is to be very careful about asking someone to change "for you" or for other supposed payoffs. The payoff you're offering may end up being downgraded in order to justify a return to the behavior you asked the person to change. (And remember – this applies to you as well. Be careful about agreeing to change your own behavior "for someone else." You're putting yourself in the same position, and potentially putting the relationship in future peril.)

Behavior Management Strategy #5: Remember that understanding behavior doesn't always make you able to change it. As noted earlier, physical changes in the brain take place when behavior has gone on for a long time, and those changes take time to reverse. Also, the payoffs for the behavior may be very powerful, or the behavior may be an offshoot of a deeply-held belief. Understanding the reason for the behavior, therefore, may not be sufficient to help you change it quickly.

However, it's still worth trying to understand it. In many situations, you *will* be able to change the behavior. And even if you can't change the behavior in question right away, understanding the reasons for it will work in your favor. Just don't lose sight of the fact that understanding the behavior is a separate thing from changing it.

Behavior Management Strategy #6: If you're determined to try and change behavior, first ask the following four questions. If you really do need to change someone's behavior, knowing the answer to these four questions will give you your best shot:

1) *What's the payoff for the behavior?* As noted earlier, this can be tricky because the payoff may be internal, and it may be about avoiding something. But if you find the payoff, you'll know what's been driving the behavior.

2) *How long has the behavior been going on?* This is important because it will give you a sense of how much the brain has changed to "engrain" the behavior. Generally, the longer a behavior has been going on, the more time and effort will be required to change it. (There are exceptions to this; sometimes an extreme change in a situation will cause a sudden change in long-term behavior. But trying to trigger a change of that magnitude by yourself can have drastic, unforeseen consequences.)

3) *Is the behavior physically addictive?* Changing behavior connected to a physical addiction requires a very high level of effort and expertise. When a physical addiction is involved, changing the behavior will almost certainly require professional assistance.

4) *Is the behavior the result of a deep-set belief?* If it is, the behavior is unlikely to change until the belief changes – and people's deep-set beliefs can be extremely difficult to change. Usually, if they change at all, they will follow the SEICR cycle described in Chapter 1. That means they won't change unless a long series of developments and problems related to the belief occur over a period of time, resulting in a collapse of the belief system.

So, if the behavior you'd like to change is the result of a deep-seated belief system, you're wise to skip trying to change it and find some other way to deal with the behavior. It's very unlikely that you'll be able to change it single-handedly.

Behavior Management Strategy #7: Take advantage of the many resources that are designed to help you understand behavior and/or

change it. Read a few of the many books written about these topics. Talk to friends who have insight into behavior. If your own behavior is at issue, try talking to a psychologist or social worker.

The reality is that we human beings desperately need to stop judging each other – and stop judging ourselves – and start trying to understand our behavior instead. Thanks to the technology at our disposal today, any one of us can easily do something that will affect millions of other people, for better or worse. That makes the need for this kind of understanding greater than ever.

So, make the effort to understand behavior. Doing so will not only benefit you and give you greater control over your own life, it will also help our entire planet move in a direction that just might save us all one day.

❋ ❋ ❋

Once more, in brief:

Here are the key points to remember from Chapter 8:

- Making the effort to understand behavior has multiple benefits:
– It gives you a fighting chance to change it;
– It can provide real motivation for change;
– It makes it much easier to get what you need from other people;
– It minimizes the temptation to judge others;
– It lets you know whether trying to change the behavior is a waste of time;
– It can reduce your anxiety and frustration;
– It helps you understand your own behavior better;
– It draws other people to you as "someone who has a clue."

- Using punishment to try and change someone's behavior has many serious drawbacks. For example:
1) It's most effective when it happens immediately after the behavior, which is rarely possible.
2) Punishment encourages the person who is punished to avoid the

punisher instead of changing the behavior.

3) The meaning of punishment is in the eye of the beholder. You may see it as just, but the person being punished may see it differently, leading to anger and retaliation.

4) Delivering punishment is unpleasant for most people, so it tends to be put off until things get out of hand.

5) Punishment sends the message that punishment in general is an appropriate way to try to change someone else's behavior. That can lead to unfortunate consequences later on.

6) Punishment can have very negative long-term consequences for the person who is punished – especially when that person is a child.

• Whatever behavior people engage in, they're getting a payoff or they wouldn't be doing it. The payoff can be nearly invisible in some cases, because it may be internal, or the payoff may simply be avoiding something. Even the person exhibiting the behavior may have no conscious awareness of what the payoff is – or even realize that there *is* a payoff.

• When our own behavior conflicts with something positive we believe, we'll often eliminate the conflict by redefining what we're doing so we don't have to change the behavior. This can have very negative consequences for us and those around us.

• People's behavior is often not based on a rational assessment of the facts; we tend to cherry-pick the evidence we acknowledge as legitimate in order to support whatever we already believe.

A few suggestions:

• Make it a habit to think about why you're doing the things you do.

• Treat behavior as separate from the person.

• If you have an emotional reaction to behavior you don't like, don't use those emotions as the basis for choosing what you do in response.

• Be wary of making a deal in which you change your behavior in exchange for a payoff (or ask the other person to change his behavior in exchange for a payoff). Making this kind of "deal" can backfire big-time.

- Remember that understanding behavior won't always make you able to change it – but trying to understand it is still worth the effort.

- If you need to change behavior, ask four questions:
1) What is the payoff?
2) How long has the behavior been going on?
3) Is a physical addiction involved?
4) Is the behavior the result of a deeply held belief? The answers to these questions will help you determine what might change the behavior – and whether it's even *possible* to change it in the short run.

- Use the resources that are out there to help you understand and change the unwanted behavior.

❋ ❋ ❋

NOTES for Chapter 8

1. For lots of helpful information about this, check out *The Brain The Changes Itself* by Norman Doige, MD.
2. Main M, George C. Responses of Abused and Disadvantaged Toddlers to Distress in the Day Care Setting. *Developmental Psychology* 1985:21;407-412.
3. For example, see studies conducted by Murray A. Straus, Professor of Sociology and Co-Director Family Research Laboratory University of New Hampshire. (After two decades of research, Straus has found that children who are spanked are two to six times more likely to be physically aggressive, to become juvenile delinquents, and later, as adults, to suffer from depression. A list of his studies on this topic can be found at http://pubpages.unh.edu/~mas2/CP-Empirical.htm.) Also see Berlin, L.J et al. Correlates and Consequences of Spanking and Verbal Punishment for Low Income White, African American, and Mexican American Toddlers. *Child Development*, Sept-Oct, 2009;80:5:1403-1420.
4. Afifi TO, Mota NP, Dasiewicz P, MacMillan HL, Sareen J. Physical punishment and mental disorders: results from a nationally representative US sample. Pediatrics 2012:130:2:184-92.
5. Napier JL., Jost JT. Why are conservatives happier than liberals? *Psychological Science* 2008:19;565-572.
6. For example, see *Why Marriages Succeed or Fail (and how you can make yours last)*. John Gottman, PhD. Simon & Schuster, 1994.
7. For more on this, see the work (books and articles) of Redford Williams, MD, at Duke University.

9.
Let Go of Certainty.

Remain flexible: Assume that everything you have accepted as a "fact" – scientific, religious, or otherwise – is at least partly wrong. And keep asking questions.

"A new scientific truth does not triumph by convincing its opponents and making them see the light, but rather because its opponents eventually die, and a new generation grows up that is familiar with it."
  – Max Plank, Physicist

"It infuriates me to be wrong when I know I'm right."
  – Moliere

"When the facts change, I change my mind. What do you do, sir?"
  – John Maynard Keynes

If there's one thing people hate, it's uncertainty. Uncertainty makes people uncomfortable, and most of us will go to pretty great lengths to avoid being uncomfortable. That may be the reason that human beings have always behaved as if their current state of knowledge is the final truth. If it seems to work and the people we care about agree with it, what's to doubt? Heck, even if the people around us don't agree with us, who cares what they think?

Ironically, any study of history reveals that the ideas we accept as the ultimate truth are inevitably replaced at some later time. In fact, it's just about impossible to find anything that has been accepted as "absolute fact" at some point in history that didn't turn out to be at least partly wrong. The sheer scope of erroneous beliefs that were considered indisputable fact for thousands of years (the Earth is at the center of the universe, heavy objects always fall faster than light objects, etc.) makes it hard to believe that anyone can still think we've reached the final understanding in any area.

Sometimes a set of ideas really does hold up over the centuries, but then turns out to be true only as long as you stay in one framework or set of conditions. Isaac Newtown's laws of physics were considered pretty much indisputable for more than 200 years, but it turns out his laws only apply as long as you're dealing with ordinary day-to-day experience. If you start dealing with incredibly high speeds, tiny sizes or intense gravity, his rules don't work any more, as Einstein deduced.

Occasionally a scientist will claim that our current understanding is the top of the knowledge ladder – insisting that it's impossible to travel faster than the speed of light because the laws of relativity say so, for example – but I think most scientists realize that today's indisputable fact is likely to be replaced or revised eventually. Many top scientists in the past expressed certainty about "facts" that turned out not to deserve certainty after all – such as Lord William Thompson Kelvin, the physicist who (among other things) contributed to our ability to measure temperature. (The Kelvin temperature scale is named after him.) He is reputed to have declared that heavier-than-air flying machines were impossible. Back in his day, very few people would have disagreed with him.

Religious beliefs can be even more difficult to challenge. That's because many religions claim that their information comes from a higher source and must therefore be accepted as the ultimate, indisputable truth. I'm not an authority on all of the world's religions, but I do know that if you study the historical development of most religions over the centuries you find changes in the interpretation of each religion's key ideas over time – and sometimes major editing of whatever book lies at the center of that religion. Pretending that this has not happened, or claiming that the "literal" interpretation of one generation is exactly the same as the "literal" interpretation of the next generation, does a disservice to the universal truths that those religions contain.

There are countless things that people become certain about over the course of their lives, ranging from the meaning of current events to who said what during a recent argument. Having certainty about something that happened while you were present certainly seems

Chapter 9: Let Go of Certainty

justifiable, but there's plenty of evidence that even that type of certainty may not be realistic. Many studies have shown that human memory is highly fallible.

An excellent example of this comes from a study conducted in the late 1980s by Ulric Neisser, a professor of psychology at Emory University.[1] In an attempt to evaluate the accuracy of "flashbulb" memories – memories of extremely unusual or emotional events – Neisser had students write a detailed account of how they heard the news about the Challenger space shuttle explosion that occurred on January 28, 1986. (This was a major national event, predisposing people to recall it for years afterwards.) Their accounts were written the morning after the event, when everything that happened was still fresh in their minds.

Two and a half years later, he interviewed the students again about how they heard about the shuttle explosion. He discovered that what people recalled was, in most cases, very different from what they had written down the day after the event. In fact, one quarter of the students recalled scenarios that were *completely* different from what they had written down the day after the event, and half of the students' stories only agreed with the earlier description in a few details. Fewer than 10% of the students told almost the exact same story they had written down the day after the tragedy – and even among those students, no one's story agreed with the original report in every single detail.

The study authors then showed the students their own handwritten accounts, created the day after the event. How did the students react? Seeing what they'd written, in their own handwriting, you might expect them to have said, "Oh that's right – now I remember." That's not what happened. Instead, most said they still believed their current recollection of those events was correct! They had certainty about their recollection, *even in the face of indisputable evidence to the contrary, written in their own handwriting.* Like certainty about most things, certainty about memories is a questionable premise.

Given that the feeling of certainty can lead people to overrule indisputable evidence, can we really be sure that we know the final truth about anything? Obviously, some "facts" can easily be checked: the number of days in a year, the number of United States presidents, and so forth. But once you go beyond that type of easily checked information, you can make a pretty good argument that the answer is no. Absolute certainty about anything – including events that happened to us in the past – is seldom justifiable.

"So what?" you may ask. Perhaps some of the things we have certainty about are not actually true, or are only partly correct. What does that have to do with staying off the Wheel of Misfortune?

Actually, it has everything to do with it, because certainty – whether it's certainty about our recollection of an event, or certainty about what we believe to be true in science or politics or religion or anything else – brings with it a host of drawbacks. Of course, I'm not talking about being "fairly certain" about something; I'm talking about being absolutely sure that you're right, with no room for debate. As we will see shortly, that kind of certainty can act as a major roadblock to our success, trapping us in dead-end situations, depriving us of support from others and preventing us from learning the very things that would allow us to overcome the obstacles we face.

Certainty that you're right about something is a very comfortable feeling, but during hard times it's one of the greatest disadvantages you can burden yourself with. In contrast, letting go of certainty – assuming that what you believe to be a fact could turn out to be at least partly wrong – sidesteps the problems created by certainty and dramatically increases your chances of staying off the Wheel of Misfortune.

Certainty: It's Not What You Think

Most of us assume that certainty is the end result of a logical thought process; in other words, that we evaluate the evidence and when we're sure that our conclusions are correct, we feel certainty. As it turns out, that's not what's actually happening when we experience the feeling of certainty. Instead, certainty is a type of internal feedback the mind/brain uses to help us manage our thinking. Certainty is a feeling that we have in response to a thought, much like the feeling of familiarity or strangeness. Brain scans have shown that the feeling of certainty doesn't even originate from the reasoning centers of the brain. In fact, it can be evoked by electrical stimulation of the brain, without any thoughts being involved at all.

If the feeling of certainty is not the endpoint of a logical thought process, then why do we experience it? It turns out that it serves a number of purposes. In terms of mental processes, certainty does at least three things for us. First of all, the feeling of certainty provides us with internal feedback that confirms that a connection we've made or a conclusion we've drawn agrees with our previous experience of what is correct. When we answer a question and the feeling of certainty comes along with our answer, it reassures us that we're on the right track. In a way, it's a shortcut our brains use to save us from having to sift through our past memories and experiences to consciously confirm that we're right.

If the feeling of certainty is missing when we answer a question, our answer may still be correct, but the absence of the feeling will affect our confidence and our willingness to stake a lot on our answer. (When a game show contestant answers a question, for example, it's usually not hard to tell whether he has the feeling of certainty about his answer.) This can happen when we have a "hunch" about something or a strong impulse; our brain may have come to an accurate conclusion about whatever is happening, but because our brain came to the conclusion outside of normal consciousness, the feeling of certainty may be missing. *(For more on this type of thinking, see Chapter 6.)* As a result, we may be unsure whether or not to trust the hunch or impulse. That's one reason learning to work with intuitive information such as hunches can be challenging: The information we receive is often correct, but without the feeling of certainty it's not always easy to know whether the hunch is real intuitive information or meaningless noise.

A more offbeat example of being correct without the confirming feeling of certainty is "blindsight," a phenomenon in which certain functionally blind individuals are able to identify the location of a visual event such as a flashing light despite having no awareness of seeing the light. The person doesn't "see" the light in the usual way because the signal coming from the eyes is not reaching the visual cortex. Nevertheless, the person can still identify the location of the light because other parts of the brain are picking up on the signal from the eyes and are able to interpret it. A person using blindsight will usually deny that he knows where the flashing light is, even though he correctly identifies its location. He denies it because he's not experiencing the *feeling of certainty* that he would have when confirming a normal visual experience. Without that feeling, the person simply can't accept that he's right about the location of the light – even though he is.

The feeling of certainty is incorporated into many of our mental processes. For example, it's part of the internal process that good spellers use. When a good speller is asked to spell a word, he or she sees a mental image of the word and then has a feeling about what he sees. If the feeling the image evokes is the "certainty" feeling, he knows the image in his mind is consistent with his previous experience and is therefore probably correct. People who use other internal processes when trying to spell a word – such as basing the spelling on the way the word sounds – tend to be poor spellers. (For a more detailed discussion of how the internal process of spelling works, check out the book *Frogs Into Princes: Neurolinguistic Programming*, by Richard Bandler and John Grinder.)[2]

When the feeling of certainty is present, we usually assume we're correct, whether the evidence supports that conclusion or not. (Remember the story of the students who were certain their memories of what happened to them on the day of the Challenger disaster were correct, even though their recollection contradicted what they themselves had written at the time.) The feeling of certainty reassures us that our thinking is accurate, and that's a very useful mental function. Unfortunately, it is *not* proof that we really are correct.

A second way that certainty helps our mental functioning is by giving us an indication that we've reached the end of a line of thought. When we think something through, such as trying to recall a location or trying to solve a problem, we stop when we have the feeling of certainty in response to our conclusions. For example, if we're trying to remember someone's name and a name pops into our head, but it's *not* accompanied by that feeling of certainty, we're likely to assume we haven't found the correct answer yet and keep trying to think of another name. Without that bit of feedback – the feeling of certainty – the process of mentally searching for the solution to a problem could go on endlessly.

A third way the feeling of certainty helps us is by rewarding us for making progress when we're working on a problem and it's taking a long time. When we're puzzling over a question or trying to make headway on a project, we need a reward from time to time to keep us from becoming frustrated and giving up pursuing the problem. An occasional "Yes, I got it!" feeling of certainty provides us with a little reward; it keeps us interested and feeling that we're making progress. It helps motivate us to keep going. By doing that, the occasional feeling of certainty helps us accomplish many things that we might otherwise never complete.

By serving these three mental functions – reassuring us that we're right about something, telling us that we've reached the end of a line of thought, and providing a little mental reward from time to time to keep us going when we're working on a problem – certainty helps us evaluate the world around us, make decisions and solve problems. It's a mental tool that most of us rely on.

When a Mental Strategy Becomes a Belief

At some point, however, many of us come to believe that certainty is something very different from a simple feeling that helps us to think clearly. Instead, *we assume it's a sign that our thinking is absolutely correct and not subject to revision or debate*. Unfortunately, the feeling of certainty is not a sign that we are correct. The fact that it *feels* that way helps our thinking process work effectively, but when we assume that our feeling of certainty is a guarantee that our beliefs or conclusions are correct, we start veering into potentially dangerous territory. That assumption triggers a long list of negative consequences.[3]

One important note: *The issue here is not whether you are actually correct.* The beliefs or conclusions that you're certain are true may very well be correct. But if you don't realize that certainty is not a *guarantee* of accuracy, you're putting yourself and those around you at a major disadvantage, because certainty closes down an open mind. And, it can make a person very self-righteous. It's certainty that leads people to say things like, "I know for a fact that so-and-so caused all of my problems." Or, "My religion is the word of God and is literally true, and if you don't agree, you're going to hell." Or, "This scientific finding is the final word on this, and the only reason you disagree is because you don't know what you're talking about." Or, "That group of people is inferior (or sinful, or dangerous, or stupid); it's just a fact, and if you don't see it, that's your problem." Or, "Everyone who disagrees with me is dangerous and a threat to me, so I have to prepare for the worst and not trust anyone." A closed mind can't see evidence that contradicts what it already believes.

Even if the idea we're certain about is actually correct, things change over time – and certainty can cause us to miss those changes, leaving us stuck with outdated ideas that we're still certain are true. If the world changes and we don't, the odds of landing on the Wheel of Misfortune skyrocket. People who are certain about their beliefs often charge fearlessly ahead based on "facts" that are no longer accurate (or in some cases never were). As a result, they encounter obstacles and setbacks they could have avoided, leaving them a long way from where they want to be. If we understand that certainty is not a guarantee of accuracy, we're more likely to notice when we're on dangerous ground and proceed more carefully and thoughtfully.

It's true that some consequences of absolute certainty can be beneficial.

At a psychological level, having certainty about what we think or believe provides us with stability. Once we feel certain about something, we don't need to think further about it and we can turn our attention to other matters. We don't have to work so hard at being observant, and we don't have to change in response to new information. And sometimes, being certain that we're right can help us to take action by giving us confidence about our choices. In contrast, living with uncertainty can be very uncomfortable.

Unfortunately, this one potential advantage of certainty is offset by the simple reality that *we may not be right!* If that's the case, taking bold action based on our feeling of certainty can have very unfortunate consequences.

It's worth noting that the tendency to insist on certainty may in some cases be connected to mindset, the phenomenon discussed in Chapter 2. When a person is in the "fixed mindset" mode, much of that person's energy goes into defending his or her current position in life because the possibility of changing doesn't seem real. The connection to certainty comes in because one way to defend your current position is to *refuse to admit any possibility of being wrong about your current ideas*. So changing from the fixed mindset to the growth mindset can remove some of the temptation to rely on certainty, and thus help the individual by making him far more open to new evidence and learning.

The Perils and Pitfalls of Certainty Syndrome

When people become determined that their understanding of something is the final, ultimate truth, they suffer from what I call *certainty syndrome*. Certainty syndrome puts us at a huge disadvantage by changing the way we interpret what's going on around us, as well as changing the way we interact with others and the choices we make.

Here are 14 good reasons to avoid certainty syndrome:

1. **Certainty stops learning**. People who are certain they possess the truth about something stop responding to new information in that area of their life.

2. **Certainty eliminates flexibility.** Being certain causes people to continue outmoded behavior, even though the situation around them has changed.

3. **Certainty leads to poor choices.** Choices based on certainty are not based on an accurate assessment of what's happening.

Chapter 9: Let Go of Certainty

4. ***Certainty makes people [inappropriately - LYNN] judgmental.*** People with certainty syndrome tend to negatively judge everyone who doesn't agree with them, pushing away potential friends and allies.

5. ***Certainty is contagious.*** Insisting on the infallibility of your own beliefs gives credence to the idea that certainty is a valid basis for action; that, in turn, reinforces that belief in others – who may be acting on the basis of certainty about very destructive ideas.

6. ***Certainty eliminates your ability to sway others.*** People with certainty syndrome are seldom able to change other people's behavior or opinion on that topic, either by force or by argument.

7. ***Certainty undercuts problem-solving.*** People with certainty syndrome are very bad at solving problems because they see things in black and white – especially by dividing the world into "those who agree with me and those who don't."

8. ***Certainty encourages fear and anger – which then encourage even more certainty.*** Because people with certainty divide the world into "those who agree with me and those who don't," their world view supports being angry and fearful of those who don't agree with them. They then reinforce their certainty in order to justify the fear and anger.

9. ***Certainty justifies abuse.*** Despite coming up with less-than-ideal solutions to problems, people who have total certainty feel justified in forcing their "solutions" on everybody, because they're certain they're right!

10. ***Certainty makes people overlook consequences.*** People who believe they have a lock on the truth stop paying attention to the consequences of their actions.

11. ***Certainty becomes ingrained.*** Certainty is a mental pattern that's very resistant to change and can therefore last a lifetime.

12. ***Certainty causes people to accept bogus supporting "evidence" without questioning it.*** This allows others to spread false ideas and "facts" that support their cause, knowing that those who have certainty will accept their "facts" without careful examination.

13. ***Group certainty is even more problematic.*** Certainty becomes even more entrenched when shared by a group, leading to additional disadvantages and dangers.

And, perhaps most ironically:

14. ***Certainty makes it easy for others to manipulate you.*** People who are certain that they know "the truth" are more easily controlled

(especially when they're part of a group that shares their certainty).

Let's consider each of these points in more detail.

Problem #1: Certainty stops learning. People who are certain they possess the truth about something stop responding to new information in that area of their lives.

Human beings are often willing to trust the feeling of certainty more than evidence that their understanding is wrong – no matter how persuasive and undeniable the evidence is. People with certainty syndrome simply dismiss or ignore evidence that they're wrong – just as the students dismissed the very persuasive evidence that their recollections about the Challenger disaster were wrong. And if people with certainty syndrome can't dismiss or ignore evidence that they're wrong, they'll invent a reason to claim the evidence isn't valid.

Unfortunately, once we begin to dismiss new experiences and evidence simply because they conflict with the thing we have certainty about, we stop learning. Certainty can blind us to important information that's right in front of us. After all, if you already believe you have the final word on something, why would you need to hear anything else? Hence the popular saying, "Don't confuse me with the facts!" In reality, *the surest way to become blind to the truth is to believe that you already possess it.*

Certainty may actually derail us from using the brain centers that we would normally use to analyze information. A 2004 study by psychologist Drew Westen at Emory University found that when politically partisan subjects were presented with negative information about the political candidate they favored, brain activity largely occurred in the limbic system (associated with emotion and the fight-or-flight response), not in the frontal cortex where logical thinking takes place.[4] No wonder evidence is easily discarded when certainty is present; it appears that contradictory evidence simply evokes a negative emotional response instead of a careful evaluation of the facts.

Again, the real question here is not whether you're right or wrong about what you believe to be true. The question is: *Are you open to new information?* If you've decided that your current knowledge is final, then no, you're not. You will not learn from new experience in that area. And when you're trying to stay off the Wheel of Misfortune, that will put you at a huge disadvantage.

That's why, regardless of whether you are certain about your current beliefs regarding God, or science, or people, or morality or anything

Consequences of Certainty Syndrome

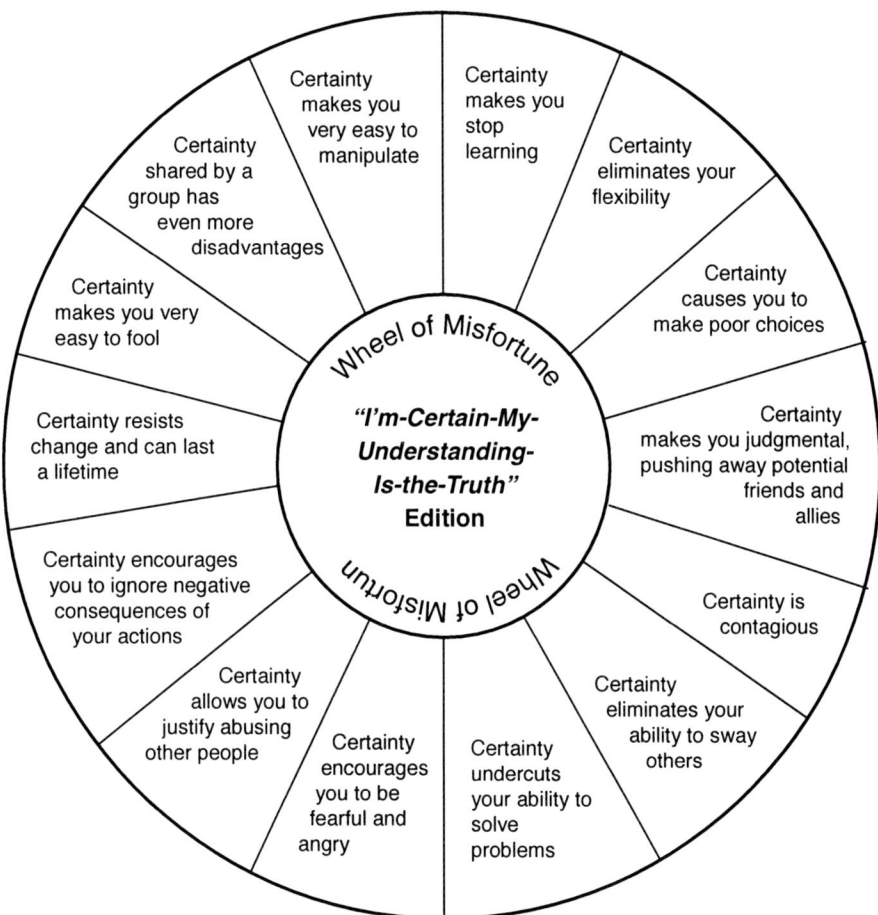

else, it's wise to act as though your ideas might possibly be *slightly* mistaken. If you act as though your world view is a belief, not a fact – even when it's based on overwhelming evidence – then, when new evidence contradicts what you thought was true, you can evaluate it with reason instead of denial. Perhaps that new input will lead you to conclude that your idea of the truth needs a little revision. If so, that revision might make it possible for you to get out of a bad situation and get much closer to achieving your goals.

Problem #2: Certainty eliminates flexibility. Being certain causes people to continue outmoded behavior even though the situation around them has changed.

The feeling of certainty is flexibility's worst enemy. When times are good, being flexible – able to change your actions when your circumstances change – doesn't matter as much, because you've got a comfortable situation. If you're wrong about something, and your certainty makes you inflexible, it may not sink your boat.

However, when times get tough, that changes. Being able to adapt to tumultuous circumstances is essential to surviving when you're in the middle of a crisis. Even more important, being able to *learn* in a new situation is critical – and as we've already discussed, people who have certainty about something stop learning in that area, even if learning might save their life.

It should be no surprise that when people look back on crises and hard times that happened earlier in their lives, they often realize that the best thing that came out of the experience was discovering that something they believed to be immutable fact wasn't accurate after all; it wasn't serving them well, and needed to be revised. That's why when you feel like you're on the Wheel of Misfortune it's an especially good idea to act as if everything you have accepted as a "fact" is at least partly wrong. Being willing to question your own certainty might save your life.

Problem #3: Certainty leads to poor choices. Choices based on certainty are not based on an accurate assessment of what's happening.

In the last decades of the past century, psychologist Philip E. Tetlock conducted a study of nearly 300 individuals who made their living as public media figures.[5] These people earned their pay as pundits, commenting on political or economic trends. He had noted that in the past no one actually bothered to check to see how accurate the predictions made by these individuals were. After doing a small-scale study in which a handful of such commentators did miserably, he decided it was important to see how well a larger group of these people did over a longer stretch of time – and if some were better at making predictions than others, to try and figure out why.

His study found that most of the media pundits did *worse than random guessing* would have done. In other words, although touted for their political and economic savvy, they weren't as accurate as, say, a chimp throwing darts at a board. Even more startling, the pundits who were the best known and most popular did the worst.

However, the commentators were not all equally bad at making predictions. Because Tetlock had gathered a lot of background data about the people he included in the study, he used that data to look for correlations that might explain the more accurate predictions. Did the person's political ideology affect their accuracy? No. Did their experience or expertise make a difference? No. It turned out that what *did* make a difference was the way they *thought* – in particular, their level of certainty.

The pundits with certainty syndrome furiously and confidently defended their ideas while dismissing evidence that failed to support their conclusions. (They also were masters of rationalizing away their bad predictions after the fact.) In contrast, the few commentators who did better at predicting the future were skeptical of assuming too much and listened to a broad variety of ideas and evidence. They rarely ruled out anything as being impossible. Their willingness to acknowledge that they might be wrong allowed them to avoid the kind of mistakes the others made.

Those who made the least accurate predictions were also the slowest to revise the ideas that had led them to make their failed predictions – another symptom of certainty syndrome. In contrast, those who made better predictions often pointed out evidence that seemed to contradict their own ideas. As Professor Tetlock says, they were more willing to entertain "self-subversive scenarios." And they were reluctant to make extreme predictions, which are easy to make when you're certain you're right. As Tetlock notes, the group that did better at predictions about the future had a "more balanced" style of thinking – "a style of thought that elevates no thought above criticism."

Interestingly, another key characteristic of those pundits who did better was that they *thought about how they were thinking*. In other words, they paid attention to their analytical reasoning process; if they caught themselves drawing a conclusion that seemed questionable, they stopped and reconsidered. The others were so certain of their ideas and ideologies that they ignored any mental, internal warnings that something about their reasoning didn't make sense.

Sadly, as already noted, the pundits who exhibited the most symptoms of certainty syndrome were the most popular media figures. As Tetlock notes, the same style of reasoning that impairs the good judgment of so-called experts seems to boost their attractiveness to the mass market. Apparently, the people who listen to these pundits want to believe the world is straightforward; they shy away from listening to people who are willing to admit they don't know everything. Certainty on the part of people in the media seems to make their listeners comfortable, perhaps because it reinforces the listeners' own certainty – even though it means that the pundit is giving them worse advice about the future.

Problem #4: Certainty makes people judgmental. People with certainty syndrome tend to negatively judge everyone who doesn't agree with them, pushing away potential friends and allies.

Many years ago I worked with a fellow who had a very mechanistic view of health; in essence, he believed that the human body is a biological machine, and if it gets sick, it just means something in the machine has broken and needs to be fixed. Of course, there's plenty of evidence that much more is involved in maintaining or losing health, particularly in terms of a mind-body connection – i.e., what goes on in our thoughts can have a powerful effect on our health. But my coworker would have none of it. He gave stern lectures on how everyone should be eating and behaving, and when most of us didn't live according to his dictates, he lowered his opinion of us. I often heard him make disparaging remarks about others, describing them as either lazy or lacking in intelligence because they disagreed with his idea of "the facts about health."

Most of us have known someone like this, who lectures everyone about his or her understanding of things, with absolute certainty that his ideas are correct and anyone who disagrees is a fool. Unless you happen to be in total agreement with the person, it can be a real turn-off. That's why the tendency to judge others that comes along with certainty syndrome leads to alienating many of those around you – not a good thing if you're trying to stay off the Wheel of Misfortune.

Problem #5: Certainty is contagious. Insisting on the infallibility of your own beliefs gives credence to the idea that certainty is a valid basis for action; that, in turn, reinforces that belief in others – who may be acting on the basis of certainty about very destructive ideas.

Plenty of people get frustrated when a political or religious fanatic causes death and destruction and justifies it with his certainty. But it doesn't occur to most of us that a big part of the problem is the culturally accepted underlying idea that *personal certainty means you're right.* (It doesn't occur to most of us because we're used to depending on our *own* certainty.) In fact, if we were taught that "facts" are *always* open to scrutiny – *no exceptions* – and that personal certainty has nothing to do with a guarantee of being correct, people would be far less likely to use their feeling of certainty to justify death and destruction.

This is equally true for science. As author Robert Burton has noted, many of those who put their faith in science are frustrated when a scientific premise such as Darwin's theory of evolution is attacked by others simply because those others are *certain* that Darwin can't be right, rather than because of conflicting scientific evidence. But scientists can undermine their own argument if they insist on certainty about what science says at any given time. To the extent that science is an accurate representation of "the truth," it's because of the weight of the evidence – not because a group of scientists have certainty about it. And it makes a far stronger argument to present it in those terms.

In fact, one of the criteria for an acceptable scientific theory is that *it must be disprovable*. If there's no way to disprove it, then there's no way to test it. As Steven Jay Gould has said, "In science, 'fact' can only mean [something has been] confirmed to such a degree that it would be perverse to withhold provisional assent." In other words, the label "scientific fact" should only be given to ideas that are supported by so much evidence that it doesn't make sense to disagree with them. Certainty should have nothing to do with it.

So, one of the ways that clinging to our own certainty works against us is by supporting the underlying idea that certainty equals truth. Spreading that idea encourages others to justify all kinds of bad things.

The solution? Assume that everything you have accepted as a "fact" – scientific, religious, or otherwise – will eventually turn out to be at least partly wrong. If you make this assumption, you won't use certainty to justify your own actions, and those around you won't be encouraged to go down that road.

At a practical level, one of the best ways to make this alternate assumption real for yourself and others is to substitute the word "believe" for the word "know," whether you're talking about religion, science or anything else. Robert Burton puts it nicely: "Substituting 'believe' for 'know' doesn't negate scientific knowledge [for example]; it only shifts a hard-earned fact from being unequivocal to being highly likely.... It is in the leap from 99.99999% likely to a 100% certain guarantee that we give up tolerance for conflicting opinions, and provide the basis for [other people's] claim to pure and certain knowledge."[6]

Problem #6: Certainty eliminates your ability to sway others. People with certainty syndrome are seldom able to change other people's behavior or opinion on that topic, either by argument or by force.

This is true for three reasons. First, people with certainty syndrome can't fathom the reasons for people disagreeing with their ideas about what's "right" (except to conclude that the person in question is ignorant or evil). That's a problem, because if you can't understand the reason someone disagrees with you, you'll never be able to change his mind.

Second, people who suffer from certainty syndrome tend to *judge* others who disagree with them, which pushes them away. Once people sense that you're judging them from a position of righteous certainty, or simply have no respect for them or their opinion, the odds of your being able to change their opinion or behavior drop to near zero.

The third reason people with certainty syndrome lose the ability to sway others is that arguments based on seeing things in black and white are totally unconvincing. Yes, people who already agree with you will be happy to know you share their conviction, but those who disagree are likely to be appalled and completely turned off. The insistence that "my viewpoint is inarguably correct" convinces the people who disagree with you that you're closed-minded and not worth listening to. In contrast, if you make it clear that your opinion is based on good evidence but is flexible, most people will listen to you with an open mind. That will make it possible for you to influence their opinion.

Problem #7: Certainty undercuts problem-solving. People with certainty syndrome are very bad at solving problems because they see things in black and white – especially by dividing the world into "those who agree with me and those who don't."

The thinking goes like this: "If I'm absolutely right about what I believe and you disagree with me, then you are absolutely wrong. And if I have certainty about my system of ethics or my religion and you disagree with me, then I am *good* and you are *bad*." Most of us know that the world doesn't work that way, but if you have no doubt about the truth of what you think, it's easy to see the world in those terms.

When it comes to morality, seeing things in black and white can be especially dangerous, because once you see everyone who disagrees with you as evil you can justify doing terrible things to them. History is full of mass slaughters, from the Spanish inquisition to the Crusades to the Salem witch trials to suicide bombings and terrorist attacks, that have been justified by this kind of black and white "you're either with me or against me" kind of thinking.

Chapter 9: Let Go of Certainty

This kind of thinking is reflected in the insulting names people come up with for groups they don't like – whether they apply to other religions, races, sexual orientations, or even the opposite gender. Once you've lumped someone into a category that has an offensive name, you don't have to think about that person any more. Your certainty about that group takes over, and the insulting name for the group reconfirms your certainty that the group is inferior and bad or stupid – a description you have now extended to this new person by lumping him or her into that group. Derogatory group names reinforce the idea that the world can be divided into "us" and "them." Furthermore, by creating pigeonholes for people you don't like (or are afraid of) they make it even easier to ignore evidence that you're partly or completely wrong.

Why does this make people with certainty syndrome bad at solving problems? Because their analysis of problems isn't accurate – at least in the area in which they have certainty. They see people and things in terms of the negative stereotype that's supported by their certainty, instead of seeing them as they are. Often, the only solution to a problem they can imagine is to eliminate anyone in the group that disagrees with them or whose behavior they don't like. This may lead to "solutions" like trying to banish or kill anyone who exhibits the behavior they are certain is wrong.

One manifestation of this kind of thinking is the idea of legislating morality. If I believe my convictions are ultimate truth, then I am justified in making them into the law of the land so everyone else is forced to follow them. There was a lot of this kind of thinking behind the prohibition of alcohol that was enacted in the United States in the 1930s. Many religious groups were absolutely certain that drinking was a sin and therefore should be summarily outlawed. There was no careful analysis of the behavioral payoffs or the addictive elements of drinking. To many of these people, it was a black and white issue.

Of course, the consequences of Prohibition were terrible. Alcohol was still available in nearby countries, so illegal importation instantly became a way to get rich, and many notorious gangsters like Al Capone became millionaires, leaving a trail of death and lawlessness in their wake. Crimes such as theft and murder increased. Racketeering led to corruption of law enforcement agencies. The potency of the alcohol being smuggled increased dramatically, since that was more profitable, leading to *increased* alcohol abuse and drunkenness. It cost the government a fortune to attempt to enforce the law, while at the same time the government lost all of the tax revenue it could have been getting from the sale of alcohol.

Despite this, some continued to argue that prohibition was a good thing, because they were certain it was God's will, and you can't argue with God! And many still argue that the best solution to any behavioral problem (at least the ones that they have certainty about) is to outlaw the behavior. Actually, that is *never* the best solution to a behavioral problem. But people with certainty syndrome see outlawing behavior they don't like as perfectly justified, even when all of the evidence says that doing so will backfire.

***Problem #8**: Certainty encourages fear and anger – which then encourage even more certainty.* Because people with certainty divide the world into "those who agree with me and those who don't," their world view supports being angry and fearful of those who disagree with them. That's partly because certainty makes it hard to understand *why* others disagree with you – and if you don't understand something, it's a lot easier to fear it. Then, once fear and anger are present, people are inclined to reinforce their certainty to help make the fear and anger seem reasonable to themselves and others. This becomes a vicious circle that can easily escalate.

This is another consequence of black and white thinking. When your certainty causes you to see some person or group as a threat, you'll dismiss any evidence to the contrary, and your ideas about how to deal with the "threat" will be very limited. Your ability to analyze a situation realistically will be dramatically impaired. As a result, your level of fear will escalate along with your anger, and anything that appears to confirm your fear will feed the fire and reaffirm your certainty that the other person or group is a threat.

It's not too hard to see that this side effect of certainty can have dire consequences, leading people to take drastic action and then justify it on the basis of their certainty. Which leads us to the next point.....

Problem #9: Certainty justifies abuse. Despite coming up with less-than-ideal solutions to problems, people who have total certainty feel justified in forcing their "solutions" on everybody else, because they're certain they're right!

This is the kind of thinking that makes it easy to justify slaughter in the name of "facts." Political leaders kill millions on the basis of absolute certainty about their ideas; religious fanatics have done the same throughout history. People who slaughter others in the name of a cause are not allowing for the possibility that their ideas might be even slightly wrong. In contrast, individuals who recognize that "the facts" evolve over time seldom wreak havoc on others in the name of their beliefs about what's true.

Problem #10: Certainty makes people overlook consequences. People who believe they have a lock on the truth stop paying attention to the consequences of their actions in that area. They think, "I know I'm right. So if I take action based on my ideas, my actions will be right as well." And when negative consequences happen and become inescapably obvious, they still feel justified in continuing because of their certainty.

Sadly, some people make enormous amounts of money and/or gain enormous power as a result of actions and choices that have terrible consequences – actions that are justified by certainty. Indeed, the fact that their actions are so profitable encourages them to avoid questioning their certainty, because at some level they know that their certainty is protecting their wealth and power.

When people owned slaves, for example, they usually had certainty that the enslaved people were inferior or in some way deserved their fate. In that situation, questioning your certainty is inviting an end to all the free labor your slaves are being forced to provide. Or if you're CEO of a multinational corporation that's destroying the environment while making staggering profits, having certainty that you're not really hurting anything is convenient, to say the least. If you stopped being so certain, you might undermine your wealth machine. (The latter situation is ironic, because destroying the planet is going to cause the people responsible for the destruction just as much suffering as anyone else. There are some things no amount of wealth can protect you from.) The point is that certainty, in many cases, goes unchallenged because those who are certain about their opinions are gaining wealth or power as a result of that certainty – and the selective blindness encouraged by certainty keeps the money and power rolling in.

Even worse, if people with power realize that certainty will encourage other people to overlook the negative consequences of their actions – to their financial benefit – they may "reinvest" some of their profits by using the money to encourage certainty in others, often by spreading misinformation. Those people who are swayed by this misinformation and buy into the certainty end up with the same blind spot, overlooking the sometimes horrifying consequences of those profit-producing actions.

Of course, consequences do matter – even if you have immense wealth or power. And consequences matter for all of us when we're caught on the Wheel of Misfortune. If you insist that your point of view is infallible, you'll fail to respond appropriately when choices you make have negative consequences. To respond appropriately and get things moving in your favor again, you'll have to be willing to stop falling back on certainty.

Problem #11: Certainty becomes ingrained. Certainty is a mental pattern that's very resistant to change and can therefore last a lifetime.

Once we associate the feeling of certainty with a given thought or set of ideas, the neural connections that form in the brain can be very persistent and difficult to change; they don't simply fade away over time. People who buy into the arguments made by a political party, for example, will often refuse to acknowledge faulty reasoning in those arguments over the course of an entire lifetime, no matter how much the evidence and the consequences of implementing that political philosophy may contradict them. That's why, once we have certainty about something, we can be stuck with that certainty for a lifetime. (Hence the observation made by physicist Max Planck, quoted at the beginning of this chapter, that new scientific ideas only take hold when the people who believed the previous ideas die.) And when certainty becomes a permanent part of our lives, so do all of the disadvantages that come with it.

This can also cause us to trust memories more than we should. As already noted, our memories are notoriously unreliable; the details of our recollections tend to change over time without our even realizing it. But once the feeling of certainty is attached to a memory, the feeling stays attached, even as the memory changes. That can backfire, because we often make significant choices based on a faulty memory of some past event. On the other hand, if we understand that the feeling of certainty that accompanies a memory is not a guarantee of the memory's accuracy, we won't be nearly so quick to make those choices – and in some situations that could turn out to be a very good thing.

The fact that certainty tends to stick with us for a very long time is another good reason to avoid buying into it in the first place.

Chapter 9: Let Go of Certainty   247

Problem #12: Certainty causes people to accept bogus supporting "evidence" without questioning it. This allows others to spread false ideas that support their cause as "facts," knowing that those who have certainty will accept those "facts" without careful examination.

People who want to influence your behavior are usually well aware of this. So, they'll gladly encourage you to have certainty about issues that work to their advantage. Then, once you've joined the certainty pool, they'll feed you bogus supporting evidence. They know that certainty causes people to accept bogus evidence without a second thought. Furthermore, the bogus evidence reinforces people's certainty even more. It's a vicious circle that can be used against you.

Cult leaders use this tactic all the time – and so do politicians and special interest groups. During elections, for example, people are sometimes paid to generate false information about opposing candidates and circulate it. In recent years e-mail has been a particularly popular way to do this, because it's nearly impossible to trace the original source of a lie. Those who have bought into a politician's ideology will accept these lies as further proof that the politician is right and his (or her) opponents are wrong. If you point out to someone who's caught up in this certainty cycle that some of the evidence he's holding up to support his belief is simply false, he'll just dismiss what you're saying. So certainty is a powerful weapon, and one that's regularly used to undermine a democracy by getting people to accept false information and vote against their own interests.

In short, certainty makes people *gullible* – a very good reason to "just say no" when it comes to being absolutely certain that you're right about something.

Problem #13: Group certainty is even more problematic. Certainty becomes even more entrenched when shared by a group, leading to additional disadvantages.

Certainty can play a major role in the way we interact with other people. It feels good to have certainty about something you believe, but it's even more rewarding to know that other people share your certainty. In addition to reinforcing our certainty, it helps us bond with the other person or people. It creates a sort of family, and that generates a sense of safety and security.

One of the biggest downsides to group certainty is that it makes us even more resistant to opposing points of view and evidence. Consider, for example, religious sects that have predicted the end of the world on a specific date. This has happened numerous times (most recently in 2011 when Christian radio host Harold Camping predicted that Judgment Day would take place on May 21, 2011, and that the end of the world would take place five months later on October 21). So far, of course, the end has failed to occur on the predicted dates. You might think such blatant evidence would shake the certainty of any rational person regarding the tenants of that religious sect, but certainty causes people to discard conflicting evidence, and when group certainty is involved, even the most in-your-face evidence may be discarded. In most cases – if the members of the sect haven't already committed suicide in preparation for the event – members of the group either decide that their faithfulness caused God to change his mind, or they conclude that their calculations about the timing must have been wrong and they come up with another date. (That's what happened in the case of Harold Camping).

Perhaps more important, group certainty tends to increase and add solidarity to the us-versus-them mentality, with all of its attendant hostility. That's especially true if others outside the group happen to disagree *strongly* with whatever the group has certainty about. (You don't have to look far to find examples of this in religion or politics.)

In short, having certainty shared by a group takes all the disadvantages and negatives that come with being certain and amplifies them into a cultural force.

Problem #14: Certainty makes it easy for others to manipulate you. People who are certain that they know "the truth" are more easily controlled (especially when they're part of a group that shares their certainty).

As already noted, individuals with certainty syndrome tend to divide the world into *those who agree with me and those who don't*. So if you have certainty syndrome, people who want to manipulate you can simply claim to agree with you and emphasize the importance of despising – and/or attacking – a particular outside person or group that has a different viewpoint. By claiming agreement, the manipulator frames himself as being one of the "good guys," and by portraying the other person or group as "the enemy," the manipulator funnels your anger toward that target.

Certainty can be so blinding that followers of a politician may miss warning signs of trouble – such as evidence that the politician's claim doesn't really reflect his personal beliefs. When group certainty is involved, the potential for manipulation is even greater because everyone in the group sees the other members of the group agreeing with the manipulator.

The vicious circle that's created when certainty, fear and anger feed on each other is bad enough by itself, but it can become deadly when special interest groups use it to manipulate people. Once that vicious circle exists – and in some cases, it exists almost entirely because of the efforts of the special interest group – the leaders of the group can deliberately flood their target audience with misinformation designed to heighten fear, anger and certainty. The target audience doesn't notice that the information is bogus because their certainty causes them to accept almost anything that agrees with what they already think. Meanwhile, the bogus evidence feeds the flames, as it were, causing the target audience to have much higher levels of fear and anger.

This is the strategy Hitler used in 1930s Germany: He created group certainty around the idea of Aryan racial supremacy. This was well-received by a populace suffering under the harsh conditions imposed on Germany as punishment after World War I. The resulting group certainty allowed Hitler to whip people into a deadly frenzy of fear, anger and certainty.

When a special interest group does this, two things happen. First, the people in the target audience become gung-ho about the special interest group, seeing the group as their protector against whatever they're afraid of. That not only gives the group ever-greater power, influence and credibility, it also causes the target audience to funnel money to the group, enriching the people at the top and adding to their power and influence.

Unfortunately, the second thing that happens is that the heightened fear and anger leads members of the target audience to make extreme choices, believing that drastic action against those they're afraid of is necessary. This is the reason hate groups have proliferated in America in recent years. This is also what leads to mass shootings and other deadly outbreaks of violence.

You would hope that this increase in extreme behavior would cause the people running the special interest groups to stop deliberately inflaming their target audience by spreading bogus and biased information. But it doesn't stop them. That's partly because the money and power they gain is a potent motivator – but it's also partly because they have certainty, too. Their own certainty encourages them to deny and/or rationalize away the negative consequences of their actions.

A related strategy is often used to keep people from hearing a message that a politician or special interest group doesn't want followers to hear; they use certainty to discredit the messenger. Basically, the politician or group loudly claims that the person spreading the message is a member of some category the followers already see as a "bad" category. Lumping the person into that category is sufficient to get the followers to stop listening to the message.

For example, if your followers have certainty that all members of one political party or ethnic group are bad, all you have to do is convince them that the person you don't want them to listen to is a member of that political party or ethnic group – whether he actually is or not. Then your followers will ignore whatever the person is saying. Special interest groups use this strategy all the time, first demonizing a category and then portraying everyone they don't want you to listen to as being a member of that category.

Certainty syndrome also works to the manipulator's advantage because it keeps the group's attention focused on fighting against those who don't agree with them – *a great way to keep the members of the group from paying attention to what the manipulator is doing.* It's the magician's trick of misdirection: Keep people focused on the shiny coin in your left hand so they don't notice what your right hand is up to. (Misdirection is especially effective if the shiny coin represents "the indisputable truth.") Focus on fighting the force of evil! Focus on the danger posed by that other group of people! Don't pay any attention to what *I'm* doing – you know I'm on your side!

Some individuals have so much certainty that a particular group or thing is a monstrous evil that they will vote for any political candidate who says he is opposed to that thing – *regardless of anything else the politician stands for, and anything he might do once elected.* That's a perfect set-up for being manipulated into electing someone who plans to run roughshod over your rights once he gets into office.

The bottom line here is that the more certainty you have that your beliefs are the final, inarguable truth, the easier it will be for others to manipulate you, getting you to act against your own interests and the wellbeing of everyone around you. If that's not a good reason to stop indulging in certainty, I don't know what is.

Chapter 9: Let Go of Certainty

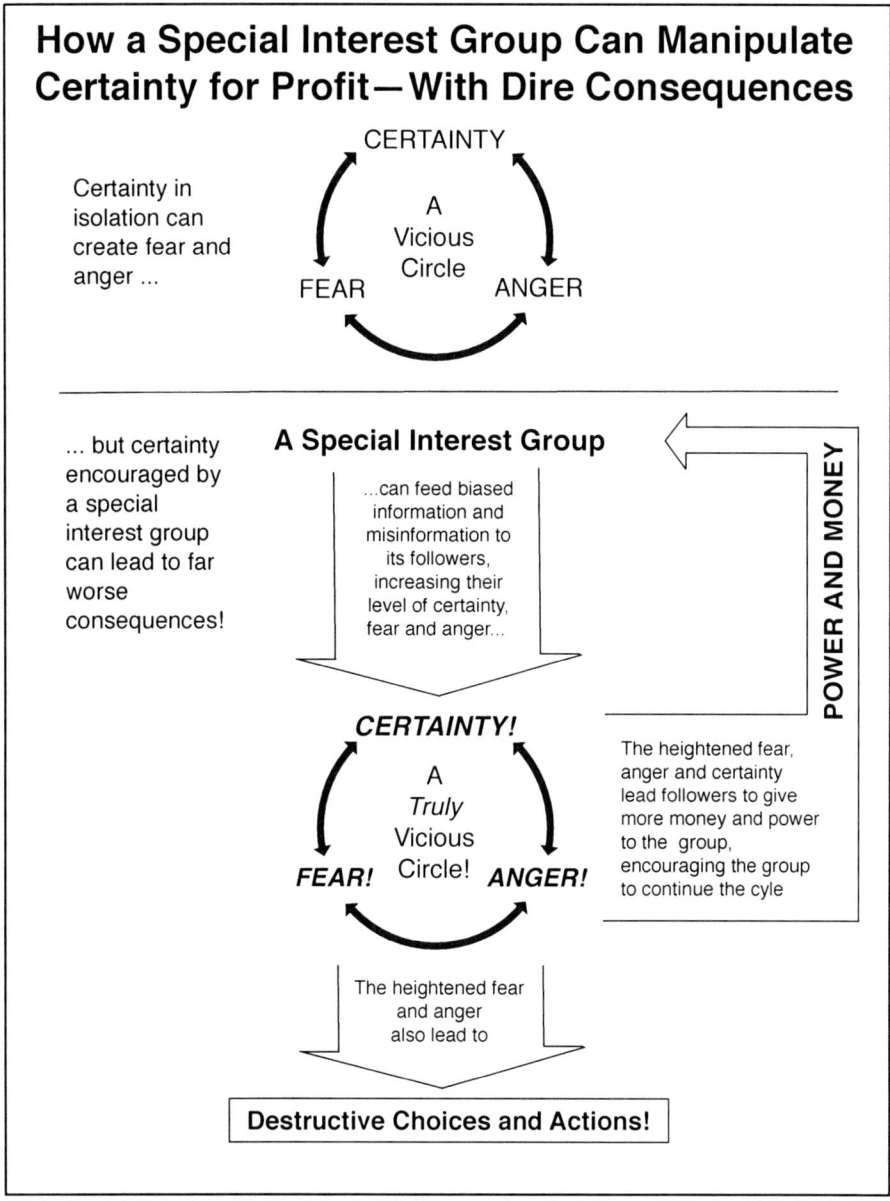

Real-World Consequences of Certainty Syndrome

How much do these disadvantages matter? It shouldn't be hard to see that at a personal level certainty puts you at a tremendous disadvantage in life, and the more certainty you allow yourself to hold, the greater the disadvantage. So making a conscious decision to forego certainty – to declare yourself open to the possibility that anything you accept as the truth might not turn out to be 100-percent correct – is one of the best ways to keep yourself off the Wheel of Misfortune.

The negative impact of certainty, however, extends far beyond our personal experience. In fact, a good argument can be made that certainty is at the heart of many of the worst problems facing our world today.

For example:

• A number of giant corporations are destroying large segments of our planet and creating massive pollution. Some companies are altering the Earth's climate in ways that are likely to be catastrophic; some are altering our food supply in ways that are setting the food chain up for a potential collapse. Many are squashing desperately needed innovation as a way to avoid competition.

• Some bankers are stacking the deck and rewriting the rules of the finance game to enrich themselves – while bringing economic ruin on others and hardship on everyone (except perhaps the wealthiest individuals).

• A number of wealthy individuals are using their money to buy politicians and judges in order to rewrite laws and tilt the playing field in their direction. Others are using their financial power to set up media empires that deliberately misinform people about what's happening, striving to make people angry and fearful, and most important, make them *certain* that what they're being told is accurate (so they'll be easier to manipulate).

• Some political parties now insist that their elected officials *never compromise*. Without compromise, a democracy cannot function. Nevertheless, this seems perfectly justifiable to people who have certainty about their opinions. They *know* they're right and everyone else is wrong, and therefore they see themselves as being within their rights to try to force their political beliefs on everyone else.

• Certainty is also behind much of the destructive behavior exhibited by some governments around the world. Whenever sensible options are ignored and leaders angrily pursue actions that increase the likelihood of war, you can bet that personal certainty is part of the equation.

The people running these corporations and banks and political parties and countries are presumably intelligent and capable, so why would they use their power to set us up for catastrophe? After all, the consequences of their actions are likely to cause them grave harm as well. Greed could be a factor, but certainty syndrome is clearly a big part of the explanation. In fact, greed – an addictive desire for ever more money – would be hard-pressed to exist without the help of certainty to justify its negative side effects. Certainty syndrome causes people to ignore evidence that something is amiss, accept bogus justifications for continuing down a problematic path, ignore consequences, and see anyone who sounds the alarm as one of "the bad guys." Add in the positive financial rewards these disastrous policies bring to the people implementing them and you have a recipe for very shortsighted and destructive choices and actions.

These actions and choices have another consequence that can be even more deadly in the long run. As already noted, spreading fear and anger is a part of this process. If fear and anger continue to be deliberately heightened for corporate or political gain, a country will slowly become more unstable and unsafe – part of the SEICR cycle that eventually leads to a system collapse (as discussed in Chapter 1). The last time America went through a SEICR cycle collapse that involved anger, hatred and fear was the Civil War – the bloodiest war in history up to that time. This is not something we should be aiming to recreate. Unfortunately, the people who are setting these wheels in motion and keeping them in motion are completely caught up in their own certainty, which makes them happy to ignore the consequences of their actions.

This idea of using misinformation to manipulate people – and the fact that it eventually backfires – was nicely summed up by Joseph Goebbels, leader of the Nazi party's propaganda unit during World War II. He said, "If you tell a lie big enough and keep repeating it, people will eventually come to believe it. [However,] *The lie can be maintained only for such time as the State can shield the people from the political, economic and/or military consequences of the lie.*" Unfortunately, by the time the "political, economic and/or military consequences of the lie" have created a catastrophe, it may be too late to do much about it. The individuals whose certainty allowed them to buy into the big lie would have been better off if they had been a little less certain about their beliefs earlier in the game.

The behaviors described above are a danger to all of us because they have potentially dire consequences. It's certainty syndrome that makes these actions seem acceptable and allows people to be blind to their consequences. Without certainty, none of these individuals or groups would behave this way – and our world would be in far less danger.

Separating Church and State? The Certainty Factor

This brings us around to another issue that's profoundly impacted by certainty: the separation of church and state in America. Although this was championed by the Founding Fathers, some religious groups still believe that their religion should become the basis for our government. Certainty syndrome makes them see this idea as entirely justifiable.

There's no question that religion can be a powerful force for good – especially in the life of an individual person. But as any student of history knows, at the societal level many religions have been connected with instances of large-scale abuse and mass slaughter during the past several millennia. The reason for this isn't usually the content of those religious belief systems; the problem is the *certainty* that is taught as part of these religions. That certainty leads to all of the negative consequences listed earlier – seeing things in black and white, misjudging causes, trying to solve problems in ways that don't work, believing it's okay to force your beliefs on anyone who disagrees, ignoring the consequences of your actions, and so forth. When combined with a few politically ambitious religious leaders, certainty syndrome can easily lead to mass suffering and slaughter.

Consequently, I'd like to humbly suggest that religions that still promote certainty as part of their doctrine seriously consider implementing the following change, for purely practical reasons: Instead of saying "Our interpretation of this book (at the heart of our religion) is the ultimate truth directly from God," why not say: "This is our current understanding of these words, which we believe to be correct." Removing the unwavering certainty doesn't mean you're wrong. It means you're acknowledging that you might someday learn new things about the words in question. Such an attitude might well have prevented most of the past abuses and wholesale slaughters that were justified by religious certainty. And that acknowledgment – which is not such a huge step to take – could potentially eliminate a mountain of horrible consequences for society that continue to affect us all even today.

I believe the tendency for religions to encourage certainty syndrome is also the best justification for the separation of church and state. There's nothing wrong with political leaders being religious; in fact, most American presidents have considered themselves to be religious. But there *is* something wrong with a political leader *being caught up in certainty syndrome*. A political leader who suffers from all the negative side effects of certainty described above has the capacity to lead his (or her) country into grave trouble. In contrast, a leader who is open to new knowledge and ideas – who doesn't assume that he or she has the final answers in any area of life – will make far better choices, find better ways to solve problems, and won't insist on pushing his beliefs onto everyone else. A leader who is not caught up in certainty will notice the consequences of his actions and make changes accordingly. A leader suffering from certainty syndrome will not.

As long as a religion makes certainty a part of its doctrine, putting it in charge of a country is likely to have very unhappy consequences.

The Importance of Doing What Works

Despite all of the problems with certainty, some will still insist that their certainty is OK, because they know they're right. In fact, they *may* be right. However, the practical reality is that it doesn't matter whether what you believe is the truth or not. What we're talking about here is *what works* – which strategy will serve you and those around you, and help you reach your goals.

Acting as if everything that you've accepted as a "fact" is at least partly wrong passes that test – it *works*. It will serve you extremely well, especially when times are tough and you're striving to stay off the Wheel of Misfortune. Conversely, having certainty about your beliefs will subject you to all of the disadvantages of certainty syndrome – *even if it turns out you were right*. So, whether you're wrong or right, certainty syndrome will act as a huge roadblock to your success and happiness.

The bottom line is that your attitude about what you consider to be the truth will either help you or hurt you. If you take the attitude that you've found the truth and that's the end of the matter, you'll suffer from a host of negative side effects. You'll be on your way to the Wheel of Misfortune. On the other hand, if you act as if your opinion is open to future adjustment, you'll do far better – regardless of whether you turn out to have been right or wrong.

Hopefully, it's clear by this point that certainty has all kinds of bad consequences. The next question is: If certainty is a problem, what is the solution?

This question can be broken down into three separate sub-questions.

1) How can we deal with our own certainty?

2) Is there anything we can do to change the mind of someone who has certainty about a specific issue?

3) How can we shift the public consciousness away from the idea that certainty is perfectly acceptable, so we have a fighting chance to eliminate all the negative consequences and side effects that certainty has brought with it?

Managing Your Own Certainty, Part 1: Keep an Open Mind

Clearly, the first step along this road is grasping the reality that certainty often backfires and making a decision to stop accepting your own certainty as a sign that you're right. Stepping away from certainty syndrome allows us to learn from experience, be less judgmental, win more friends and allies, be more effective at changing other people's behavior and beliefs, solve problems more effectively, really understand the consequences of our actions, and avoid being easily manipulated by others on the basis of group certainty. It also stops encouraging others to buy into the idea that being certain is the same as being right.

Making the decision to stop buying into certainty will start you down the road to side-stepping all of the problems certainty brings with it. And whenever you catch yourself exhibiting the signs of certainty – seeing the world in black and white, dismissing evidence that contradicts what you think is true, and so forth – an alarm should go off in your head that makes you stop and look more carefully at what's going on in your thinking.

Here are some examples of ways to reframe thoughts and statements that are based on certainty:

• Instead of saying "Don't tell me you didn't start this argument, I was here and I heard you say such-and-such before I said anything," say: "The way I recall it, you said such-and-such first."

• Instead of saying "I know for a fact that this person caused all of my problems," say: "I believe this person has caused all of my problems."

- Instead of saying "My religion is the word of God and is literally true, and if you don't agree, you're going to hell," say: "I believe my religion is the word of God; it has helped millions of people, and millions of people agree with me."

- Instead of saying "This scientific finding is factual, and the only reason you disagree is because you don't know what you're talking about," say: "This scientific finding is supported by an overwhelming amount of evidence, so I don't believe disagreeing with it is justified."

- Instead of saying "That group of people is inferior [or sinful, or dangerous, or stupid] – it's just a fact, and if you don't see it, that's your problem," say: "My experience has been that that group of people is inferior [or sinful, or dangerous, or stupid]."

In other words, make a decision that from now on you'll leave room for the possibility that your understanding of the facts might eventually shift a little bit when new evidence presents itself. And then, take the next step: Be open to new evidence if it turns up, so your idea of what's true actually reflects your experience, not just your internal sense of certainty.

Admitting that you may not have the final word about something may seem like admitting that you're wrong, but it's nothing of the sort. It simply tells the world that you're not walking around with a closed mind; you're paying attention and willing to consider new evidence if it appears. And you'll reap enormous benefits at a personal level, because acting on this assumption – that everything you believe to be true will eventually turn out to be at least partly mistaken – will dramatically increase your power and vision. Ultimately, it will remove a huge roadblock from the path to a better future for yourself and those you care about.

Managing Your Own Certainty, Part 2: Ask Questions

Adopting the idea that everything you believe to be fact will turn out to be at least partly wrong is a powerful tool for staying off the Wheel of Misfortune, but it's an internal tool. The active, external way to implement this idea and enhance your openness to learning is to make it a habit to *keep asking questions*.

A few years ago, a thoughtful and observant acquaintance of mine –

let's call him Tom – told me about an encounter he had with a friend he hadn't seen for a while. Here is the story, as Tom told it to me:

"When my friend came over to visit, I discovered that he'd become involved with a religious cult. One of the attractions for him was that it made him feel like he belonged to a family. However, once in the group he was also subjected to a number of pressures that discouraged him from leaving. For one thing, there was tremendous pressure to 'behave' – which meant doing what the group said to do, and never challenging the group's beliefs which were spelled out by the leader. Conditions were also arranged to keep the members of the group very busy, so there was little time or energy left for sitting around and examining the leader's ideas critically. Furthermore, using a time-honored strategy, anyone outside the group who questioned the dictates of the group was portrayed as either ignorant or as 'the devil.'

"My visiting friend was a pretty intelligent individual, so I was somewhat surprised to learn of this development. It didn't seem logical to me, but of course, his decision was swayed largely by factors that had little to do with logic. And once inside the confines of the group, logical challenges to the group's beliefs were derailed using well-practiced arguments – or punishments.

"As we talked, he told me about his new life, perhaps partly to see whether I was a candidate for joining the group. Constant recruitment is obviously important to keep a group like that going. As he detailed some of the group's beliefs about the nature of life and what they claimed was necessary to be acceptable in the eyes of God – and acceptable to the cult's leader – I felt compelled to point out some glaring logical inconsistencies in those beliefs.

"If my friend had been talking to anyone else, pointing out these inconsistencies might have torpedoed the conversation, but we were friends and had a good opinion of each other. So, he tried his best to counter the points I was raising. That wasn't easy because I'd thought a lot about these kinds of things, and he found that he couldn't dismiss my challenges with prepackaged answers. Once that became clear, he fell back on the ultimate defense: 'How do I know you're not lying to me?' he asked. 'How do I know you're not the devil?'

"I knew this question was impossible to answer. How can you prove to someone that you're not the devil? So I said, 'This is not about me versus your group's leader. I'm not saying that you should take my word instead of his. This is about using the mind and intelligence that God gave *you*.

Chapter 9: Let Go of Certainty

Your leader says he speaks for God, and you have to take his word for that. But you *know* that God gave you your mind and heart and curiosity and ability to think clearly. He gave you those resources for a reason – so you could use them. You don't have to take anyone's word for that.'

"I told my friend that *my* doubts didn't really matter. But I also told him, '*Your doubts do matter.* It's not sacrilege to ask questions when your heart and mind say that something is fishy. So, don't take my word for anything – or your leader's word either. Instead, trust the intelligence you were given. If you accept a set of ideas about the world, do it because your heart and mind say they make sense. And if your heart and mind say that maybe they *don't* make sense, then don't commit yourself to those ideas until your doubts are fully resolved.'

"My friend admitted that challenging the leader's ideas was not exactly encouraged. I told him that when someone says you can't challenge something, even if he says he's speaking for God – *he is claiming a higher authority than God, because God gave us the desire to find answers in the first place.* The truth doesn't need to be protected. When you challenge it, you force it to demonstrate that it really is true, and that makes it stronger. I told my friend that any time someone tries to discourage you from questioning what he claims are 'the facts,' I would take that as an indication that his 'facts' are not as solid as he would have you believe."

The point Tom was making is well-taken: Making it a policy to keep asking questions will serve you well. This means doing three things:

1) First, it means being inquisitive; keeping your curiosity alive so you continue to grow.

2) Second, it means challenging beliefs and ideas that strike you as ineffective or downright wrong.

3) Third, it means being willing to extend your questioning to include areas that *you yourself* think of as a closed book. In other words, for this idea to be most helpful in hard times, you need to be willing to challenge anything – even the things *you* have certainty about.

In terms of that last point, consider the case of Charles Darwin, creator of the theory of evolution. Charles Darwin wrote down every fact he encountered that seemed to contradict his theory so that he could remember them and use them to refine his theory. In other words, *he went out of his way to seek out challenges to his own ideas*. He was smart enough to know that understanding contrary evidence would work in his favor by making his theory more solid as he took the new evidence into account. He didn't defend his ideas as inarguably correct; he assumed they would need to be revised and was open to revising them. He did the *opposite* of what people with certainty do, and the fact that his theory ended up becoming one of the foundations of modern biology speaks to the power of this open-minded strategy.

Of course, it's tough for most people to remain open to the possibility that some of their pivotal ideas about the universe might be even partly mistaken. Being willing to *actively question* things you see as the absolute truth is even harder. In addition, being willing to question your own "absolute truth" can also put you at odds with friends and allies; in some cases, those around you will see your willingness to question things that they consider to be the truth as heresy.

Nevertheless, questioning something that really is true does it no harm – quite the opposite. If that "truth" stands up to questioning, you'll have even greater faith that it's correct. And if it doesn't stand up to questioning in some respect, then you've gained knowledge and a more accurate understanding in that area. That new understanding may put you in the position of disagreeing with people you used to agree with, but it also puts you in a position of greater strength. And when you're fighting to stay off the Wheel of Misfortune, greater strength makes a difference.

Why Don't We Ask Questions?

If asking questions is such a powerful thing to do, why do we so often fail to ask them? One reason is certainty syndrome; but even people who are not locked into certainty about their ideas may avoid asking questions that badly need to be asked. Here are just a few reasons:

• *We don't ask questions because it's easier not to.* Asking questions often forces us out of our comfort zone, opening up a can of worms, so to speak. People sometimes make a conscious choice not to challenge things, simply because it's easier to avoid "rocking the boat." This strategy may not cause you any grief when times are good, but when times get tough, asking questions can be the key to making changes for the better – maybe even the key to saving your life.

• *We don't ask questions because we're not paying attention.* Once we feel comfortable with our picture of the world, it's easy to shut out evidence that should be alerting us that something is wrong, even if we don't have certainty syndrome. Needless to say, if you find yourself on the Wheel of Misfortune, and things aren't going the way you'd like them to, it's a good time to start paying attention – and a good time to start questioning the assumptions that you and those around you have been making.

• ***We don't ask questions because we believe that the current situation is the way things are supposed to be.*** In other words, it's always been this way, so let's leave well enough alone. The big problem with this approach to life is that things in the world are changing faster and faster. Given that reality, refusing to question "the way it's always been" can end up putting you into a perilous situation. As Albert Einstein once observed, "The release of atomic energy has not created a new problem. It has merely made more urgent the necessity of solving an existing one." Not questioning old beliefs when everything around you is changing – and perhaps putting you in danger – is a bad idea. Many time-honored ideas and beliefs *desperately* need to be questioned for the safety of our own lives and future. And that's just as true at the personal level as at the global level.

• *We don't ask questions because we're afraid of being punished.* The punisher in question might be a parent, your peers, your boss, a religious leader or the government. Your fear of being punished could be legitimate, but the important issue is, *what are the consequences of not asking the questions?* At some point, the consequences of not asking questions may become far worse than the consequences of asking them. So, when the negative consequences of keeping your questions to yourself start to escalate, make sure you re-evaluate the situation. You don't want to lose everything because you were afraid to ask a question.

• *We don't ask questions because we've been told that God doesn't want us to.* Unless God tells you this personally, you're taking the word of an intermediary. In most cases, the intermediary is benefiting from having you believe this (for instance, he or she may be gaining or maintaining power over you). Think of it this way: A being capable of creating a universe is not likely to be offended by the asking of questions. In fact, you can make a good argument that if human beings were created by God, then He gave us the ability to ask questions because He knows that questions lead us to the truth. The idea that God would be angry because we're asking questions doesn't really make sense.

• ***We don't ask questions because it doesn't occur to us that a conclusion we've reached might be wrong.*** It's remarkably easy to mistakenly assume that an assumption we've made or a conclusion we've drawn is a fact, even when it's not based on any evidence at all. For example, if your spouse leaves you for another man or woman, you may be tempted to draw all kinds of terrible conclusions: "This is the worst thing that ever happened to me," "I'll never be happy again," "My wife (or husband) never really loved me," "I've wasted the best years of my life," and so on. If the economy crashes and your life savings disappear, you may think, "This is the worst thing that ever happened to me," "My future is ruined," "Without that money I'm nothing," "I've lost everything that matters to me," "My life is over," and so forth.

The problem with these conclusions is that they're unwarranted. Most likely, *every one of them will turn out to be wrong*. And yet most of us tend to accept these kinds of emotional reactions as the truth instead of questioning them. Then we base our perspective on them, and react accordingly.

There's nothing wrong with having a legitimate emotional reaction to a devastating turn of events. But if you want to keep your wits about you and make optimum choices that will keep you off of the Wheel of Misfortune, you need to see your thinking for what it is: an emotional reaction, *not* a statement of the truth.

Instead of accepting this kind of emotional assumption without question when you have an emotional reaction to a negative event, make it a point to *question your assumptions and conclusions about what happened*. Conclusions you reach in the heat of emotion are legitimate as feelings, but they may NOT be accurate, factual evaluations – and you shouldn't make important choices on the basis of them.

The tendency to not question our assumptions and conclusions can be even more devastating when they involve what we see as our limitations. If you tell yourself that you can't out-think an opponent, or accomplish a goal, or find a way to make a difficult situation manageable, *you need to question the accuracy of your thinking*. If you don't, you will effectively prevent yourself from solving the problem or reaching the goal. Any time you catch yourself thinking that you don't have the skills or intelligence to solve a problem or reach a goal, an alarm should go off: *You're accepting an assumption that may be false.*

The bottom line is: Assume that anything you feel absolutely certain about might not be 100% correct – and keep asking questions.

Two Caveats About Asking Questions

It's important to note two things regarding this strategy:

1) Asking questions isn't the same as demanding answers. There are times when you can demand an answer, and times when you're better off just being patient. The important thing is to *keep asking questions.* The answers will show up eventually – if you're really looking for them.

2) When you recognize the value of asking questions, remember that it's a two-way street. If someone questions the things that *you* believe to be true, don't be offended. Instead, think of it as an opportunity to "re-certify" whatever you believe. If you can successfully answer challenges to your beliefs, that's evidence that you're on the right track. On the other hand, if someone's question pokes a hole in what you believe, that means it's time to consider the possibility that your "truth" may need some revision. At the least, it means you need to increase your understanding of what you believe so you can defend it more adroitly.

Having to rethink beliefs that we're comfortable with is never entirely pleasant, but it may lead us to clearer knowledge and a greater understanding – and those will go a long way toward keeping you off the Wheel of Misfortune.

Challenging Certainty Syndrome in Others

Keeping your own mind open is one thing, but what can you do when you want to change someone else's mind and their opinion is protected by certainty?

As we've already noted, when people are certain about something, they are quite capable of ignoring, denying or rationalizing away evidence that their belief is faulty. Of course, there's nothing wrong with presenting the person in question with contrary evidence. However, the way you present it will determine whether you have any chance of changing the other person's mind.

On the one hand, if you present your evidence in a way that shows you're already certain the other person is wrong, your presentation will be interpreted as an attack. Defenses will fly up, and the other party will dismiss your evidence – and you. You'll be wasting your time.

On the other hand, if you present your evidence nonjudgmentally, showing an authentic curiosity about the other person's reaction, you may have a chance to influence his opinion. Furthermore, certainty comes in degrees; we've all experienced the difference between being absolutely certain about something and feeling *pretty much* certain. So how certain the other person feels will also make a big difference in how successful you are at changing his opinion.

Unfortunately, as a general rule, the odds are extremely slim that your evidence, no matter how good it seems to you, will eliminate the other person's certainty completely. No one gives up certainty on the basis of one or two pieces of conflicting evidence. As noted earlier, contrary evidence often simply bypasses the rational mind and goes straight to emotion-related parts of the brain, where it generates feelings like anger instead of a thoughtful response.

Back in Chapter 1 we spoke about the repeating SEICR cycle. (In a nutshell: A system is Stable, followed by a period of Expansion, then a period of Instability, then a system-wide Collapse, and finally, a Rebirth.) An inaccurate belief that has profound certainty attached to it will often follow this cycle. Certainty makes a belief very resistant to change, thus creating a stable belief system; but over time, as experience relating to that belief accumulates, flaws in the belief can become more and more problematic until at some point that belief system crashes, allowing an improved and more accurate belief to replace the previous one.

In practical terms, what this means is that when someone has profound certainty about an inaccurate belief, the belief may only change when the problems arising from the inaccuracy of the belief become so obvious and overwhelming that the believer simply can't escape seeing them. In other words, the evidence that the belief is at least partly wrong may have to pile up for quite a while, until the comfort and stability of maintaining certainty is outweighed by the problems the belief is causing.

Depending on the belief in question, this can take a long time! The collapse of a belief system from the weight of its flaws might not even happen during the person's lifetime. It's even possible for a person to go through a belief-system collapse and *still* refuse to alter a belief, although that's pretty rare. (The SEICR cycle is very effective at causing major changes, which is probably why nature relies on it.)

So is it worth presenting the person with evidence that his certainty may not be justified? If you do it nonjudgmentally, yes – as long as you don't expect it to change the person's mind on the spot. If you're correct about the other person's belief not being accurate, you can at least add to the weight of the conflicting evidence; you might hasten the arrival of the moment at which the evidence is so overwhelming that the person throws in the towel and changes his mind. But if you want to change a person's belief quickly, and he or she has profound certainty about it, you're not likely to succeed.

One other thing to keep in mind: If you have absolute certainty about your own ideas – the ones you're trying to convince the other person about – you're almost sure to fail at changing the other person's mind. Losing the ability to sway other people's opinions is one of the many disadvantages you bring upon yourself by buying into certainty.

Also, remember that the presence of *group* certainty can be a strong deterrent to the impact of conflicting evidence. The person in question will have the support of the group that agrees with his belief – and that will add many extra reasons not to change the belief, including the sense of belonging that comes with being part of a group. That's one of the reasons it's notoriously difficult to talk a believer into leaving a religious cult.

The nottom line is that it *is* possible to change someone's mind, even when the person in question has certainty. But you have to present the conflicting evidence slowly and nonjudgmentally, and you have to be willing to be patient, because the process can take a long time. And, you have to accept the possibility that you may not succeed at all.

Helping the World Rise Above Certainty Syndrome

Getting past certainty on our own is a good thing, and changing someone's mind when they hold a destructive belief is also a good thing. But the damage caused by certainty extends across the entire world. So the last question we need to be asking is: What can we do to help people around the world move past certainty syndrome?

Changing someone's mind about a specific belief that's protected by certainty is tough. But getting people to understand the drawbacks of this type of thinking doesn't necessarily require breaking through a barrier of certainty. Yes, some people do rely on certainty as a psychological support, and many others share certainty with groups that are like family to them. For these individuals, the idea of letting go of certainty may seem very threatening. But most people simply haven't thought about certainty as a concept, even though they rely on certainty out of habit.

Whether or not an individual sees giving up certainty as a threat, opening people's eyes to the limitations they've placed upon themselves by indulging in certainty can be a little tricky. So, if you want to help spread the word that certainty backfires, here are four helpful suggestions:

1) One key to getting people to realize that certainty isn't going to serve them well is to keep driving home the point that this is not an issue of whether they're right or wrong. Saying that certainty backfires is not the same as saying "your idea of the truth is wrong." Make sure they understand: The problem with being certain about something doesn't arise from the belief itself, *it arises from refusing to allow any questioning of it.*

2) Although it's important to emphasize the concrete downsides of certainty, it's a good idea to use examples that don't directly relate to the person you're talking to. If you use the person's own beliefs as an example, he's likely to think you're attacking him; that will quickly bring the discussion to a halt. But if you can illustrate the problems caused by certainty using examples that your listener doesn't have a personal investment in, he'll (hopefully) get the message. Then, once he sees the downsides of insisting on certainty, he'll realize that the disadvantages apply to *everyone's* ideas about what's true – even his own.

3) Emphasize how much this realization has helped you – and has helped you *without* forcing you to change your beliefs about what's true.

4) Always come back to the positive. Certainty is a huge roadblock in our lives; deciding to let go of certainty is like moving a huge boulder out of your path. And you don't have to change what you believe to move that boulder; you just have to change your attitude about certainty.

Ultimately, as physicist Max Planck noted in the quote at the beginning of this chapter, many new ideas are only accepted when a new generation grows up with them. The older generations sometimes can't get past their certainty and refuse to consider them. When Dr. Ignaz Semmelweis realized that doctors needed to wash their hands to prevent the spread of disease back in the mid-1800s, the doctors of the time were scandalized. This idea implied that they might be causing people to get sick and die, and they would have none of it. It took several decades for a new generation of doctors to grow up accepting the idea. (Hopefully, such a scenario won't be repeated when it comes to grasping the idea that certainty backfires.)

So what can we do to help the world get past certainty syndrome? First, we can make sure that we stop falling back on certainty in our own lives. That will not only help keep us off the Wheel of Misfortune, it will also set a good example for those around us.

Second, we can make sure that the problems inherent in relying on certainty are out there for everyone to see. Certainty syndrome is not a topic that has received much press, and it's time to change that. When a worthy new idea does survive and is picked up by the next generation, it's partly because the new idea works. But it's also partly because the idea is widely spread, enough so that up-and-coming generations know about it and can make up their own minds about it. Refusing to rely on certainty really does work – it's one of the best ways to keep yourself off of the Wheel of Misfortune. So spreading the word, and encouraging up-and-coming generations to avoid falling into the trap of relying on certainty the way previous generations have, could make a huge difference in the way the future of our world unfolds.

In the meantime, I have great hope that even adults who have relied on certainty all their lives may be able to break that habit and start looking at the world from a less-comfortable but far more effective, certainty-free perspective that says, "I'm open to learning; I'm not going to be so quick to judge others; I'm not going to be swept up in fear and anger; I'm not going to pretend that I can ignore the consequences of my actions; I'm not going to accept evidence without careful examination just because it seems to support what I already think; and perhaps most important, I'm not going to let other people manipulate me just because they appear to agree with me."

All that's required to make this change happen in your own life is to forego the comfort of certainty. And if enough people make that change, we'll be on the road to a much less dangerous and far more tolerant world.

Once more, in brief:

Here are the key points to remember from Chapter 9:

• People hate the discomfort of uncertainty. It's much more comfortable to assume that what we believe is the truth, despite any evidence to the contrary.

• Almost everything that human beings have accepted as indisputable truth has eventually turned out to be at least partly wrong.

• Certainty is not the end-product of a logical thinking process. It is a *feeling* that we attach to certain thoughts because it serves several valuable purposes in our thinking processes. Furthermore, the feeling of certainty is absolutely *not* a guarantee that we are correct – although we often assume that it is.

• Accepting that certainty is a feedback mechanism and not a guarantee of accuracy doesn't mean "admitting you're wrong." It's a very effective, practical strategy, especially when times are tough. It will spare you from a host of self-imposed problems that come along with certainty.

• There are at least 14 good reasons to avoid certainty syndrome:
1. Certainty stops learning.
2. Certainty eliminates flexibility.
3. Certainty leads to poor choices.
4. Certainty makes people judgmental.
5. Certainty is contagious.
6. Certainty eliminates your ability to sway others.
7. Certainty undercuts problem-solving.
8. Certainty encourages fear and anger – which then encourage even more certainty.
9. Certainty justifies abuse.
10. Certainty makes people overlook consequences.
11. Certainty becomes ingrained and can last a lifetime.
12. Certainty causes people to accept bogus supporting "evidence" without questioning it.
13. Group certainty has even more pitfalls.
14. Certainty makes it easy for others to manipulate you.

• The best reason to separate church and state is certainty syndrome. A person with certainty about his religious beliefs – regardless of what they are – will suffer from all of the side effects of certainty syndrome. If that person is given political power, those side effects can result in disastrous choices that affect millions of people.

• At a personal level, assuming that everything we believe to be a fact will eventually turn out to be at least partly mistaken increases our power and vision and removes a host of obstacles to making our lives better.

• One of the best ways to avoid the pitfalls of "absolute certainty" in yourself is to keep asking questions – even when it's easier to avoid asking them. However, asking questions isn't the same as *demanding answers*. There are times when you can demand an answer, and times when you're better off being patient.

• When someone challenges *your* ideas about the truth, think of it as a chance to grow.

• It can be difficult or impossible to change someone else's certainty, especially quickly – and especially if you're trying to do so based on your own absolute certainty about the opposing viewpoint. However, if you present conflicting evidence in a nonjudgmental way, you may eventually help to move the other person to the point at which he no longer sees the belief as tenable, and he finally does change his mind.

• Eliminating certainty from the world could change the world dramatically for the better, but may take generations to accomplish. Spreading the word about the dangers and pitfalls of certainty syndrome can help.

NOTES for Chapter 9

1. Described in *Phantom flashbulbs: False recollections of hearing the news about Challenger*, by Ulric Neisser and Nicole Harsch, in *Affect and Accuracy in Recall: Studies of "Flashbulb" Memories.* Eugene Winograd and Ulric Neisser, editors. Cambridge University Press, 1992.
2. Bandler R & Grinder J (1979). Frogs Into Princes. Moab, Utah: Real People Press.
3. For a much more detailed discussion of these ideas, check out the book *On Being Certain: Believing You Are Right Even When You're Not*. St. Martin's Press 2008.

4. Westen D, Blagov PS, Harenski K, Kilts C, Hamann S. Neural bases of motivated reasoning: an FMRI study of emotional constraints on partisan political judgment in the 2004 U.S. Presidential election. J Cogn Neurosci. 2006 Nov;18(11):1947-58.
5. As described in his book *Expert Political Judgment: How Good Is It? How Can We Know?* Princeton University Press 2005.
6. In his book *On Being Certain: Believing You Are Right Even When You're Not.*

10.
Create the Future You Want.

***Avoid being trapped by your feelings about
the past or future. Instead, use the power you have
in the present to begin achieving your goals.***

"Do what you can with what you have, where you are."
  – Theodore Roosevelt

"Unhappiness is not knowing what we want and killing ourselves to get it."
  – Don Herald

"Patience is bitter, but its fruit is sweet."
  – Jean Jacques Rousseau, in Emile (1762)

In 1977, actor LeVar Burton became famous – at the age of 19 – for playing the lead role in the groundbreaking television miniseries *Roots*, which portrayed the kind of experiences shared by many Africans who were captured and sold into slavery in America before the Civil War. The resulting success and fame Burton experienced at this age overwhelmed him. In a 1988 interview he notes that in the midst of this success he seemed to have everything – but he was not at all happy. Eventually, that contributed to his career sliding downhill. In a way, he became trapped by his recent past; everything about his life was shaped by his success, whether he liked what was happening or not.

Finally, he began psychoanalysis and started taking a more positive, spiritual view of life. One of the things he did was decide that he needed to be specific about what it was he really wanted and start focusing on it, instead of being caught up in everything that was less than ideal in his life. After some thought, he realized that what he most wanted to do was to star in a television program, so he got a pad of paper and wrote down a detailed description of the hypothetical program he wanted to be part of: a one-hour dramatic series with lots of action, adventure and romance, successful and popular with both the audience and the critics. He even listed the starting salary he wanted. He taped the description above his bed and focused on this goal every day. At night, he said in the interview, "I dreamed on it."

The strategy worked: Two months later he was hired as a featured member of the cast of *Star Trek: The Next Generation.* The job description was a perfect match, and the series was extremely successful.[1]

This is a great example of the power of switching from a world view that says, "I'm trapped by my past" to a worldview that says, "I'm a free agent in the present. I'm going to find ways to change what I'm doing here and now so I create the future I want."

Creating the Future You Want

All of us experience our lives in the context of the passage of time; that's a basic part of being human. Furthermore, most of us think of the past as being set in stone, but see the future as changeable; we believe that we can change it via the choices we make today. (In fact, the ability to determine our future by making wise choices in the present is arguably the greatest power we have in our lives.)

Unfortunately, our ability to create the future we'd like to experience is easily undercut by beliefs about our limitations (for example, as reflected in the fixed mindset we talked about in Chapter Two). Our ability to create the future can also be undercut by certain beliefs about the past and the future – what we might call "time traps." Furthermore, our attempts to reach our goals can misfire simply because we don't have the proper tools and strategies at our disposal. Creating the future is like creating anything else: If you don't know what you're doing, the result of your efforts is probably not going to be what you hoped for.

In this chapter, we'll address these concerns in two sections. In the first half of the chapter, we'll talk about how to avoid being derailed by time traps. In the second half of this chapter, we'll address the problem of not having the right tools and strategies to create the future you want.

In that section we'll outline a detailed roadmap for success – 12 specific strategies you can use to make it very likely that you will, in fact, reach your goals and end up with the life you want to have.

There are four main time traps – four ways your beliefs about the past and future can keep you from achieving your goals in life:

Time trap #1: Believing that you're controlled by the past. For example, you might believe that past events have pushed your life in directions that you have no power to alter. That belief can very effectively prevent you from changing direction.

Time trap #2: Spending too much time "living in the past" because you remember it as being better than the present. This can become an energy sink, and that will work against you when times are tough. Furthermore, your recollections and conclusions about the past may not be accurate.

Time trap #3: Fearing the future. This is a common experience, especially when times are tough. Most of us know that this is counterproductive and based purely on assumptions about events that may not actually happen, but it can be a very hard habit to break.

Time trap #4: Seeing your happiness as only being possible in the future after some condition is met or some event comes to pass. This belief backfires in multiple ways, and (ironically) it can be a major impediment to actually ending up with the result you think will make you happy! Even worse, if you ultimately do find yourself in those circumstances you were pinning your happiness on, there's a very good chance that you won't be as happy as you expected.

Let's talk about each of these in detail.

Time Trap #1: Believing you're controlled by the past

Believing that the past controls us – i.e., that events that happened in the past have put limitations on what is possible in the present – is one key way that we can trap ourselves in a life that makes us unhappy. It allows past events (or more accurately, our *recollection* of those events) to set the agenda for what we can do, or think we should be doing, now.

Unfortunately, believing that we are limited by anything, including the past, becomes a self-fulfilling prophecy. Richard Bach put it succinctly in his book *Illusions*: "Believe in your limitations, and sure enough, they're yours."

The idea that our current problems are being caused by past events is an illusion. Your past experiences may have led you to where you currently find yourself – but that's very different from saying that your past *is causing* your current problems, and in some way preventing you from solving them. We are, and always will be, independent agents in the present. (Ironically, that independence includes the right to see yourself as being controlled by past events, if you choose to. You can also choose to believe that you're being controlled by sentient lizards who live on the other side of the galaxy, but in either case, you're allowing yourself to be influenced by a belief, not an accurate analysis of your situation.)

To fully appreciate the fact that the past is *not* causing or controlling your current situation, it's very important to make a distinction between the question, "How did this situation get started?" and the question *"Why is this situation continuing?"* The second question is the one you need to answer if you want to change things for the better.

For example, suppose you were mistreated or abused as a child. Clearly, that kind of experience can be life-altering. But if you're now passing the same abuse on to others, or if you're living your life afraid to be close to others because of that past abuse, *blaming your behavior on your past is pointless.* It's like driving down a road and saying "I can't turn off of this road because I started driving down this road a long time ago." That may be the reason you're driving down the road right now, but seeing that as preventing you from making a turn onto a different road is completely self-defeating – and completely false. You can *always* stop and decide to change what you're doing, regardless of what happened in the past.

An excellent thought relating to this comes from the late author Jane Roberts, who said *the present is the point of power*. In other words, NOW is when you have the power to change things. Not tomorrow or next year, not yesterday or at some distant point in your past.

Taking this idea to heart is one of the most important antidotes for powerlessness. We are always couched in the present moment, and the present moment is where our power lies – whether we choose to realize it and use that power or not.

NOTE: Sometimes, when people have undergone extreme traumas, the psychological impact and repercussions can also be extreme, and may call for more help than this book can provide. These cases are usually considered to be post-traumatic stress disorder, or PTSD. If you find that your life is being severely hampered by recurring nightmares or fears that make it difficult or impossible to function, you may have PTSD and should seek professional help. The suggestions in this section are aimed at those of us who feel limited by our past, but not to such an extreme level.

Breaking the Chains of the Past

If you feel that your current life is being controlled or negatively influenced by your past, here are five strategies that can help:

1) Don't simply accept the idea that the past can control you in the present.

2) Make a commitment to changing your current situation.

3) Look for present-day "leftovers" from your past that may actually be triggering the situation you don't like right now, so you can take steps to eliminate them or change your relationship to them.

4) Look for *payoffs* you may not realize you're getting for remaining stuck in your unhappy situation.

5) If you need help to break out of your cycle of self-limitation, get that help.

Let's consider each of these in more detail.

Strategy 1: Don't simply accept the idea that the past can control you in the present. This is just the first step, but it's a crucial step. If you've accepted the idea that the past has the power to control you, you have to challenge that idea in order to give yourself the freedom to make the changes you want to see in your life.

Many of the beliefs we carry with us – beliefs that shape our choices and actions – are invisible to us. They've become such a standard part of our internal landscape, so to speak, that we stop being aware that they're there. (This is especially true if we have certainty about them, as discussed in Chapter 9.) So if you feel that your past is holding you back in some way, stop and consider what that means. Are you buying the argument that you can't turn off a road because you started driving down it a long time ago?

Your past only has as much control over you as you give it. So, if you've bought into the idea that you're at the mercy of your past, put that idea front and center and consider whether it truly makes sense. (Hint: It doesn't.)

Deciding that you're actually not at the mercy of your past won't automatically change your life – but until you challenge that belief, it may very well keep you trapped. Once you consciously decide that your past can't really control your present – that something else is going on – it will be like opening a door that you've been keeping shut without realizing it. Then you'll be free to find ways to step through that open door.

Strategy 2: Make a commitment to changing your current situation. It's much easier to complain about what you don't like than to make changes in your life. Furthermore, blaming what you don't like right now on the past provides justification for doing the easy thing: *nothing*. Also, there's the phenomenon of "learned helplessness" described in Chapter 3: Once you've been in a bad situation for a while, the natural tendency is to become pessimistic and ignore ways to escape from it, even when they're staring you in the face. This also helps to trap us.

So, a key part of getting back your power in the present is making a commitment to solving your problems. Once you've acknowledged that change is possible, make an official proclamation to yourself – and to at least one person close to you – that you're going to make the effort to bring about the changes you need. This "makes it official" that you understand the need for a change, and that you're making it a goal to take concrete steps and make those changes happen. Without making this commitment, you're almost certain to remain stuck in your unhappy situation.

Strategy 3: Look for present-day "leftovers" from your past that may actually be triggering the situation you don't like right now, so you can take steps to eliminate them or change your relationship to them. If you're feeling controlled or limited by past events that are no longer happening, something in the present – some "leftover" from your past – needs to be addressed. This could be something internal or something external.

To deal with this, you first have to identify what remnant of the past is still with you. What is causing you to act as if those events were still happening? Are you still rerunning them in your mind? Are others in your life reminding you of those events?

One kind of "leftover" from the past that may still affect us years later is negativity picked up from others – especially if that negativity was a low opinion of us. Perhaps a family member or some of your peers always said, "No one is ever going to like you," "You're not very smart," "You're not a real man," "You'll always be ugly," etc. Absorbing and internalizing these kinds of comments is a normal human tendency; we often accept others' negative opinions of us (especially when we're growing up). Unfortunately, those claims can then become part of our consciousness for years afterward.

In fact, those negative opinions can remain with us long after the people who showered us with them have disappeared from our lives. For example, a critical parent could leave you going through life with low self-esteem. But you're not *stuck* with low self-esteem unless you're still carrying that parent around inside your head. Or perhaps other kids taunted you as a child. If some of your current behavior – things you're still doing – amount to trying to prove that those kids were wrong, who are you trying to prove it to now? Yourself, basically, because you've internalized those putdowns and you're carrying them around with you.

It shouldn't be hard to see that it's a losing battle to try and prove something to people who aren't around any more. It makes far more sense to recognize that you've unwittingly internalized someone else's negativity, and then take steps to remove those ideas from your mental landscape. You can do that by learning to notice when you're internally repeating those negative thoughts. When you catch yourself doing that, challenge them. Ask yourself where those ideas came from and question their validity. Remind yourself of the evidence that contradicts those negative beliefs. If you get in the habit of doing this, slowly but surely those negative ideas from the past will fade.

Another "leftover" that we may be carrying from the past is anger over previous mistreatment. That can easily shape our present by sapping our energy, spreading our resulting bad feelings onto other people and into other events, and keeping our focus on old issues instead of on the possibilities that are in front of us right now. If the cause of your anger is truly in the past, then letting go of that anger is the answer, although this can be difficult if the offense was profound (for example, child abuse or rape). If you can't let go of your anger on your own, get help. Eliminating this baggage from the past will make a huge difference in your ability to create the life you want. (For more on the importance of letting go of anger, see Chapter 3: Hold On To Your Personal Power.)

Yet another present-day "leftover" that can cause you to feel that you're controlled by the past is people or things around you that, for one reason or another, remind you of the past. If a parent was abusive when you were growing up, for example, you might find yourself now associating with someone who is abusive in the same way, causing you to have a resurgence of the old feelings and doubts about yourself that you had back then. Once you identify that something like this is triggering negativity in your life, take steps to change your relationship with the person (or people) in question. This might entail talking to them about how they interact with you, or altering your circumstances so you don't interact with them in the same way – or so you don't interact with them at all. (Actually, the simplest solution is to change your perception of your relationship with them so that they no longer have a negative effect on you, but that's not always easy to do.)

Strategy 4: A fourth way to free yourself from the idea that your past is limiting you is to **look for payoffs you may not realize you're getting for remaining stuck in your unhappy situation**. Locating the leftovers from your past that are causing your feelings of limitation will only reveal half of the problem. The other half is that something has been dissuading you from making changes – some kind of payoff you're getting from staying in the current situation. Given that we're talking about a situation you don't like, the payoff is very likely an avoidance payoff. In other words, by leaving the unpleasant status quo alone and just feeling bad about it, you're avoiding dealing with something you perceive as even more unpleasant or scary. For example, if a past emotional trauma has left you angry or fearful, to get past that you may have to confront those feelings and think about the trauma – and avoiding that confrontation could be the payoff you've been getting for letting the status quo continue.

Either way, to free up your ability to move on you'll have to determine what payoff you're getting from remaining in your situation. If you realize that it's an avoidance payoff, you'll have to make a conscious decision about whether avoiding that scary thing is worth the suffering you're enduring with the status quo. On the other hand, if you realize you've been getting a *positive* payoff for staying in your less-than-ideal situation – for example, someone in your life rewards you with approval for staying in your unpleasant situation – you'll have to decide whether the reward you're getting is a good tradeoff for the situation you don't like. Once you've consciously made a decision, you'll be in a much better position to take action.

In either case, the key factor here is becoming *conscious* of what's really going on. Bad situations – especially those that seem rooted in the past – often continue because of fears, anger and other factors that we're not consciously looking at. Such things are far less scary and much easier to deal with once we bring them into the light of day.

One last point about freeing yourself from the belief that your past is limiting you:

Strategy 5: If you need help to break out of your cycle of self-limitation, get that help. Making these kinds of changes can be totally life-altering. It can also be very challenging. In short, the bigger the issues involved, the more you may need outside help to make the change. Asking for help can be embarrassing, but it's vastly preferable to spending the rest of your life suffering because you were afraid to ask for help.

Time Trap #2: "Living in the past" – devoting too much energy to remembered "better times."

Hard times, by definition, are less desirable than good times. If you have strong memories of good times in the past – say, before economic or political changes, or before you lost someone you loved – it's easy to spend a fair amount of mental time "reliving" that previous situation. Done to excess, however, this can become a roadblock to creating a better future. (As folksinger Tom Paxton has said, "It's okay to look back, as long as you don't stare.") Dwelling on better times in the past diverts your energy away from improving your current situation, and the sense of loss it generates in the present can lead to depression and despair, making your current life even more unpleasant than it already is.

This is a very different problem from feeling controlled by your past, but it can derail your energy just as surely. It's a question of what you choose to focus on – and no matter how much you miss the past, it's up to you how much time and mental energy you devote to thinking about it.

Here's another way to look at this. If you're spending a lot of mental energy reliving what you think your life was like at some point in the past, you are, in essence, trying to recreate it. There are three problems with this:

First, the past doesn't repeat itself, so the best you can actually hope to create in the future is a variation on the situation you miss. Even in the best of all possible worlds, the future will never be identical to your recollection of the past.

Second, when you use your energy to replay the past, you're not using it to create the future – and a positive new future situation would serve you much better than mental excursions into past situations that no longer exist.

Third, your recollection of the past is probably not as accurate as you believe. Human memory is designed to eliminate unpleasant memories (unless we constantly rehash them to keep them alive), leaving us with a rosier picture of the past than what we actually experienced. So if you *did* actually recreate the past that you miss, you might be shocked by all the negatives you've forgotten about. (It would be like remarrying someone you divorced years ago, only to be reminded why you divorced them the first time around!)

The important thing here is to make an honest appraisal of your thinking habits. If you know you're spending too much time thinking about the past, remind yourself that you have a limited amount of time and energy. Although you can't recreate the past, you can create a new situation that brings you the same benefits the previous situation brought you – for example, love, enough money, power over certain aspects of your life – whatever it was that made that past time seem so ideal. It makes a lot more sense to use your limited time and energy creating a new situation that has those benefits, instead of allowing the past to take up all of your time and energy.

PS: Don't fall into the trap of believing that nothing could ever be as good as what you experienced in the past. Nothing in the future will be exactly like it – but future possibilities are only constrained by your imagination and by how much effort you put into creating what you want. So appreciate the past for the good things it brought you – but put your energy into creating what you want in the future.

Time Trap #3: Fearing the future

Human brains have a very large frontal lobe (the section of the brain right behind the forehead). At some point it was discovered that damage to this area didn't turn people into vegetables, so it was thought that the frontal lobe might not serve any important purpose. In fact, it now appears that the frontal lobe is the part of the brain that imagines the future – a capability that's pretty much uniquely human. It certainly is key to creating the future you'd like to experience and moving toward a chosen goal.

Most people have heard the term "frontal lobotomy," which refers to surgically removing the frontal lobe of the brain. This type of surgery, among other things, makes a person very calm. That's what originally led to the idea that a frontal lobotomy might be a good thing for some highly anxious psychiatric patients. Of course, knowing what we know today, it's not hard to see how losing your ability to think about the future might eliminate anxiety.

Like most things in life, our unique frontal lobe is a mixed blessing: It apparently gives us the ability to choose our future in a way few other creatures on Earth can, but it also makes it possible to become filled with fear and anxiety over what we think the future may hold. That fear and worry can rob us of our energy and health and undercut our ability to make decisions. Fear can certainly prevent us from taking actions that would help us create the future we want to experience. So if you have fears about the future, addressing them consciously can make a big difference in your happiness *and* your ability to end up where you'd like to be.

There are many different ways we can experience fear and anxiety about the future, and many different reasons we might do so. Here are a few different kinds of future-oriented fears you may have experienced, and some strategies for dealing with them.

• ***Fears and anxieties that you can't pin down.*** "Worrying" can be thought of as fearing some possible unpleasant future situation. It's bad enough that we run through future scenarios with scary endings in our conscious minds; what makes fear and worrying even more problematic is that we often run through those scary scenarios *outside of consciousness.*

While that might sound like a good thing (at least better than thinking about the possibilities we're afraid of consciously) it's actually a bad thing, because even if we aren't *consciously* thinking about them, their unpleasant endings can trigger fear or concern that's very conscious. This can lead to a general state of anxiety or dread that we can't even explain, because the thing that's triggering the anxiety is outside of our conscious focus. All we notice is the feeling of dread, and the emotions can be just as disabling as if you were devoting your full conscious attention to what you're afraid of.

Suppose you react with overwhelming fear to the idea of encountering a snake. A likely explanation is that whenever the subject of snakes comes up, you start running through a terrifying encounter with a snake (or snakes) in your mind – but outside of your normal consciousness. Since the mental process triggering the fear reaction is mostly outside of your awareness, your reaction may seem mysterious and uncontrollable. In reality, it's not.

To interrupt this mental chain of events and stop the fear response, you just have to make your "mental movie" of a scary encounter with snakes conscious. Then you can do something to prevent your mind from running that "movie" and triggering fear every time the subject of snakes comes up. (Practitioners of neuro-linguistic programming have developed techniques to interfere with this type of mental process, thus eliminating the automatic fear reaction. To learn more about their methods, check out the book *Frogs Into Princes*.[2])

Now, let's say instead of snakes, you're very worried about the possibility of someone you care about being hurt or killed. You may not be consciously imagining the worst, but if you're feeling fear and anxiety about this possibility, it's likely that you're running through that kind of scenario in your mind outside of consciousness.

Again, the antidote to this kind of worry is to first make this "mental movie" of undesirable events conscious. It's not difficult to do: You just have to realize that a mental process is taking place that you may have been consciously ignoring. *Stop ignoring it* and address it directly. (Remember, it's mostly scary *because* you haven't been addressing it consciously.)

That brings us to the next type of future-oriented fear....

• ***Fear that if something happens you won't be able to deal with it.***
In my experience, what makes a scary mental scenario generate fear or worry (whether it's conscious or unconscious) is that is has no ending

in your mental "movie" except the scary one. Fears are always about a theoretical outcome: If I quit this job I hate, my family will starve; if my child goes into a bad neighborhood without my protection, he could be hurt or killed; if I do what I really want to do, my true love will leave me; if I take steps to protect my rights, I'll be punished; and so forth. The mind is quite capable of creating scary mental movies about the possible future in which bad outcomes occur, and those movies may be running over and over just outside of your conscious focus, generating fear and anxiety.

In reality, there are probably many things you could do that would salvage a bad situation if it actually occurred. The problem is, when you're running through a "crisis movie" (inside or outside of consciousness) you're probably just accepting the scary ending without questioning it. So, the antidote is to consciously decide what *specific actions* you would take to make things better if the scary possibility actually occurred. In other words, watch your scary mental movie consciously – and then *write a different ending.* What would you really do if the thing you're scared about actually happened? How could you make something good come out of it?

The point is that these kinds of mental movies are troubling because they leave us stuck with a scary outcome; they have no hopeful resolution. *That's what makes them scary: the idea that this could happen – and if it does, you have no way to deal with it.* If you can demonstrate to yourself that you *do* have some resources that would help you deal with it, a lot of the anxiety will drop away.

Of course, this doesn't mean you'll be *happy* if the scenario you're afraid of actually happens, but it will let you see clearly that you have some resources and some ideas about what to do. If your worst fears happen, the world will not end. There is something besides "the void" at the end of that scary tunnel.

Not only can defusing this kind of thinking eliminate a lot of fear and worry, it can also go a long way toward keeping you from creating the very chain of possible events that you're reacting to with fear and anxiety. Ironically, the more nervous we are about the possibility of something happening, the more likely we are to say things and take actions that help to create those events. So, defusing the mental process that's generating your fear and anxiety may not only help give you back a little piece of mind, it may help to steer your future away from those undesirable, scary situations.

- **Obsessive fears.** What if a fear spirals out of control, even when you know it doesn't make sense because you've already taken steps to prevent what you're worried about? In extreme form, this might be considered a psychiatric disorder, but I think most people have experienced being moderately obsessed about something in a way that becomes irritating or counterproductive. Fear can be particularly unpleasant if it becomes obsessive. However, it is possible to break an obsessive mental circle.

To my knowledge, the best work in this area has been done by Jeffrey Schwartz, MD, a psychiatrist and researcher in the field of neuroplasticity. Dr. Schwartz is the author of *Brain Lock: Free Yourself from Obsessive-Compulsive Behavior*.[3] He's shown that under ordinarily circumstances, fear triggers three different centers in the brain: one that makes us uncomfortable, one that motivates us to act, and one that turns off the alarm once action has been taken. When we obsess about something, that cycle becomes rewired so that the third part doesn't happen. Instead, we continue to be alarmed and try to take action – assuming we can, or at least think we can. (This explains repetitive behaviors such as constantly washing your hands because of a fear of germs; the third brain center isn't doing its job and turning off the fear once your hands have been washed.)

Dr. Schwartz's success in treating this type of obsession has come from focusing on the processes that are happening in the brain, instead of focusing on the specifics of the fear. In other words, the problem isn't really the thing we're obsessing about; it's the way our brain is working. So he teaches people to begin by thinking of their obsessive behavior as a brain-process problem, not a problem about whatever they're afraid of. In fact, the more these people focus on the content of their fears, no matter how positive their intention, the more the faulty brain process is reinforced. (Many traditional psychological approaches to curing obsession focus on content, and they don't usually produce high levels of success.)

Schwartz teaches people to think of managing the obsession as an issue of *derailing the process*; he doesn't have them focus on the content of their fears. So, following this model, when you feel obsessive fear, realize that it's a process unfolding in your brain. If you can actually do something that may address your obsessive fear and prevent a bad thing from happening (whether it's locking the door, washing your hands, turning off the oven, or whatever) *do it – but pay close attention, so you know for certain that you've done it.*

Then, make it your mission to shift your mental gears so the faulty pattern in your brain doesn't keep recycling. When the fear pops up again, instead of acting on it again, remind yourself that you know for certain you've done something about it, and then deliberately set the fear aside to deal with at another time. Finally, force yourself to engage in something else that's pleasant, so your thoughts have something else to occupy them. After a while your brain will learn to stop running through that obsessive pattern, and the cycle of obsessive fear will stop.

• **Fears that make us feel alive.** Despite the negative connotations we usually associate with fear, fear can have positive side effects as well. For example, we may be getting some kind of emotional payoff for remaining in a state of fear or worry. If we are, that payoff can undercut our efforts to eliminate the fear.

Emotions make us feel alive, whether they're emotions we usually think of as positive (e.g., happiness) or emotions we tend to think of as negative (e.g., fear). As strange as it seems, people often prefer feeling anxious, upset and unhappy to simply being calm and dealing with life, because the emotion creates a sense of *being alive*. It can actually be reassuring.

Needless to say, there are better ways to experience your aliveness! This is the kind of trade-off that people usually only buy into because they don't see it for what it is. Once you realize that fear can actually have this positive side effect, you can decide whether or not that's a factor in the fear that you're experiencing. If it is, you can make a conscious choice about whether you want to continue making that trade-off.

One last helpful strategy when dealing with fear of the future: If you're frustrated because you feel the thing you're worried about is completely out of your control – i.e., nothing you can do can possibly have any effect on what will happen – put your energy into *visualizing* a different outcome – one that you want. Despite skepticism among some who believe that events can't be influenced by thought alone, plenty of people have experienced the opposite. Furthermore, vividly imagining a positive outcome will remind you that a more positive outcome is possible, and that will help keep your perspective from becoming totally negative.

Time Trap #4: Believing your happiness depends on one specific future situation.

If there's one mistake we human beings seem to make regularly, it's this one: believing that our happiness depends on some particular set of circumstances that could possibly happen at some point in the future. Believing this can lead to enormous unhappiness and wasted time. It can even lead to a wasted life.

Here are three reasons this belief backfires:

Reason #1: *If you're depending on future events to make you happy, you're going to spend much of your life unhappy.* If you decide that you'll only be happy when something happens in the future, you're basically deciding that *you can't be happy now* because the situation you're waiting for hasn't happened yet. You are choosing to be unhappy until then. This is totally self-defeating.

Think of it this way: Life is a journey that keeps going until we die. (And who knows – maybe after we die!) Your goal should be to be happy *during the journey*, not just when and if you reach some specific point in your journey.

Reason #2: *People are very bad at knowing what will actually make them happy.* The things we are certain will make us happy often turn out to not make us happy at all. (Comedian and actor Jim Carrey once said, "I think everybody should get rich and famous and do everything they ever dreamed of, so they can see it's not the answer.") One reason that's true is that we tend to believe generally accepted ideas about happiness, like the idea that having more money will make us happier. Such ideas are not usually based on our own experience – and they're often simply not true.

If you ever get to spend time with people who have a great deal of wealth, for example, you'll quickly discover that most of them are not any happier than the rest of us. People who have won millions by playing the lottery are often the first to express disappointment that the windfall didn't bring them happiness. I'm sure there are exceptions to that, but the reality is that massive quantities of money do not come with happiness attached. (Yes, it is true that being very poor does often correlate with being *less* happy. But having enough money to meet your needs is quite different from having enormous wealth. We'll talk more about this later in this chapter.)

Other examples of people being bad at knowing what will make them happy can be seen in relationships and career choices. Some people decide that they won't be happy until they end up with the person of their dreams. Unfortunately, there are countless stories of people who fought to end up with a particular partner, only to find out that being with that person wasn't anything like what they imagined it would be. And plenty of people have devoted their lives to a career path they didn't really enjoy, thinking it would make them happy because it would win someone else's approval – a parent or spouse, for example. But because they spent their lives pursuing something they didn't really enjoy, they were never very happy; and in many cases, even if they achieved great success in their chosen field, it didn't win the other person's approval anyway!

It's true that we're not always wrong; sometimes what we think will make us happy does turn out to make us happy. Unfortunately, even when it turns out we guessed right and reaching our goal wasn't loaded with unforeseen downsides, there's another catch: Being in that situation will not maintain your happiness endlessly. Human beings get used to things after a while. Elation wears off and boredom sets in.

In short, setting up a future situation as your source of happiness not only postpones your happiness until you get there, it puts all of your eggs in one basket – one that, by definition, you haven't experienced first-hand. Assuming that you actually succeed in creating that situation, everything you believed about it could turn out to be wrong, or could be offset by unforeseen problems. And, eventually, whatever happiness it does bring you will wear off.

Again, the solution is simple: Instead of pinning your happiness on reaching a goal, *make it your mission to be happy during the journey to the goal.* Doing this won't diminish the satisfaction you feel when you get there, but you'll be much more likely to have a happy life in the meantime. And if for some reason you don't make it to your goal, you will have had fun on the journey anyway!

Reason #3: A third reason that believing your happiness depends on one specific future situation backfires is that **seeing your happiness and/or satisfaction as lying in the future can actually make it harder to get there.** There's nothing wrong with using a future focus to create the future you want – in fact, that's part of the game. The problem arises when you see happiness as being impossible to achieve until you reach that future goal. This creates the perspective that *the present is not okay.* That perspective backfires. In fact, it helps keep you stuck where you are.

If you insist on labeling your present circumstances as horrible, you'll waste a lot of energy resisting your current experience. That means you'll be focusing a lot of your energy on what you *don't* want, which will actually help to perpetuate it. It will also divert your energy away from creating what you do want.

Furthermore, seeing what you have right now as unacceptable can add a sense of desperation to your desire to reach your goal – i.e., *if I don't make this happen I'm going to be miserable forever!* To enlist the universe's help in reaching your goal (not to mention anyone else's help), you need to be communicating what you want clearly and calmly. Desperation acts like static, interfering with the message you're trying to put out there.

That's why one of the best ways to create the future you want is to make peace with what you have right now – in other words, to decide that the present, with all of its inadequacies, *is okay.* If you can manage to see your current circumstances that way, you'll free up a tremendous amount of energy which can then help you move more quickly towards the situation you'd rather be in.

Here's another way to say this: If you want to be happy later, *maximize your happiness now*. Doing so will not only make you happier now, it will remove a lot of obstacles that will otherwise slow your journey towards a better situation.

I know that sometimes being happy during the journey to your goals may seem like a tall order, depending on your ideas about happiness and how you feel about your current circumstances. Nevertheless, it's really important to try. (If you need further help getting to that place, I recommend checking out the book *Happy For No Reason* by Marcy Shimoff.)

12 Strategies for Creating the Future You Want

Even if you manage to avoid these four "time traps," you still won't be very effective at creating the future you want unless you use strategies that make time work to your advantage.

The reality is that we're creating our future all the time; what we

Chapter 10: Create the Future You Want

don't always do is create the future we *want*. That's because in order to effectively create the future, we have to use the future-creating process in the right way. It's like learning to drive a car. To become a driver you have to learn a whole series of actions to take; you have to learn to take them in the right order; you have to learn which things you need to pay attention to when the car is moving; and so on. If you don't master the basics of driving, or do them in the right order, you're likely to end up lost or in an accident.

Creating your future is much the same; to do it well and end up where you want to go, it's very helpful to master a number of effective strategies and learn how and when to use them. If you plunge ahead without any strategies or plan, you may very well end up being one of those people who never realize their dreams.

Think of it this way: You're creating your future all the time, every day, whether you want to or not. So you might as well figure out how to make the process produce the results you want – instead of results you don't want.

With that in mind, here are 12 strategies that will help you to create the future you'd like to experience:

1) Choose your goal carefully, and be specific!
2) Describe your goal carefully.
3) Make a commitment to achieving your goal.
4) Create a game plan.
5) Create specific proactive strategies.
6) Create specific reactive strategies.
7) Set up favorable conditions that will help you create the result you want.
8) If your goal is to create a specific thing, and a good outcome is extremely important, perform a "pre-mortem."
9) Maintain effective attitudes and expectations.
10) Use visualization and focus.
11) Take action!
12) Stop periodically and think about the choices you're making on the way to your goal.

There's a lot to say about each of these, so let's look at them in more detail.

Creating the Future You Want – Strategy #1: Choose your goal carefully, and be specific! As Lilly Tomlin once said, "I always wanted to be somebody, but now I realize I should have been more specific." If you have no destination in mind, you're going to wander aimlessly. So the first rule in creating what you want is to *know what it is*. As the saying goes, "You have to name it to claim it."

This is actually not quite as straightforward as it sounds – there are several pitfalls you need to avoid in order to avoid making a choice you'll regret later.

– *Pitfall #1*: **Don't overlook the reality that you're picking a journey, not just a goal.** You'll probably spend a long time working to reach your goal; depending on the goal, it could be weeks, months, years or decades. It's a huge mistake to ignore the kind of experience you'll be having during that time because you think you'll be happy when you reach your goal. In other words, pick goals that will provide you with satisfaction *while you're working to create them*. If your goal is to become rich, make sure your goal involves doing something you enjoy that will make you rich. If your goal is to win the heart of one specific person, find a way to work toward that goal that will be fun, not some way that will make you miserable. (Your chances of winning someone's heart, by the way, go up enormously if the person can see that you're already happy!)

If you pick a goal that will bring you some level of happiness during the journey, you won't be setting yourself up to suffer all the way to the goal. Besides, as we already discussed, when you reach your goal you may find that it's less thrilling than you expected. If you choose an enjoyable journey, at least you won't be sorry you made the trip. In fact, you should be having such a good time making the journey that reaching your goal might spoil the fun you're having! That's a far better setup than hoping achieving your goal will make up for the misery of the journey.

As noted in my song *Piece of the Puzzle*, George Burns once observed that he'd rather fail at something he loved than succeed at something he hated. He understood that if you're on a journey you enjoy, you've already won the game, whether you win the grand prize or not. If you're on a journey you're not enjoying, you've already lost, regardless of whether you reach your goal or not.

– **_Pitfall #2_: Don't assume a particular goal will make you happy if you achieve it.** Once you have a specific goal in mind and start working towards it, there's a good chance you'll reach it. That makes it *very important* to take your time, do some homework and think carefully before you begin devoting your time and energy to creating a new situation.

As mentioned earlier, people are very bad at predicting what will really make them happy. One reason we tend to have poor judgment about what will make us happy is that we usually choose our goal by imagining ourselves in that situation. If we imagine being happy and satisfied when we reach our goal, it seems like a good thing to aim for.

Sadly, this method for choosing where we want to end up is fraught with peril. There are a number of reasons for this, many of which are spelled out in Daniel Gilbert's book *Stumbling on Happiness*. Here are just a few reasons imagining yourself in your desired situation can backfire.

The first problem with assuming a particular goal will make us happy is that when we imagine what will make us happy in the future, we only incorporate whatever we already know about the experience in question. Actual experience is made up of millions of details, and until we're in a specific situation, we can't possibly know what all the details of that experience will be. So we base our imagined future on the details we do know about. For example, we might imagine that if we have lots of money we'll be able to live where we want, buy the things we want, get people to do what we ask, etc. Or, you might believe that if you become a successful surgeon, everyone will treat you with respect; and so forth.

As an outsider, it's not too hard to see that once people actually put themselves into these positions, all kinds of problems and downsides will also be part of the experience, and those downsides may easily offset the parts of the experience that we expected to make us happy. If you end up with an enormous amount of money, for example, friends and relatives and strangers may hound you to get some of it. You may find it hard to tell when people actually like you and when they're just hoping to get favors from you. You may be targeted by dishonest people looking to scam you. In the other example, if you become a successful surgeon, you may find that you're not getting as much respect as you thought you would; and meanwhile you *are* working long hours, stressing your body, not getting to see your family, and so on.

Of course, it's easy to dismiss this possibility. You may think, "I'm different – those downsides won't bother me!" But for most people, that kind of assumption would be based on bravado, not experience. The reality is, just imagining how you'll feel after achieving your goal is a dangerous way to choose your goal – especially if it's a big goal that will take you years and a lot of effort to achieve.

A second problem with assuming a particular goal will make us happy is that when we imagine a future situation and how we'll react to it, what we imagine is strongly influenced by how we're feeling at the time. Plenty of studies have shown this to be true. A simple example would be judging how enjoyable it will be to eat a particular food the next day. People's judgment about this is largely based on how hungry they are when you ask them. (Eating a plate of spaghetti won't sound so great if you're full, leading to a prediction that you won't enjoy it that much; but it may sound great if you're hungry, leading to the opposite prediction.) The same rule applies with larger, more important issues in life; our ideas about what situation will make us happy – and should therefore be our goal – are heavily influenced by how our lives are going at the time we're making the decision. Which, of course, has nothing to do with the reality we'll actually face once we achieve the goal.

A third problem with assuming reaching a particular goal will make us happy is that we fail to consider that pleasure is likely to wear off over time. We tend to think about the pleasure and satisfaction we'll feel when we reach a long-desired goal, but the reality is that things that start out being pleasurable become less pleasurable when we experience them over and over again. So even if you aren't bothered by downsides after you reach your goal, chances are good that the thrill will wear off after a while.

Ironically, the same is true of negative experiences, but in reverse; situations that are painful, such as a major loss or disaster, often become less painful than we would have predicted, and do so fairly quickly. That's because the human mind is very good at putting events into contexts that take the sting out of them. People often believe that they'll be emotionally destroyed by a huge loss or disaster, should it happen; but if it actually does happen, they deal with it and move on – even when they didn't think they'd be able to.

In any case, it's important to remember that even if you reach your goal, the pleasure you get will almost certainly be temporary. Knowing that could make a big difference in which things you decide are worth devoting years of your life to achieving.

A fourth problem with assuming a particular goal will make us happy is that we tend to buy into widespread beliefs about what makes people happy. As noted earlier, cultural beliefs about happiness are notoriously unreliable. One reason for that is that memory is easily distorted, with negative experiences being minimized or forgotten. As a result, people who have been where you're trying to go may give you reports that don't accurately reflect the negatives you're likely to encounter.

For example, if lots of people tell you that having children is the ultimate source of happiness, that's going to factor into your decision about whether or not to have kids. But in reality, people living with a teenager are likely to give you a very different report about the happiness that comes from raising children than someone who is recalling the experience after the kids have grown up and left home. The former parents are in the middle of one of the toughest parts of being a parent; the latter parents have already filtered their memories to focus on the most pleasant parts of the experience.

Furthermore, communal beliefs tend to be treated as fact simply because they're widely shared. So, if everyone around you says that money will make you happy, you may decide to make wealth one of your goals. However, widely-accepted ideas about what will make you happy can turn out to be wildly inaccurate.

So what's a good way to check your goals against reality? The best way is to find someone who is currently in the situation you think you'd like to experience and ask that person about the details of his or her life. (Asking before or after the person is actually in that situation will not necessarily give you reliable information; so, talk to them *while they are having the experience*.) This strategy is the one most likely to help you find out whether your goal really will make you happy.

For example, after I had spent 15 years living in New York City working as a musician, I was visited by a student at one of the schools I had attended who was interested in becoming a successful pop musician – essentially the same dream I had been following. By visiting me, he got to talk to someone who was right in the middle of what he thought was the kind of life he wanted. I told him about my experiences in great detail – the good parts and the bad. Afterwards, he wrote to me and told me that seeing what I was going through was causing him to have second thoughts about his goal of being a pop musician. However, he also said that he now realized he didn't have to follow the dictates of his friends and family about how to be happy in his life. In short, by talking to someone who was currently in the situation he had chosen as a goal, he got some useful information that his imagination could not have provided.

Most of us don't bother to do this kind of reality check. One reason we don't is that we believe in our own uniqueness. ("Just because *he's* not happy being rich doesn't mean *I'll* be unhappy as a rich person.") Of course, there could be some truth to that. However, it's risky to choose your life's goals making the assumption that you won't be as bothered by negatives as someone else is. Besides, even if you *would* react differently to the downsides associated with achieving your goal, doing your homework is still the best way to see what you might be getting into.

That's why it makes sense to talk to others who are currently having the experience you think you'd like to have. If that's not possible, read or listen to interviews that were done when the person being interviewed was in the position you'd like to be in. This should help shed some realistic light on what you'll find if you reach your goal – and maybe lead you to revise your goal for the better.

Here are a few strategies that will help when choosing your goal:

• ***For the most part, pick goals that won't take years or decades to achieve.*** Actually, there's nothing wrong with having a long-term goal, but studies suggest that you're much more likely to achieve short-term goals.[4] So, if you choose a very long-term goal, make sure to also pick short-term goals that will move you towards your bigger goal – goals that won't require years or decades to achieve. Make those your immediate goals. Achieving them will give you encouragement and satisfaction that will help keep you on track toward your bigger, long-term goal.

• ***Pick a goal that's realistic, in terms of what is physically possible.*** You can look younger, but you can't change your chronological age. You can learn to swim, but you may be too old to make the Olympic team. Keep it real!

• ***Beware of pinning your happiness on wealth and/or success.*** If you create wealth or success but not happiness, you haven't done yourself much of a favor. Plenty of studies have been done on the connection between wealth and happiness. Generally, they have concluded that money increases happiness up to a certain basic income level at which your needs are being met; once your income goes above that level, the correlation tends to disappear.[5,6] I would put it this way: Having less money than you need to meet your basic needs increases *unhappiness*; but having more money than you need for basic comforts does not necessarily lead to greater happiness.

One recent study surveyed more than 136,000 people living in 132 countries.[7] The study separated "happiness" into several different categories. It found that when people evaluated their "satisfaction with their lives," they tended to give higher marks if they had more wealth. But when asked about other factors such as positive and negative feelings, the correlation largely disappeared. Positive feelings, instead, were strongly associated with what the authors of the study call "social psychological prosperity." This category was based on questions like: Are you treated with respect by others? Do you have family or friends you can count on in an emergency? People who responded in the affirmative to these kinds of questions also reported higher levels of positive feelings in their lives – and that's not a bad definition of being happier.

The study authors note that economics professor Tibor Scitovsky may have been correct when he distinguished between comfort and pleasure: He believes that being comfortable is mostly about simply having your needs and desires met. Pleasure, on the other hand, is more about being involved in stimulating and challenging activities, being with friends and learning new things.[8]

The reality is that many things get called "happiness," but some of them may not be as deserving of the title as others. (To this day, I still see articles in the popular media proclaiming that "a new study finds that being richer does make you happier." If you stumble across one of those, look carefully to see whether the study in question made a distinction between being satisfied, being comfortable and actually being happy.)

Here's another way to think of it: Life is all about working within limitations, and limited financial resources is one limitation that almost everyone has experienced. Depending on your perspective and how serious your financial limitation is, it can definitely lead to frustration, stress and unhappiness. But that's just one type of limitation people encounter in life. Having money can reduce or eliminate that concern, but there are lots of other limitations you may face in life that have nothing to do with money – health problems, relationship problems, fears, physical limitations like blindness or deafness, limitations imposed by your current circumstances, and so on. All the money in the world won't offset some of those limitations. Furthermore, extreme wealth can bring limitations of its own, such as undermining your privacy, making you a target, even undermining your relationships. So it's unrealistic to think that having a lot of money will necessarily bring you happiness.

The bottom line is that happiness and money are different animals. So make sure your personal goals are based around increasing your *happiness*. If your wallet gets fatter or your "street cred" goes up as a result of reaching your goal, that's great. But if your goal is simply to be rich or very successful, happiness may not be a side effect of reaching your goal. No matter how rich or successful you are – if you're miserable, you're miserable. As 18th-Century English author Charles Kingsley said, "We act as though comfort and luxury were the chief requirements of life, when all that we need to make us really happy is something to be enthusiastic about." Choose your goals accordingly.

Creating the Future You Want – Strategy #2: Describe your goal carefully. Spelling out the details of what you want is a critical part of creating it – both to help bring it about, and to make sure that you end up with a situation that's very close to what you wanted, not just an approximation.

Here are a few suggestions that will help you clarify exactly what you want:

– Suggestion #1: Don't be too general or abstract about your goal. The universe will never bring you an abstraction. Saying, "I want to be successful and loved by everyone!" doesn't give you a specific direction to go in or a specific end point to reach. It's equally pointless to state your goal as "being happy." If you want to create something, you have to be as specific as possible! Take your lead from LeVar Burton, whose story I recounted at the beginning of this chapter: Specify the job you want to have, or the details you'd like to see in your future partner, or the place you'd like to live. And if there are quantities involved in your goal – money, for example – be specific. (When Jim Carrey was starting out, he wrote himself a check for 10 million dollars from a hypothetical movie company and kept it in his wallet. Within a few years, he had a real check for that amount in his wallet.) Also, *make your goal measurable*;

that way you can tell how far along you are, and you'll know when you've achieved it.

This isn't just a nice-sounding idea; studies have shown that being specific about your goals makes a big difference. People produce better results when they set themselves specific goals than when they set vague goals.[9]

– Suggestion #2: *Frame your goal in positive terms rather than negative terms.* Studies have found that when your intention is to create something rather than to *prevent* something, the result is more likely to occur.[10] That may be partly because you tend to get whatever you focus your thoughts on – *even if it's something you don't want*. For that reason, it makes sense to focus your energy on the thing you *do* want to end up with, rather than focusing on not getting something you don't want. For example, if you decide that your goal is to live "anywhere other than this lousy town," the fact that you're focused on the place you *don't* want to live will actually encourage the universe to keep you right where you are. If you focus on the idea of moving to a specific other place, and imagine yourself there, you're more likely to end up there.

– Suggestion #3: *Make sure that the way you want to feel when you achieve your goal is part of what you're aiming for.* It's important to distinguish between wanting a thing and wanting to experience the way you believe it will make you feel. Don't restrict yourself to wanting one specific job or lover or home or income level when the *feeling* you think you'll get from it is the real payoff. In most cases, we want something specific because we believe it will make us happy, but as already noted, people are not good at predicting what will make them happy. So if a part of your bottom-line goal is to be happy, or loved, or secure, or respected, remember that a specific achievement or change of circumstances *might not create that for you*, even though it seems like it should.

The way to make sure you really do get what you want is to be clear about the real bottom line (i.e., that you want to be happy, loved, secure or respected) and see the other specific goal as a step in that direction. That way, if you achieve the other goal and it fails to produce the feeling you wanted – or it produces the feeling, but it doesn't last – you'll know that you simply haven't reached your emotional goal yet, and you'll be able to keep moving forward.

However, remember that your goal has to be more than *just* the feeling you want to experience – that's too abstract by itself. The key is to include the feeling you want as part of the concrete, specific goal: for example, "I see myself having such-and-such a job, and I am happy and fulfilled in it."

*– Suggestion #4: **When you're spelling out the details of your goal, make sure you aim to create the <u>optimum</u> result – the one that works best for you – rather than the <u>maximum</u> result.*** Not long ago, San Francisco's Bay Bridge (normally little noticed by visitors due to the popularity of the Golden Gate bridge) was adorned with 25,000 LED lights designed to create a light show visible from much of San Francisco. When I was in that city recently, a friend who lives in the area met me for dinner. He picked me up at my hotel in his vintage convertible and after dinner suggested we drive around town and find a spot from which I could see the new light show. (San Francisco being a very hilly city, this was not an easy task.) We drove up and down the famously tilted streets until we finally found a dead-end street overlooking the bridge. The bridge was clearly visible, but my friend wasn't satisfied. "We can do better than this," he said, and immediately drove us off to reach the high point of the city where Coit Tower is located. Unfortunately, when we got there, every parking space around the tower was full, and it was impossible to see a thing from the parking lot itself. And, we had no time to try and relocate the street we'd found before. So I never got to watch the light show!

You may have heard the saying "Perfection is the enemy of the good" (or one of its many variations). The point, of course, is that insisting on not settling for anything except the maximum possible result often leaves you with a less-than-optimum result – or no result at all.

In terms of choosing the goal you want to reach, this can be restated as: *Be wary of wanting to create too much of something.* That's the difference between maximizing and optimizing. Maximizing something means getting as much of something as possible; optimizing means getting the amount that works best for you. My friend had found us a perfectly good place to see the bridge lights, but because he was determined to have the best possible view, we ended up with no view at all.

In the real world, the scale of something is part of what makes it good or bad; getting too much of the thing you want can backfire. Is your goal to never have to work for a living? To be the biggest star in the world? To be unbelievably rich? To become a titan in the business world? The truth is, endless leisure becomes boring; constant adoration from fans can make your life miserable; incredible wealth brings with it huge problems that moderately wealthy people never have to deal with; and achieving incredible business success may destroy your personal life. You get the idea.

In fact, the consequences of maximizing instead of optimizing can be pretty serious. Consider the prospect of eating the maximum possible amount of food. This is partly the idea behind "supersizing" portions at fast food restaurants. Going for the maximum amount of food is crazy – too much sugar will leave you with diabetes and too many calories can make you obese. During the housing boom at the turn of the 21st Century, many people thought it was a great idea to buy the biggest house they could possibly afford, whether they needed that big a house or not. If those folks had purchased the optimum house, not the maximum house, they would have saved themselves a whole lot of pain and suffering when the housing market collapsed.

So, when you're figuring out what your specific goal is, don't make it your goal to have the greatest amount of whatever-it-is that it's possible to have. Aim for the amount that will serve you best. In short, *optimize, don't maximize*.

Creating the Future You Want – Strategy #3: Make a commitment to achieving your goal. A goal isn't much more than a daydream until you make a conscious decision that *this is your goal and you're going to work toward achieving it*. So, once your desired outcome is clear and vivid in your mind, make a declaration to yourself – and at least one person you trust – that this is the result you are now in the process of creating. Making that commitment changes your goal from just a nice idea to a part of your probable future.

Johann Wolfgang von Goethe, the well-known German writer and scientist, made these observations about the positive results that are produced when you make a commitment to achieving your goal:

"*Until one is committed, there is hesitancy, the chance to draw back, always ineffectiveness, concerning all acts of initiative (and creation). There is one elementary truth, the ignorance of which kills countless ideas and splendid plans: that the moment one definitely commits oneself, then Providence moves too. All sorts of things occur to help one that would never otherwise have occurred. A whole stream of events issues from the decision [to make a commitment to reach your goal],* raising in one's favor all manner of unforeseen incidents and meetings and material assistance which no man could have dreamed would have come his way."

In other words, making a commitment to achieve your goal invites the universe to help you get where you're going. Without that commitment, you're just toying with an idea.

One important caveat: You probably shouldn't make a major public announcement about your commitment. Doing that adds a new concern to your list: trying to maintain your credibility with friends and acquaintances. That shifts some of your focus and energy away from moving toward your goal. In fact, some studies suggest that a public declaration of your goal may backfire; in some situations people work harder towards their goals when they keep them to themselves.[11])

Nevertheless, I think it's a good idea to share your commitment with one person you can trust. That helps to make it real, and gives you a potential ally if you need advice or moral support.

Creating the Future You Want – Strategy #4: Create a game plan. It's tempting to think that just having a clear-cut goal is sufficient to make it materialize, but the reality is that you have to *create* it. You don't get a free ride. Since you're going to have to take a series of steps to get to the place you want to be, you need to have a pretty good idea of what those steps are going to be.

Of course, no plan is perfect, and the universe will undoubtedly throw obstacles in your path along the way to your goal. (That's not always a bad thing; some of the detours you end up taking may turn out to be very important to helping you reach your goal!) In fact, the way you plan to reach your goal at the outset may not even be the best way to get there. So you'll need to be flexible and not throw in the towel if your plan has to be revised over time.

Despite these caveats, trying to reach a goal without having any kind of plan is not a wise move. So, come up with a plan, and just remember not to be alarmed if you have to change it occasionally as you get closer to your goal.

Creating the Future You Want – Strategy #5: Create specific proactive intentions, detailing when and where you'll take action. Psychologist Peter Gollwitzer has done extensive research into what helps people reach their goals. A key strategy that he has written about is what he calls setting "implementation intentions."[12] These are specific plans that spell out what you'll do when a given situation arises on the way to your goal.

Gollwitzer makes a distinction between implementation intentions and what he calls *goal intentions*. As he explains it, goal intentions are about the end result you hope to achieve. They're usually phrased like this: "I intend to reach such-and-such a goal." In contrast, implementation intentions are all about the steps you'll take and the obstacles you'll encounter on the way to your goal. They're phrased like this: "On the way to my goal, I will do X."

I find it helpful to divide implementation intentions into two categories: *proactive* intentions and *reactive* intentions. The proactive strategies specify what you're going to do at a specific point in time – a form of self-scheduling. In contrast, reactive intentions specify how you'll react when and if a specific situation or obstacle arises on the way to your goal.

Let's talk first about *proactive* implementation intentions. If you're trying to find a job under difficult circumstances, your proactive intentions might include sending out three resumes every morning before you start the rest of your day. If you're trying to learn a new skill, you might plan to devote every Monday night to reading about the skill or practicing it in some specific way. If you're trying to get over your fear of public speaking, you might decide to meet with friends every Saturday to practice speaking in front of people you trust.

Dr. Gollwitzer has noted several interesting things about spelling out your intentions in this way. For one thing, specifying when you'll start a project can make an enormous difference in the success of the project, especially if getting started will be difficult. For example, when asked to write a paper during their Christmas vacation, college students who specified when and where they would write the paper were far more likely to actually write the paper than students who didn't specify these details.[9]

Laying out proactive intentions also makes a huge difference when a goal is long-term – for example, when you're planning to do something to improve your health. (That's long-term because you may not see quick results.) Spelling out your proactive intentions can make the difference between actually doing what you hope to do and not getting around to it. One study followed women who had a strong goal intention of performing a self-examination to check for signs of breast cancer. Of those who specified where and when they would do this, virtually all of them actually did the exam. Of the women with strong goal intentions *but no specific proactive intentions* about when they'd do the exam, only 53% actually did it.[13]

An interesting sidelight: Forming proactive implementation intentions appears to be a far more effective motivator than fear. One experiment focused on trying to get college students to exercise once a week. When they were given a fear-based reason to exercise – in this case, education about heart disease and information about how the exercise would reduce their chances of developing heart disease – the number of people in the group who actually started exercising increased from 29% to 39%. In contrast, when the group laid out *specific proactive intentions* about when and where they'd do the exercises, the percentage of people exercising jumped to *91%*.[14]

Other studies have found similar results: In most cases, fear only gets people to take action if implementation intentions are also specified.[15] As Dr. Gollwitzer says, fear may cause us to *set* goal intentions (i.e., I'm going to take this action so I avoid that bad outcome); but unless we also set proactive implementation intentions (i.e., I'm going to do this every week at this specific time and place), the fact that we fear the bad outcome, by itself, is very unlikely to help us to reach that goal.

So, if you really want to reach your goal, decide on specific actions you'll take to help move toward your goal, and specify when and where you'll take those actions. Doing this will make it far more likely that you'll actually follow through. And that, in turn, will make it far more likely that you'll reach your goal.

Creating the Future You Want – Strategy #6: Create specific reactive strategies to prepare for possible situations that may arise on the way to your goal. In contrast to proactive strategies, which involve planning specific things you're going to do and when you'll do them, *reactive* strategies involve planning how you'll respond if specific things (such as roadblocks or opportunities) arise on the way to your goal.

Suppose your goal is to get a certain type of job. When you apply to companies on your list, you may get rejected. So, you should plan how you'll respond if that happens. You might decide that if you're turned down you'll react by being upbeat, thanking the person for his or her time and going out of your way to leave the person who rejected you with a positive impression. Or, if you're looking for a life partner, you might consider possible situations (positive and negative) that could arise as you meet people, and then think of positive ways to respond if those situations occur.

As Dr. Gollwitzer notes, there are multiple advantages to planning out reactive strategies before you set off to reach your goal:

– *Advantage 1*: *You won't be caught off guard.* When you think a situation through ahead of time, you can consider lots of scenarios that might arise and plan for each of them. You can take your time and decide what the best reaction would be. If you *haven't* thought about the situation ahead of time, you have to "wing it." That makes it much more likely that you'll respond in a way that doesn't help you out.

For example, in the situation described above in which you're rejected by a company rep while job hunting, the temptation might be to react with anger or despair. But if you've thought about this possibility ahead of time when you planned your reactive strategies, you'll already know that reacting in a positive way is more likely to work to your advantage. If you conceal your dismay or anger and react politely, the person will have a positive recollection of you; then, if another opening arises later, he or she may offer you *that* job. Because you planned for the possibility of being turned down ahead of time, you'll be prepared to do the most useful thing instead of just reacting emotionally.

– *Advantage 2*: *If you plan reactive strategies ahead of time, you won't miss opportunities.* Opportunities often appear and disappear very quickly. If you've thought about how you'll react to an opportunity, you'll be ready to take action as soon as one materializes. Or, perhaps, you'll already know that you *don't* want to take advantage of a particular type of opportunity that might otherwise seem tempting. If you want to get a promotion at your job and you get a chance to do a favor for your boss, for example, you're much better off if you've considered such a scenario ahead of time. You'll already have some idea about the consequences of saying yes or no.

– *Advantage 3*: *If you plan reactive strategies ahead of time, you'll be able to stay focused when obstacles arise.* If you're working toward your goal and a situation arises that you never thought about, you'll have to stop and consider your options and what the consequences might be. This diverts your mental resources away from whatever is happening, making you more likely to miss something important while you're trying to make a decision. On the other hand, if you plan reactive strategies ahead of time, you'll already have a good idea of what to do when any of those situations arise. You can remain focused on what's happening right now, which can work to your advantage, big-time.

- *<u>**Advantage 4**</u>: **If you plan reactive strategies ahead of time, you won't be easily sidetracked from moving toward your goal.**** If you've thought about different situations that could arise on the way to your goal that might distract you or derail your efforts – things like bad habits, competing goals or temptations – you'll know what to do the moment they appear.

This works particularly well if your goal is to break a habit, because you can decide ahead of time how you'll react when whatever triggers your bad habit occurs. For example, if you want to lose weight or stop eating a particular category of tempting food, you can decide ahead of time what you'll do when you find yourself faced with the food you want to stop eating. Or, suppose you tend to react with anger to certain types of comments, and you know that an angry reaction could cost you a job or a relationship. Planning ahead of time to react differently can make a huge difference. If you *don't* plan your reactive strategy ahead of time, all of your good intentions are likely to become meaningless as soon as the situation occurs.

Yes, it's true that we can't anticipate every single thing that might happen to us. And even when we foresee something that does end up happening, it may happen a bit differently than we expected. No one can be prepared for everything. But the more prepared you are, the better off you'll be. In short, the more concrete your plan is in terms of what you're going to do, when you'll do it, and how you'll do it – both in terms of what actions you'll take to move forward and how you'll react to situations that arise – the more likely you are to succeed.

Creating the Future You Want– Strategy #7: Set up favorable conditions to help you create the result you want. Instead of setting out blindly, give some thought to the conditions in which you're working. If you optimize certain aspects of your situation you may be able to increase your chances of success even before you begin.

For example:

• ***Surround yourself with people who appreciate your abilities in the area relating to your goal– and who appreciate the value of your goal.*** If you want to become an artist, make sure the people around you value your artistic talent and will encourage you. If you want to own your own business, make sure you spend time with people who agree that it's a good goal for you. It's also a good idea to surround yourself with people who have already mastered or achieved what you're striving for so you can learn from them (unless your achievement would be a threat to them – which might be the case with a competitor, for example).

• *Get rid of obvious obstacles.* If your goal is to eliminate something unwanted from your life – to stop smoking, drinking or gambling, for example – don't spend your time hanging around with people who smoke, drink or gamble! Remove the tempting items from your surroundings. Do as much as possible to create conditions that will help you get where you want to go.

• *Write your goal down and post it where you can see it often.* Remember how actor LeVar Burton changed his life by writing down the details of what he wanted and posting it where he could see it every day? Writing something down is a great way to remind yourself of what you want to be focused on, and posting the written version where you can see it will keep it on your mind. It's a concrete reminder that will help you avoid getting sidetracked by all the other things – good and bad – that are clamoring for your attention every day.

Creating the Future You Want – Strategy #8: If a good outcome is extremely important, perform a "pre-mortem." As you may know, a *post-mortem* is performed to determine why someone died. In a play on that idea, author/scientist Gary Klein came up with the term "pre-mortem" to describe his method for avoiding future problems when setting out on a project. (It's described in detail in his book *The Power of Intuition*). A pre-mortem a way of figuring out ahead of time what might go wrong as you pursue your goal.

To do this, you (and any others involved in achieving your goal) have to imagine a future in which your project was a dismal failure – i.e., the worst possible outcome occurred, and you didn't reach your goal. Next, you brain-storm about what went wrong that led to this hypothetical worst-case outcome. This exercise will usually reveal all sorts of pitfalls that may be awaiting you that you would otherwise never have thought of. Once this process has made those pitfalls visible, you can take steps to avoid them.

Why is it valuable to do this? When we start out towards a goal, we strive for optimism; we don't want to be deflated before things get rolling, so we imagine the most positive possible series of events unfolding in the future. That's not a bad thing; without optimism, you'll never reach your goal. It's just that optimism has a downside – it tends to make us unprepared for obstacles. This process can help you avoid that. Another reason to do this is that other people involved in your project probably won't want to appear critical, so even if they see potential problems, they may not mention them. The result is that you're set up for a fall because you're trying to imagine the best possible outcome – *not* the obstacles you're likely to face.

Yes, doing this "pre-mortem" exercise sounds depressing. But the idea is not to squash your optimism; the idea is to make sure you're really well-prepared for anything. If you think of all the grand projects that have gone awry throughout history – some of which led to huge disasters – it's not hard to see that those terrible outcomes could have been avoided if the people involved had simply done this pre-mortem exercise. So if your goal is to create something big, and the consequences of failure would be large, do the pre-mortem exercise. It's probably not necessary for many kinds of personal goal you might set for yourself, but when the stakes are high, it's a good way to avoid potential obstacles. It could dramatically increase your chances of achieving success.

Creating the Future You Want – Strategy #9: Maintain effective attitudes and expectations. Here are a few ways you can do this:

• ***Don't demand that the world bring you what you want.*** People who demand things are, in essence, admitting that they're afraid they won't get what they want. They're trying to "force the issue" by making demands. Furthermore, the fact that they're fearful enough to make demands means that fear is a big part of the equation.

That's bad, because the emotion of fear tends to produce what you're fearful of instead of the outcome you'd prefer. You're putting emotional energy into the wrong thing, which can backfire even if you're doing it outside of your conscious focus (for example, in a "mental movie" with a scary ending that you keep replaying just outside of consciousness, as we described earlier). So by insisting that the universe give you what you want, you're actually creating a giant obstacle to reaching your goal.

How can you reverse this? If you realize that you've been demanding that God or the universe give you what you want, do two things:

1) Make peace with what you already have instead of resisting it or fearing it or being angry about it. This doesn't mean dropping your plan to change things – it means changing your focus. If you're expending energy on how much you hate the situation you're in now, you're not only wasting energy that could be put into creating a better situation, you're actually prolonging the situation you don't like. Remember: You get more of what you focus on and put your energy into, *whether it's something you like or not.* If you make peace with a current situation that you don't like, you'll stop putting energy into it and the situation will change much faster.

2) Make peace with the possibility that you might not end up with exactly what you want. If you're afraid of not ending up with exactly what you want, you'll be putting energy into resisting that possibility, which is counterproductive. Fretting about the possibility of an unwanted outcome in the future backfires just as badly as resisting your current situation, and for the same reason. Resisting what you don't want – in the present or in the future – wastes your energy and tends to bring you more of it.

So, make peace with the possibility of a less-than-perfect outcome. Tell yourself you're going to do your best to create what you want, but you'll be okay if it doesn't work out. Although it sounds strange, deciding that any outcome will be tolerable – even if it's not exactly the outcome you want – *increases the likelihood that you WILL get what you want.*

For example, you could say: *What I have isn't what I want, but that's okay because I'm headed toward the thing I want. The possibility of ultimately not ending up with what I want is scary; but that's okay, too. I'm not going to waste my energy fretting about that. The calmer and more clear-headed I am about what I want, the more likely I am to get it.*

Here are two more things that will free up your energy and help you move toward your goal much more quickly:

• ***Don't demand that you reach your goal by a specific route.*** Depending on the nature of your goal, there may be a million different ways to reach it. As noted earlier, it's important to have a plan – but your plan may not turn out to be the best (or only) way to reach your goal. Most successful people will tell you that their road to success was full of unplanned turns and detours. Once you've reached your goal, you may look back and realize that many of those detours were necessary side trips that helped you reach your goal, even though they didn't seem that way at the time.

So, be open to alternate ways of reaching your goal. If you get too single-minded about how everything should work, you'll automatically reject unexpected opportunities that don't fit into your plan – even ones that might turn out to be your key to creating what you really want.

• ***Don't demand that things happen by a certain time.*** In other words, don't put a time limit on getting your result. Some experts will advise the opposite – give yourself a time limit to reach at least part of your goal to make sure you're motivated. In my experience, however, this strategy backfires. There's no telling how many steps will be involved in creating the better situation you'd like to be in.

Some goals are really big and will require that you learn new skills or go through major shifts in your life before they become real. If you want to find a lasting relationship with a partner, for instance, you're trying to achieve something that requires a significant amount of experience and special skills. (Anybody can get into a relationship. You're looking for one that will *last*, and that doesn't happen without work.) If you insist that the next relationship you find be "the one," you're putting a time limit on the result. In fact, that next relationship may be happening just so you can learn some key things that will make a lasting relationship possible with a different partner farther down the line.

So, instead of being impatient, be observant. You may find that you're moving toward your goal after all – you've just chosen a goal that takes time to create. As noted in Chapter 2, success results from persistence far more often than from talent or luck.

One of the most important reasons not to put a time limit on reaching your goal is that if you set a time limit, you could be setting yourself up to fail. After all, you may be halfway to your goal when the self-imposed deadline rolls around. At that point, just because you've missed your deadline, you've failed! You didn't fulfill your arbitrary criteria for "success." This is completely unnecessary and self-defeating – and it's an easy trap to fall into. The way to avoid it is to decide up front that reaching your goal will take as long as it takes, and you're not going to set arbitrary deadlines for reaching it.

Chapter 10: Create the Future You Want

You can also put other kinds of qualifications on reaching your goal that can backfire. For example, you can say, "If I fail to achieve this after I've tried three times [or 10 times or 100 times], I'll throw in the towel, admit I've failed and move on to something else." Yes, this might make sense in some situations, just because you may stop enjoying the effort it's taking to move toward your goal. But if you stop enjoying the journey, *that* should be your reason for giving up, not the number of times you failed. When Thomas Edison was trying to develop a working light bulb, he went through thousands of filament materials and bulb designs before one worked. His comment? "I have not failed," he said, "I've found 10,000 ways that won't work." The only reason we have electric lights is that he refused to set any limit that would "officially" mean he had failed.

So, be patient and stay focused on what you want. The experience of thousands of people suggests that you can and will create the experience you want if you relax, stay focused and give it a chance to unfold at its own speed.

NOTE: There's one important caveat to this. If you decide not to put a time limit on reaching your goal, be careful how you define *continuing to work toward your goal*. For example, suppose you're married and your spouse agrees to support you for a year while you quit your regular job and pursue your dream to succeed as a sculptor. I'm not suggesting that your spouse should support you indefinitely if one year turns out not to be enough time for you to become successful as a sculptor. Nor am I suggesting that you use this idea to justify burning through all of your life savings, destroying relationships or going into mind-boggling debt in order to keep working toward your goal. All I'm suggesting is that you should decide ahead of time that you won't be a failure if you haven't succeeded by the end of the year, the deadline that you and your spouse agreed upon. If your goal really matters to you, when the end of the year rolls around you can find other ways to continue moving toward it.

Remember: Working toward a goal is not an all-or-nothing proposition. That's why so many artists have day jobs! If you have to split your focus with other necessities while you're on the way to your goal, so be it. The vast majority of people who reach their life goals ended up doing other things on the way. They made it in spite of that, and so can you.

Creating the Future You Want – Strategy #10: Use "visualizing" and focusing techniques. We discussed the importance of focus back in

Chapter 5. Here, the issue is exactly *how* you focus on what you want to create. (Note that the word *visualization* is the popular term for focusing on something using your imagination, but not everyone is visually oriented; while many people think in images, some think primarily in sound or even touch. If you're not a visually oriented thinker, think of the word "visualization" as simply meaning *creating a situation in your imagination*, in whatever sensory form your imagination prefers.)

Whether or not you believe in the more "metaphysical" explanation for the value of visualization – i.e., the idea that your thoughts can influence what happens in physical reality – there's plenty of experimental data showing that visualizing makes a difference, at the very least for the person doing it. Consider a study done in the 1970s (described by Ellen Langer in the book *Mindfulness*): At a retreat for men between the ages of 75 and 80, the men were divided into two groups. One group was asked to vividly imagine themselves in the year 1959. To help them visualize it, they were shown pictures of each other as they looked at that time. The other group was simply asked to talk extensively about what 1959 was like.

Within four or five days of doing this, physical changes began to be evident in the first group that was actively using visualization. The men in this group became more active and independent; furthermore, their finger length and sitting height increased and their manual dexterity improved, along with their vision. None of these effects occurred in the other group. In other words, visualizing themselves as younger men *changed them physically*.

So, whether or not you believe visualization can alter events directly, visualizing yourself as successful in your field could make a significant difference in your physical appearance and demeanor – and even without any other impact, that could have a significant effect on your chances of actually ending up as the version of yourself you're imagining.

However, if you hope to use this strategy to your advantage, it's important to do it *in the right way.* This can make a big difference in whether or not you succeed in creating the experience you want. With that in mind, here are several suggestions that will help you use this type of thinking to your advantage:

– *Visualizing suggestion #1: DON'T focus on the fact that you want something.* Why is it so bad to focus on the idea that you want something? If you focus on thoughts like these:

– *I want to lose weight;*
– *I want to be rich;*
– *I want so-and-so to stop abusing me;*

what you're really focusing on is:

– *I'm too fat.*
– *I'm not rich.*
– *So-and-so is abusing me.*

Basically, you are saying: I want these things *because I do not have them.* You're imagining yourself *without* what you want. The universe will respond by saying: "Okay! You see yourself as a person who doesn't have those things! I can give you more of that!"

Instead of concentrating on the idea that you really want something, focus on the *result* you want, as if it were already happening. Visualize yourself as the version of you who *doesn't need to want* that situation because you already have it! So, in the three examples above, to reach your goal you would:

– *Imagine yourself as a skinnier person*
– *Imagine yourself as a person with more money and resources*
– *Imagine yourself in a healthy, non-abusive relationship.*

Here's the secret to creating what you want, in a nutshell:

You don't get something because you want it so badly; you get something because you **see yourself having it.** (It's worth going back and reading that sentence again!)

An important note: If imagining yourself as having reached your goal is too difficult – for example, if your goal is to be rich but you have a hard time believing you'll ever be rich – try focusing on the idea that you're in the process of getting there. In fact, that's a great way to say it to yourself: "*I am in the process of becoming successful in this field,*" or "*I am in the process of becoming myself at my ideal weight,*" or "*I am in the process of getting out of an abusive relationship.*" This is very different from falling into the trap of saying "I want to be successful, skinny, out of this relationship, etc.," which reinforces the idea that you *are not where you want to be* and unintentionally helps to perpetuate the situation you don't like.

– *Visualizing suggestion #2: Imagine yourself <u>in the situation you want to experience.</u> Perspective counts.* This is a very important caveat. There's a big difference between 1) just imagining the better situation you'd like to be in; 2) imagining yourself in that situation as if you were watching yourself from across the room, and 3) imagining yourself *in the situation as if it were happening to you right now*. When you're visualizing the situation you want to create, be *in your body in the scene you're imagining*, looking out at the situation. Don't just imagine the scene without you in it, or imagine the scene from an outsider's perspective, as if you were watching it happen to someone else.

For example, suppose you were a prospector, and your goal was to find a large nugget of gold. You could imagine that outcome in your mind in three different ways. First, you could simply imagine the big gold nugget you'd like to find. Second, you could see yourself standing with a nugget of gold in your hand, the way the scene would look to another person standing nearby. Third, you could imagine your hand in front of you, holding the gold nugget, as if it were happening to you right now.

These three approaches are likely to produce very different results. Assume for a moment that your thoughts really can influence your future experience. If you just visualize the gold nugget you want intently for several minutes every day, the universe might oblige you by having you find a *picture* of a gold nugget that looks very much like the one you've been imagining. That would make sense, because that's what you visualized: the image of a gold nugget. You weren't part of the scene you visualized.

Similarly, if you visualize the image of yourself holding the nugget as seen by an outside observer, you'd probably find yourself one day looking at *someone else* holding that gold nugget. You'd be in the position you were in when you imagined the scene – watching it happen to someone else. However, if you used the third technique – if you imagine that you're inside your body and looking down at your hand holding a gold nugget – that's the experience the universe would try to bring you.

So, if you're going to use visualization, make sure you imagine the outcome as if it were happening to you right now, looking out at the situation through your own eyes.

– *Visualizing suggestion #3: Devote a short period of time every day to visualizing your desired end result.* This keeps your focus clear, and it's an important part of bringing the result you want into your experience. If you've posted your goal where you can see it, as discussed earlier, thinking a little about it every day should come naturally. As TV and movie star Henry Winkler once said, "If you know what you want, and you brush your teeth with what you want, it will come to you like a magnet."

It's worth repeating that this is the reason "counting your blessings" – i.e., spending a few moments every day or so dwelling on the things you do like in your current experience – is actually a smart thing to do. Most of us have parts of our experience that we do like, things that we want to continue when the rest of our experience changes to something better. By dwelling on those positive things and reflecting on how nice they are from time to time, you're helping to perpetuate them in your experience – just as you can unintentionally perpetuate things you *don't* like by dwelling on them.

– *Visualizing suggestion #4: Don't visualize your goal constantly.* This is a very important point. Visualizing your goal constantly won't work in your favor, for several reasons. First of all, if you think about your goal constantly, sooner or later you'll start thinking about the distance between where you are now and where you want to be. As we discussed back in Chapter 5, once you start to focus on that gap, you get into trouble. You'll become frustrated and impatient and start directing your energy in ways that undercut your journey toward your goal.

Another reason not to focus on your goal all the time is that you don't *need* to focus on your goal that much. As discussed in Chapter 6, you have many more mental resources than just the ones found in your conscious mind; and those resources are there, in part, to take over thought processes so your conscious mind can deal with other important things – like whatever is happening right now in your immediate environment. Instead of constantly imagining your goal, it's far more productive to be clear about what you want, vividly imagine yourself in that situation for a few minutes every day, and then turn the process over to your greater mind and go on about your business.

Another reason not to obsessively visualize your goal is that obsessing often reflects fear – fear that you won't be able to achieve something, fear that you'll lose something you have, and so on. As we discussed earlier, this can be very unhelpful because it keeps your energy pointed toward what you *don't* want instead of what you *do* want. If you find yourself worrying obsessively, try the strategies discussed in the section on *Fearing the Future*, earlier in this chapter.

– Visualizing suggestion #5: Make sure to visualize your proactive and reactive intentions. Visualizing proactive intentions (i.e., "I'm going to send three resumes out every morning") will make your plan more real and help remind you to do it. Visualizing reactive intentions (i.e., "When Sue makes one of her nasty remarks, I'm going to remain calm and tell her that she's being hurtful instead of lashing back at her") will help you practice your planned response internally. It will also help you recognize the cues associated with that situation as soon as they appear in day-to-day life, so you'll be ready to respond the way you planned.

Creating the Future You Want – Strategy #11: Take action. Here are some tips to help you do this:

<u>*Action tip #1*</u>: *Every day take one small step toward your goal.* Remember Joe Simpson, the climber who had to make his way across an expanse of rugged terrain after being gravely injured? (His story was told back in Chapter 5.) Taking one small step at a time saved his life.

Examples of the usefulness of this strategy in other circumstances aren't hard to find. In Japan a version of this small-steps-toward-your-goal concept, called "kaizen" (pronounced "ky-zen"), is used as a fundamental guide for employees in many organizations and companies known for their excellent products and workmanship. Kaizen loosely translates as "continuous improvement." The idea is to take a small step toward your goal every day, noting the result of each effort and making changes in what you do next based on the result of your last step.

Taking a small step toward your goal every day has become something of a cliché, but there are several good reasons to make a conscious effort to do this.

First of all, major goals are almost never achieved magically, all at once. They usually result from a lot of different elements coming together, all of them building towards the change you want to see. So, tackling one small step each day makes perfect sense. If you wait around for huge opportunities to appear or big changes to happen all at once,

12 Strategies for Creating the Future You Want

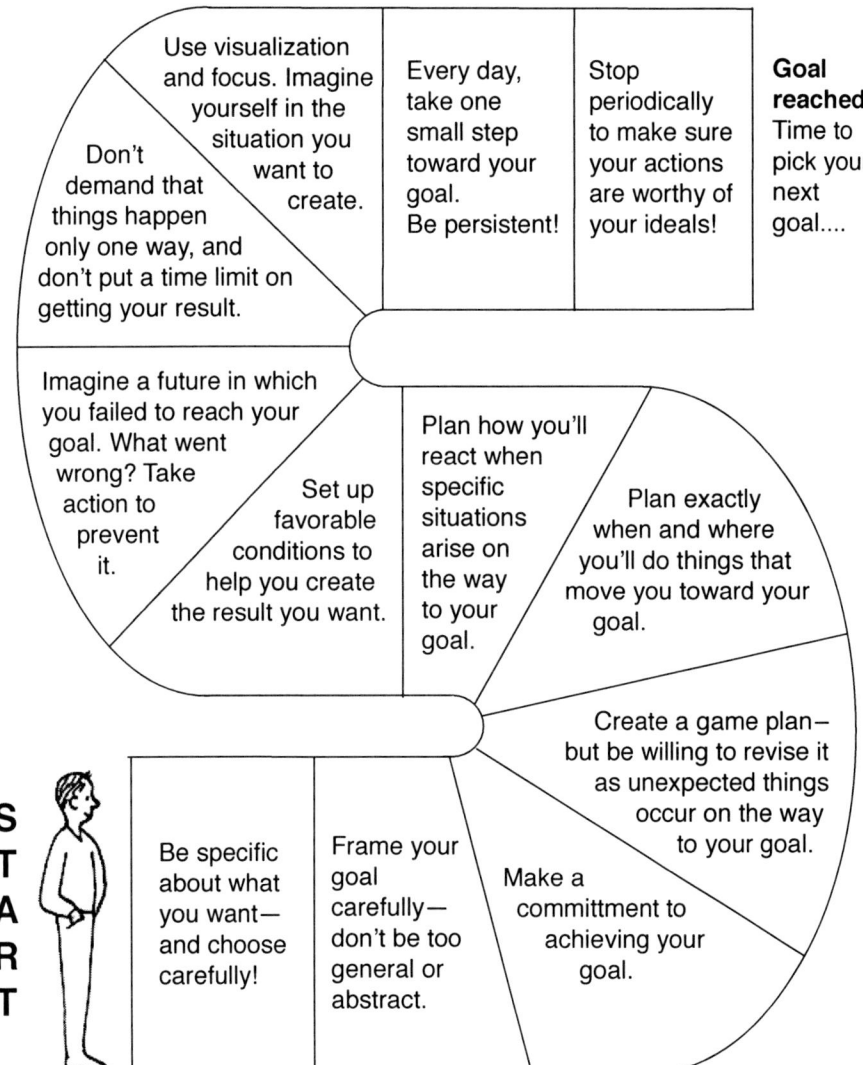

you're simply wasting time. You're pushing your goal farther into the future – maybe even past the point of being achievable.

A second reason taking small steps towards your goal every day works is that taking big steps toward a goal (assuming big steps are even possible) often ends up being overwhelming. In fact, human beings usually resist big changes, partly because we know that when big changes happen to us we'll have to make a lot of changes in our daily lives and our behavior, and they may suddenly trigger a lot of unexpected, unpredictable additional developments – all of which we'll have to respond to in some way. Just thinking about it can be exhausting! Small changes, in contrast, don't come with all of that baggage; we don't have to worry about rearranging our lives as a result of them. So by making a steady series of small changes, we don't freak ourselves out.

A third reason taking small steps towards your goal every day works is that every giant leap we try to take that *fails* acts as a huge psychological setback. In contrast, making a little progress each day is encouraging. Yes, you may get tired or discouraged from time to time, but you'll also see progress from time to time. And, you'll avoid the kind of huge letdown that can derail your efforts completely if you try to make a huge leap forward and it doesn't turn out the way you expected.

A fourth reason taking small steps towards your goal every day is a good idea is that small steps can actually produce huge results when conditions are right. This is sometimes referred to as the "butterfly effect," which gets its name from the idea that the flapping of a butterfly's wings can potentially alter the weather on the other side of the globe a week later. It's like an avalanche that begins when one stone slips into another stone, which knocks a group of rocks loose, which cause a ledge to break off, and so on, resulting in an avalanche; each event triggers a bigger one until the impact is huge.

Here's an ancient proverb that captures the same idea, following the increasing impact of a small negative event:

For want of a nail the shoe was lost.
For want of a shoe the horse was lost.
For want of a horse the rider was lost.
For want of a rider the battle was lost.
For want of a battle the kingdom was lost.

Professor Randy Pausch, who became known for his Last Lecture video and book (named for the lecture he gave shortly before he died from pancreatic cancer), told a story that also illustrates this concept. His parents took him and his sister to Disney World when he was 12 and she was 14; they let the kids have some time on their own together, and the kids decided to spend some of their savings buying a present for their parents. At one of the Disney World stores they bought a ceramic salt and pepper shaker set, but shortly thereafter they dropped it, breaking the salt and pepper shakers into pieces. A stranger saw the upset kids and suggested they take the broken gift back to the store. They did, and to their astonishment, the manager replaced the set, free of charge.

When they told their parents what had happened, the parents were amazed by the kindness of the store manager, and they realized that it had a lot to do with the policies of Disney World. So, they decided that from then on they would bring their busloads of English-as-a-second-language students to Disney World – all the way from Maryland! They did so for 20 years, eventually spending more than $100,000 on tickets, food and souvenirs at the park.

All because of a single act of kindness.

Again, you never know what the consequences of one small action may be, so if you're trying to create something in your life, do something small to move you toward that goal every day. One day's actions may have little or no effect, but the next day's actions may have a huge impact. Since you can't be sure when the circumstances will line up to cause your actions to result in a big change, it makes sense to keep taking small steps towards your goal every day. That way, when circumstances are aligned in your favor, even if you don't realize it at the time, you'll automatically take advantage of them.

This same idea is captured in the proverb that says *success results when opportunity meets readiness.* If you sit around waiting for something to motivate you, opportunities may come and go while you're waiting. So don't wait! Take a small step toward your goal every day.

<u>*Action tip #2:*</u> A second thing to remember when taking action to move toward your goal is to **be persistent**. Of all of the factors that can help you reach your goal, persistence may be the single most important one. Many of the most successful people in history have said that without being persistent they would never have reached their goals.

Professor Pausch, who told the story about Disney World, achieved numerous life goals by simply refusing to give up. One of his goals was to become one of the "Imagineers" who create the spectacular rides and attractions for the Disney theme parks. Once he had finally earned a PhD in computer science, he applied repeatedly to become an Imagineer, but the company turned down his applications over and over again. So, he backed off for a while – but he didn't give up. A few years after that, he became an expert in creating virtual reality programs, and he heard that the Disney people were working on a project involving virtual reality. So he applied again and persisted until he ended up talking to the project's team leader on the phone. Prof. Pausch said he was coming to California; could they get together for lunch? The fellow said sure. (In reality, Pausch wasn't being entirely truthful; he had no plans to go to California unless he got the lunch meeting!)

Next, Pausch spent 80 hours talking to everyone he knew in the field to get their thoughts on the type of project the Imagineers were working on. His resulting expertise impressed the other fellow deeply at their lunch meeting. So, Pausch said he had a sabbatical coming up (six months off from teaching when he could do whatever he wanted to advance his academic work). The fellow agreed to let him work with the team for those six months.

Then Prof. Pausch had to go back to Carnegie Mellon and convince them to give him the sabbatical! (You probably won't be surprised to hear that he succeeded.)

Prof. Pausch had a saying that captured his attitude about getting what he wanted: "Brick walls are NOT there to keep us out," he said. "They are there to give us a chance to show how badly we want something." Persistence is one of the ways you get over those walls.

Action tip #3: A third helpful strategy when taking action to move toward your goal is to **try behaving as if you are the future self who has already reached your goal.** As noted earlier, you don't get something because you want it so badly; you get something because you *see yourself having it*. Acting as if you have it can be part of that process.

Humorist Allan Sherman was popular in the early 1960s for his song parodies. (He was best known for his hit "Hello Muddah, Hello Fadduh," about a child writing a letter home from camp.) For years before he became well-known, he and his wife lived in a tiny apartment on East 66th Street in New York, often out of work and struggling to pay the bills. He'd had some small successes in show business in the past, so to help make life more bearable, he and his wife created a little game they would play. Whenever the phone would ring, they'd both jump up and yell, "I'll get it – it's Darryl Zanuck!" (Darryl Zanuck was an Academy Award-winning movie producer, director and studio executive – one of Hollywood's most powerful and influential people at that time.) They pretended that Mr. Zanuck was calling to say he'd discovered Sherman's work and needed his services immediately. This game helped buoy their spirits during difficult times.[16]

It also sent a message to the universe. A few years later, after Sherman had finally become known as a humorist, his wife answered the phone and burst into tears. Alarmed, he asked her what was wrong. "It's Darryl Zanuck," she said, handing him the phone.

Acting as if your goal is already real is a way to help yourself imagine yourself as the person you want to be. It also says to the universe, "I am the person who has achieved this goal in the future – I'm just waiting patiently for reality to catch up to what I already know on the inside." So, even though it may be difficult or feel absurd, try acting as if you're already in the situation you want to create, even if you do so in only a few small ways.

Creating the Future You Want – Strategy #12: Stop periodically and make sure your choices and actions are worthy of your best nature. One of the greatest dangers we face as we work to achieve a goal is the danger of becoming impatient or fearful and, as a result, taking actions that are not worthy of our ideals. Often, this is the result of focusing too much on the gap between where we are and where we want to be. When it seems like we'll never make it to our goal, or when we simply get weary of the amount of time and effort it's taking to get there, it's tempting to take actions that we wouldn't take under ordinary circumstances. The unfortunate reality is, those actions tend to backfire – sometimes badly. In some cases, they may even start a chain of negative events that undermine all the work we've done to get where we are. So it's important to stop now and then and take stock of what we're doing.

One of the most clear-cut wake-up calls that you may be heading down that road is finding yourself having to justify something you've done – or are thinking of doing. If you catch yourself justifying your actions, an alarm should go off in your head. That's when you need to stop and consider whether you're acting out of fear, impatience or desperation. If you're doing something you wouldn't have chosen to do at the outset, you may be using the end to justify the means – and that's a strategy for failure.

The Bottom Line

If every action you take to move toward your goal is worthy of your ideals, you'll move yourself – and the world – in a positive direction. And, you'll increase your chances of success. So, even if that alarm hasn't gone off in your head, make it a habit to stop from time to time and think about the actions you're taking. That way, you won't wake up one day and realize you've allowed yourself to get off course – or worse, wake up at your goal and realize you sold your soul to get there.

✳ ✳ ✳

Once More, in Brief:

Here are the key points to remember from Chapter 10:

To use time to your advantage, you need to avoid four "time traps:"

1. Don't buy the idea that you're controlled by your past. You're not. If you feel like you are, remember that the key question is not "How did this situation get started?" but *"Why is this situation continuing?"* Look for "leftovers" from the past that are triggering your feelings of limitation. Determine if there's a payoff in the present that's keeping you locked into the behavior or current situation that you don't like. Get help if you need it.

2. Don't devote too much energy to remembered "better times." Don't use too much of your mental energy to replay the past (which may not have been as glorious as you remember anyway). Instead, use your mental resources to help create the future you want to experience.

3. Don't waste too much energy fearing the future. If your fears seem nebulous, you may be running scary movies about the future in your mind, just outside of consciousness. First, bring those scary movies into your conscious mind where you can examine them. Then, write different endings so those mental movies have legitimate, less-scary outcomes.

4. Don't fall into the trap of believing that your happiness depends on something in the future. Seeing your happiness as lying in the future guarantees that you'll spend much of your life unhappy. And remember that human beings are very bad at knowing what will make them happy.

Use these 12 strategies to create the future you want:

1) Choose your goal carefully, and be specific! Talk to people who are currently in the situation you want to achieve, to find out what it's really like. Pick goals that will provide you with satisfaction *while you're working to create them,* not just after you achieve them. And beware of pinning everything on wealth and/or success.

2) Describe your goal carefully. Don't be too general or abstract. Make sure that the way you want to feel when you achieve your goal is part of what you're aiming for. And always aim to create the *optimum* result – the one that works best for you – rather than the maximum result.

3) Make a commitment to achieving your goal. Make a declaration to yourself – and at least one person you trust – that this is the result you are now working toward.

4) Create a game plan. Generate a concrete set of steps you can take to move toward your goal. However, be willing to revise your plan as unexpected things happen along the way.

5) Create specific proactive intentions, detailing when and where you'll take action. Lay out exactly when and where you're going to do specific things that will move you toward your goal.

6) Create specific reactive strategies to prepare for possible situations that may arise on the way to your goal. This will help you make good choices when you find yourself in those situations, and help you be ready to grab opportunities as soon as they arise.

7) Set up favorable conditions to help you create the result you want. Surround yourself with people who appreciate the value of your goal. Eliminate as many obstacles as you can. Write your goal down and post it where you can see it often.

8) If a good outcome is extremely important, perform a "premortem." Imagine a future in which your project was a dismal failure; then backtrack to deduce what went wrong that would produce such an outcome, so you can avoid letting those mistakes happen.

9) Maintain effective attitudes and expectations. Follow these three rules: Don't make demands; don't insist that you reach your goal by a specific route; and don't put a time limit on getting your result.

10) Use visualization and focus. Devote a short period of time to imagining yourself in the situation you want to experience every day, as well as imagining yourself taking the steps to get there. *Don't* focus on the idea that *you want something.* You don't get things in life because you want them so badly; you get them because you *imagine yourself having them.*

11) Take action. Every day take one small step toward your goal, and be persistent!

12) Stop periodically to make sure your choices and actions are worthy of your best nature. Actions that require justification are probably not in sync with your ideals and will undermine your chances of reaching your goal.

❋ ❋ ❋

NOTES for Chapter 10

1. As recounted in an interview with TV Guide magazine, August 13, 1988, pgs 12-15.
2. For example, see Section I in Bandler R & Grinder J (1979). *Frogs Into Princes.* Moab, Utah: Real People Press.
3. J. M. Schwartz and B. Beyette. *Brain Lock: Free yourself from obsessive-compulsive behavior.* New York: ReganBooks/Harper Collins.
4. Bandura A, Schunk DH. Cultivating competence, self-efficacy and intrinsic interest through proximal self-motivation. *Journal of Personality and Social Psychology* 1981:41;586-98.
5. Diener E, Seligman MP. Beyond Money: Toward an Economy of Well-Being. *Psychological Science in the Public Interest* 2004:5;1-31.
6. Blanchflower DG, Oswald AJ. Well-Being Over Time in Britain and the USA. *Journal of Public Economics* 2004:88; 1359-86.
7. Deiner E, et al. Wealth and Happiness Across the World: Material Prosperity Predicts Life Evaluation, Whereas Psychosocial Prosperity Predicts Positive Feeling. Journal of Personality and Social Psychology 2010:99;1;52-61.

8. Tibor Scitovsky. The Joyless Economy: The Psychology of Human Satisfaction and Consumer Dissatisfaction. Oxford University Press 1976.
9. Locke EA, Latham GP. A theory of goal-setting and task performance. (1990) Englewood Cliffs, NJ: Prentice Hall.
10. Higgins ET. Beyond pleasure and pain. American Psychologist 1997; 52:1280-1300.
11. Gollwitzer PM, Sheeran P, Michalski V, Seifert AE. When Intentions Go Public: Does Social Reality Widen the Intention-Behavior Gap? *Psychological Science* 2009:20:5:612-18.
12. Gollwitzer. Implementation Intentions: Strong Effects of Simple Plans. *American Psychologist* 1999:54;7;493-503.
13. Orbell S, Hodgkins S, Sheehan P. Implementation intentions and the theory of of planned behavior. *Personality and Social Psychology Bulletin* 1997:23;945-54.
14. Levanthal H, Singer R, Jones S. Effects of fear and specificity of recommendation upon attitudes and behavior. *Journal of Personality and Social Psychology.* 1965:2;20-29.
15. Levanthal H, Watts JC, Pagano F. Effects of fear and instructions on how to cope with danger. *Journal of Personality and Social Psychology* 1967:6;313-21.
16. As recounted in his autobiography, *A Gift of Laughter.*

Afterword

"That which does not kill us makes us stronger."
  – Friedrich Nietzsche, 19th-Century German philosopher

Each of the ideas discussed in this book comes with a lot of detailed information – more than most people can remember without multiple readings. So, here are the most important ideas that I hope you'll take away from this book, corresponding to each chapter, boiled down to make them a little easier to remember:

1. When times are hard, don't despair. Remember that hard times are part of a natural cycle designed to cause circumstances to evolve into something better. A major breakdown in the course of our experience is nature's way of allowing significant problems to be solved. It's not the end of the world; it's leading – hopefully – to a new and better beginning. In fact, a crisis gives us a unique opportunity to make really big changes for the better – changes that are almost impossible to make when everything is stable.

2. Remember that you have nearly limitless capacity for growth and change. Knowing this will impact the choices you make and the consequences that flow from those choices. It's been well demonstrated that "talent" is the result of thousands of hours of focused practice, not some magical gift that you have to be born with.

This is especially important to remember when you find yourself with an opportunity to move ahead in your life or career, or to learn something new. If you're tempted to turn down such an opportunity, ask yourself why. Is it because you believe you can't learn or change enough to be successful at it? If that's your reason for saying no, you may be doing yourself a major disservice, especially if you're striving to stay off the Wheel of Misfortune. Learning, growing and moving ahead may be the best things you could do for yourself.

Also, remember that when you have the opportunity to give feedback to others about their efforts – especially young people – the way you give your feedback has a profound effect on the reaction you'll inspire. Always reward people for their hard work and perseverance, not for "being smart" or "being talented."

3. Even if you've been victimized, don't take on the role of victim. Taking on that role causes you to give up much of your personal power and can trigger a long list of negative consequences in your life. If you're already in that position, changing your attitude will eliminate a host of problematic relationships and consequences from your experience, bringing more good people into your life and improving your mental and physical health.

At the very least, if you catch yourself blaming others for your problems, remember not to make that idea the basis of your reality. Instead, focus on the idea that you control your life. You may have been victimized, but you don't have to be a victim.

Finally, remember that forgiving someone who has wronged you is not about letting that person off the hook. It's about ending your own suffering. Furthermore, it clears your vision, so if action needs to be taken your judgment about what action to take is more likely to be sound.

4. Good communication is crucial to creating the life you want, so pay attention to how other people are reacting to your message. That will tell you whether or not you're being understood. If you're *not* being correctly understood, *change the way you're communicating until you get the reaction you want*. And if your communication is in a form that won't be received until later, run it by a feedback person before you put it out into the world; that way you can make sure your message is coming across correctly before it's too late to change it.

Also: When asking someone to do something, be sure to clearly communicate the goal your request is supposed to achieve. Then, if something goes wrong and the person fulfilling your request has to improvise, his or her choice of what to do is more likely to be appropriate and helpful.

5. Choose the things you focus on with care. Your life is not made up

8. Tibor Scitovsky. The Joyless Economy: The Psychology of Human Satisfaction and Consumer Dissatisfaction. Oxford University Press 1976.
9. Locke EA, Latham GP. A theory of goal-setting and task performance. (1990) Englewood Cliffs, NJ: Prentice Hall.
10. Higgins ET. Beyond pleasure and pain. American Psychologist 1997; 52:1280-1300.
11. Gollwitzer PM, Sheeran P, Michalski V, Seifert AE. When Intentions Go Public: Does Social Reality Widen the Intention-Behavior Gap? *Psychological Science* 2009:20:5:612-18.
12. Gollwitzer. Implementation Intentions: Strong Effects of Simple Plans. *American Psychologist* 1999:54;7;493-503.
13. Orbell S, Hodgkins S, Sheehan P. Implementation intentions and the theory of of planned behavior. *Personality and Social Psychology Bulletin* 1997:23;945-54.
14. Levanthal H, Singer R, Jones S. Effects of fear and specificity of recommendation upon attitudes and behavior. *Journal of Personality and Social Psychology.* 1965:2;20-29.
15. Levanthal H, Watts JC, Pagano F. Effects of fear and instructions on how to cope with danger. *Journal of Personality and Social Psychology* 1967:6;313-21.
16. As recounted in his autobiography, *A Gift of Laughter.*

Afterword

"That which does not kill us makes us stronger."
  – Friedrich Nietzsche, 19th-Century German philosopher

Each of the ideas discussed in this book comes with a lot of detailed information – more than most people can remember without multiple readings. So, here are the most important ideas that I hope you'll take away from this book, corresponding to each chapter, boiled down to make them a little easier to remember:

1. When times are hard, don't despair. Remember that hard times are part of a natural cycle designed to cause circumstances to evolve into something better. A major breakdown in the course of our experience is nature's way of allowing significant problems to be solved. It's not the end of the world; it's leading – hopefully – to a new and better beginning. In fact, a crisis gives us a unique opportunity to make really big changes for the better – changes that are almost impossible to make when everything is stable.

2. Remember that you have nearly limitless capacity for growth and change. Knowing this will impact the choices you make and the consequences that flow from those choices. It's been well demonstrated that "talent" is the result of thousands of hours of focused practice, not some magical gift that you have to be born with.

This is especially important to remember when you find yourself with an opportunity to move ahead in your life or career, or to learn something new. If you're tempted to turn down such an opportunity, ask yourself why. Is it because you believe you can't learn or change enough to be successful at it? If that's your reason for saying no, you may be doing yourself a major disservice, especially if you're striving to stay off the Wheel of Misfortune. Learning, growing and moving ahead may be the best things you could do for yourself.

Also, remember that when you have the opportunity to give feedback to others about their efforts – especially young people – the way you give your feedback has a profound effect on the reaction you'll inspire. Always reward people for their hard work and perseverance, not for "being smart" or "being talented."

3. Even if you've been victimized, don't take on the role of victim. Taking on that role causes you to give up much of your personal power and can trigger a long list of negative consequences in your life. If you're already in that position, changing your attitude will eliminate a host of problematic relationships and consequences from your experience, bringing more good people into your life and improving your mental and physical health.

At the very least, if you catch yourself blaming others for your problems, remember not to make that idea the basis of your reality. Instead, focus on the idea that you control your life. You may have been victimized, but you don't have to be a victim.

Finally, remember that forgiving someone who has wronged you is not about letting that person off the hook. It's about ending your own suffering. Furthermore, it clears your vision, so if action needs to be taken your judgment about what action to take is more likely to be sound.

4. Good communication is crucial to creating the life you want, so pay attention to how other people are reacting to your message. That will tell you whether or not you're being understood. If you're *not* being correctly understood, *change the way you're communicating until you get the reaction you want*. And if your communication is in a form that won't be received until later, run it by a feedback person before you put it out into the world; that way you can make sure your message is coming across correctly before it's too late to change it.

Also: When asking someone to do something, be sure to clearly communicate the goal your request is supposed to achieve. Then, if something goes wrong and the person fulfilling your request has to improvise, his or her choice of what to do is more likely to be appropriate and helpful.

5. Choose the things you focus on with care. Your life is not made up of the things that happen to you; it's made up of your experiences, and what you experience is determined by what you pay attention to.

What you choose to focus on is particularly important when you're striving to stay off the Wheel of Misfortune. A few key things to remember:

First, you get more of what you focus on. So, don't focus too much on the things you don't like. Instead devote at least some of your attention to things you *do* like in your current experience.

Second, don't focus on the seemingly huge distance between where you are and where you'd like to be. That focus will cause you to end up feeling anger and frustration, causing you to make desperate choices that will undermine your journey towards your goal.

Third, be sure to focus on small steps you can take to move toward your goal. That focus will keep you energized, help you avoid frustration, and allow you to experience yourself actually making progress.

Remember: Your conscious focus is a powerful tool. Use it wisely.

6. Treat impulses and gut feelings as valuable information coming from outside of your normal consciousness. There's a lot more to your mind than just the conscious part most of us identify with. Your "greater mind" can do an enormous amount to help you out, especially when you're trying to stay off the Wheel of Misfortune. Take the time to learn how your greater mind works, so you can make the most of the help it's trying to provide. Among other things, pay attention to your impulses, which are often your greater mind's way of trying to help you out. However, remember the big caveat about impulses: Impulses to do violence spring from repressed emotion, *not* from your greater mind. Those impulses are a warning sign, not a message to be followed.

7. Learn to manage (and if possible, prevent) emotional "stacks." A key to keeping relationships working smoothly is to communicate and/or take some kind of action when a recurring situation is upsetting. Doing nothing causes the emotion to backlog until either A) some minor thing causes an emotional explosion, or B) the backlog begins to undermine your health. So, learn to notice when you're not expressing your feelings. It may not always be appropriate to express them on the spot, but it's very important to find some way to prevent your feelings from simply being squashed and turning into stacks of pent-up anger.

Furthermore, develop strategies for avoiding this kind of emotional backlog in the future, both in yourself and (if possible) in those with whom you have a relationship.

8. Make the effort to try to understand behavior that doesn't seem to make sense, whether it's your own or someone else's. This will give you a fighting chance to change that behavior. It will also make it easier to get what you need from others, increase your peace of mind and help you stay off the Wheel of Misfortune.

Four key points to remember:

• Punishment is seldom an effective way to change behavior; there are too many ways it can fail to produce the desired result.

• Human behavior – including our own – is often not based on a rational assessment of the facts. If you learn to recognize that reality in yourself, you can avoid making some poor choices.

• All behavior happens because there's a payoff. However, the payoff may be difficult to observe because some payoffs result from our internal interpretation of events – and sometimes, just *avoiding something* is the payoff. That's a particularly difficult payoff to see.

• Be wary of the "trade-off trap" – making a deal in which you change your behavior in exchange for something (or ask the other person to do so). This can backfire big-time.

9. Beware of certainty syndrome, in yourself and others. Certainty is seldom warranted and brings with it a host of disadvantages, including preventing you from learning, undercutting your judgment, making you unable to influence others who disagree with you, causing you to see things in black and white, leading you to push your ideas onto everyone else, and – perhaps most important – making it easier for other people to manipulate you. Instead, get in the habit of admitting that you may not have the final truth – about anything. This is not "admitting you're wrong;" it's a way of telling the people you encounter that you really do care about the truth, not just about your own opinion, and that you're still open to learning. Instead of indulging in certainty, *keep asking questions.*

10. Use time to your advantage; don't let it work against you. Don't accept the idea that you're trapped by your past; that your best days are behind you; that some future event may devastate you; or that you must reach some specific future situation before you can be happy.

Instead, learn effective life strategies that will help you use time to your advantage. Then, slowly but surely create the future you want to experience.

Key points to remember about creating what you want:

• Choose a *journey* that will make you happy, not just a goal.

• Aim to create the *optimum* amount of what you want – the amount that will work best for you – rather than the maximum amount.

• Don't make demands of people or of the universe, or insist that you reach your goal by one specific route or in a specific amount of time.

• Every day, devote a short period of time to visualizing yourself in the experience you want to end up with. Remember: *You don't get things in life because you want them so badly; you get them because you see yourself having them.*

• Don't be shy about expressing gratitude for the things you like in your life. Doing so helps to keep them in your experience. And if they disappear, it helps ensure that they'll return.

• Every day, take one small step toward your goal. This is by far the most effective way to get where you want to go. And, *be persistent.*

• Make sure every action you take is worthy of your ideals. If you find yourself having to justify your actions, stop and make sure you're not acting out of fear, anger or desperation.

Being Passionate, Effective, Adaptable and Caring

The strategies in this book can do a lot more than just keep us off the Wheel of Misfortune. They can have a dramatic, positive effect on our lives:

They can make us more ***passionate*** about our lives, by helping us to choose goals that take us on inspiring journeys; by reminding us that obstacles and setbacks are a natural part of the growing process; by reassuring us that we have unlimited capacity to learn and grow; and by keeping us focused on the positive aspects of our journey rather than the negatives.

The strategies can make us more ***effective*** by keeping us from taking on the role of victim; by helping us communicate clearly so we get what we need from others; by ensuring that we make the most of our internal and external resources; by helping us to understand our own behavior and other people's behavior so we have a fighting chance to change behavior we don't like; by helping us prevent the emotional stacks that undermine close relationships; and by keeping us moving steadily toward our goals until we reach them.

The strategies can help us remain _**adaptable**_ by making us less afraid of sudden sweeping changes; by keeping us from indulging in certainty, which reduces flexibility and stops learning; by reminding us that our potential is unlimited; and by encouraging us to be prepared for obstacles along the way to our goals – both the likely obstacles and the unexpected ones.

And, the strategies can allow us to remain _**caring**_, by giving us a positive perspective; by providing insight into behaviors that would otherwise seem inexplicable; by helping us see ourselves as non-victims who can afford to assist others; and by side-stepping the kind of black-and-white, us-versus-them thinking that accompanies certainty syndrome.

Being passionate, effective, adaptable and caring in a challenging world is no small feat, but it pays huge dividends. In the meantime, if we play our cards right, getting caught on the Wheel of Misfortune – unpleasant by definition – can make us stronger and more resilient by challenging us to learn new skills, pushing us to our limits and making us realize we have more strength than we knew. Then, when we find ourselves surrounded by good fortune, we'll be ready to reach greater heights than we ever dreamed we could, thanks to the wisdom and strength we gained on our journey.

✸ ✸ ✸

Bibliography

Books

Agor W. (1986) The Logic of Intuitive Decision Making: A Research-Based approach for Top Management. Westport, Conn: Greenwood Press.

Bach R. (1977) Illusions: The Adventures of a Reluctant Messiah. New York: Dell Publishing.

Bandler R & Grinder J (1979). Frogs Into Princes. Moab, Utah: Real People Press.

Bandler R & Grinder J. (1982) Reframing: Neuro-Linguistic Programming an the Transformation of Meaning. Moab, Utah: Real People Press.

Bennis W. (2009) On Becoming a Leader (Fourth edition). Philadelphia, PA: Basic Books.

Bloom BS, ed. (1985) Developing Talent in Young People. New York: Ballantine Books.

Burton, RA. (2008). On Being Certain: Believing You Are Right Even When You're Not. New York: St. Martin's Press.

Cohen H. (1982) You Can Negotiate Anything. New York: Bantam..

Colvin G. (2008) Talent is Overrated: What Really Separates World-Class Performers from Everybody Else. New York: Portfolio/Penguin.

Damasio AR. (1994) Descarte's Error: Emotion, Reason and the Human Brain. New York: Penguin Books.

Diamond, J. (1997) Guns Germs and Steel: The Fates of Human Societies. New York: W.W. Norton & Company..

Doidge N. (2007) The Brain That Changes Itself. New York: Viking Penguin.

Dweck, CS. (2006) Mindset: The New Psychology of Success. New York: Ballantine Books.

Dyer WW. (1995) Your Erroneous Zones. New York: Avon Books.

Edwards B. (1999) The New Drawing on the Right Side of the Brain. New York: Tarcher/Penguin.

Elkman P, Friesen WV. (1978) Facial Action Coding System, Parts 1 and 2. San Francisco: Human Interaction Laboratory, Dept. of Psychiatry, University of California.

Elkman P. (1995) Telling Lies: Clues to Deceit in the Marketplace, Politics and Marriage. New York, Norton.

Ferguson M. (1980) The Aquarian Conspiracy: Personal and Social Transformation in the 1980s. Los Angeles: J.P. Tarcher.

Ferguson M, Coleman W & Perrin P. (1990) Marilyn Ferguson's Book of Pragmagic. New York: Pocket Books/Simon & Schuster.

Frankl VE. (2006) Man's Search for Meaning. Boston: Beacon Press.

Frazier GD. (2007). Hell's Guest. Williams & Company.

Gardner C & Troupe Q. (2006) The Pursuit of Happyness. New York: HarperCollins.

Gigerenzer G. (2007) Gut Feelings: The Intelligence of the Unconscious. New York: Viking Penguin.

Gilbert D. (2006) Stumbling on Happiness. New York: Vintage Books.

Gladwell M. (2005) Blink: The Power of Thinking Without Thinking. New York: Back Bay Books.

Goldberg E. (2006) The Wisdon Paradox: How Your Mind Can Grow Stronger as Your Brain Grows Older. New York: Gotham Books.

Goldberg P. (1983) The Intuitive Edge: Understanding Intuition and Applying It in Everyday Life. New York: G.P. Putnam's Sons.

Gonzales L. (2003) Deep Survival: Who Lives, Who Dies, and Why. New York: W.W. Norton & Company.

Gottman JM. (1994)Why Marriages Succeed or Fail (and How You Can Make Yours Last). New York: Simon & Schuster.

Gottman JM, Gottman JS & DeClaire J. (2006) 10 Lessons to Transform Your Marriage. New Yor: Three Rivers Press.

Hamada T. (1991) American Enterprise in Japan. Albany, NY: State University of New York Press.

Justice B. (1988) Who Gets Sick: How Thoughts, Moods and Beliefs Can Affect Your Health. Los Angeles: Jeremy P. Tarcher, Inc.

Kiley DS, with Noonan M. (1995) Albatross. New York: Bantam Books.

Klein G. (1999) Sources of Power: How People Make Decisions. MIT Press.

Klein G. (2003) The Power of Intuition: How to use your gut feelings to make better decisions at work. New York: Currency/Doubleday.

Langer EJ. (1989) Mindfulness. Cambridge, Mass: Da Capo Press.

Lehrer J. (2009) How We Decide. New York: Houghton Mifflin Harcourt.

Levine N. (2003) Dharma Punx: A Memoir. New York: HarperCollins.

Levine N. (2007) Against the Stream: A Buddhist Manual for Spiritual Revolutionaries. New York: HarperColFlins.

Libet B, Kosslyn SM. (2004) Mind Time: The Temporal Factor in Consciousness (Perspectives in Cognitive Neuroscience). Cambridge, Mass.: Harvard University Press.

Locke EA, Latham GP. (1990) A theory of goal-setting and task performance. Englewood Cliffs, NJ: Prentice Hall.

Marmot M. (2004) The Status Syndrome: How Social Standing Affects Our Health and Longevity. New York: Holt Paperbacks.

McGraw PC. (1999) Life Strategies: Doing Wha Works, Doing What Matters. New York: Hyperion Press.

Merzenich MM, Tallal P, et al. Some neurological principles relevant to the origins of—and the cortical plasticity-based remediation of—developmental language impairments. In J. Grafman and Y Christen, eds., Neuronal plasticity: Building a bridge from the laboratory to the clinic. Berlin: Springer-Verlag, 169-87.

Miller DP. (2004) A Little Book of Forgiveness: Challenges and Meditations for Anyone with Something to Forgive. Berkeley, Calif.: Fearless Books.

Nicolis G, Prigogine I. (1989) Exploring Complexity: An Introduction. New York: W.H. Freeman & Company.

Prechter RR. (2002) Conquer the Crash: You Can Survive and Prosper in a Deflationary Depression. Prechter RR. Hoboken, NJ: John Wiley & Sons, Inc.

Prigogine I. (1989) Exploring Complexity: An Introduction. W.H. Freeman & Company;1989.

Roberts J. (1981)The Individual and the Nature of Mass Events. Amber-Allen Publishing. San Rafael, Calif.

Roberts J. (1994) The Nature of Personal Reality: A Seth Book. San Rafael, Calif:

Amber-Allen Publishing.

Schwartz JM & Beyette B. (1996) Brain Lock: Free Yourself from Obsessive-Compulsive Behavior. New York: Harper Perennial.

Scitovsky T. (1976) The Joyless Economy: An Inquiry Into Human Satisfaction and Consumer Dissatisfaction. New York: Oxford University Press.

Sharp K. (2010) Starting Over: The Making of John Lennon and Yoko Ono's Double Fantasy. New York. Gallery Books.

Sherman A. (1965) A Gift of Laughter. New York: Fawcett World Library.

Shimoff M & Kline C. (2008) 7 Steps to Being Happy from the Inside Out. New York: Free Press.

Siegel BS. (1986) Love, Medicine and Miracles: Lessons Learned about Self-Healing from a Surgeon's Experience with Exceptional Patients. New York: Harper Perennial.

Simpson J. (2004) Touching the Void: The True Story of One Man's Miraculous Survival. New York: Perennial.

Strauss W & Howe N. (1991) Generations: The History of America's Future, 1584 to 2069. New York: William Morrow & Co.

Tetlock, PE. (2005) Expert Political Judgment: How good is it? How can we know? Princton, NJ: Princeton University Press.

Williams R & Williams V. (1993) Anger Kills: 17 Strategies for Controlliing the Hostility That Can Harm Your Health. New York: Harper Paperbacks.

Winograd, E & Neisser, U., Eds. (1992) Affect and Accuracy in Recall: Studies of "Flashbulb" Memories. New York: Cambridge University Press.

Published Studies and Presentations

Afifi TO, Mota NP, Dasiewicz P, MacMillan HL, Sareen J. Physical punishment and mental disorders: results from a nationally representative US sample. Pediatrics 2012:130:2:184-92.

Ambady N, Rosenthal R. Half a Minute: Predicting Teacher Evaluations from Thin Slices of Nonverbal Behavior and Physical Atttractiveness. Journal of Personality and Social Psychology 1993;64:3:431-41.

Aronson J, Fried CB, Good C. Reducing the Effects of Stereotype Threat on African American College Students by Shaping Theories of Intelligence. Journal of Experimental Social Psychology. 2002:38;113-125.

Bandura A, Schunk DH. Cultivating competance, self-efficacy and intrinsic interest through proximal self-motivation. Journal of Personality and Social Psychology 1981:41;586-98.

Baumeister R, Bratslavsky E, Finkenauer C, Vohs K. Bad is Stronger than Good. Review of General Psychology 2001;5:4: 323–370.

Bechara A, Damasio H, Tranel D, Damasio AR. Deciding advantageously before knowing the advantageous strategy. Science. 1997:28;275(5304):1293-5.

Beilock SL, Carr TH. On the fragility of skilled performance: what governs choking under pressure? J Exp Psychol Gen. 2001;130(4):701-25.

Beilock SL, Carr TH, MacMahon C, Starkes JL. When paying attention becomes counterproductive: impact of divided versus skill-focused attention on novice and experienced performance of sensorimotor skills. J Exp Psychol Appl. 2002;8(1):6-16.

Beilock SL, Bertenthal BI, McCoy AM, Carr TH. Haste does not always make waste: expertise, direction of attention, and speed versus accuracy in performing sensorimotor skills. Psych on Bull Rev. 2004;11(2):373-9.

Beilock SL, Bertenthal BI, Hoerger M, Carr TH. When does haste make waste? Speed-accuracy tradeoff, skill level, and the tools of the trade. J Exp Psychol Appl. 2008;14(4):340-52.

Berlin, L.J et al. Correlates and Consequences of Spanking and Verbal Punishment for Low Income White, African American, and Mexican American Toddlers. Child Development, Sept-Oct, 2009;80:5:1403-1420.

Betsch, Tilman et al. Different Principles of Information Integration in Implicit and Expicit Attitude Formation. European Journal of Social Psychology 36;2006:887-905.

Blackwell L, Trzesniewski K, Dweck CS. Implicit Theories of Intelligence Predict Achievement Across an Adolescent Transition: A Longitudinal Study and an Intervention. Child Development. 2007:78;246-263.

Blanchflower DG, Oswald AJ. Well-Being Over Time in Britain and the USA. Journal of Public Economics 2004:88; 1359-86.

Chase WG, Simon HA. Perception in Chess. Cognitive Psychology 1973:4;55-81.

Diener E, Seligman MP. Beyond Money: Toward an Economy of Well-Being. Psychological Science in the Public Interest 2004:5;1-31.

Deiner E, et al. Wealth and Happiness Across the World: Material Prosperity Predicts Life Evaluation, Whereas Psychosocial Prosperity Predicts Positive Feeling. Journal of Personality and Social Psychology 2010:99;1;52-61.

Dijksterhuis A Bos M, et al. On making the right choice: The deliberation-without-attention effect. Science 2006;311:1005-07.

Dijksterhuis A, van Olden Z. On the benefits of thinking unconsciously: Unconscious thought can increase post-choice stisfaction. Journal of Experimental Social Psychology 2006;42:627-631.

Draganski R, Gaser C, et al. Neuroplasticity: Changes in grey matter induced by training. Nature 2004: 427;6972;311-12.

Ehrlinger J, Dunning D. How chronic self-views influence (and potentially mislead) estimates of performance. J Pers Soc Psychol. 2003 Jan;84(1):5-17.

Ericsson KA, Kintsch W. Long-term working memory. Psychol Rev. 1995 Apr;102(2):211-45.

Falko Rheinberg. Achievement Evaluation and Motivation to Learn. Gottingen: Hogrefe, 1980. 87, 116. Also reported at the conference of the American Educational Research Association, Seattle, April 2001.

Flora C. The Grandmaster Experiment. Psychology Today July/August 2005.

Goldman L, et al. Prediction of the Need for Intensive Care in Patients Who Come to Emergency Departments with Acute Chest Pain. New England Journal of Medicine 1996:334;23;1498-1504.

Gollwitzer. Implementation Intentions: Strong Effects of Simple Plans. American Psychologist 1999:54;7;493-503.

Gollwitzer PM, Sheeran P, Michalski V, Seifert AE. When Intentions Go Public: Does Social Reality Widen the Intention-Behavior Gap? Psychological Science

2009:20:5:612-18.

Good C, Aronson J, Inzlicht M. Improving adolescents' standardized test performance: An intervention to reduce the effects of stereotype threat. Applied Developmental Psychology 2003:24;645-62

Grove W, et al. Clinical versus Mechanical Prediction: A Meta-Analysis. Psychological Assessment 12 (2000): 19-30.

Higgins ET. Beyond pleasure and pain. American Psychologist 1997; 52:1280-1300.

Isenberg DJ. How Senior Managers Think. Harvard Business Review. Nov-Dec 1984;80-90.

Jenkins WM, Merzenich MM, et al. Functional reorganization of primary somatosensory cortex is adult owl monkeys after behaviorally controlled tactile stimulation. Journal of Neurophysiology 1990:63;1;82-104.

Johnson JG, Raab M. Take the first: Option generation and resulting choices. Organizational Behavior and Human Decision Processes 91:215-29.

Jones CM, Miles TR. Use of Advanced Cues in Predicting the Flight of a Lawn Tennis Ball. Journal of Human Movement Studies. 1978:4;231-35.

Kiecolt-Glaser JK, et al. Hostile marital interactions, proinflammatory cytokine production, and wound healing. Arch Gen Psychiatry. 2005;62:12:1377-84.

Kray L, Haselhuhn M. Implicit Theories of Negotiating Ability and Performance: Longitudinal and Experimental Evidence. Journal of Personality and Social Psychology 2007:93:49-64.

Levanthal H, Singer R, Jones S. Effects of fear and specificity of recommendation upon attitudes and behavior. Journal of Personality and Social Psychology. 1965:2;20-29.

Levanthal H, Watts JC, Pagano F. Effects of fear and instructions on how to cope with danger. Journal of Personality and Social Psychology 1967:6;313-21.

Lusk CM, Hammond KR. Judgment in a Dynamic Task: Microburst Forecasting. Journal of Behavioral Decision Making 1991:41;55-73.

Maguire EA, et al. Navigation-related structural change in the hippocampi of taxi drivers. Proc Natl Acad Sci USA 200:97;8;4398-4403.

McBeath MK, Shaffer DM, Kaiser MK. How baseball outfielders determine where to run to catch fly balls. Science 268:569-73.

Mechelli A, Noppeney U, et al. A Voxel-Based Morphometry Study of Monolinguals, Early Bilinguals and Late Bilinguals. Presented at the ninth annual meeting of the Organization for Human Brain Mapping, New York City in 2003.

Main M, George C. Responses of Abused and Disadvantaged Toddlers to Distress in the Day Care Setting. Developmental Psychology 1985:21;407-412.

Miller G. "The Magical Number Seven, Plus or Minus Two: Some Limits on Our Caapacity for Processing Information." Psychological Review 63 (1956): 81-97.

Mueller CM, Dweck CS. Praise for intelligence can undermine children's motivation and performance. J Pers Soc Psychol. 1998 Jul;75(1):33-52.

Muller SB, et al. "How Do World-Class Cricket Batsmen Anticipate a Bowler's Intention?" Quarterly Journal of Experimental Psychology 29: 2162-86.

Napier JL., Jost JT. Why are conservatives happier than liberals? Psychological Science 2008:19;565-572.

Nilsson U. The anxiety- and pain-reducing effects of music interventions: A systematic review. AORN J. 2008;87:4:780-807.

Orbell S, Hodgkins S, Sheehan P. Implementation intentions and the theory of of planned behavior. Personality and Social Psychology Bulletin 1997:23;945-54.

Patterson ES, Woods DD, Sarter NB, Watts-Perotti. Patterns in Cooperative Cognition. Coop '98, Third International Conference on the Design of Cooperative Systems. Cannes, France, 1998.

Pesenti M, Zago L, et al. Mental calculation in a prodigy is sustained by right prefrontal and medial temporal areas. Nature Neuroscience 2001:4;1;103-7.

Rozin P, Royzman EB. Negativity bias, negativity dominance, and contagion. Personality and Social Psychology Review 2001;5:296–320.

Schneider P, Scherg M, et al. Morphology of Heschl's gyrus reflects enhanced activation in the auditory cortex of musicians. Nat Neurosci 2002:5;7;688-694.

Solomons L, Stein G. Normal Motor Automatism. First published in Psychological Review, September 1896.

Stewart TR, Heideman WR et al. Effects of Improved Information on the Components of Skill in Weather Forecasting. Special Issue: Experts and Expert Systems. Organizational Behavior and Human Decision Processes. 1992:53;2;107-34.

Straus, MA and Paschall MJ. Corporal punishment by mothers and development of children's cognitive ability: A Longitudinal study of two Nationally representative age cohorts. Journal of Aggression, Maltreatment, and Trauma. 2009;18:5: 459 – 483.

Straus, MA.. Differences in Corporal Punishment by parents in 32 Nations and its Relation to National Differences in IQ. Paper Presented at the 14th International Conference On Violence, Abuse And Trauma, 25 September2009, San Diego, California.

Westen D, Blagov PS, Harenski K, Kilts C, Hamann S. Neural bases of motivated reasoning: an FMRI study of emotional constraints on partisan political judgment in the 2004 U.S. Presidential election. J Cogn Neurosci. 2006 Nov;18(11):1947-58.

Wilson T, Schooler J. Thinking Too Much: Introspection can reduce the quality of preferences and decisions. Journal of Personality and Social Psychology 1991;60;181-192.

Wilson T, et al. Introspecting about reasons can reduce post-choice satisfaction. Personality and Social Psychology Bulletin 1993;19:331-339.

Wood RE, Williams-Phillips K, Tabernero C. "Implicit theories of ability, processing dynamics and performance in decision-making groups." Australian Graduate School of Management, Sydney, Australia.

Wrezesniewski, A., McCauley, C., Rozin, P., and Schwartz, B. 1997. "Jobs, careers, and callings: People's relations to their work." Journal of Research in Personality 31: 21-33.

Articles

Jay Leno says: Persistence Pays Off. Parade magazine, September 6, 2009, p 5.

Meditation? Fire Walking? Yogic Breathing? He's a Believer. TV Guide, August 13 1988, p 12-15.

Queen Takes All. Serena Allott. The Telegraph, January 16, 2002.

Supercharged. Joshua Davis. Wired Magazine, October 2010, p 138-180.

The Spiritual Connection. Martha Sherril. Oprah magazine, May 2008. p 286.

About Christopher Kent

Christopher Kent is a long-time singer-songwriter and recording artist; he is also a professional writer and editor who has authored more than 150 published how-to, science and general-interest articles. *Help and Hope* is his first book and CD set.

As a young musician Christopher spent four years touring North America, Europe and Japan with the American Boychoir, where he received intensive training in voice and music theory. In high school and college he taught himself to play guitar and began writing songs and performing in local venues. During this time he also began writing essays and short novels and developed a lifelong interest in human behavior, leading to a bachelor's degree in psychology at Haverford College.

After college he moved to New York City where he continued to nurture his twin interests in music and writing. In the ensuing years he became a winner of the New York Songwriters' Competition, held at that time by the major music publishers of New York, and performed in clubs throughout the region; he also taught a highly praised songwriting course for five years. Meanwhile, he helped pay the rent by creating educational materials for several companies, eventually becoming a staff writer for two science/medical trade magazines.

Christopher has previously released two albums and two CD singles, most recently an original Christmas carol called *Songs of the Season*. He is currently working on his second book & CD set, as well as a how-to songwriting book based on the course he taught in New York. He lives in Pennsylvania with his wife Lynn.

(To learn more about Christopher, sample some of his articles, read lyrics and hear some of his previous recordings, visit *christopherkent.com*.)

✹ ✹ ✹

CPSIA information can be obtained at www.ICGtesting.com
Printed in the USA
BVOW03s2031220714

360001BV00006B/21/P